The Grammar Schools of Medieval England: A.F. Leach in Historiographical Perspective

The greatest single contribution to the history of the grammar schools of medieval England – including Winchester and Eton – was made between 1890 and 1915 by Arthur Francis Leach. Leach's research led him to take issue with accepted views of English educational history. In particular, he challenged the widely held view that Edward VI, during the Protestant period, founded most of the better-known educational institutions. He argued that not only were schools widespread throughout England before the Reformation – far exceeding what was available for the youth of his own generation – but that these derived from the secular, although church-related, colleges of Anglo-Saxon time. Showing this would, he hoped, eliminate the persistent "myth" that the monks had been the schoolmasters of pre-Reformation England.

Miner argues that previous readings of Leach which suggest that his main concern is to take issue with the Reformation and to argue that this great watershed in history was – at least with regard to education – a retrograde step rather than a great movement forward have not taken into account the full range of his publications. The aim of the present study is thus to place both Leach's achievements and his more controversial theses in historical context. A separate chapter devoted to unpublished material from the Charity Commission reveals Leach's method of work and provides an analytic survey of opinions on his work by reviewers and historians. The author also supplements Leach's lack of material on the school curriculum with descriptive analysis of grammatical manuscripts from the fourteenth and fifteenth centuries, showing the presence of an educational Christendom of which Leach was evidently unaware.

John N. Miner was a member of the Department of History of the University of Windsor.

Arthur Francis Leach

The Grammar Schools of Medieval England

A.F. Leach in Historiographical Perspective

JOHN N. MINER

McGill-Queen's University Press
Montreal & Kingston • London • Buffalo

McGill-Queen's University Press 1990
ISBN 0-7735-0634-9

Legal deposit first quarter 1990
Bibliothèque nationale du Québec

∞

Printed in Canada on acid-free paper

This book has been published with the help of a
grant from the Social Science Federation of Canada,
using funds provided by the Social Sciences and Hu-
manities Research Council of Canada.

Material in chapter 3 and appendix 1 which is under
crown-copyright in the Public Record Office is repro-
duced by permission of the Controller of Her Majesty's Stationery Office.

The author and publishers wish to thank the following for permission to reproduce the illustrations contained in this book: The British Library, London, for
nos. 3, 4, 5, 7, 8, and 9; Trinity College Library,
Cambridge for nos. 1, 2, and 6.

Canadian Cataloguing in Publication Data

Miner, John N. (John Nelson), 1920–
    The grammar schools in medieval England: A.F.
    Leach in historiographical perspective
    Includes index.
    Bibliography: p.
    ISBN 0-7735-0634-9
    1. Leach, Arthur Francis, 1851–1915. 2. Public
    schools, Endowed – England – History. 3. Education,
    Medieval – England. I. Title.
    LA634.M46 1990   370'.942   C89-090146-5

Contents

Abbreviations

PUBLICATIONS BY ARTHUR
FRANCIS LEACH

EEW   *Early Education in Worcester*
ESR   *English Schools at the Reformation*, part 1
FRP   "The Foundation and Re-foundation of Pocklington Grammar School"
HWC   *A History of Winchester College*
M   "Memorandum ... on the History of Endowed Schools"
MS   *Memorials of Southwell*
RE   "The Reformation in England"
SME   *Schools of Medieval England*
SS   "School Supply in the Middle Ages"
TP   *The Protectorate*
VCH   *Victoria Country History of the Counties of England*

OTHER WORKS

RAC:C   Report of the Assistant Commissioner: Chichester Prebendal School
RAC:S   Report of the Assistant Commissioner: Southwell Collegiate Grammar School, Nottinghamshire
RAC:Y   Report of Assistant Commissioner: School of the Cathedral Church of St. Peter of York

PUBLISHER'S NOTE: John Miner died unexpectedly on 23 May 1987. At the time of his death, his manuscript was still in editing. His brother Edmund, a member of the Department of Modern Languages at King's College, allowed us to continue with publication by taking over the tasks of approving editorial suggestions, proofing, and indexing. He was aided in this by Marilyn Mason, who was of great help in the preparation of the index and proofing.

John Miner had retired in 1984 from the University of Windsor, where he had been a member of the Department of History for seventeen years. He was a careful and painstaking researcher whose devotion to duty and inspiring search for the best won the respect and trust of both colleagues and students. Those of us who worked on the final stages of the book without his aid hope that we have been faithful to his intentions and that he would have been pleased with the result.

Preface

The present study began as a doctoral dissertation at the University of London some twenty-eight years ago and expanded or contracted with the library facilities available to me as I went about my university teaching responsibilities. The work has gone through at least three stages: an early emphasis on the manuscript evidence for the later medieval grammar school curriculum; a developing interest in A.F. Leach himself stimulated by a new wave of analysis and criticism associated in part with the focus on social history during the 1960s; and, recently, the resolve to track down all Leach's extensive and scattered writing on the history of the grammar schools.

While the research for the first stage was confined mainly to the libraries of London, Oxford, and Cambridge, that of the second and third stages found a congenial climate in the excellent range of pre-World War I periodicals available in Wayne State University and Detroit's public library and at the University of Michigan, Ann Arbor. Two sabbatical leaves, generously arranged through the Department of History at the University of Windsor, allowed me to integrate these three phases of the work. During the first leave, in 1973–74, I was able to view Leach's basic research from a wider perspective than the strictly English one. On the second leave, 1980–81, spent as a research associate at the Pontifical Institute of Mediaeval Studies in Toronto, I was able to unify the different parts of the total project.

For the constant encouragement essential to sustaining my interest in seeing this work to completion, I am indebted to many persons. Brother Ernest Gauthier, visitor of the Toronto District of the Brothers of the Christian Schools, first arranged for me to go to Europe for study before I assumed teaching duties at the University of Alberta under the auspices of St Joseph's College, Edmonton. Dr Helen

Chew, Dr Richard Hunt, and Dom David Knowles were my supervisory and resource personnel throughout the formal preparation of the dissertation. Professor S.T. Bindoff was, up to a few weeks before his much-lamented death, an almost constant source of help and inspiration.

Several persons in the academic world have in one way or another contributed to the successful conclusion of this work. They include my colleagues in the Department of History at the University of Windsor, latterly under the chairmanship of Dr Ian Pemberton and Dr Larry Kulisek; J. Ambrose Raftis, csb, president of the Pontifical Institute of Mediaeval Studies, and his colleagues: Michael M. Sheehan, csb, Leonard E. Boyle, op, P. Osmund Lewry, op, and the late James A. Weisheipl, op; the late Dr John E. Wrigley; Dr Jo Ann Hoeppner Moran; my brother, Dr E.J. Miner, fsc; and a close friend and fellow historian for more than thirty years – Dr John Durkan.

For particular services connected with the research and publication I am grateful to the Social Science Federation of Canada for its grant-in-aid; to the University fo Windsor for bearing the initial costs of the word-processing services, a summer research grant in 1982, and a separate financial contribution; to Mr M.J. McManus of the Charity Commission, London, England; to Mr Peter B. Blaney, officer, Aid to Publications Programme, Social Science Federation of Canada; to Mr Philip J. Cercone, executive director, McGill-Queen's University Press; to Brother Francis McCrea, provincial superior, sharing the prepublication costs of the manuscript; and to Mr James W. Leach, grandson of A.F. Leach, who kindly sent me a photograph of his grandfather and some personal correspondence relative to Leach's death. Finally, I wish to express a special word of thanks to a former secretary in the Department of History at the University of Windsor, Cathy Paige who, with the aid of the university's wordprocessing team, worked long hours to help me bridge the gap between the early outline on a dozen cassette tapes and a second and workable draft of the manuscript. Her skill, energy, and unfailing good humour ultimately helped to make the difference between a seemingly unending "process" and the satisfaction of glimpsing the finished product.

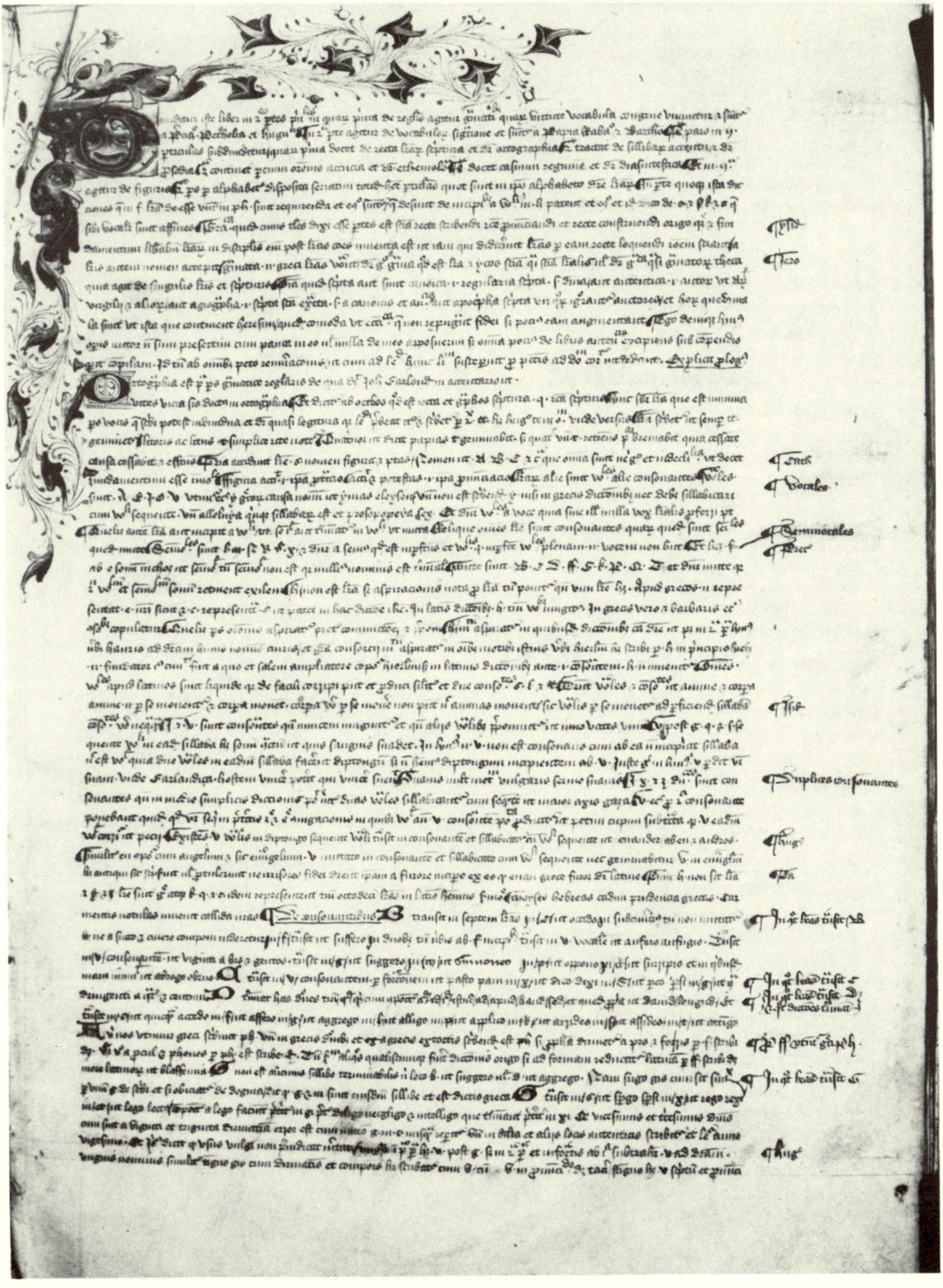

1 Orthography. Ms Trin. 0.5.4, fol. 80.

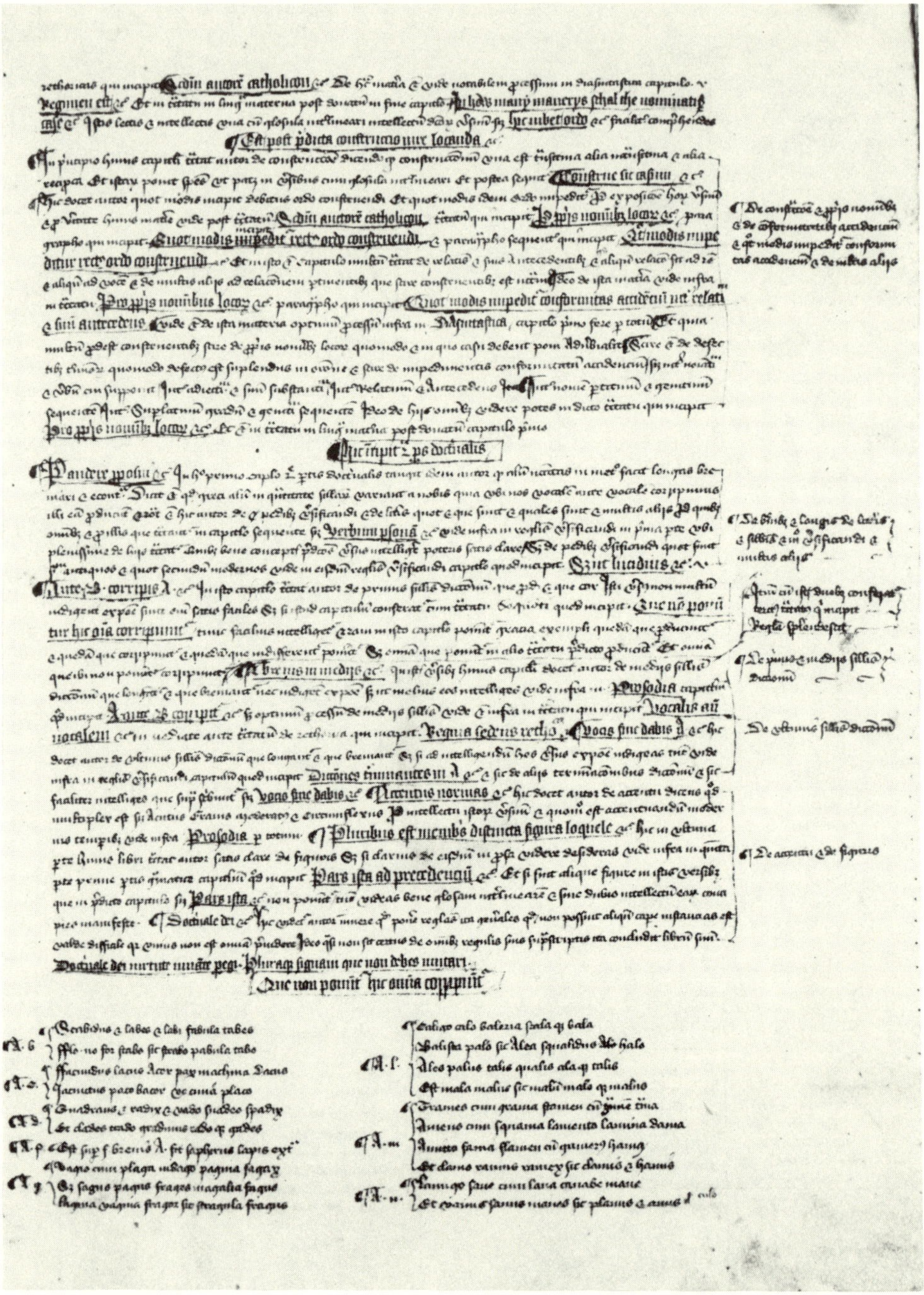

2 Prosody and syntax. Ms Trin. O.5.4, fol. 12

3 The "small" Cato. Ms Harl. 1002, fols. 11v–112

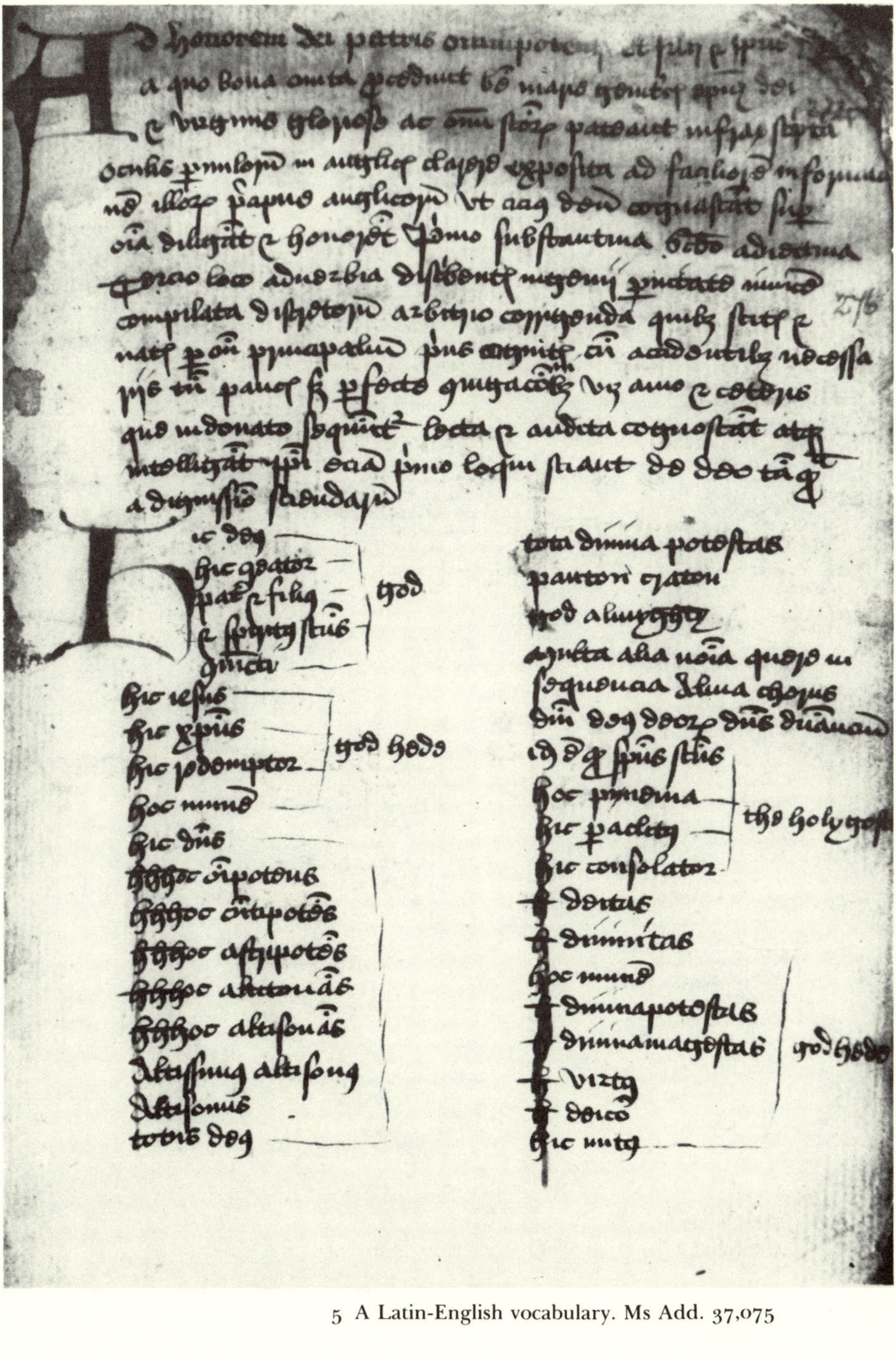

5 A Latin-English vocabulary. Ms Add. 37,075

6 Verse vocabulary: Deux nichil fecerat frustra. Ms Trin. o.5.4, fol. 34

7 *Right*: *Questio* on the Gospel. Ms Harl. 1587, fol. 51

Noftun queda derelm

... questiones ... phe pwas totu definicunt
... sic expo que e declaraciunt has se
... ille mtn q definicunt totu phas p
... ymo pimo ... ut parem ... e ...

... ut ventu ... e sesar augusto
... nt discbeixt ... vmusq orbis ... sic expo edin ... ma
... data ... ceyt a sesar augusto nt vmusq ... de
... cebeixt ... be mdd ... Audieues aut ... del
sebat in cordibz finis e stridebat detibz ... eu
... sic er ant ... inder audiee q diserabat ... cabat
m cordibz fuo e fciebat detibz ... eu ... cot eu
... no ... em l v omes e q ... eu die ... venetis
... cas ... e disseree ... fecno sn cave ...
... se ... nd ... secta ... ane a ... e ...
... secta ... cas ... e au ... blyndy e ... ve ... ca
... e q ... e ane a blyndmt ... secta e ... feste
... blynd ... Amen dico vobis q mul-
te manfiones in domo patris mei fi quo
minus dixesse vobis vado parare vobis
locum ... fic ... dico vos ame ... die ...
... mee ... q no ... mtta ma ... no fuisse
... mee dixiste vos q ... mo va pa vo com
Anen an ... o fit ... e no vado parare
... fic ... cotu ... q ... a ... poynt ... one q
... fic ... monone ... e poftq ... q ...
... hic no fic ... dico q q ... e ... fere
... q fac ... e ... deg ... t fe
q no ... cortari ... vctlas ... cotes

Vt cotta q vi cramaticor
... cape fil dic mltq mm cor

colit ōeō Iacobus. vt ad locū denotatū
eō noīe. Sed Deus cōferūt eū alio ōdio
sicut psonā. vt colo ꝗ diligo scm̄ iacobū.
istam psonam. vñde versus

Philippo bn̄ia p noxinā non tolerat
expiano noīe illi sue ꝗm simulat
Ille ōō ōtio ꝗm stꝫsit pecte p̄sit
Sed ōtio libriū ꝗm stōsit nemo p̄sit
ciūꝗ p̄oīta pciauo teste locat
Ihesū suo alsū cui nata famulat
Sed scm̄ Iacobū teūo sapiēuo ita sit
Sed tibi Iacobe teūo diciuo reꝓbat

Deuetio qnid est pars ōeō signifi
ratio mentis affectum boce mcondita
Qñd est ītilectio dico ꝓdm̄ ꝑciaum est ꝑ
ōeō mdeclmabilis alnē ꝑtibꝫ ītilectia ad ba
pos ān affectiuo mdicatuost Qñd est ꝓit
ītilectio mentis affectū v ān passioūe sub
boce mcondita v mꝓstit significare contra
descriptōem ītilectio qñā ponut donatꝫ arguit
sit ōio ꝓ ōeō vt dicit pciaum sigt mentio
conceptu sꝫ mentio affectū secd̄m donatū qʒ
ītilectio nō est ꝓ ōeō. Ad istud dicendū est
ꝗ licet ītilectio sigt mentis affectū pones p̄so

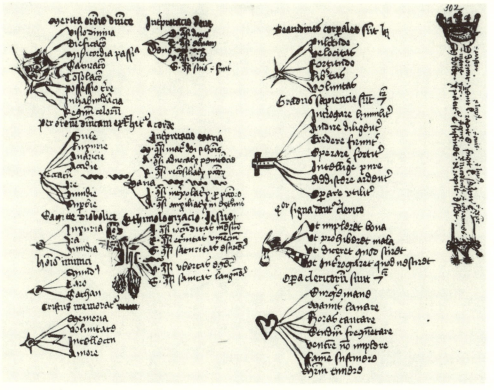

9 Virtues and duties of a clerk. Ms Harl. 5751, fols. 301v–302

8 *Left*: Philosophical grammar. Ms Add. 32, 425, fol. 81v

The Contribution of A.F. Leach

Introductory Survey

The present study owes its origin to a longstanding interest in, and sense of indebtedness to, an energetic and controversial writer of the later nineteenth century, Arthur Francis Leach, an historian of education in England and especially of its medieval development.[1] In spite of the central position Leach held in one of the great educational controversies of his day – the place of England's public schools in an increasingly democratic society – he has remained a virtually unknown figure, especially within the historical profession with which he would willingly have identified if given any encouragement. Foster Watson's biographical notice in the *Dictionary of National Biography* contains the main landmarks in his career and this sketch has so far not been enlarged upon.[2] Born in London in 1851, Leach was educated at Winchester College and at Oxford, enjoying a Fellowship at All Souls College from 1874 to 1881. His scholastic ability was recognized early: in 1872 he won the Stanhope Historical Essay Prize and in the following year he obtained a First Class in *Literae Humaniores*. Three years later Leach was called to the Bar by the Middle Temple. Of this period of his life we know little or nothing except that he published two or three short treatises.

If there is a turning point in Leach's career, it is his appointment in 1884 at the age of thirty-three as an assistant charity commissioner with the Endowed Schools Department. Between 1901 and his death in 1915 Leach held the posts successively of administrative examiner at the Board of Education, assistant secretary, and, for the last nine years of his life, second charity commissioner.[3] A quick perusal of these dates and the publishing details of his works reveals that Leach's historical writing was not the fruit of a detached and independent situation but the product of a remarkably active career in public administration.

Leach is known to readers of educational history in the English speaking world – and to a limited extent beyond it – mainly on the basis of his three books: *English Schools at the Reformation 1546–48*, published in 1896; *Educational Charters and Documents, 598–1909*, published in 1911; and *The Schools of Medieval England*, which came out in the year of his death, 1915. It is no exaggeration to say that Leach's fate at the hands of both the reading public and the scholarly community mirrored the fate of these three publications.

The first of these books sparked a controversy that has helped to cast serious doubt on Leach's methods of research and inter-pretation generally. *English Schools at the Reformation* was the first serious analysis of the impact of the Reformation on the educational life of England. In it he focused on the extent and purpose of medieval schools as no previous writer had done. In his single-mind-ed attempt to expose Edward VI and his councillors as the destroyers, rather than the creators, of educational institutions, however, Leach revealed a tendency to exaggerate the basis for his claims. He too easily identified schools with chantries and consquently believed that Edward VI had a disastrous effect on educational development when he dissolved these religious institutions.

The second of the three publications, however, gives the measure of Leach's failure. The subject of *Educational Charters and Documents* was promising as well as ambitious – an edited collection of educa-tional documents throughout most of England's recorded history. Leach said of it: "This book aims at doing, so far as the scantier space allows, for the educational history of England what Bishop Stubb's *Select Charters* did for its constitutional history."[4] The author's stated purpose went unfulfilled.

The last book, *The Schools of Medieval England*, has had a curious history. Put together under restrictions imposed by the publishers on the series in which it appeared, the book apparently includes all that the author had discovered about education from the earliest Anglo-Saxon times to the reign of Henry VIII. It has, therefore, been accepted in many quarters as a ready reference to the whole range of England's medieval educational experience. The book's structure, however, is governed by Leach's predominant theses. One of these is his emphasis on secular collegiate churches as educational centres to the virtual exclusion of monastic contributions. Another is his implied belief in the continuity of medieval schools despite the intermittent and fragmentary nature of much of the documentary evidence. Leach does not submit these generalizations to any critical analysis – indeed, it would have been difficult for him to do so since no footnote references were allowed within the terms of publication.

Leach is thus vulnerable to criticism, while the reader remains relatively unaware of the extensive documentary research that had contributed to so many of the ideas the author discusses in his very
readable book.

Leach's publications are listed in a bibliography included in *The
Schools of Medieval England*. Though by no means complete, the compilation is impressive, ranging over a dozen or more scholarly and
semi-popular journals in addition to more than forty encyclopaedia
articles and a remarkably sustained series of contributions to the
Victoria History of the Counties of England (VCH). The bibliography
includes eleven books, five written by Leach and six edited by him.[5]
The readership Leach was aiming at is clear enough from this bibliography: a relatively wide sector of the reading public – educators,
government employees responsible for educational decisions, professional historians, and teachers of history and related subjects.

Considering Leach's writing as a whole, it is easy to isolate a few
dominant themes. His writing can be divided into three chronological periods: 1890–1900, 1901–10, and from 1911 to his death in
1915. The first of these periods is dominated by the basic question
of the antiquity of the nation's schools, in particular the grammar
or Latin schools. This question was not merely academic for Leach.
With a missionary zeal, he attempted to convince his fellow countrymen of both the antiquity and the continuity of a considerable
number of England's educational institutions. There is no single
theory that Leach enunciated more persistently and none that appears, at least to him, more difficult to convey effectively. In this
matter Leach is conscious that he is setting himself against the current
– that he is questioning what might be called the "Reformation tradition" and a particular aspect of Whig historiography. In particular,
Leach is challenging the widely held view that it was Edward VI, a
Protestant, who had founded most of the better-known educational
institutions, including the majority of the great public schools, Winchester and Eton alone excepted.

English Schools at the Reformation, published in 1896, is a full-length
study of the antiquity of England's schools and related issues. Leach
had already revealed his beliefs on the subject four years earlier in
an article in the *Contemporary Review* entitled "Edward VI: Spoiler
of Schools." Late in 1894 Leach published in the same journal an
article, "School Supply in the Middle Ages," which, together with the
designation of Edward VI as the "spoiler," was to embroil him in
almost continual controversy in his own lifetime and until the present
day. In a contribution to the *Archaeological Journal* in 1898 entitled
"Sherborne School: Before, Under, and After Edward VI," Leach

again reveals his conviction that this particular watershed in educational history had been misinterpreted by generations of Englishmen. He considers this basic misunderstanding within the wider
context of the antiquity of the nation's schools. Leach had written
an article on the subject for the *Fortnightly Review* in 1892, attempting
to decide whether York or Canterbury was the oldest school in
England. He returned to this topic from 1896 to 1898 in letters to
the *Times* and the *Guardian*.

To a wide segment of the population, an issue of greater relevance
than the antiquity of the schools was the legal interpretation of the
term "free schools." Some parents were then claiming that the public
schools, in becoming the preserve of a wealthy few, had been un-
faithful to their original purpose of providing education gratis for
those who wished to avail themselves of the opportunities established
by the earliest charters of foundation.

There were few contemporary issues that engaged Leach's attention more closely than this one. His "Memorandum" on the history
of endowed schools was included in the report of the Royal Commission on Secondary Education in 1895. This memorandum was
soon followed by two articles in the *National Observer*, both entitled
"Free Grammar Schools." Some twelve years later, in 1908, Leach
wrote an article, "The True Meaning of 'Free School'," that appeared in two successive issues of the *Journal of Education*. He often
referred to this subject in his writings on more general themes,
including numerous chapters in the *VCH*. It is not surprising, then,
that an entry written by Leach under the heading of "Free Schools"
found its way into the American publication *A Cyclopedia of Education*.

During the period 1890–1900 Leach concentrated mainly on
schools in the north of England, working on the early schools of
Yorkshire with particular emphasis on Southwell Grammar School
and Beverley. Throughout his reseach and writing, Leach never lost
sight for long of his principal themes. The price he paid for this was
considerable repetition, but Leach clearly believed that many of the
erroneous and unfounded opinions then current with regard to the
earlier history of England's schools were extremely obdurate.
Perhaps he was right, for the "Oldest School" controversy featured
in his *Times* and *Guardian* articles was still being discussed in the
Times Educational Supplement in 1911.

During the period 1901–10 Leach wrote a lengthier work on Warwick School and an informative study on the Schools of Lincoln, one
version of which appeared in the *Journal of Education* in 1906. Of
even greater importance to Leach during this period was the history

of St Paul's School in London. His article on Colet and St Paul's the *Journal of Education* in 1909 sparked a new line of controversy, for in it Leach attempted to prove that the supposedly new and innovative school was not founded by John Colet but was a continuation of the older cathedral school. During this period Leach wrote numerous chapters for the *VCH*. Some twenty volumes include Leach's summaries of education in the counties concerned. He also edited the second volume on Essex, the second on Northamptonshire, and the fourth on Worcestershire – editions not included in the bibliography in *The Schools of Medieval England*.[6] These chapters in the *VCH* are not, of course, confined to medieval foundations but bring together the more relevant and scattered material on the historical development of a particular school from its earliest days to the nineteenth century.

In the third and last phase of his work – up to 1915 – Leach's research and publication proceeded on different levels. While he was completing the study he regarded as his most enduring contribution, *Educational Charters and Documents*, he began to write on a broad variety of educational and related topics for the *Cyclopedia of Education*. At this time Leach also began to give more thought to the broader context within which so much of his research had been conducted. Leach appreciated both his limitations and the light he had let fall on the entire scope of educational history. This is clear in one of his most scholarly essays, an address to the British Academy published in that body's proceedings in 1914 as "Some Results of Research in the History of Education in England; With Suggestions for Its Continuance and Extension." Unfortunately for his subsequent reputation, however, it is not this paper, but *The Schools of Medieval England* that is better known.

Considering Leach's remarkable range of writing and thought-provoking questions on educational history, there is little doubt that his *Schools of Medieval England* has done its author and its subject a disservice. In his ninth chapter, for example, Leach considers the relative abundance of school statutes available from the fourteenth and fifteenth centuries. However, instead of explaining the statutes themselves, as we might have wished, he ranges over a variety of topics, including the position of the schoolmaster in some of the ancient churches, the function of bachelors in particular grammar schools, and the decline of French in the classroom. One of the main drawbacks to Leach's writing is his tendency to try to prove something from isolated selections. Leach, unfortunately, did not tidy up his work. Nor did he clearly identify the features of his research that were basic to an understanding of medieval education as distinguished, for example, from current issues. Whatever their intrinsic merit, current issues did not necessarily bear directly upon the broader principles of inquiry that could inform the history of education in medieval and early modern England.

The net result of all this is that no scholar has yet studied all of Leach's publications. Merely compiling everything that he wrote on the subject of education is a formidable task. No single library contains such a collection, and most of the persons who have consulted Leach have been content to draw upon one or more of his three books generally available in libraries: *English Schools at the Reformation, The Schools of Medieval England,* and *Educational Charters and Documents.*His only other writing that is readily available is that in the *VCH* volumes, but there is little evidence that researchers have consulted these books the better to understand Leach's total contribution.[7]

Reference has been made above to Leach's involvement in the current issues of the day. Leach began ransacking ancient libraries searching for material on early school foundations when he was appointed assistant charity commissioner of the Endowed Schools Department in 1884. The bibliography that appeared in *The Schools of Medieval England* is correctly designated as "Works on the History of Schools."

Leach's initial writing, however, was not concerned with educational matters at all. It is worth considering at this point what his early writings had in common with his later work on education. Leach's earliest known work is an essay for whch he won the Stanhope Prize in 1872. His paper, entitled "The Protectorate," which he read in the theatre at Oxford on 12 June of that year reveals more than one strand of thought that would also characterize him in later years. Although the work is a serious attempt to use analysis and narrative to evaluate Oliver Cromwell within his historical context, Leach reveals all too clearly his admiration for both the man himself and the republic of virtue that he tried to establish. Leach begins with the expulsion of the Long Parliament on 20 April 1653 and ends with the death of Cromwell on 3 September 1658.[8] The Royalists, as might be expected, are given short shrift. The fact, for instance, that they were excluded from the first "free and general election for Parliament" in fourteen years, Leach ascribes to their general perversity: they had upheld, in a bloody war, "the right of the king to enslave the nation" and, moreover, "still professed these principles in favour of a dissolute exile" (*TP* 32). This view of the Stuart cause, coupled with the "hated rule of the Bishops" (*TP* 95), pervades the entire essay, while the cause of the Protectorate, and of Cromwell in particular, is presented as the greatest good. Even the factionalism of the professed supporters of the new regime serves to enhance Cromwell's stature. Leach singles out, in particular, the Levellers, led by Lilburne and Harrison, who were mostly "Anabaptists, Fifth Monarchists, and holders of every form of fervid and enthusiastic religion," and who, as Leach says, "added the fanaticism of religion to political insanity." Cromwell had to bring together these elements and others whose enthusiasm urged them into "an unnatural alliance with the Royalists"(*TP* 23).

The virtue that Leach believes best characterizes Cromwell is fairness. Leach believed him particularly devoted to toleration. We are told, for instance, that Cromwell "had never shown an intolerant spirit" (*TP* 21), that he defended freedom of worship (*TP* 27), that he was "the apostle of toleration in religion" (*TP* 75).

Cromwell could not, of course, view Catholics in the same light, especially during the war with Spain. With men's minds filled with "the horror and hatred" associated with the massacres in Ireland, and more recently those in Piedmont, Cromwell had no alternative but to maintain the severity of the law against them, but he "never encouraged persecution" (*TP* 78). Leach contends, moreover, that Cromwell extended this sense of fair play to the Royalists themselves. Cromwell had to punish them, but his action was tempered with "mercy and magnanimity" (*TP* 38). Even in dealing with them, he was averse to bloodshed, despite the fact that "they were at once more selfish, more hostile, more bloody in their projects" (*TP* 31). Leach's somewhat impassioned rhetoric may seem uncharacteristic, but the writing does reflect an intensity and self-confidence that never abandoned him.

Throughout the essay, Leach attempts to show how Cromwell remained tolerant despite the self-interest of contending parties who made the exercise of this virtue especially difficult. Leach believed, for example, that Cromwell "succeeded better in Church than in State," because he decided to let the established Presbyterian form of government stand without encouraging or discouraging it, and because he published two church ordinances designed to regulate the bestowal of benefices (*TP* 75). The first ordinance set up a commission to insure that only fit persons be endowed with a stipend for preaching; the second provided for commissioners in each county to depose from office not only poorly instructed and indifferent ministers but inadequate schoolmasters as well (*TP* 76).

Underlying Leach's assessment of Cromwell is the view that his hero was, in the social sense, "a solid English country gentleman," who "represented the firmest and most English portion of the party, the ardent religion of the age and nation" (*TP* 26). Placing him in the context of those surrounding him early in the Protectorate, Leach makes the following suggestive remark: "He must no longer be a Presbyterian, or an Independent, a Monarchist or a Republican, but simply an Englishman, and the chief of Englishmen, to harmonize their conflicting interests, caring equally for the interests of all, and ruling each party in the nation for the welfare of the whole" (*TP* 27).

Two observations, at least, may be drawn from Leach's admiration for Cromwell. Leach's sympathy for Cromwell and his policies is consistent with his later efforts to equate the interregnum period with notable advances in education, in contrast, for instance, with the debilitating effect of the restored Stuart monarchy on the same area of activity. Also, Leach's emphasis on Cromwell's distinctively English qualities supports his contention that the groundwork of the nation's educational enterprise had been laid in the pre-Norman period, specifically, in connection with the early collegiate churches. He believed these collegiate churches were both secular and English, in contrast to later monastic and Norman institutions.

As far as can be ascertained, Leach's earliest publications were two legal essays, *Digest of the Law Relating to Probate Duty* and *Club Cases*, published in 1878 and 1879 respectively.[9] In the first, Leach refers to himself as "of the Middle Temple, Barrister at Law and Fellow of All Souls' College, Oxford," while in the second he omits the reference to the Middle Temple. In his preface to the *Digest on Probate Duty*, Leach observes: "The Law relating to Probate Duty is a typical example of the confusion characteristic of English Law in general, without having the same long history to account for, even if not to some extent to justify such confusion ... It is ... impossible to conceive a subject so slight and simple plunged into a more hopeless state of muddle."[10]

Leach conceived his task in this essay to be one of organization and clarification. The work is fifty-five pages long, with a seventy-page appendix of statutory provisions relating to probate duty. He intended the work to be a digest of the law in general and, more precisely, a "clear and exact statement of fiscal laws." In a broader context, he hoped to make "a mite of contribution to the great work of digesting and codifying the Law of England."[11]

In the second work, fifty pages long with an appendix of five more pages containing rules for a club, Leach explains that clubs had now become an important element in social life and court cases relating to them a subject of much attention. He thinks, therefore, that "a more or less popular treatise" on the principles of law governing clubs, as well as the legal decisions already arrived at, might prove useful.[12]

Even at twenty-seven, Leach considered himself a codifier whose purpose was to dispel the confusion surrounding the unorganized growth of an institution or a concept. Leach is aware that, in an effort to be both readable and accurate, he may not have succeeded in being either "technical and concise" enough to be of use to lawyers, or "plain and diffuse" enough to be of interest to laymen. His treatise is, nevertheless, intended for both groups and he hopes that each will find it to its liking.[13]

It is difficult to account for any other material that Leach published before his appointment as assistant charity commissioner in 1884. But some time within the next three or four years he published an essay entitled "The English Land Question" in which he frequently cites examples from Ireland, France, Belgium, Australia, and the USA.[14] He states that the essential feature of England's present system is that it was "a gigantic monopoly in the ownership of the land."[15] With the aid of statistical data he shows that in England there is one landowner for every 220 persons.[16] His solution is the abolition of the law of primogeniture.[17] He has no hesitation in stating when things went wrong: "Primogeniture was unknown to our English forefathers, who divided the land equally. It was brought in by the Normans."[18]

Although the subject of these essays is different from the educational issues that occupied Leach for the remainder of his career, the methodology is not. Like the educational climate considered from a historical standpoint, the legal climate of his fellow countrymen is characterized by "confusion," and, however explained, confusion is a malady which ought to be dispelled as quickly as possible. Moreover, he intended such clarification not only for the legal profession but equally for the reading public. Leach believed he had the necessary historical background and instructional ability to communicate his findings to all those concerned with the origins of the nation's formative institutions.

Some of these aims and abilities were later put to the test when Leach attempted to win the approval of a well known contemporary, Frederic William Maitland (1850–1906). Founder of the Selden Society, which was devoted to the study of the history of English law, Maitland not only edited several of its volumes but also published (partly in collaboration with Frederick Pollock) the two volume *History of English Law Before the Time of Edward I*. This study, embodying a new reconstruction of the development of medieval English government, provided an alternative to the widely accepted view presented by William Stubbs in his three volume *Constitutional History of England*, first published in 1874–78. With the almost simultaneous publication of *Domesday Book and Beyond* (1897) and his *Roman Canon Law in the Church of England* (1898), Maitland had, by the time he encountered Leach, established himself as the foremost historian of medieval law in his day.

In 1898 Leach suggested to Maitland that he edit the Book of the Provost of Beverley (based on the Manor Rolls of 1416) for the Selden Society.Having written *English Schools at the Reformation* two years earlier, Leach was intent, it would appear, on being accepted as a competent editor in the difficult field of medieval Latin.[19] Maitland's negative reaction was compensated for by his suggestion that Leach do something with the material dealing with the town of Beverley that he had noticed in Leach's house. Leach offered to work up the town ordinances of Lincoln as well. He abandoned this latter project at Maitland's recommendation when it became clear that Leach had produced an abundance of material on Beverley alone.[20]

Beverley Town Documents was published in 1900 as volume 14 of the publications of the Selden Society. Leach refers to himself on the title page as "of the Middle Temple, Barrister at Law, Assistant Charity Commissioner." Maitland had no problem with the body of the text itself. Neither Maitland, nor the Society's honorary secretary, Lock, questioned Leach's ability to edit such a work. Maitland's biographer probably captured their opinion quite accurately in his comment that "with the text Leach was on comfortable terms."[21]

Unfortunately Leach's fondness for reading too much into the text exercised Maitland's patience. Moreover, in Maitland's opinion, the introduction was too rambling and even the grammar itself was "hardly respectable." As he remarked, "I should much like to tell him that this won't do for the Selden." However, especially disconcerting was the way in which Leach "gives the rashest judgment about the most disputable matters."[22] Maitland would not endorse Leach's plan for a companion volume on Lincoln since he had failed to persuade Leach "not to plunge into speculations about the craft guilds" of the twelfth century. As he said, Leach was "perfectly civil, nay jovial" but at the same time "sweet on his own stuff" and was one who "has not read enough to know how thin it is."[23]

A glance at Leach's introduction enables the reader to appreciate the validity of Maitland's criticism. Almost from the first pages, Leach reveals his fondness for large, bold strokes of comparison, frequently enlisted in support of the central importance of the medieval church.

Beverley today is a small market town with a parish church a great deal too big for it ... In the days with which we are dealing the East Riding was by far the most populous, the wealthiest, and the busiest of the Ridings. The minster was the East Riding cathedral of that great ecclesiastical and secular potentate the Archbishop of York, with a Provost and a Chapter of canons of its own, invariably drawn from the ranks of the greatest eccle- siastics and state officials of the day, and a large staff of clergy – chancellor, precentor, treasurer, grammar schoolmaster, vicars choral, chantry priests, clerks, and others; while the town itself was one of the greatest seaports and mercantile towns in the kingdom.[24]

In his general observations Leach reveals his exasperation at what he considers undue ecclesiastical influence. In his account of the agreement reached in 1536 between Edward Lee, the archbishop of York, and the burgesses of Beverley, he states that the archbishops, as lords of Beverley, had "hung round the necks of the burgesses for centuries," preventing them from attaining that freedom that burgesses in other towns of similar size and importance had long since achieved.[25] Although in this and later publications Leach cor- rectly insisted upon the central importance of the church's role in medieval education, he also exhibited a persistent annoyance with what he perceived to be ecclesiastical authority operating in its own self-interest. Maitland, in his initial reaction to Leach's introduction, remarked on this when he wrote to Lock: "I don't like suffragan or other bishops, but Leach's gird at them can hardly stand."[26] An example of Leach's excess is his account of a dispute involving Car- dinal Wolsey and Sir Ralph Ellerker, a knight, accused of being "an arrant poacher." Leach both generalizes and anticipates by noting that "the scandalous way in which the spiritual power of St John of Beverley was brought to bear on the unhappy knight makes it easy to understand why the bulk of the upper classes of the laity looked on with ready glee at the spoliation of the spiritual lords."[27]
Equally well founded was Maitland's concern with Leach's spec- ulations on the twelfth-century craft guilds. Although Leach had stated initially that their history was "extremely obscure," he went on to make several far-reaching claims. Leach insisted that, at least in the later Middle Ages, the merchant guild was but one of the craft guilds – "though indeed the premier one" – no more to be identified with the town government than any other craft guild. On this im- portant point Leach was taking issue with writers whose work on this and related topics was more extensive than anything that he had done himself. He seems, nonetheless, to have been quite keen on

exposing their work as both fallacious and misleading. Poulson's statements with respect to the identification of the merchant guild and Beverley's municipal government, for example, "are absolutely without authority and are totally inconsistent with the evidence he himself adduces." Leach regards even Charles Gross as misleading in his estimate of the weavers' position in fourteenth-century Beverley and inaccurate in his appraisal of them in the twelfth century.[28]

It can be seen that Leach thought of himself as a revisionist, as well as a codifier. His concern with the meaning of specific terms and his efforts to define and redefine important words and phrases is commendable in itself. He was concerned, for instance, with whether there was any distinction intended between the "men of Beverley" and the "burgesses" of the town in the twelfth century charter and with the force of the word "community" in the town's Magna Carta of 1359. Less commendable is his consideration of specific terms while he remains determined to maintain some overriding generalization. In such instances he frequently abandons moderate and judicious enquiries in favour of a more polemical approach that he too readily equates with well-founded conclusions.

Since Leach, as has already been mentioned, did not identify with the academic community, or even the legal profession for which he had been trained, one might easily infer that, at least as far as his research and writing were concerned, he pursued a quite isolated career. He was, however, an active and well-respected member of the Society of Antiquaries in London. There are several references in the society's proceedings between 1894 and 1910 to his communications and occasional interventions. Early in 1894, for instance, Leach gave a lengthy description of the foundation deed of a chantry in Beverley Minster dating from 1352, with the seal of the local Corpus Christi Guild attached. He included in his presentation the historical background of the complete Latin text.[29] A similar but shorter presentation in 1897 centered on his exhibition of the original charters granted by Humphrey de Bohun, Earl of Hereford and Essex, to the borough of Saffron Walden, some time between 1298 and 1321.[30] Probably the most controversial paper was that read to the society in 1909 in which he maintained that Colet's foundation at St Paul's was in reality a continuation of the ancient cathedral grammar school.[31]

To dwell for a moment on the more positive side of Leach's intentions, consider his industry, his ability to keep to his topic and finish it for publication, and his emphasis on basic source material, especially unpublished manuscripts. This argues an easy familiarity not only with Latin but also with palaeography, accomplishments to which Leach referred on occasion in dealing with school charters. Leach apparently considered at least part of his strength to lie in his capacity for bringing the essential elements of a process to the surface in the interests of simplicity and communication to others. He was at the same time distressed with the way in which material only half true, or at best a series of conjectures, passed for substantiated conclusions among so much of the reading public. Finally, Leach aimed at a broad spectrum of this reading public, however specialized his writing may appear to be.

Leach believed his primary task was to convince people that there actually were schools in England before the Reformation and that they were widespread throughout the country: "Wherever a grammar school now exists, ancient documents are likely to throw the history of the school back beyond the Reformation."[32] These documents were, however, not always known – not to mention made use of – by their custodians: "The town clerks of ancient boroughs, the incumbents of ancient churches, particularly those which have been collegiate or in which there have been several chantries, are very likely to have, even without suspecting it, documents bearing on the ancient history of schools."[33] Although admittedly the historical records for these schools are less than complete, Leach is more than convinced they are sufficient to establish that the commonly accepted notions of the provision for the education of England's medieval population "are extremely erroneous" and that the history of many of these schools "is much longer than is commonly supposed."[34]

Leach cites a wide range of examples, among them St Paul's. He confesses that to ask people to consider that St Paul's is older than Colet will, for the most part, appear "pure absurdity." Yet, he says, any difficulty attending the placing of St Paul's before Colet arises "not from a deficiency but from a superfluity of material."[35] He refers also to the grammar school at Northampton, where the pre-Reformation origins of that institution have been concealed by those who for "some obscure reason" have been reluctant "to admitting this antiquity of the provision of secondary schools in England."[36] In regard to St Albans, he notes that the origin of the school, lost "in the immemorial past," was recently incorrectly ascribed in that institution's "official account" to an action of the town corporation as late as c. 1569.[37]

Leach says that he has even come across the term "public school" in several pre-Reformation instances. As early as 1364, in a letter from the Bishop of Winchester to the Prior of Canterbury, the late schoolmaster of that monastery's almonry school is mentioned as having accepted the office of master of the public school at Kingston on Thames.[38] Similarly, the grammar school of Lincoln is referred to in 1436 as the "Public School."[39] Finally, discussing the cathedral grammar school at Durham, Leach claims that public grammar schools existed at Canterbury, Winchester, and Worcester as grammar schools of the city.[40] In spite of such examples, however, Leach sees an increasingly larger reading public falling victim to a traditional and uncritical attitude of mind with respect to a great chapter in England's past.[41]

An example of how Leach clarifies the history of many schools is the case of Newbury in Berkshire. He mentions that the Schools Inquiry Commission report listed Newbury as dating from "before 1677" on the strength of a Crown payment for that year in connection with the sale of Crown lands as equivalent to the stipend of the master of the town's grammar school (*ESR* 114). Although Lord Brougham's commission had acknowledged an earlier existence for the school, Leach points out that the commission had been unable to obtain the relevant chantry certificate that had continued the school. This certificate, he is now able to say, has since become available. It shows that a town grammar school was provided for in the will of Henry Wormestall in 1466. Wormenstall's lands and tenements in Newbury and Greenham were to provide not only for a priest to pray for his and all Christian souls forever, but also a sum equal to £12 2s. 4 1/2d. to be available to "Thomas Evans, Schoolmaster, teaching a Grammar School there, whereof that town hath great need" (*ESR* 114–15).

The evidence for the existence, continuation, or dissolution of schools provided by the chantry certificates is at the very centre of Leach's controversial main argument in his *English Schools at the Reformation*. Probably his most succinct explanation is the following:

These returns, known as the Chantry Certificates, are the main and in a number of cases the only source of our knowledge of the schools which existed in England before the Reformation. So completely extinct had this knowledge become before the publication of the educational items in these certificates in 1896, that the very existence of grammar schools before Edward VI was denied, and he was regarded as the founder of the institutions which his advisers set themselves to reform, and in only too many cases succeeded in disendowing and destroying."[42]

The central position Leach gave to these chantry returns in his investigations into the early history of the schools provided him with the very incentive that he needed, the overwhelming conviction that to establish his main line of argument he had to demolish the hitherto unquestioned view that Edward VI was the founder of England's school system. Not that the Chantry Acts were directly responsible for the destruction of schools. As Leach admits, "it is perhaps the case even that the statesmen of the day did not realize the full effects of their action in taking away the lands of the schools and substituting fixed stipends from the Crown." This would be even more probable, Leach says, if they had really intended to re-endow these schools at the first favourable opportunity. Nevertheless, the procedure, in Leach's view, "did in fact sign the death-warrant of scores of Schools" (*ESR* 114).

It is not a question of the school being put out of existence: at Newbury, for example, the chantry certificate makes it clear that, whereas the Crown took over the lands in virtue of the Chantries Act, the school itself was continued. Compared to nearby St Bartholomew's Hospital, which was exempt from the Act and flourished, Newbury School languished for a century or so with the schoolmaster left with a fixed stipend instead of an endowment (*ESR* 115). In another instance, Edward VI's commissioners suppressed a school established in the early sixteenth century at Week in Cornwall by the wife of Sir John Percival, Lord Mayor of London. The arrangement there had consisted of a chantry in the parish church to provide for a priest who would not only fulfill the usual obligation of prayers for her soul but also "teach children freely" in a school founded by Dame Percival not far from the parish church. The chantry would also provide for a maniciple, who, as Leach explains, combined boarding-house duties with teaching elementary pupils (*ESR* 116). Although, as Leach points out, a memorandum speaks of the chantry as a real need for the children in the area "for that they that list may set their children to board there, and have them taught freely, for the which purpose there is an house and officers appointed by the foundation accordingly," the commissioners refer to it as "in decay by reason it standeth in a desolate place and far from the market for provision of scholars." They recommended, therefore, that the school be suppressed in Week itself, but continued at Launceston, the shire town, which is "a very meet place to establish a learned man to preach and set forth the word of God to the people, and also to teach children their grammar, and other necessary knowledge," the two places being, as they remarked, only seven miles apart (*ESR* 116–17). Leach views this as another plan to replace an endowment with a fixed stipend, since the arrangement for the Launceston stipendiary was abolished in favour of one whereby "the pension of the priest [was] to be borne by the inhabitants of the town, because the Schoolmaster of S. Mary Week, by their own suit,

is removed hither." Leach thinks that there must have been difficulties over this transaction for the entry in the commission report
refers to the endowment of Launceston, by Queen Elizabeth out of
the revenues of the Duchy of Cornwall, to the master "who has always
been appointed by the Corporation." Leach's ironical comment is
that "thus was Queen Elizabeth credited with the good deeds of
Edward VI, who took the School endowment, but gave a fixed stipend instead" (*ESR* 118).

While Leach refers to this and other similar cases as instances of
the "Edwardian spoliation," he has nothing but praise for the principles involved in the transaction described above. He regards this
case, in fact, as "a remarkable instance" of Protector Somerset's "advanced views" in applying a founder's endowment to the best educational advantage, with the endorsement of enlightened local
authorities in the two centres concerned (*ESR* 118).

Bodmin, also in Cornwall – where, as Leach remarks, "new founders have not come forward, as in other parts of the country, to
make up for the Edwardian spoliation" (*ESR* 119) – experienced the
same melancholy fate. Lands and a priest's salary had been provided
for the grammar school in what Edward's commissioners themselves
described as "the greatest market town that is in all the shire" and
"a very meet place for a learned man ... for the Lord knoweth the
said 2,000 people are very 'ignorant'" (*ERS* 121). But all that was
provided for the continuance of the school was the salary (£5. 6s.
8d.). This Crown payment, however, "credited as usual to Queen
Elizabeth" as Leach observes, was listed as discontinued in Lord
Brougham's commission of 1837 and was identified in the 1867
School Commission Report as one "formerly held in St Thomas'
Chapel" and now in abeyance (*ESR* 121).

The reader, Leach says, would only be wearied if confronted with
a succession of such examples illustrating Edward VI's method of
founding schools. Nonetheless, he "can turn over the documents
and see for himself how the 226 Schools recorded fared, many of
them destroyed at once," and, with a touch of irony, "many more
fading away under the tender attentions of that careful educational
planter" (*ESR* 122).

Leach is prepared to clear up several points connected with the
chantry certificates and the misleading notions that have been based
on them. One is that Henry VI deserves more credit than is usually
accorded him for educational foundations. Leach describes the munificence that attended the founding of Eton College. He begins with
Henry's signed warrant of 3 June 1446, reciting his grant to the
college that "it might always have in its precinct a public and general
grammar school" (the first time, Leach remarks, that the term "public

school" was used of Eton) and that the same school, as it surpassed all other grammar schools of the kingdom "in the affluence of its endowment and the pre-excellence of its foundation," was to be recognized as such by its name of the King's General School "and be called the lady, mother and mistress of all other grammar schools" (*SME* 258).

Leach asserts on some occasions that the sovereign most deserving of praise as an educational founder is Edward VI's father, Henry VIII. This view is based on Henry's conversion of a number of dissolved monasteries into collegiate churches with grammar schools attached to them, as well as a similar conversion of several hospitals into schools – entirely or in part – after they, too, had been dissolved. Leach goes on to estimate that "not less than 200 grammar schools and a larger number of song schools" were connected with Henry VIII's intended suppression of clerical foundations along the lines of the previous monastic suppressions. He points out, however, that whereas an act of Parliament had been passed in the winter of 1545–46 giving Henry this power, he died before he had time to suppress more than a score of them. Only in the new reign of Edward VI could the fruit of this act be realized with the passing of the Chantries Act, which vested all the endowments of these institutions in the Crown after Easter 1548.[43] As Leach, of course, was aware, the schools that came under the Chantries Act represented only a fraction of the total number of school foundations, but what he is concerned to show is how particular educational institutions fared under this Act. He explains this by stating that the commissioner in question charged a yearly stipend for the schoolmasters to the Crown revenues in each county from the net amount he realized from a dissolved college or chantry.[44]

The trouble was, Leach says, "the sum was fixed" and no allowance was made for incidental sources of revenue, including the holding of another chantry, as at a collegiate church, to augment the regular stipend of the schoolmaster. Leach remarks that this kind of arrangement "had added to the attractions of the office and of course ceased with the change in religion and the destruction of the collegiate churches." Leach cites instances to illustrate how this worked in practice. In Southwell Minster, the stipend of the schoolmaster had been £10 a year, but in 1504 he had been given in addition the richest chantry in the Minster, worth £13. 6s. 8d. a year, thus doubling his income. The effect of the chantry commission was to reduce his successor's income to £10 again.[45]

Another case cited is that of Birmingham, where the land given became urban and the "unearned increment" accordingly much greater. Birmingham was deprived of the chantry grammar school at Deritend because no foundation deed could be furnished to show that one of its priests was required to keep a school, although, as Leach claims, one actually did so at £5 a year salary. Birmingham did, however, acquire two-thirds of the lands of the Holy Cross Guild – it is not clear precisely how, whether by purchase or gift – producing £25 a year. Leach goes on to observe that this sum had increased by 1907 to more than £40,000 a year, enough to provide schooling for more than 1,450 boys and 1,267 girls in two high and seven grammar schools.[46]

Leach asks his readers to compare this prosperous achievement with what happened at the neighboring school of King's Norton, a "much larger and better endowed school" than Deritend was in the early sixteenth century. King's Norton was continued by the chantry commission at the fixed salaries then received – £10 for the master and £5 for the usher – the total reduced by fees of the Crown officials to £13 9s. As a result, Leach says, "the school was at the time of the Schools Inquiry Commission in 1867 a sham grammar school in which three boys learned Latin and some forty the three R's."[47]

Leach concludes that if any of the reforming rulers is entitled to credit for educational foundations, it is Henry VIII, not his son, Edward VI (*SME* 277). With regard to Henry VI he writes: "Henry VI, far more than Edward VI, deserves to be remembered as a founder of English schools and as an eminent promoter, though by no means creator, of English education" (*SME* 251). With this claim Leach has seemingly pushed back the chronological focus of English education by a full century, but the reader may well question the force of his conviction.

The unwary reader might easily get the impression that one of Leach's main concerns is to take issue with the Reformation and to argue that this great watershed in history was – at least with regard to education – a retrograde step and not the great movement forward that it has been depicted to be. This view of Leach's intention, although consistent with some of his statements, does not stand up to closer inspection. For Leach, the two most important aspects of the Reformation in England were the rejection of papal jurisdiction and the suppression of the monasteries. Leach is careful to note any advantages to education accruing from the latter. This is why he can speak of a "record in the history of the schools" with some degree of consistency when he refers to the addition in a single year of ten richly endowed public boarding schools supplied with ample university scholarships, no fewer than twenty-four of these at Canterbury and twelve at Worcester. Leach makes his point quite explicitly: "This is a remarkable refutation of the views of the feeble-minded semi-Reformers of the day and their lately resuscitated theories that the Reformation did not advance but retarded education."[48]

Other monasteries, Leach claims – he cites as an example Thornton Abbey in Lincolnshire – were converted into collegiate churches "with similar grammar schools attached." But these, Leach says, are useless to mention except in vindication of Henry's action as they were abolished again under Edward VI, Cranmer "regarding the canons of collegiate churches as drones little more useful than monks."[49]

Finally, after establishing to his own satisfaction how ancient England's schools actually were, Leach moved naturally to a consideration of their extension and geographical distribution around this country. In this matter Leach became involved in controversy over two related issues: the comparison of educational provision before the Reformation with that in his own day and the relationship of medieval education to the church. Remarking on the "deplorable deficiency of the supply of public secondary schools throughout the country" as revealed at the Conference on Secondary Education that had met at Oxford in 1893, Leach quotes a summary of the Report of the Schools Inquiry Commission to the effect that in 1865–66 there were about 800 secondary schools of all grades. These included, he notes, a large number that were hardly more than elementary schools – "as elementary school was then understood" – and many of these, he claims, were "decrepit" and not far from "extinction." What this means, then, is that for the population of 19,000,000 at that time there was only one secondary school for every 23,750 persons.[50]

Leach has no doubts about when the country was more liberally supplied with schools. "There is not the smallest doubt that the provision for secondary education was far greater in proportion to population during the Middle Ages than it has ever been since" (SS 675). Although Leach admits that "it is difficult to arrive at a precise estimate of the proportion of schools to population," partly owing to our uncertainty about England's population at a given point in the Middle Ages, (SS 683) he feels confident enough to suggest some broad comparisons. He takes the county of Hereford to serve as a practical example of what may well have existed on a national scale.

Leach reckoned the population of Herefordshire at some 25,000; that of the town of Hereford 3,568; and of Ludlow, "then seemingly reckoned in Herefordshire," 2,198 – making some 30,000 in all. Leach then notes the presence of the cathedral grammar school in Hereford, a guild school in Ludlow, and a collegiate grammar school in Ledbury. He states that, in addition to these, at the time the colleges and chantries were suppressed there were fourteen grammar schools in the county. That is, for a population of some 30,000 there were seventeen grammar schools. Leach's question is, "Where should we find in 1877, or 1893, a population of 30,000, or even 60,000, with 17 grammar schools at its command?" Although conceding that Herefordshire might have had more than the average number of schools normally found in a single county, Leach posits a minimum of ten schools for each of forty counties. This would suggest a maximum population of 2,250,000, one grammar school "for every 5625 people," in marked contrast to the findings of the Schools Inquiry Commission of one "to every 23,750" (SS 684).

Leach's full argument about the range of educational resources at the disposition of people in pre-Reformation England is contained in "School Supply in the Middle Ages," probably one of his best studies. His main line of argument is that from the introduction of Christianity to the Reformation, education was an ecclesiastical concern. "Education was, if not a first charge on the endowments of the Church, at all events a well-recognised part of the duties for the performance of which the endowments were given." Since the Church was ubiquitous, so education was in some form ubiquitous, "if not universal" (SS 675). All that has to be done, therefore, is to locate those kinds of ecclesiastical institutions that would require a school of some kind and proceed to a geographical survey of their extension throughout the whole country.

In this connection Leach identifies the larger centres of population with two institutions: the cathedral and the collegiate church. He remarks that "the cathedral cities were then, what they are not now, the great towns of England," and the cathedral schools might be considered the ancestors of the modern public schools. There were seventeen cathedral cities. Even towns like Salisbury, Chichester, and Wells were still important, the last-mentioned being larger in 1377 than Southampton or Derby (SS 676, 678, passim). Leach is confident that all such centres were active: "Every cathedral church maintained in early days a small university, and, to the last, afforded instruction in what was regarded as the highest faculty, theology" (SS 675).

Leach is equally confident in regard to the educational facilities provided by the much larger number of collegiate churches: "Every collegiate church kept a secondary school" (SS 675). At times he identifies collegiate churches with towns of "secondary size," such as Beverley, Wolverhampton, and Warwick, but he also speaks of them as located in small towns. Leach estimates there were at least 200 such collegiate churches. Together with the seventeen cathedrals, he regards them as the backbone of the entire educational system of the country. Repeatedly noting the canonical obligation of these collegiate churches to maintain grammar schools, Leach tends, nevertheless, to base his contention on the more ancient among them, apparently leaving open the question of the educational facilities provided by the numerous later examples. For instance, from 1269 to 1340 there is, in the chapter act book of the minster, "repeated mention" of Beverley's grammar school and the appointment of the master by the church's chancellor. So too at Leicester where the grammar master is mentioned in 1242, and at the collegiate church of Ottery St Mary in Devonshire in 1399 when Bishop Stafford, in assigning the distribution of a bequest from two citizens of London, includes both the grammar and song schoolmasters (*SS* 678–9).

Leach also points out that, in the absence of a collegiate church, grammar schools in towns were conducted in connection with three different kinds of institution: corporations or guilds, hospitals, and chantries. Many country villages possessed grammar schools as well, through the benefaction of a pious founder whose wish to adorn his manor or to commemorate his birthplace frequently bore little relation either to the school's chances of success or the requirements of the population (*SS* 676). At Oxford there were "crowds of grammar schools," those of Merton and Magdalen College being only two among many. He also states that there was a regular faculty or subfaculty of grammar at Oxford and degrees were awarded in the subject. As far as the guilds themselves are concerned, Leach is confident that "in those towns where there was no collegiate church there was, nevertheless, nearly always ... a grammar school maintained; most often by a guild, often by or in connection with a hospital, failing that by a chantry created for the purpose." He cites instances of such guild schools at Stratford-on-Avon, at Ludlow, and at Ashburton, where the Guild of St Lawrence was entrusted with the school founded by Bishop Stapledon of Exeter in his native place (*SS* 679).

Leach is equally confident of the contribution of the schools maintained in connection with hospitals and chantries. Identifying a later medieval hospital more with an almshouse than with a modern institution of that name, Leach mentions grammar schools at London's St Anthony's Hospital at Exeter (where the grammar school was originally established in the Hospital of St John in 1332), and at Reading, where the almshouse was converted into a grammar school in 1486. As for chantry schools, "it is unnecessary to give instances" since, as Leach contends, "nine-tenths of the grammar schools of Edward VI's foundation (so-called) were continuations of pre-existing chauntry schools" (*SS* 680).

Because other schools kept by great nobles in their households "probably did not affect the mass of the people," Leach does not discuss them (SS 682). Turning to the poll tax of 1377, however, Leach delves into the relationship of town populations to the estimated number of schools at that time. London, with 44,000 people, is credited with at least six known grammar schools; York, with 13,500, is credited with at least three; and Bristol, with 12,000 people, probably had three (SS 683–4).

Leach notes that all the other towns contained a population under 10,000, with twenty-six of them having fewer than 4,000 residents. With hardly an exception, every one of these towns – "which would not make a decently sized nineteenth-century village" – possessed a grammar school, in some cases two or three. Leach also notes that the schools were well attended: there were 120 students, for instance, at Bruton, sixty at Kynnersley in Herefordshire, and a limit of twenty-six at a tiny place like Wollaton, near Nottingham (SS 684).

Leach, therefore, is confident that there was a widespread network of grammar schools extending throughout pre-Reformation England, that the backbone of the school system was the cathedral and the collegiate churches, and that this provision of schools in pre-Reformation England far exceeded what was available in the way of educational provision for the children and youth of his own generation. Leach was encouraged and confirmed in his views of the relatively widespread provision for education in later medieval England by his conviction that education was at that time closely identified with the church. As it had been from the earliest times, "education was the creation of religion, the school was an adjunct of the church, and the schoolmaster was an ecclesiastical officer."[51] He cites the grammar school at Oswestry (c.1423) as "one of the earliest instances of a school entrusted to a mixed body of laymen and clerics, and not part of, or dependent on, an ecclesiastical foundation, college, hospital, or chantry" (SME 235).

Leach was especially motivated to establish the ecclesiastical character of pre-Reformation England by what appeared to him to be widespread ignorance of this central historical fact. Nowhere did he see this more clearly than in the commonly held assumption that the great public school of Winchester was a secular or lay institution from the beginning. "It has been said and repeated that Winchester College was not an ecclesiastical foundation. This is a fundamental error. All educational foundations were then also ecclesiastical."[52] Statements like the above do not advance his argument with any precision, but, as he frequently does, Leach goes directly to the document(s) in question. He finds that the statutes of New College,

of which Winchester is a dependent preparatory school, are sufficiently clear: the very first clause, in fact, reveals that Wykeham's
intention was "to fill up the gaps" in the educated secular clergy
"caused by the Black Death."[53] As might be expected, therefore,
Leach lays great stress on the bishop's responsibility for the conduct
of the schools in his diocese, the keeping of a public school being
the concern "not of the monks, but of the secular clergy." A case in
point is Worcester, where, Leach says, the earliest records show that,
although, as in other cathedral cities, monks had replaced secular
canons as the cathedral staff, the school itself was under the control
of the bishop and was situated, not on monastic property, but "outside it in the city."[54] In 1312, in Worcester, the bishop of that city,
Walter Reynolds, conferred the direction of the city's grammar
school on a Master Hugh of Northampton with the concluding
words: "Whether the collation of the same belongs to us in right of
our bishopric or as archdeacon, saving always the rights and dignity
of our church of Worcester."[55]

Leach also relates instances of excommunication exercised to prevent rival schoolmasters from encroaching on the rights of the recognized teacher. He considers this as perhaps "the most salient
proof" of the extent to which "schools, scholars, and learning were
in pre-Reformation times matters of ecclesiastical ... law and under
the cognisance of the ecclesiastical courts."[56] Leach cites an instance
from 1410 in which two grammar school teachers brought a writ of
trespass against a third master who had opened a school without the
collation of the prior of Llanthony. The case was heard at common
law, but the ruling was that the action could not be tried there for
two reasons. One was that the plaintiffs had no estate at common
law in their office but only a ministry of office that depended on the
grant of the prior. The second reason was, Leach says, because
"teaching and information of children was a spiritual matter; ... Education was a matter of ecclesiastical law, and therefore for cognizance
of the ecclesiastical courts."[57]

Leach is not in any doubt in regard to the ecclesiastical nature of
the schools. "The earliest school in England of which we have definite
information is precisely where we should expect to find it, viz., in
the earliest ecclesiastical foundation in the country, the Cathedral
School at Canterbury" (SS 676). In spite of some of the social changes
affecting the educational structure of the later Middle Ages, described later in this study, Leach sees this basic relationship of the
church and the school as continuing from the earliest Christian communities in England until the period of the Reformation. During
this period education was the responsibility of the clergy and was "a

matter of cognizance in the ecclesiastical courts." From the university to the village school, Leach contends, "every educational institution was an ecclesiastical one" and, allowing for some degree of exaggeration, asserts that "those who governed it, managed it, and taught in it were ecclesiastics" (*SS* 675).

Leach was equally at pains, however, to distinguish the secular ecclesiastical jurisdiction from that of the monastic order. There were, in fact, few topics which exercised Leach's patience more than monastic education. His fellow countrymen had shown an uncritical acceptance of what he regarded as an historical myth – the identification of most of the educational life of pre-Reformation England with the monks and the monasteries. At the beginning of the century a writer like Nicholas Carlisle had tried to provide historical validity for this view, while at the end of the century an historian of Winchester College could still say: "One of the chief novelties of Wykeham's school was that it was not, as most previous schools had been, a monastic school."[58] The myth did not reflect admiration of the monks and their schools. Quite the contrary: in an article published in the *Edinburgh Review* an historian describes monasticism as a system that not only severely restricted the exercise of one's mental powers, but militated against "all natural affection," a system that promoted "the keenest intellectual subtlety" while at the same time it crushed "the slightest movement in any forbidden direction."[59]

When, in the closing pages of *The Schools of Medieval England*, Leach invites the reader to reflect on the long-term effects of monasticism on English medieval education, he speaks of the quiet thinker as being "lured into the cloister" and the progressive thinker as being "under a ban" owing to a climate of repression that, especially in the fields of theology and philosophy, is "most dangerous." From the perspective of his own personal religious convictions, Leach regards the monk as a formative influence in the area of superstition, the kind of religious practice that Leach associates with the chantry. From the perspective of national history, he views the monk as an unfortunate and unhealthy by-product of the Norman Conquest.

It must, therefore, be recognized that Leach's concern with monasticism reaches much deeper than merely showing whether the monks taught school themselves or paid others to do it for them. He dissociates the monks from the world of learning itself, even suggesting that they are foreigners to the English way of life. Henry VIII's dissolution of the monasteries is then seen by him as a long-awaited retribution for the monks, who had supplanted secular clergy in the first place through their Norman connection, both before and after the Conquest.

Leach's major study of this topic was his publication in 1913 of *Documents Illustrating Early Education in Worcester, 685–1700*. After remarking that it was usual before 1896 for people to ascribe practically all education before the Reformation to the monasteries, he contends that he has searched the monastic archives at Worcester for every possible reference to education but has found remarkably little. This will not, however, come as much of a surprise, he remarks, to persons familiar with his articles in the *VCH* pertaining to schools connected with the great abbeys of Reading, Abingdon, St Albans, and Bury St Edmunds, or the cathedral priories of Durham and Winchester. It will be even less of a surprise to readers of his history of Winchester College, "in which the vague talk about monastic schools was subjected to scientific scrutiny and tested by records." This paucity of educational material ought, in fact, to dispose of any notion that monks were the main educators of the Middle Ages.[60]

In order to help sever the association of monasteries and education once and for all, Leach has recourse to several related arguments. One of these has to do with the earliest historical records of the cathedrals. He says: "The Cathedral Chapter at Worcester was originally one of secular clergy, as it was everywhere in England as elsewhere, till the monastic movement connected with the names of Dunstan and Oswald at Worcester."[61] The experience at Worcester, therefore, will, in Leach's view, dispel any notion that the monasteries were responsible for education. The sources of what might be called "the monastic educational thesis" are not far to seek. A former minor canon of Worcester, Leach asserts, had argued that the school there had owed its inception to St Oswald's introduction of the Benedictine rule. In his *Life of St. Oswald*, however, Eadmer does not connect the saint with the actual founding of the school, contends Leach, but rather with the restoration of learning on the part of the monks whom Oswald had brought in to replace the secular canons (*EEW* xv).

Leach comments that Eadmer was merely a romantic writer viewing events a century and a half after they had happened and more than half a century after the Norman Conquest. Here, as in other places, Leach assumes he is on firmer ground than medieval or early modern writers. In his view, a much better authority was the nearly contemporary biographer, the Saxon monk at Ramsey, who, writing within twenty years of Oswald's death, makes it quite clear that what was in question was not grammar or any other of the liberal arts but merely "the monastic custom" for the benefit of "intending monks" (*EEW* xv).

Leach notes that the first definite document mentioning Worcester Grammar School dates only from 1291. This document, he says, "shews us the schoolmaster and the school boys in the parish, and no doubt on the very spot in which the schoolmaster is found 300 years later at the dissolution of chantries, in the centre of the city, far outside the monastic precinct, and under the jurisdiction of the bishop, not of the prior or monks" (*EEW* xix). Similarly, a second instance is cited from 1429 when a bishop, Thomas Pulton, again appointed a chaplain, Sir John Bredel, to "our grammar school in our city of Worcester." Leach infers from this that the bishops in those days not only exercised their functions as school governors in regard to patronage "but also in seeing that the school was well conducted, and removing a master who conducted it ill." In this particular instance, Bredel replaced a former chaplain who had been accused of, among other things, "negligence ... want of attention and idleness" (*EEW* xxiv-xxv).

Leach insisted that the Benedictine monks could not have kept grammar schools in medieval England, if for no other reason than that their own rule, as well as canon law, forbade their accepting outsiders into their precinct. They could not, then, have kept a public school. And, he also argues, when monks did teach other monks in novices' schools, they were really teaching them the rule of the monastery and "the peculiar monkish services by heart." As Leach claims to have shown from the *Obedientiary Roles* of Winchester, such a school was frequently very small indeed, ten students at the most, frequently fewer than that, and sometimes none at all (*EEW* ii).

To eliminate any lingering notion that the monasteries somehow conducted grammar schools, Leach argues that the majority of monastic candidates would have received their Latin education before entering the monastery. Even in cases where they still had to learn Latin after entering the monastery, there would not have been enough of them to make a school. He emphasizes that the majority of monks entered the monasteries when they were already mature young men. Eighteen years was the specified minimal age, for instance, at the abbeys of St Augustine (Canterbury) and Westminster in the fourteenth century.

To illustrate this further, Leach cites particular examples, such as Prior Selling of Canterbury (1472–95), who, he says, was a fellow of All Souls College, Oxford, and had already studied Greek in Italy before he entered the monastery, and Henry Holyman, bishop of Bristol, who had been a scholar of Winchester and fellow of New College before becoming a monk of Reading around 1530 (*EEW* ii).

While Leach is ready to concede that novices entering religion with the benefit of a university education would not be very numerous, he is quite convinced that most of them would have completed their grammar school education before coming to a monastery. He argues that while the not infrequent entry *ad religio-nem* placed against a scholar's name in the Winchester register, for example, might imply that a large number of monks entered religious life as boys and therefore required further education, very few were in need of it. Leach points out, for instance, that at Winchester, where the full complement of monks was "theoretically" sixty, the rolls disclose that the novices never exceeded ten in number and more often than not scarcely half that figure. Citing forty as typical of Worcester's size from 1290 onwards, Leach argues that eight novices would have been that monastery's maximum. Most of these would have needed only the more specialized instruction related to the rule and the liturgy, since "a considerable proportion had been educated before they came" (*EEW* xlv).

Finally, Leach discredits the monks as educators by trying to show that their attitude towards university life was at the very best ambiguous. He states that "a curious illustration of the disregard of the monks to any form of learning" is to be found in two letters written in 1305 by the abbot of Westminster, who was president of the general chapter of Benedictine monks. In the first letter the abbot complains that the prior of Worcester neglected to provide for the theological lectures in the cathedral prescribed by canon law; in the second letter he objects to the renewal of these lectures being made to depend on the prior's withdrawal of one of his two university scholars for the purpose before the latter had finished his course. The evidence, however, goes in both directions, and Leach is honest enough to admit that the records show that, at least from 1300 onwards, "Worcester Priory seems to have maintained with fair regularity two monk-scholars at Oxford" (*EEW* xxxviii).

Leach attached to his quite lengthy study of Worcester a collection of representative documents, including one of 5 July 1423 concerning the failure of particular monasteries to provide student facilities at Oxford or Cambridge for one or more of their monks. The prior of students at Cambridge, for example, not only cited the abbot of Colchester for withdrawing a scholar of his monastery from the university for an entire year without sufficient reason, but also called upon the president of the assembly discussing these matters to urge upon the various abbots concerned the need for money to provide a hall for monks studying at Cambridge. Others cited for negligence included the abbots of Abbotsbury, Tavistock, Burton, and Hyde; in one way or another they had withheld support for university studies for from one to seven years. The abbot of Chester was cited in particular for his not having had a scholar at university for nearly twelve years (*EEW* 66–8, passim).

With a high degree of satisfaction, Leach concludes his introductory account of Worcester, insisting that "after this exposition of the facts" there is no further ground for the traditional identification of monks with schools or education. If the priory of Worcester is any example, in fact, all its educational activity was confined "to instructing its three or four novices in the Rule, and such preliminary learning of Latin as they had not acquired before entering the monastery" (*EEW* lv).

An especially good example of the lengths to which Leach would go to sever any connection between a monastery and one of England's better known schools is furnished by his extensive study of Sherborne School in Dorset, published in 1898. Leach's study was intended to be a critical response to the *Short History of Sherborne* published two years earlier by one of the school's housemasters, W.B. Wildman. Although obviously well disposed towards him and thankful for the help Wildman has afforded him in his own research into the history of Sherborne, Leach is, nevertheless, concerned to show that Wildman's identification of the early school with the local abbey is historically untenable.[62] Leach begins by going all the way back to Bede, who mentions that in 705 the West Saxon province was divided into two parishes, one at Winchester, the other at Sherborne. Since there undoubtedly was a college of clerks at the cathedral centre of Winchester, Leach claims "we may be quite certain" that a similar college was established at Sherborne, and "if a college of clerks, then a grammar school." Satisfied by a similar line of inference that there had not been any monks at Sherborne before this development, Leach considers the late eleventh century in a somewhat fruitless attempt to identify precisely the school that Stephen Harding, founder of the Cistercians, had attended. Leach concedes that at the dissolution in the sixteenth century the surrender of the abbot and sixteen monks to the Crown apparently included the schoolhouse standing within the monastic grounds. Nevertheless, he continues to argue that the schoolmaster, "being a secular person outside the abbey, and not depending on a stipend from the abbey," must have continued the school somewhere else in the town.[63]

Leach's writings on this particular issue through the reign of Edward VI and the implementation of the Chantries Act shed little light on the monastic or secular origins of the grammar school at Sherborne. His argument may, indeed, impress the reader as both tortuous and obscure. Yet, Leach evidently considered it sufficient to conclude that Sherborne School had never been monastic.[64] In his study of Sherborne grammar school, Leach expresses some of his deepest convictions about monks and monasteries. He thinks of the monks as essentially feudal landlords. The parishioners of Sherborne, for example, derived no benefit whatever from the abbey church but had to build and take care of the parish church at their own cost "in a relatively humble building at the end of and outside the church of the lordly abbey." Moreover, Leach claims, monks were relatively inactive even in their religious mission among the people, as compared, for instance, with the friars. The monks were content to remain in their cloister, "praying and praising," it is true, but "cultivating their own souls." Whenever they left the cloister, it was either on business "connected with their property" or for their own pleasure, but "never for the religious benefit of the people." The inference, then, is that the reader need not be surprised to learn how little the monks actually contributed to education. They were expected to maintain grammar schools exclusively for their own novices but "they mostly failed to do even that."[65]

Leach recognized, nevertheless, that some monasteries and abbeys did have connections with particular grammar schools. To explain such relationships he drew attention to a few helpful distinctions. He explains, in connection with Abingdon School, that in the larger towns where the cathedrals were held by monks or where there were great monasteries, three different types of school were present. The only one that Leach regards as a school in any real sense was the public grammar school situated in the town, taught by secular clerks, priests, or laymen for the benefit of the general public, both clerical and lay. The other two, by contrast, were relatively small private classes, one conducted by a monk in the monastic cloister for the novices, the other for a few poor boys of the almonry who received their clothing, board, and lodging as well. This almonry school, Leach points out, was an early fourteenth-century development, under the control of the monastic almoner but taught by a secular clerk.[66]

Leach wants to make sure, though, that when schools appear to be directly related to monasteries, his reading public understands precisely what this means. In the earliest documents relating to the school in Gloucester, while it is clear that the canons of Llanthony Abbey, on the outskirts of the city, held the right of collation to the school, this amounted only to the appointment and licensing of the master to teach. There was no evidence, Leach insists, that the priory was expected to find an endowment for the master. He enlarges upon this point by stating that "the grammar school was peculiarly the bishop's child." Even in cathedral centres, Leach remarks, where the churches and their patronage became vested in the monks, as at Canterbury or Winchester, or in the regular canons, as at Carlisle, the bishop was careful not only to retain but to exercise the patronage of the school, and this he did, "either in person or through his archdeacon." In the monastic cathedral centre at Durham, Leach maintains, the true progenitor of the present cathedral grammar school was neither the almonry school nor the so-called novices' school, but a school established in 1414 by Bishop Thomas Langley. Even this foundation, however, must have had a precursor long before Langley's day, since "by all analogy" its development would no doubt have paralleled that of other monastic cathedral places such as those mentioned above.[67]

It may be said, in general, that a pronounced anti-monastic bias is evident in Leach's later writings, including his studies of Worcester and Sherborne and *The Schools of Medieval England*. In his *English Schools at the Reformation* (1896) his tone is more moderate. In this earlier work he was concerned to show that, contrary to popular belief, not all education in the Middle Ages was the responsibility of the monks. He concedes at the outset, for instance, that as ordinaries within their own limited monastic jurisdiction, as wealthy landlords, or as trustees acting on behalf of other people, the monks "may have controlled or even founded and maintained some Grammar Schools." He mentions places such as Evesham, Bruton, Cirencester, Lewes, and Bridgewater where some kind of relationship obtained between the monastery and a grammar school (*ESR* 15–19).

It is tempting to associate Leach's deepening bias against the monks with the publication of Francis Aidan Gasquet's favourable interpretation of them in his *Henry VIII and the English Monasteries*. This two volume work appeared in 1888–89, a short time before Leach brought out his *Visitations and Memorials of Southwell Minster* (1891). In *Southwell*, however, Leach pays tribute to Gasquet, referring to "Father Gasquet's brilliant book on Henry VIII and the Monasteries," and adds the following observation, with reference to his own research on Southwell: "The records of the triennial visitations of the church, held with fair regularity during the greater part of this period, supply most valuable evidence on the main thesis of Father Gasquet, that the allegations brought by Henry VIII and his Commissioners of Inquiry against the monasteries and other ecclesiastical establishments were false and scandalous."[68]

It is worth noting that Gasquet's remarks about monastic schools, expressed as they were in the most general terms, were not of a nature to upset Leach. In two footnote references in his Southwell book Leach acknowledges Gasquet's help with respect to obscure Latin terms. It could be inferred from this that, at least for a brief period, they corresponded on matters of common interest.[69] A search through the relevant sections of Gasquet's uncatalogued letters and other correspondence in the possession of Downside Abbey, however, has not revealed any written contact with Leach, while Gasquet's few notes on schools show an interest in the Latin instruction itself rather than in any institutional aspect.[70] All that can be inferred from Leach's own writing is that during the late 1890s his attitude towards Gasquet changed. This, at least, appears to be true in his 1910 debate with J.E.G. de Montmorency with respect to the education of women in medieval England. Leach refers to Gasquet's work in question as "that brilliant polemical pamphlet,"[71] and de Montmorency's integrity is assailed partly because he has relied for some of his information on Gasquet, who has cited his sources "with characteristic looseness."[72]

In conclusion, Leach did not, evidently, see any purpose in explaining his change of heart with respect either to medieval monasticism or to Gasquet. It seems probable that, as he found increasing evidence of how slight the connection was between the monks and the grammar schools, he grew increasingly exasperated at the durability of the traditional view associating the monasteries with whatever learning and education there was in pre-Reformation England. Gasquet's work could well have become an additional irritant to Leach in his constant effort to replace "myths" with "facts."

CHAPTER TWO

Background to the Endowed Schools Act of 1869

Leach was born into a generation of great educational activity. During his formative years at Winchester and Oxford, Queen Victoria's ministers took the first major steps to establish a system of national education. England was the last industrialized western nation to adopt such an educational program. Ever since Henry Brougham, an early advocate of reform and co-founder of the *Edinburgh Review* and the University of London, had attempted in 1820 to institute such a program in association with the established church, repeated attempts in this direction had invariably foundered on the irreconcilable differences between Anglicans and Nonconformists. Schools, therefore, continued to be an object of private enterprise and voluntary organization. By mid-century, however, an increasingly industrialized England had doubled its population within a single generation – to eighteen million from nine million. The majority of the new generation lived in cities and towns linked together by the new railway system, presenting a marked contrast to the predominantly rural country of 1800. What was needed, therefore, was nothing less than a new geography of education.

One of the more important pieces of legislation within the context of this educational ferment was the Endowed Schools Act of 1869. This act embodied the recommendations of the Schools Inquiry Commission of 1864–68. It addressed itself to some 782 grammar schools and 2,175 endowed elementary schools, providing for the new "schemes" connected with these schools to be transferred to an augmented charity commission. Leach was a student at Oxford when this legislation was passed, but when he became a charity commissioner fifteen years later, the Endowed Schools Act still constituted the point of departure for his subsequent historical investigations.

It is helpful to consider some of the main educational and historical questions that affected the political climate in which the act was passed – questions that Leach either includes in his publications or that probably influenced him in some direct way. When Leach later discovered the historical basis for the 1869 act to be very much in error, he attributed this to persons of his own generation having been brought up on a series of "myths" and half-truths in regard to England's educational past, not the least of which, as we have seen, was what could be termed the "monastic thesis."

One of the sources of erroneous educational history in general, and of monastic education in particular, was, in Leach's view, the early nineteenth-century historical writer Nicholas Carlisle, whose survey of schools had been drawn on for information by the framers of the Endowed Schools Act. Entitled *A Concise Description of the Endowed Grammar Schools in England and Wales*, Carlisle's two-volume work served as a handy compendium of educational history from its appearance in 1818 until Leach's day. Only occasionally does Leach refer to Carlisle, almost invariably in a negative vein. For instance, in his discussion of the origins of the grammar school at Derby, Leach claims that Carlisle repeated a mistake in Lyson's *Britannia* concerning the school's foundation deed. This error was in turn accepted in the *Endowed Schools Commission Report* in 1867, resulting in Derby's "being misplaced as the second earliest school in England" (*ESR* 124–5).

Carlisle's work, especially his style of writing, may now seem very remote indeed. More important, however, is his readiness to connect educational services with monastic foundations. This is one of the "myths" that Leach is at great pains to demolish virtually from the moment he sets out on his educational career. Carlisle says, in part: "The great increase of Religious Houses in this period [the late twelfth century], very much increased the number of Seminaries of learning, as there was a School more or less celebrated in almost every Convent. And some idea may be formed of the number added to the Schools by this means, when it is considered, that there were no fewer than 557 Religious Houses of different kinds, according to Bishop TANNER, founded in England between the Conquest and the death of King John."[1]

While acknowledging that the purpose of such monastic schools was partly fulfilled in the instruction of younger monks in the language and music of the Latin liturgy and in the production of beautiful manuscripts in the scriptorium, Carlisle does not hesitate to enlarge upon the educational scene: "In the Schools of all the larger Monasteries, besides the requisite parts of learning, several other Sciences were taught, as Rhetoric, Logic, Theology, Medicine, with the Civil and Canon law. These two last branches of learning, Law and Physic, being very lucrative, were so diligently studied and practised by the Monks, that they were almost the only *Pleaders* and *Physicians* of those times. Many persons of Rank and Fortune were also educated in these Conventual Schools, to which they frequently became Benefactors."[2]

Carlisle observes further that learning before the Reformation had been "much confined to the monasteries"; after the dissolution of these establishments it began to become diffused generally among the people, with the final result that literature itself became a measure of general policy.[3] Carlisle connects this diffusion of learning with the widespread creation of grammar schools in the generation before the change of religion. He views their establishment as "one of the Divine means for bringing about the blessed Reformation." He states that in those thirty years there were more grammar schools "erected and endowed" in England than had been the case during the preceding three centuries. But he also reserves special praise for Edward VI, under whose commission in 1549 the "regulation" of such schools was effected.[4]

If there is any topic that gives Leach as much concern as the "monastic" one, it is this unquestioning attribution of so many of the nation's grammar schools to the reign of Edward VI. Carlisle speaks of Edward as follows: "Unlike his Royal Father, his attention and solicitude were extended to every class of his Subjects, who felt the effects of his benign disposition; and his Princely endowments constitute at this day, part of the glory of the British Empire."[5] It is in this context that Carlisle then quotes with approval a comment that Erasmus had earlier made to Colet in praise of England's men of learning.[6]

Carlisle is not unaware of deficiencies in these proposed educational ventures after the Reformation. He refers, for example, to "the extreme avidity of EDWARD's ministers, which tempted them to impoverish every Ecclesiastical Foundation for their own benefit,"[7] and he mentions "the very low state of Public Education, in the middle of ELIZABETH's reign."[8] Nevertheless, he reserves most of his comments in this regard for his own generation. He states, for instance, that a select committee of the House of Commons, appointed to inquire into the education of the "Lower Orders" in London in 1816, concluded "that a very large number of poor Children are wholly without the means of Instruction, although their Parents appear to be generally very desirous of obtaining that advantage for them."[9] It must have been with some degree of satisfaction, therefore, that Carlisle could go on to recount that the same committee, in a second report of 7 July 1817, expressed the opinion "that it would be expedient to extend the instructions under which they act, so as to embrace an Inquiry into the Education of the Lower Orders generally throughout England and Wales."[10]

The government's concern with the state of education generally, both in London and throughout the country, encouraged Carlisle to examine the history of the educational foundations as carefully as he could with whatever sources were at his disposal. These sources are not impressive, for he has had to append to his preface a series of eighteen questions that he sent out to some 1,400 headmasters of grammar schools throughout England and Wales, requesting information on the origins and original endowments of their institutions.[11]

Of greatest concern to Carlisle is the decline in the original endowments, a matter that will later be discussed by Leach at some length. Carlisle does not identify any of these ill-treated institutions, but it is clear that he is referring to a situation generally well known, since he calls for a public investigation and reform of such evils, which are "only within the power of Parliament."[12]

In order to illustrate the kind of returns that Carlisle received from his inquiry, it might be useful at this point to include four or five of the schools with particular relevance to Leach's own investigations. The Free Grammar School at Sherborne, adjoining the east end of the church, "was founded, and very liberally endowed by King EDWARD the Sixth, in the Fourth year of his reign, 1551." Carlisle mentions that the governors of Sherborne School – twenty of the principal inhabitants of the town – were given, in partial support of the school, the whole of the dissolved chantry of Martok, the dissolved chantry of St Catharine in the church of Gillingham, and the Free Chapel of Thornton in the parish of Marnhull, all of these in the county of Dorset. Carlisle also mentions that the revenues of the school have formerly been "much neglected, if not abused" but that new regulations in recent years have been both proposed and adopted.[13]

In like manner, the grammar school at Durham "is coeval with the Foundation of the Cathedral Church, by King HENRY the eighth, on the 12th of May, 1541." The statutes of Durham are quoted to the effect that there shall be constantly maintained eighteen poor boys "whose friends are not able to give them education." After their admission they are to be maintained by the church "until they competently understand Grammar, and can read and write Latin, for which they shall be allowed *Four* years, or, with the Dean's assent, *Five* at the most." Carlisle notes in regard to Durham that "repeated applications have been made for information respecting this School, but no answers have been received."[14]

The Free Grammar School in Ripon "was founded and endowed in the year 1555, by King PHILIP and Queen MARY". Once again, Carlisle appears to be satisfied with this late date for the foundation of the school, mentioning in passing that the sovereigns had given over to the governors of the town and parish of Ripon all the possessions formerly associated with the late chantries of the Assumption of the Blessed Virgin Mary, of St James the Apostle, and of St John the Evangelist, all in Ripon.[15]

The account of the ancient foundation of Southwell is one of Carlisle's vaguest and constitutes a remarkable contrast to Leach's later study of the same institution. Noting that the date of foundation is not forthcoming, Carlisle mentions the will of Robert Batemanson, dated 23 June 1512, as the one document with any bearing on the topic. He points out, however, that there is nothing in the records of the collegiate chapter with regard to the fulfillment of this particular will. Moreover, he states that the chapter no longer possesses land at Egmonton, which was intended as the principal source of support for Batemanson's free grammar school in Southwell.[16]

Finally, there is a relatively extensive summary of the history of Westminster College, which, in Carlisle's opinion, ranks among the best establishments in the British Empire for the instruction of youth. Although he states that Westminster was founded by Queen Elizabeth in the year 1560, he is impressed with what he thinks is a history antedating this particular foundation. He refers, for instance, to the history of Croyland Abbey in which a school at Westminster is mentioned in the time of Edward the Confessor. He refers also to the life of Thomas Becket by William Fitzstephen in which the author speaks of the three chief churches in the metropolis as having schools attached to them. Carlisle was content with Stow's interpretation which included Westminster Abbey among such churches. He then states that from the late fourteenth century to the dissolution of the abbey the monastic almoner paid a salary to a schoolmaster, who is described as "*Magister Scholarum, pro eruditione puerorum Grammaticorum.*" Carlisle inferred from this that such a person was distinct from the one who taught singing to the choristers.[17]

Carlisle was able, then, to make a correct analysis of educational development when some of the essential documentary evidence was available to him. Leach did not acknowledge such accomplishments, convinced as he was that the repeated guesses and inferences of writers like Carlisle had helped to perpetuate false notions of educational history, including those central untruths that monasteries were centres of learning and Edward VI was a founder of schools.

Carlisle's mention of the two different teachers at Westminster, one for the grammar students, the other for the choristers, does, however, relate to one of the more specialized questions to which Leach addressed himself – the distinction in the medieval cathedrals and collegiate churches between the choristers and the grammar students. Leach frequently expressed annoyance at the confusion surrounding this point, which led so many people in his day to equate grammar schools with what he was prone to refer to as "mere choir schools." One of the persons he blamed for this confused notion was Maria Hackett, who in 1827, only a few years after the appearance of Carlisle's history, published her *Brief Account of Cathedral and Collegiate Schools.*[18]

This historical work had an immediate and practical end: to alleviate what seemed to her the distressful and difficult condition of the choristers in the cathedral churches, especially in St Paul's, London. The work consists of five parts. The first, a preface, includes a list of endowed choristers. The second part includes summaries of the various cathedral establishments throughout England and Wales. The third presents a number of letters bearing directly upon the condition of the choristers at St Paul's, London. The fourth is an appendix of documents and authorities with respect to the ancient collegiate foundation attached to St Paul's Cathedral. The fifth is a register of the almonry of St Paul's, taken from the Tower records.[19]

In the third part, Hackett calls upon the Lord Bishop of London to reflect on what she refers to as "the neglected situation of the Children belonging to St Paul's Choir". She states that whereas the choristers, from early times until quite recently, had been part of the dean's household and had been maintained and educated from cathedral funds, the fixed sum granted to the almoner in charge of them gradually, through the depreciation of money, became quite inadequate. Upon the refusal of the cathedral chapter to grant any increase, the almoner had no alternative but to give up his responsibility for instructing the choristers.

Hackett assumes that at least the main features of the history of St Paul's choristers were fairly well known to both the bishop of London and her readers. Without offering specific sources for her statements, she remarks that the children, living, for the most part, away from both church and singing master, waste much of their time loitering about the streets. Their education is much neglected, except for the instruction afforded them in connection with the required choral services and the occasional recitation of their catechism. In seeking at least a partial explanation for this state of affairs, Hackett has recourse to a historical explanation based on the confusion between the two schools at St Paul's. As she sees it, the boys of St Paul's choir are now treated as if they had no distinct claim to the property of the "ancient school" connected with the cathedral.

This stems, she asserts, from confusing Dean Colet's early sixteenth-century foundation, dedicated to the Child Jesus, with the continuation of the older St Paul's school. She insists that the two foundations are in reality quite distinct, the property belonging to Saint Paul's School not having been conveyed to the School of the Child Jesus.[20] Whatever the merits of this interpretation, it is diametrically opposed to that of Leach, who never tires of trying to show that Colet's foundation was actually a continuation of the older one, however new its direction may have been.

While much of the correspondence in the third part of her book involves Hackett's insistence on the rights of the choristers to their proper endowment and the corresponding efforts of the chancellor to explain his inability to accede to her request, her explanation for being so persistent is worth considering. Addressing the chancellor early in 1813, she dissociates herself from any popular clamour against sinecures. What she does insist upon, though, is that the endowments of the *magister scholarum* were intended expressly for the upkeep of his school. All she asks, therefore, is that the chancellor recognize his duty to restore the school to its "former respectability."[21]

Although civil enough, the chancellor's reply offered little encouragement to anyone campaigning on behalf of the choristers.[22] He claimed that the chancellorship brought in less revenue than that stated by Hackett – scarcely more than £60 a year, in fact – a sum insufficient for current purposes. She responded, saying that she feared all the estates belonging to the cathedral had been "sadly managed by the ruinous system of granting long leases on nominal rents."[23]

In April of the same year Hackett wrote the dean of St Paul's, saying that the more she pursued her inquiries, the more convinced she became that the boys of St Paul's choir had a right to a "Classical Education" from cathedral funds.[24] Three months later the chancellor communicated to her his own personal belief that teaching had little to do with the total scheme of things. Although he was ready to concede that his predecessors in office had at one time the duty of supplying, out of the endowments, a "a proper master" to teach the choristers grammar and "Morality," this duty had long since lapsed. He added that the revenues attached to the office for that purpose had been reduced to the equivalent of "a perfect sinecure."[25]

There appears not to have been any marked progress towards a resolution of the issue over the next decade, for in late August of 1826 Hackett once again pressed her case on behalf of the choristers to a new dean of St Paul's, the Right Reverend Charles Richard, Lord Bishop of Llandaff. She had devoted some effort in the intervening years to a broader and deeper study of the historical development of England's ecclesiastical institutions. She mentions in particular that she is now presenting her esteemed correspondent with an "Essay on Cathedral and Collegiate Schools, with an Abstract of their Statutes and Endowments." It is evident that it is a more competent and knowledgeable person who is now arguing the case for the choristers.[26]

Hackett thus returns with added credibility to the charge she had made more than a dozen years before. Her assessment of more contemporary developments recalls that of Carlisle:

It can scarcely be doubted that it was the degraded state of the Capitular School which induced the Dean to transfer his bounty to a new foundation, on a more liberal scale, and to place it under the government of *lay* patrons.

But, though the Ecclesiastical Grammar School survived for a time this invasion of its name and dignity, it ultimately sunk into a state of neglected obscurity. The secular establishment soon rivalled its less fortunate precursor in public esteem, and the periodical examinations of the pupils educating (sic) under the Mercers' Company are at this day honoured by the Dean and Chapter of St Paul's with that sanction and encouragement for which the School under their own jurisdiction languishes in vain.

I spare myself the painful task of pursuing the history of the School through its gradual decline, down to the lowest point of degradation, at the beginning of the present century.[27]

In summary, she argued that the school under the administration of the cathedral chapter had already reached a "degraded state" by the time of Colet. In transferring his bounty to a new foundation on a more generous scale and under the direction of lay patrons in the form of the Mercers' Company, Colet ultimately doomed the older, ecclesiastical school to a state of "neglected obscurity," which reached its nadir at the beginning of the nineteenth century.

The foregoing correspondence is sufficient to show that Hackett closely connected grammar schools with schools for the choristers of a cathedral or collegiate church. As with Carlisle, such a view was but one more challenge to Leach. His almost endless repetition can be traced, at least in part, to what he considered to be the unfounded assertions of these two writers.

In 1818, the same year in which Carlisle's historical work appeared, the Rev. W.L. Bowles published a letter entitled *A Vindication of Winchester College*, addressed to Henry Brougham, Esq. and occasioned by Brougham's letter to Sir Samuel Romilly on charitable abuses.[28] Identifying the *Edinburgh Review* as the principal source of repeated attacks on the great public schools of England,[29] Bowles attributes this attack to a perception that the original endowments of the college at Winchester had been diverted from the founder's original intention of providing for the "poor and indigent" to an enrichment of the warden and fellows. Bowles will have none of this, pointing out that Wykeham in employing the phrase *"pauperes et indigentes scholares"* could not have meant "mean, destitute, charity children" for three reasons. First, there is no stated provision for their maintenance during the first two years of their fellowship at New College, unless they are related to the founder. Second, if they had been poor in any but a comparative sense, they would not have had any means of arriving at the first level of education at which they were designated as scholars. Finally, Bowles says, it could hardly have been the founder's idea to leave them at Oxford afterwards without his seeing to their upkeep.[30]

Bowles then takes up a series of charges against Winchester, stemming, for the most part, from what was perceived as the easy living of an affluent student body in contrast to the poorer sections of the population for whom the school, it was charged, had been originally intended. After responding to these criticisms, Bowles mentions that he, himself, is one of those who have benefited from "the munificence of such a founder."[31] In a postscript he states that the main question is "whether the establishment, founded by William of Wykeham, has been diverted from those objects for which he intended it, and given to others, whom he had not in his contemplation."[32]

There is little question that Leach would have written a "vindication" of his *Alma Mater* in much the same way that Bowles did. The political and social import of the term *pauperes et indigentes scholares* was an essential element of the educational ferment in which Leach first took up his position as an assistant charity commissioner. The response to the question formulated by Bowles would be not only a principal concern of the charity commissioners in their implementation of the Endowed Schools Act, but also a sharp incentive to Leach personally to investigate the historical basis of the allegation that the poor and indigent were threatened with the loss of their rightful educational heritage.

As has already been stated, Leach cites Carlisle and Hackett on occasion as among the progenitors of the "myths" that, in his view, continued to plague the understanding of educational history throughout the nineteenth century. While he does not mention Bowles by name, the central issue raised by that writer – the true intent of the founder of Winchester's original endowments – was one that Leach was at constant pains to clarify over a much wider field than Winchester college. Disparate and unconnected as these writers appear to be, they mirror at least part of that climate of opinion from an earlier generation that provided the stimulus for Leach to initiate a fundamental questioning of his country's educational past.

In describing the educational developments that preceded Leach's entry on the scene as a charity commissioner, it is necessary to account for the spate of governmental intervention between 1849, when a royal commission was appointed to examine the conditions at the universities of Oxford and Cambridge, and 1870, when W.E. Forster's Education Act was passed. Both ends of the educational spectrum were confronted with formidable difficulties. Oxford was still governed by the seventeenth-century statutes of Archbishop Laud and Cambridge by the sixteenth-century statutes of Queen Elizabeth. There were no local authorities to deal with the administration of schools. The report of the royal commission, issued in 1852, was followed by the Oxford and Cambridge University Acts of 1854 and 1856 respectively. The acts did away with existing handicaps and left the universities free to develop without government interference. The Education Act, confined to elementary schools, provided for the local election of school boards, who were empowered to establish schools and levy rates to pay for them in areas where churches and other voluntary organizations had not done so.

At the university colleges, a number of ancient restrictions related to the founders' kin were removed to open scholarships and fellowships to competition, while the religious tests for the BA degree – subscription to the Thirty-nine Articles of the church of England – were no longer required. Measures like these inevitably drew attention to the entire range of secondary school education, beginning with the great public schools which were so closely associated with the universities. A particularly good illustration of this concern is contained in a lengthy article in the *Edinburgh Review* of 1861 on recent works about Eton College. The writer introduces the subject as follows:

It is now exactly fifty years since Sydney Smith, in the pages of this Review, entered his earnest protest against the system upon which the public schools of England were at that time conducted, – against a system of education avowedly based upon the dangerous principle of rearing a maximum of lambs with a minimum of shepherds.

Fifty years, as we have said, have elapsed since Sydney Smith put forth these wise and brave words. ... During that period, education has been elevated into a science, and all classes of Englishmen, save the wealthiest and highest, have largely benefited by its influence. When he wrote, bad as our public schools were, they were probably the best schools to be found in the kingdom; at the time at which we are writing, we are very much inclined to suspect that they are nearly the worst.[33]

The writer points out that it would have been impossible to know with any certainty how the duties outlined by the founder of Eton were currently being discharged had not Henry Brougham, "presiding in 1818 over his famous committee for inquiring into the education of the lower orders, bethought him of the friendless condition of the poor scholars of Eton and Winchester, and called upon the administrative bodies of those two foundations to come forward and render up an account of their stewardship." The college authorities protested against this summons, stating that they considered themselves under a moral and religious obligation not to reveal the secrets of their foundations, enjoined on oath by their statutes. Only under the pressure of parliamentary authority did the fellows of Eton agree to send their provost, Dr. Joseph Goodall, to be interrogated by the committee.[34]

At the committee hearing the committee members were surprised to learn that the provost's stipend for 1817 was only £279, the stipends of the fellows but £52, and that of the headmaster £58. By comparison, in the year 1625, for example, the offices were valued at a much higher income. The explanation was that whereas the stipends constituted a relatively negligible part of the remuneration of the headmaster and fellows, by a "time-honoured" custom the main source of income had been from fines levied on college property on the understanding that lapsed leases would be renewed at the old rents. This practice resulted in the provost's income, for example, occasionally reaching £2,500 a year and that of each fellow £1,000, apart from the college livings, of which, in defiance of their statutes and their oaths, they held one apiece.[35]

There were other practices current in early nineteenth-century Eton that contravened the statutes of Henry VI, the founder. The main substance of the oath taken by the provost and fellows was that no dispensations from the statutes were to be allowed and that the provost and fellows were not to avail themselves of any dispensations. The article then expands upon "the utter disregard" which the governing body of Eton College exhibits towards the intentions of their founder and the oaths which they have taken. Attention is drawn, in particular, to their practice of holding college livings contrary to their oaths "not to hold any ecclesiastical preferment with their fellowships" – and this on the grounds of a reputed dispensation from Queen Elizabeth.[36]

Although admittedly some changes for the good have been effected in recent years at Eton, especially for the benefit of the boys on the foundation,[37] the fact remains that the headmaster and the lower masters are expressly enjoined by statute 14 "to educate the foundation boys themselves." They are committed to instruct the oppidans, if they have the time to do so, but their care and attention is to be primarily bestowed on the scholars and choristers. The lower master of Eton, however, is not instructing a single boy on the foundation, spending all his time instead on the oppidans, who pay him well although they are entitled to his services free of charge. The collegers, then, on whom "by statute" he ought to bestow the greater part of his time, have to pay as much as £700 a year to assistant masters for the instruction to which they are entitled without cost.[38]

The *Edinburgh* article furnishes several details concerning the outlandish fees for services, which are not rendered as promised. However, the quality of the teaching itself is evidently central to any overall reform of the public school system as practised at Eton. In particular, the narrow and stifling climate of the Eton-King's relationship is assailed. Certainly, prior to the "regeneration of the colleges in 1843" the fellows of King's College, "grossly neglected and ill educated" at Eton, tended to keep to themselves later on at Cambridge, exempt even from the university's public examinations. On returning to Eton with only Latin and Greek to their credit, and scornful of the other fields of learning, they were placed in charge of much greater numbers of students than even the most experienced teachers could have handled.[39]

A commentary follows on the poor quality of the classical program itself – its grammar "a mass of monkish doggerel" – and on the fact that while sixty-five of the more advanced students are now reading both Latin and Greek literature, the rest of the school is left relatively neglected. The other subjects, including mathematics, geography, history, modern languages, and English composition, are poorly taught. In short, an Eton graduate might be "quite unable to pass the common tests of the Civil Service Examiners."[40]

It is clear that the economic reality of the situation had overridden and affected all other aspects of the school. It has not been, however, an easy task to get to the truth of the situation at Eton. For one thing, no history of the college is available. For another, until 1818 only the provost and the fellows were in a position to state anything certain with regard either to revenues or to the duties enjoined upon the governing body of the founder. The statutes were kept secret, and although they were available in a manuscript copy in the British Museum along with other relevant college documents, they were discredited at Eton as "garbled and imperfect."[41]

The writer in the *Edinburgh* acknowledges that the original statutes of Eton College can not be applied in their primitive vigour in nineteenth-century England. The change in the country's religion, for instance, is sufficient justification for the considerable reduction already made in the ecclesiastical part of the college.[42] He does insist, though, that the "enormous revenues" willed by a king for the education of the "upper and middle classes" of England should not be diverted from their initial purpose "into the pockets of a small number of individuals who are not entitled to them."[43] He concludes, therefore, with a call for a royal commission, supported by Parliament if necessary, with "full visitatorial powers," and including not only Eton but also the great public schools of Westminster, Winchester, Harrow, and Rugby.[44]

The above critical estimate of Eton College illustrates the main problems that a royal commission was soon to confront when it was directed to investigate revenues, management, and curriculum in connection with the nine "chief" public schools. Established in 1861 under the chairmanship of Lord Clarendon, and extending its inquiry to Shrewsbury, Charterhouse, Merchant Taylors', and St Paul's schools in addition to those called for by the writer in the *Edinburgh Review*, the commission published its report in 1864. The commissioners recognized an improvement in the discipline and moral tone of the schools – a tribute, in many ways, to the legacy of Thomas Arnold at Rugby. They also held firm for the retention of the classics as the central core of the curriculum, though they expressed dissatisfaction with the relatively low level of achievement among those exposed to classical studies. They were at least equally distressed by the widespread indifference among the teachers to the inclusion of more "modern" subjects in the program.[45]

To ensure the efficiency of a form of education intended, as Gladstone expressed it, for "that small proportion of the youth of any country who are to become in the fullest sense educated men,"[46] the Public Schools Act of 1868 provided for new and more representative governing bodies in all the schools considered, with the exception of Merchant Taylors' school and St Paul's. While a governing body in each school was to control the fees, the curriculum, and the appointment or dismissal of the headmaster, government policy was basically that of decentralization. Each school was to remain free from governmental inspection and to all intents and purposes independent.[47]

In the *Edinburgh Review* of July 1864, there appeared a commentary on the report of the royal commission of that year. The writer takes encouragement from the fact that the commissioners had recommended the abolition of the taking of fines and their division among the provost and fellows and the extraction of payments from the scholars on the foundation "contrary to the intentions of the founder.[48]

The curriculum commands most of the writer's attention. At contemporary Eton a small minority of boys leave the school as "very good classical scholars" with those special mental traits and good taste that such a training confers. An even smaller number graduate as "tolerable mathematicians." Apart from a larger number who acquire some degree, at least, of familiarity with one of these subjects, the majority leave Eton with very little knowledge not only of the classics and mathematics, but also of modern languages. The majority is destitute in every other respect of those habits of mind "which can conduce to their usefulness or happiness in after life."[49]

He then makes the point that circumstances have greatly changed since the sixteenth century when the classical languages – the key to all the then known philosophy, history, science, and dramatic poetry, not excluding the Bible itself – became the basis of education. And "it was as the key to these treasures that the languages were then taught: not as a system of philological gymnastics" – an idea that arose at a later period, he states, when it had become necessary to justify a great expenditure of time and energy on a program that had come to be regarded as of "little intrinsic value."[50]

One obvious result is that the great majority of English gentlemen have read "under coercion" a few extracts from a limited number of Greek and Latin poets, but are ignorant of Shakespeare and Milton. Whatever level of culture this may represent, "high poetic culture, with reference to the poetic literature of the present day, it assuredly is not."[51] Long possession is an acceptable argument against the sudden "dethronement" of classics by the fiat of a royal commission, but "it is no more a good argument against a gradual change now than it was in the sixteenth century, when the scholastic system was relinquished and the classical system was introduced in its place."[52]

Finally, in considering the size of Eton – 800 boys, compared with fewer than 500 at the largest of the other schools, Harrow and Rugby – the writer pertinently observes that Eton's popularity does not derive primarily from its scholastic reputation but, rather, from its "great aristocratic connexion." The *nouveaux riches*, especially, are far more likely to send their sons to Eton to obtain a "social diploma" than to seek instruction in Latin and Greek, or for that matter anything else. As he remarks, a light cavalry regiment more often than not is "the conclusion of the educational course."[53]

It is reasonable to assume that others among the great public schools of the country experienced problems similar to those at Winchester and Eton. Be that as it may, Carlisle, Hackett, Bowles, and the writer in the *Edinburgh Review* all believe the scholastic decline to be related, in whole or in part, to a diminution of revenue intended for specific educational purposes. This was one of Leach's main concerns, both as a charity commissioner and as an educational historian.

In his *Encyclopaedia Britannica* article, Leach presents a tightly reasoned analysis of the decline of the grammar schools prior to the nineteenth century. His view of Elizabeth's reign is mixed. He sees as quite positive the fact that many of the Elizabethan school foundations, even though in most cases they were probably replacing older ones, were the product of joint effort in annual subscriptions and donations of land or ready money, from not one benefactor but several. This is the case, he says, in many schools which have been attributed to the Queen herself or to other individual founders. He cites examples such as Wakefield and Halifax in Yorkshire, Ashbourne in Derbyshire, Sandwich in Kent, Hexham in Northumberland, and St Saviour's and St Olave's in Southwark, as well as Nottingham, which, as he says "after an existence of at least 300 years as a fee school, was refounded as a free school in 1512."[54]

He views as negative the strong tendency in Elizabeth's reign to make the grammar schools do double work: replace the loss caused by the suppression of the song schools and serve as elementary schools teaching the three Rs. This, in Leach's view, was a forlorn attempt, always renewed and generally resulting in "degrading the secondary school while not making the elementary school efficient." A particularly good example is Wellingborough in Northamptonshire. The school, founded by joint effort and out of common town estate, languished until in recent years "it shook off the elementary school and became one of the most flourishing secondary schools in the county".[55]

Leach views the period of the Civil War, and especially that of the Commonwealth, as particularly good for the schools: "Many new schools were created, many old schools obtained an increase of endowment and efficiency."[56] He is drawn particularly to the act of Parliament, 30 April 1649, by which deans and chapters were abolished. He states that, in spite of this, the schools were expressly saved by a clause which declared that all payments from their revenues

that either had been or ought to have been paid towards the maintenance of a grammar school or scholars before 1 December 1641
should continue to be paid.

Leach explains that although the temporal estates were put up for
sale, the "spiritual property,"[57] including livings and tithes, was directed in part to the provision of salaries and salary increases for
preaching ministers and schoolmasters. The result was that all the
cathedral grammar schools were left intact. Some, like Canterbury
and Rochester, received repairs to their buildings. Others, like Chester, Salisbury, Chichester, and Durham, received increases in teachers' salaries of 50 per cent to 100 per cent over the fixed amounts
first set by Henry VIII's statutes (if not earlier) and left unchanged
by successive cathedral chapters.

Leach's view of the Restoration is not flattering. He states that the
Restoration Parliament put a stop to both new schools and new
endowments and, by virtue of the Act of Uniformity in 1662 and
the Five Mile Act in 1665, prevented anyone but a member of the
Church of England from teaching in a public or private school. A
series of court decisions resulting from the acts freed a large number
of schools from the control of the bishops. The outstanding exceptions were the endowed grammar schools, which continued to be
the sole preserve of the Church of England. In Leach's view, by the
end of the eighteenth century this condition had led to the schools
being "in a more decrepit condition than they were at any time in
their long history," with only those institutions that were in command
of great resources and could attract the aristocracy flourishing.[58]

Whereas Leach softens his picture of the Restoration a little by
mentioning as a great innovation the development of schools for
girls, such as those at Hackney and Chelsea, he reserves his most
stringent criticism for the period of the Georges and the first half
of Queen Victoria's reign. He claims that the condition of the nation's
public schools was at its worst between 1750 and 1840. This fact, he
states, emerges clearly from a reading of the Victoria County Histories, Carlisle's *Endowed Grammar Schools*, and the reports of Lord
Brougham's Commission of Inquiry with respect to charities (1818–
37). Although "great, if partial," improvement followed upon legal
and private parliamentary acts aimed at the restoration of school
endowments, "a deplorable state of things" was revealed in the reports of the Public Schools Commission and of the Schools Inquiry
Commission in 1863 and 1868 respectively.[59]

Leach remarks that this sad state of affairs had been largely improved in his own day by eliminating "religious disabilities" and by
making membership on the school governing bodies more repre-

sentative of the population as a whole. Moreover, the curriculum of both the great and the lesser public schools had been broadened by means of special commissions with "drastic powers," the former under the Public Schools Commission, the latter under the Endowed School Commissioners and the charity commissioners under the Endowed Schools Act of 1869.[60]

In order to appreciate Leach's remarks on the above educational activity of the government, some background is useful. In 1864, the Schools Inquiry Commission was appointed to examine the schools not covered by either the Clarendon Commission or the earlier Newcastle Commission (1858–61); that is, all the schools other than public and elementary ones, "those large classes of English society which are comprised between the humblest and the very highest."[61] The Commission was under the chairmanship of Lord Taunton and included a wide range of political affiliation – former members of the Clarendon Commission as well as radical leaders like the Liberal W.E. Forster and the Nonconformist Edward Baines. The Commission set to work with great energy, and, depending mainly on the personal visitations of twelve assistant commissioners, examined close to 800 endowed schools and 122 proprietary schools.[62]

The proprietary schools, organized in many respects on the public school model, were maintained by joint-stock companies. Of recent vintage, they catered to a middle class interested primarily in professional and business careers. Without as a rule neglecting the classics, schools such as Cheltenham and Wellington managed to maintain a high standard in mathematics, science, and modern languages.[63] By contrast, most of the endowed grammar schools impressed the commissioners as very unsatisfactory, with only a number of those catering to the upper-middle class earning high marks. In addition to poor teaching methods, lack of motivation, and defective statutes, the commissioners noted the "chaotic" geography of many of these schools – an almost complete absence of any rationalization for either their numbers or their locations.[64] The majority of the older schools, obligated by their foundation statutes to provide a classical education, now found themselves in small towns or agricultural areas where a curriculum limited to the classics was of little practical use while, by contrast, there were no endowed schools in relatively large towns such as Huddersfield.[65]

The prime objective of the Taunton Commission's report, issued in 1868, was to ensure an efficient education for the various social groups that now constituted England's middle class. To this end, the report advocated a three-tiered system, catering to those aiming at the university, those intending to join one of the professions or the army, and those who belonged to the inferior but extensive class of smaller tenant farmers, small tradesmen, and superior artisans. The schools of the first grade, as expected, would have a curriculum based on the classics, but including mathematics, modern languages, and science. The second grade schools would concentrate on subjects of practical use in business, such as English, arithmetic, and natural science, and, while not offering any Greek, would retain Latin as an option. The third grade of education would be geared to modern subjects, including English, elementary mathematics, geography, history, natural science, and a language other than English. The school-leaving ages for each category were set respectively at eighteen to nineteen years, sixteen, and fourteen, this last to be strictly enforced for the boys.[66]

There were other recommendations of the Taunton Commission that would eventually bear directly on Leach's work as a charity commissioner. These include the retention of religious instruction in all three grades of school, with the right of parents to withdraw their children from such classes if they wished; the access to masterships on the part of candidates not in holy orders;[67] and the provision for more extensive and better educational facilities for women. In regard to this last, the commissioners were favourably impressed with "the far-sighted and enlightened views" relating to the education of girls as expressed by a number of men and women whom the commissioners had consulted. They voiced the hope that many endowments not specifically designated for boys' schools would contribute to the establishment of secondary schools for girls.[68]

What was of primary concern, however, was the need not only to effect a complete revision of the constitutions and the governing body of each school, but to do so in such a way that each individual school would be considered within the context of the other schools in its area. Partly for this reason, the Taunton Commission recommended the establishment of an "Administrative Board." It was thought that the charity commission, which had been established in 1853, could be reconstituted and enlarged to serve this purpose. Responsible chiefly for educational endowments, the charity commission would appoint suitable persons to inspect the schools, draw up "schemes" for their organization, and submit these to Parliament.[69]

The Endowed Schools Act was passed by Gladstone's first government in 1869. The act did not respond to the Taunton Commission's plans for the complete overhaul of secondary education but confined itself to the matter of school endowments. Although the act fell quite short of the expectations of educational reformers, it undoubtedly contributed to the revival of many grammar schools that had been in decline. In this connection it laid the groundwork for an "educational ladder," including the availability of scholarships for elementary school pupils which allowed them to benefit from the resources of a number of endowed schools, which in turn found a greater number of their own students obtaining places at the universities. The act also encouraged the broadening of the curriculum and an improvement in teaching. Perhaps not the least of its achievements was the stimulation it afforded to the secondary education of girls.[70]

The Endowed Schools Act took shape in an increasingly polarized community. On the one side was the Nonconformist campaign dedicated to the establishment of a national system of free non-sectarian education. The campaign was centralized in the National Education League of Birmingham under the Radical and future Liberal colleague of Gladstone, Joseph Chamberlain. On the other side was the formation of the Headmaster's Conference under the initiative of Edward Thring of Uppingham, who hoped to counter what he detected as a threat to the administrative independence of the public schools and their special relationship with the established church. Under strong opposition from school patrons in church and state, a more moderate draft of the bill was enacted into law.[71]

An immediate effect of the Endowed Schools Act was the impetus it gave to grammar schools to move into the privileged class of public schools. In the long term, however, resentment built up against the way in which the commissioners were implementing these "schemes." This happened partly because the re-organization of governing bodies frequently offended the interests of the Church of England or dissenting groups and partly because local residents, long accustomed to having their sons educated free of charge on an ancient endowment, were now required to pay fees. The transfer of the functions of the Endowed School Commissioners to the charity commission in 1874 under Disraeli's government did little to allay the unrest, especially among those at the bottom of the educational ladder.[72]

As the upper middle classes throughout the country increasingly identified their future with a public school education for their sons, the commissioners looked for opportunities to transform endowed grammar schools into public schools by excluding the local foundationers, whether they were receiving a grammar school education or an elementary one. At Kendal, for instance, where opposition to the process continued into the 1880s without avail, an annual endowment of £518 that had gone toward the education of seventy-five or more poor children in the Bluecoat school was appropriated for the development of the local grammar school into a boarding school for a wealthier clientele. In this way, old-established grammar schools were "alienated from their locality." Instead of being common schools for the benefit of local families, they were changed into residential institutions "serving a single class."[73]

The commissioners defended their actions on the ground that both the Taunton and the Newcastle Commissions had actually been opposed to free education. The aim was, rather, to put "liberal" education within the reach of everyone by means of larger exhibitions to schools of higher grade, while guaranteeing the rights of the poor through the lesser exhibitions associated with the elementary schools. The commissioners maintained, moreover, that since the original founders had not designated their endowments for the benefit of a particular class, so it would ill become them to do so. In this connection they expressed their agreement with Benjamin Kennedy, the classical scholar and former headmaster of Shrewsbury, that a free school did not mean free from fees but "free from interference."[74] Interpreted in this way, the endowed schools were really intended for the sons of the middle class, and, therefore, the particular job of the charity commissioners was to return the endowments to this class.[75]

In his capacity as a charity commissioner, Leach would later endorse most of the objectives of the Endowed Schools Act. Broader representation on the governing bodies of schools, a curriculum open to modern subjects, a much greater degree of access to secondary education for girls, a geographical rationalization of school facilities – all these were to meet with his approval. There were, however, at least three areas in which Leach could not reconcile the findings of some of his predecessors with the historical documentation that he discovered to be relevant to the issues in question.

One area was church-state relations. Quite independently of his personal view in favour of Henry VIII's dissolution of the monasteries and his disapproval of the educational losses attendant upon Edward VI's dissolution of the chantries, Leach observed correctly that the claims of the Church of England to educational institutions founded before the Reformation could hardly be vindicated. Unless it could be shown that the scholastic institution in question had been established independently of any ecclesiastical obligation – an unlikely situation, as Leach was prepared to illustrate from a wealth of examples – it would be legally impossible on the basis of Elizabeth's Church settlement of 1559 for the established church to claim continuity with the doctrine and worship of pre-Reformation educational founders. As Leach noted, these distinctions were especially relevant to the issue of religious instruction in the schools within the context of the new legislation.

A second area of difference concerned the meaning of "free" education in a number of the earlier foundation statutes. In opposition even to some fellow commissioners, Leach insisted that "free" meant precisely what it appeared to mean – an education free of charge. Not only was Leach openly disagreeing with those who had, for instance, adopted the legal meaning of freedom from interference; he also had to show that the designation of early endowments in favour of "poor" scholars was intended only in a relative sense. He had a particularly good opportunity to do this in his analysis of the origins and purpose of his own school of Winchester College, where he traced the interpretation in an absolute sense to an earlier generation. In his opinion, there had been too much needless discussion over the meaning of "poor," especially during Brougham's Commission of inquiry with respect to charities between 1818 and 1835, when it was contended that "the poor labouring classes" at least were entitled to the endowments of schools such as Winchester College.[76]

Leach does not accept this argument at all. He notes that the test of poverty to qualify for admission as a scholar is found in the oath that every scholar had to take on reaching his fifteenth birthday – that his spending allowance for the year did not exceed five marks. Leach contends that this sum, equal to £3.6s.8d a year, was the limit of value for the exemption of church livings from the tax known as the tenths, payable to the papacy, and was actually "an appreciable yearly income."[77] To understand the founder's statutes correctly it is sufficient, he says, to observe that in the foundation deed itself provision was being made for those, as the text has it, "busied in school studies, whose means barely suffice to enable them to continue and become proficient in grammar." Leach concludes by remarking that the education of the labouring classes was not even thought of in the fourteenth century, and that it would be "an absurd anachronism" to credit Wykeham with establishing a college as a "ladder from the gutter to the University."[78]

Central as the above two issues were to Leach's assessment of the Endowed Schools Act and his implementation of that legislation as a charity commissioner, a third aspect of the Schools Inquiry Report exercised him most: the historical information given to the commissioners from a wide variety of sources of uneven credibility. This compilation of the origins and terms of ancient educational endowments constituted Leach's main point of departure for his first major publication, *English Schools at the Reformation*.

The practical question in the generation preceding Leach's appointment as a charity commissioner was how government could reorganize in a more equitable and efficient manner the endowments and bequests for education accumulated through many centuries, to respond to the needs of a more industrialized age. As a member of a commission designed to that very end, Leach would find, in virtually every corner of the country, numerous examples of both the decline of ancient schools and the possibility of new institutions with an expanded curriculum. To sort out the legal technicalities involved, as well as to inform local governing bodies concerning the antecedents governing their decisions, Leach would make his historical research and publications a *sine qua non* for the just and efficient reordering of the nation's accumulated educational resources.

Leach's first major work, *English Schools at the Reformation*, had as its more immediate background his own memorandum on the history of endowed schools, prepared for the Royal Commission on Secondary Education and published in 1895. The aim of his report is stated succinctly: "This Memorandum is designed to show, first, that the antiquity of the origin of our chief secondary schools is far higher than is usually supposed; and, secondly, that the ascertainment of the true origin is a matter of practical importance" (M 57).

The working paper for Leach's analysis of the subject is the list of schools published by the Schools Inquiry Commission of 1868, contained in Appendix 4 of their report and entitled "Endowed Grammar and other Secondary Schools arranged in the Chronological Order of their Establishment." The Commission cites three sources for the chronological list in question: the report of the commissioners appointed to inquire into charities, 1819–37; Carlisle's *Endowed Grammar Schools*; and, for some of the cathedral schools, the report of the cathedral commissioners of 1852.[79] As Leach notes, the list contains 389 foundations in all. The origin of eighteen of these was attributed to the period of English history prior to the reign of Henry VII; seventeen to the reign of Henry VII; sixty-three to that of Henry VIII; fifty-one to that of Edward VI; no fewer than 157 institutions to the reigns of Mary and Elizabeth; and eighty-three to that of James I. Leach's own list of schools in *English Schools at the Reformation* is confined to those mentioned in the chantry certificates and the continuance of re-foundation warrants. A quick comparison of the two lists reveals that the Schools Inquiry Commission lists eighteen schools founded before 1485, while Leach lists ninety-two. Leach reduces the sixty-three attributed to Henry VIII in the Schools Inquiry Report to thirty-nine.[80]

Leach finds that he cannot accept the Taunton Commission's list as the point of departure for his own investigation into the antiquity of the schools. Citing the Commission's entry under Carlisle Grammar School as an example, Leach places little credence either in the school's "reputed" foundation in 686 by St Cuthbert or its alleged re-establishment five centuries later by William Rufus. Leach, however, is more concerned with the inconsistency of the commissioners. He remarks that they have been willing to search out the origins, however erroneous, of this particular monastery, but are not prepared to do the same for schools attached to all the other cathedrals of the "new foundation." Accordingly, the establishment of the grammar schools belonging to Canterbury, Chester, Durham, Ely, Gloucester, Peterborough, Rochester, and Worcester is credited to Henry VIII from the year 1541 (M 61–2).

Leach surveys additional inconsistencies with respect to schools such as Derby, Ripon, Penrith, Ashburton, and the cathedral school of York, (M 62–4, passim). He then concludes that, with few exceptions, the schools attributed to the reigns of Henry VIII and his family, along with "a considerable number" ascribed to James I, were "continuations, re-foundations, or augmentations" of schools already established in connection with ecclesiastical institutions before "the great revolution" that began in 1536 (M 64).

Leach's memorandum contains a useful summary of the different kinds of schools existing in medieval England. His explanation of chantry-related schools, in particular, is central to an appreciation of the finer distinctions that he attempts to draw in this summation. Leach believes the chantries began in the thirteenth century and were generally identified with particular altars in the larger churches. In the cathedrals of London and York, for instance, there were some fifty chantries altogether. In the churches of towns like Newark, Hull, and Nottingham, Leach states that there were a dozen or so chantries, making these churches for all practical purposes collegiate. Finally, he sees the concept disseminating into various towns and villages, with the chantry attached to parish churches to assist the parish priest. He points out that in the larger churches, where the grammar school was maintained out of the general revenues of the church itself, it became common, either to increase the endowment or to ease the drain on general revenue, to appoint one of the chantry priests as the grammar schoolmaster. This was done, for example, at Southwell in 1504. Leach comments that "this practice has led, as in the case of Stafford, some of the grammar schools to be regarded as chantry schools, when they were really the schools of the collegiate church at large" (M 65–6).

Leach closely connects the chantry schools and the hospital schools. Included in his remarks is his interpretation of why this connection is significant. Since medieval hospitals were refuges for the poor rather than shelters for the sick, founders often connected their schools with hospitals. Leach thinks that this connection allowed them to evade a provision of the canon law. From at least the thirteenth century, Leach argues, the traditional manner of supporting ecclesiastical foundations, including colleges and schools, by endowing them with churches was prohibited except "when the appropriation was for the benefit of the poor." As a papal bull could be obtained to sanction such appropriation by merely inserting a clause testifying to the poverty of the body in question, a church, quite commonly, was appropriated directly to those administering a hospital or almshouse for the poor. In this way, according to Leach, the boarding school of Bishop Stapledon's foundation at Exeter was placed in the hospital of St John "under the governance of the master." Similar arrangements existed at Coventry and Ewelme in respect to the Bablake hospital and Ewelme almshouse respectively. He also mentions that almshouses were part of the foundation of Eton and that William of Wykeham solved the problem at Winchester by describing his scholars as poor clerks, Leach noting that their poverty was "mostly of a relative kind" (M 66–7). One further point of particular interest in this memorandum is Leach's discussion of the denominational character of England's schools in his own day. What was important in his view was the extent to which any of the schools of pre-Reformation England could, in the nineteenth century, be classified as Church of England schools. He points out that, even after considerable legal inroads had been made upon the traditional doctrine that every grammar school was considered an institution of the Church of England, the law still presumed "that religious instruction provided for in any foundation, and particularly one of so-called Royal Foundation by Edward VI, was a Church of England school." Since, however, one of the most important aims of the Endowed Schools Act was "to vindicate the national, as opposed to the denominational, character of the old schools," it is not surprising to learn that the Endowed Schools Act had reversed the test. Under the act, what really mattered was whether in the express terms either of the "original instrument of foundation" or of the founder's statutes, or under the founder's authority within fifty years of his death, scholars were required to be instructed according to the doctrines of a particular church. Leach states that if the original founder did not enjoin any specific religious teaching, or if the foundation document is not available or the original requirement lost sight of, "the school cannot claim to be treated under section 19 of the Endowed Schools Act, 1869" (M 70–1).

This is one of the instances in which institutions such as the chantries have a particular relevance for Leach in connection with current issues. The normal requirements of a chantry school – the participation of the scholars in Masses, prayers to the Virgin Mary, and the invocation of saints – mean that its founder cannot have prescribed instruction "in accordance with the doctrines of the Church of England as by law established." Even with regard to the colleges of Winchester and Eton, which were excluded from the Endowed Schools Act, the directives in their statutes pertaining to their scholars' attendance at mass and other related services were not observed after the Act of Uniformity in Elizabeth's reign made such practices illegal. The same is true, therefore, Leach states, "of all pre-Reformation schools of which we have the statutes" (M 71).

Leach concludes, then, that in no such case is it possible to contend that the school is one in which scholars are required to be instructed in the doctrines of the Church of England. The religious practices for which the chantries were founded are relegated to the realm of the superstitious in the act for the chantries collegiate under Edward VI. It is true that the act provides for the continuation of those chantries that supported schools, by a commission to be appointed under the act, and, as Leach says, the majority of them were so continued. "But it is obvious that the necessary disuse of the superstitious practices, whether they were strictly speaking illegal or not, has caused a breach of observance, which is fatal to the contention that the schools are, by foundation and practice, the two co-essential requisites, denominational" (M 71–2).

The discovery of a close relation between a medieval institution like the chantry and the educational issues of his own day illustrates the topical interest that characterizes so much of Leach's writing. He realized that without a sound historical background the augmented charity commission had been ill-equipped to respond to the more pressing and practical questions related to the intent of ancient educational endowments. Leach appreciated the close relation between these two aspects of the government "schemes" for educational reform. The writings of persons like Bowles and the contributor to the *Edinburgh Review* on the more famous public schools had alerted government and public alike to the necessity of both vindicating and reforming these institutions to meet the demands of a new age. What

was of serious concern to Leach, however, was that the more historical features of the educational scene had been entrusted for far
too long to writers who, like Carlisle and Hackett, had perpetuated
false notions of school history in their attempts to extend their knowledge of the past. What was needed was a more systematic and professional examination of the historical background to the nation's
educational endowments. Leach was prepared to confront the challenge of providing such an examination when, in 1884, he accepted
the position as a charity commissioner at Whitehall under Gladstone's second ministry.

CHAPTER THREE

Leach as Assistant Charity Commissioner

Leach's work as a charity commissioner consisted primarily of written reports submitted to his superiors in connection with a wide variety of schools with some grounds for financial consideration under the provisions of the Endowed Schools Act of 1869. A selection of these reports illustrates the process whereby Leach managed to channel a day-by-day occupation, stemming from a government appointment, into an extensive historical survey of the entire grammar school system. His publications were related to, but virtually independent of, the many contemporary issues that he and his fellow commissioners had to resolve.

For this purpose, a relatively detailed treatment will be afforded to his investigations into the schools of Chichester, Southwell, Beverley, and York and their connection with his central theme of the importance of the cathedral and collegiate churches in medieval education.[1] The four centres were investigated in the early years of Leach's employment – 1886 to 1896 – and have been chosen because his treatment of them reveals the way in which Leach, quite early on, succeeded in using the experience of his practical on-the-job activities as both a source and a stimulus for his more theoretical concerns in the general subject of medieval education.

In the years 1886–89 there were nine assistant charity commissioners at Whitehall. They had fifty-five assignments during these three years. Leach was assigned to prepare no fewer than twenty-four of these reports. Each report examined the educational facilities with respect to their eligibility for government financial assistance. In the course of these inquiries Leach encountered a number of situations in which post-medieval developments had either altered or confused the terms of an original educational endowment. These changes were effected not only by various Reformation statutes that modified or even eliminated the more religious and ecclesiastical aspects of medieval schools but also, in the nineteenth century, by the Ecclesiastical Commissioners, a permanent body established by act of Parliament in 1836 to ensure a new and more rational distribution of ecclesiastical revenues within the Church of England itself.

The cathedral of Chichester first set Leach on the path of investigation into the history of the nation's schools. As early as the last month of 1884, the case of Chichester's Prebendal School was referred to Leach for his inquiry and report with regard to "the establishment of a scheme under the Endowed Schools Acts."[2] The tenor of the report on Chichester's Prebendal School is a forerunner of many of Leach's reports in that the immediate question was whether the commissioners possessed any jurisdiction in the case. To answer this question Leach provides an extensive historical background, one which reveals most, if not all, of the historical authorities on whom he was disposed to rely in these early days of his educational studies. Since the school was in the charge of a prebendary of Chichester cathedral, and since the prebend in question constituted the entire endowment of the school, the problem, as he understands it, is whether the school qualified as "endowed" and whether the prebendary, as "an ecclesiastical officer" and not a schoolmaster, was outside the jurisdiction of the commissions (RAC:C 786).[3]

A second question Leach asks is whether the school qualifies as "endowed" within the meaning of section 27 of the Endowed Schools Act of 1869, which would allow the commissioners to request an increase of endowment from the ecclesiastical commissioners. This in turn, if favourably disposed of, would raise the question of whether the cathedral's dean and chapter would have to assent to any change in the governing body of the school and, still further, whether the school was within the terms of the Endowed Schools Act as outlined in section 19 (RAC:C 786). Leach begins his historical summary by observing that Chichester, like St Paul's, Salisbury, and York, belongs to the old foundation. As such its chapter has consisted "not of regular but of secular clerks or secular canons, otherwise called prebendaries" since 1075, when the cathedral was transferred from Selsey. At least two features in the history of the chapter itself are directly related to the question in hand. First, it appeared to Leach that some time towards the middle of the fourteenth century, when the residence of the canons became the exception rather than the rule, the way was open to the "usurpation by the dean and canons residentiary of the title and legislative power of the Dean and Chapter, of which, in point of fact, they only formed the resident portion." Second, all prebends in the cathedral, "as distinct from the conventual cathedrals and Henry VIII's new foundations," were in the gift of the bishop of Chichester (RAC:C 786).

With regard to the first of these points, from Bishop Storey's statutes Leach cites the requirement that any future prebendary of Highley, apart from sharing in the disbursement of the money connected with the attendance of certain clergy at cathedral funeral services, was not to consider himself entitled to "any share of the common fund of our cathedral church" on the basis of either his canonry in the cathedral or his residence in the city of Chichester (RAC:C 788). This statute has a direct bearing on one of the legal opinions, advanced only five years or so before Leach undertook the study of Chichester, that Bishop Storey's statutes were invalid because "they effected a severance of the prebend from the cathedral church," making it "a separate foundation for educational purposes." To the contrary, Leach argues, "the strongest proof of all" that the prebendary's membership of the cathedral chapter was not in question in that, since he would henceforth have to live in Chichester, it was found necessary to make sure that residence in the city would not of itself give him the right to be regarded as "a residentiary in the technical sense," thereby entitling him to share in the "common fund" over and above his "separate property" (RAC:C 803–4).

As for the second point, the nomination to the canonry and prebend of Highley was the prerogative of the dean and chapter, while the actual appointment resided with the bishop. If, however, the bishop were to put off the collation (appointment to a benefice) of the nominee for more than twenty days after the nomination by the dean and chapter, the right of collation would pass to the archbishop of Canterbury. Although the prebendary could obtain from the dean a leave of absence not exceeding thirty days in any given year in the event of ill health or for other reasons, he had to provide at his own cost a substitute teacher who would be subject to the approval of the dean and chapter (RAC:C 787).

After Leach has satisfied himself as to the accuracy of Bishop Storey's statutes, he quotes the founder's reasons for his decision to found "a perpetual grammar school" in the city of Chichester. The founder had observed "the no slight ignorance of the priests" under his jurisdiction and the excessive promotion of bad priests "on account of the rarity of good ministers of Christ" in his diocese. The direction of the grammar school was to be the responsibility of the prebendary of Highley, and the holder of such prebend was not permitted to hold any other benefice. Should he accept any, no matter the kind, his canonry and prebend of Highley would be *ipso facto* considered vacant (RAC:C 789). It is quite clear that the bishop foresaw the possibility of the incumbent neglecting his teaching responsibilities. In an amending statute of 1502, the clause forbidding the prebendary of Highley to hold any additional benefice was altered to permit him to accept a single ecclesiastical one, with or without the cure of souls, on the condition that he "provide and keep one usher fit in that capacity to teach under him in our said Grammar School, for the relief and anxiety of the master of the above-mentioned school, and for the benefit of the scholars flocking to the said school" (RAC:C 790).

Bishop Storey still had in mind a priest who would be ready to teach as well as to offer Mass, including a requiem Mass for the bishop himself and his parents, as well as for all his benefactors, and "all faithful souls departed" (RAC:C 788). When, therefore, by a statute of 1550 the then bishop of Chichester, George Day, thought it useful to extend the teaching duties attached to the prebend of Highley to persons who might not be priests – "to other literates sufficiently instructed and fit to teach" – he explained the changed circumstances as partly stemming from the fact that "the celebrations of masses" provided for in Bishop Storey's ordinance "are by no means held and performed in these days" as had earlier been the custom (RAC:C 790–1). The bishop states that this new procedure, having been the subject of mature deliberation, has the support of the dean and chapter, as well as of the canon and prebendary of Highley, Master Antony Clarke (RAC:C 790–1).

Of prime consideration is the relationship, if any, between the school of Bishop Storey and that of the cathedral. Leach's examination of the cathedral statutes convinced him that there was undoubtedly "some school connected with the cathedral in some way" before the earliest of the bishop's statutes. The chancellor's duties were contained in a 1232 statute issuing from the bishop with the dean and chapter "in chapter assembled." The duties included "some educational functions with regard to young men or minor ministers in the second form and boys in the third form," referring, continues Leach, to "the second and third rows of seats below the stalls in the cathedral choir" (RAC:C 792–3).

As this statute did not help provide an understanding of the later fifteenth century developments, and as there was no continuous documentation, Leach's consideration of the immediate post-Conquest period is based largely on E.A. Freeman's interpretation (RAC:C 794). A brief reference in the episcopal registers to the failure of the chancellor to find a teacher in grammar for the cathedral choristers on the occasion of Bishop Reade's visitation in 1402 does not keep Leach from confessing that he has not been able "to trace any definite connexion between the chancellor's school, which clearly existed at Chichester, and the Prebendal School" (RAC:C 794).

Both the statutes of 1502 and of 1550, in fact, satisfied Leach that the terms used expressly point to a new foundation (RAC:C 794). In spite of this, Leach thinks that the school site and buildings antedated Bishop Storey and that they were not originally part of the endowment attached to the prebend of Highley, but were "a separate and independent endowment of the school." Leach's examination of the architecture of the building, which still contains the "great cellar" that the prebendary was allowed to lease, led him to conclude that the building in question was not originally intended as a school and that, in his opinion, while the school buildings and appurtenances constituted a separate endowment, "there is no evidence to show whence it is derived" (RAC:C 794–5).

Leach traces the contemporary issue back to the Charitable Trusts Acts of 1854. Although the Charitable Trusts file, which Leach thinks had once existed, had disappeared, he did manage to trace an order of the House of Commons, dated 12 June 1860. The order contained the correspondence that had up to then passed between the charity commissioners, the dean and chapter of the cathedral, the prebendary of Highley, and a number of persons expressing their interest in the school. In this context, the dean and chapter stated in 1854 that the school was supported entirely out of the revenues of the prebend, with the dean and chapter having no control over either the funds or their application. Later in the same year, the Reverend T. Brown, prebendary of Highleigh, informed the commissioners that he did not know of any real or personal property belonging to the school except, perhaps, the school buildings themselves. Brown further stated that the "instrument of his collation as prebendary" required him to teach grammar in the grammar school in the city of Chichester. Since he had already rendered to the cathedral commissioner an account of his prebendal responsibilities, he had nothing to report to the charity commission (RAC:C 797–8).

After summarizing the complaints with regard to the conduct of the school between 1854 and 1860, Leach cites the recommendation made in 1864 by the prebendary to one of the assistant commissioners of the Schools Inquiry Commission – that the bad financial situation of the school could be remedied and the school itself enlarged if the said Commission could prevail upon the ecclesiastical commissioners "to give an equivalent for the property of the prebend of Highleigh." Leach further notes, however, that in 1879, shortly after the case had been referred to Mr. Fearon, an assistant charity commissioner, Canon Swainson, speaking on behalf of the dean and chapter, questioned the right of the charity commissioners to bring "the so-called Prebendal School" within their sphere of jurisdiction. The canon argued that the Chichester Grammar School was "not a school endowed with a prebend, but a prebend charged with the duties of keeping a school" and, hence, pertained to the jurisdiction of the ecclesiastical commissioners (RAC:C 798).[4]

Between the above dates and Leach's first visit to Chichester in January 1885, the situation appears to have grown even more complicated. The various interpretations of the dean and chapter stalled somewhere between the opinion that emphasized that the sole endowment of the school – the prebendal stall – was an ecclesiastical dignity or promotion that, by the Act of Uniformity of Charles II's reign, was to be filled only by one in priests' orders, and the view, expressed by the chapter clerk, that the prebendary "could not be prebendary unless he did the duty of teaching" (RAC:C 799).

The central question in the whole issue became more confused as Leach proceeded with his own analysis. What appeared to him as at least reasonably straightforward is best left in his own words:

There can be no doubt – it does not appear to be denied – that under the provisions of Bishop Storey's statutes the prebendary of Highleigh is a person "bound to teach," since he is fined if he neglects to teach for 40 days, and his prebend is *ipso facto* void "if he has ceased to teach for more than three months," and it is specifically ordained that he should "libere et gratis doceat, instruat, informet, et castiget" the "grammaticos et alios ... ad nostram venientes scholam" and he receives payment for teaching since he receives the revenues of the prebend on condition of teaching (RAC:C 803).

Even the above statutes had been contested by judicial opinion, specifically on the ground that the school had been founded before and independently of Bishop Storey's efforts to have the Highleigh prebend annexed to his foundation. On that showing, therefore, the prebend was in reality separated from the cathedral establishment, rendering the bishop's statutes invalid (RAC:C 803–4).

Leach does not accept this opinion of either Bishop Storey's intent or the effect of the statutes. To the contrary, Leach maintains that the prebendary of Highleigh, as a schoolmaster, is not only no less a member of the cathedral body than before but is equally no less a prebendary because of saying mass on Friday and attending to other ecclesiastical duties before the Reformation that "he ceased to perform" after the Reformation (RAC:C 804). Leach goes on to mention that the prebendary – in conformity with the intent of the statutes – was still called canon and prebendary of Highleigh, that he was to be collated by the bishop and admitted by the dean, and that he still paid an annual sum out of the same prebend to the dean and chapter in place of the year's revenues. But, as mentioned above, the strongest evidence, in Leach's opinion, stems from the fact that, had it been understood that after Bishop Storey's action the Highleigh prebendary was not a member of the cathedral, the chapter would not have found it necessary to remind the prebendary that residence in Chichester did not entitle him to a share in the "common fund" in addition to his separate property. And, as a further point, the very form of collation by the bishop and induction by the dean still in use makes it clear that "the prebendary is still regarded as a member of the cathedral chapter, and his prebend as a part of the cathedral foundation" (RAC:C 804).

As in many other inquiries during the ensuing years, Leach is content to rest his case, satisfied that at least on historical grounds he has provided the basis for his own interpretation. At least two other aspects of Bishop Storey's foundation demand further consideration: the governing body of the school and the religious formularies connected with the conduct of the institution. With regard to the first, if the bishop's statutes are valid, Leach contends that the bishop of Chichester, possessing both the right of collation and the power of visitation of the prebend, would govern the school. Included in the governing body also would be the dean and chapter, since they held the power of nomination as well as dismissal of the prebendary as schoolmaster and, more recently, the prerogative of nominating scholars or choristers to the school. If, on the other hand, the statutes are invalid, Leach suggests reasons why such persons as the archbishop of Canterbury and the ecclesiastical commissioners would then have to be considered as governing bodies (RAC:C 810–11).

With respect to the religious question, Leach observes that the whole tenor of the stipulated prayers, the office of matins, and attendance at the morning Mass implies that the students would receive some degree of instruction in the Roman Catholic faith. In that case, Leach remarks, "I apprehend there would be considerable difficulty in proving continuous observance to August 1869." Leach pays little attention to the not unrelated intervention of Bishop Day in Edward VI's reign to provide for the admission of laymen to the prebend and headship of the school, being content with the probable opinion that the statute, if held to be valid, "is overridden by the Act of Uniformity" (RAC:C 811–12).

It is useful to consider Leach's historical authorities as they impress him at the outset of his career with the charity commission. The

Chichester documents, both printed and manuscript, are among the more extensive collections included in Leach's reports and correspondence in the Public Record Office. An appendix, of which the first item is a copy in Latin of the statutes of Edward Storey together with the amending statute of George Day, includes a series of excerpts from a variety of sources, some of which were used by Leach in his lengthy discussion of the history of cathedral chapter prebends.

Following the first of these excerpts – a group of three quotations from an essay by the Reverend E.W. Benson, the future archbishop of Canterbury, on the relation of the chapter to the bishop – is a more extensive quotation from the Regius Professor of History at Oxford, E.A. Freeman, excerpted from his essay on churches of the old foundation. In the passages from Freeman, Leach underlines those pertaining to schools: *"During this stage* [regarding Thomas, first Norman archbishop of York] *he appointed one distinct officer only, the master of the schools, a functionary who seems to be the same as the chancellor of the church,"* and *"after these comes the chancellor, whose chief function is of an educational kind, whose business is the teaching of the younger members of the cathedral body, some add the general superintendence of all the schools in the diocese"* (RAC:C 822–3).[5]

Leach finds a few brief but hardly informative references to schools and the schoolmaster, as well as to prebends, in William Stubbs' edition of *The Foundation of Waltham Abbey*. Leach's main interest appears to be in what Stubbs says about the introduction of monastic rules into England, an echo of Leach's concern to identify a married clergy with a distinctively English experience. One of his quotations from Stubbs is: "The great stumbling-block [in England] was the custom of the common dormitory which was incompatible with the existence of a married clergy, such as continued in England for 60 years after the Conquest" (RAC:C 823–4).[6]

At the end of his appendix of sources Leach includes several excerpts from H.C. Maxwell-Lyte's *History of the University of Oxford*. The range of subjects includes the relationship of the universities of Paris and Oxford to the chancellors of Notre Dame and Lincoln respectively, to the faculty of grammar at Oxford, and the identification of the master's degree with the licence to teach (RAC:C 830–2).[7] As might be expected in view of the peculiar issues raised in connection with the prebendal school of Chichester, Leach depended on the published statutes of the English cathedrals for much of his material. He includes in the historical background under consideration a summary of documentary material from St Paul's, Salisbury, and Wells. His first excerpt, relating to the school at St Paul's in the reign of Henry I, is taken from *Dugdale's History of St. Paul's*.

This is followed by material from W. Sparrow Simpson's recent edition of the statutes and customs of London's cathedral church and additional quotations from Dugdale. It appears from the St Paul's material that Leach's main concern is to find all the historical evidence that links the early medieval chancellor with the *magister scolarum*, and then to show how the former gradually gave over his responsibilities *vis-à-vis* the grammar school to the latter (RAC:C 824–6).[8]

The even more recent publication of the statutes and customs of Salisbury Cathedral serves Leach's continuing interest in elucidating the respective responsibilities of the four chapter dignitaries, the dean, chanter, chancellor, and treasurer, but especially those of the chancellor: "*Similiter CANCELLARIUS in scolis regendis et in libris corrigendis.*" Leach refers any reader interested in the meaning of *regendis* to his extracts from Maxwell-Lyte's work on Oxford (RAC:C 826–7).[9] Additional material on Salisbury is found in the Rolls Series edition of St Osmund's register, specifically with reference to the prebend of Calne in Henry I's reign, to which the chapter dignity of treasurer was attached. Leach uses this source to unravel the prebendary situation at Chichester (RAC:C 827).[10]

The extracts from Wells contrast with the rest of the material. Leach furnishes his readers with some of the more pertinent items in his report on the cathedral to the ecclesiastical commissioners in 1883 (RAC:C 828–30).[11] Quoting the part in the report to the effect that Wells now possessed no grammar school at all, whereas for six hundred years such an institution had been integrated with the cathedral establishment, Leach draws particular attention to the request of the present dean and chapter. Their intention to re-establish the school, hampered only by want of means, is "not only recommended by historic claims, but would also be in accordance with the principles now regulating the appropriation of endowments." The report's plan for Wells, in fact, is stated very succinctly: the presumption must be that some property representing the original endowment for a grammar school attached to the cathedral "has passed into the hands of the Ecclesiastical Commission," and that a new assignment "for the same purpose," therefore, might be regarded as "an equitable act" (RAC:C 828).

Leach then summarizes the historical statement following the request of the dean and chapter, which is largely concerned with stages in the school's endowment from the thirteenth century. Leach is especially interested not only in the details of endowment but also in the distinction between the choristers as an institution separate from the grammar school and the educational responsibilities of the chancellor. He completes his series of extracts from Wells with material from a very recent edition of the cathedral statutes. To this he appends a lengthy note of his own, informing the reader of his contact with the then chancellor of Wells Cathedral, Canon Bernard, to whom he is indebted for a history of Wells by the librarian of Exeter Cathedral. He remarks that the relevant passages in this book on the chancellor's deputy, the *Archi-Schola* or *Magister Scholarum*, provide satisfactory evidence for the view that "there is properly an Endowed Cathedral School at Wells" (RAC:C 828–30).

In his reports Leach appends explanatory footnotes and references to additional authorities to help explain the significance of some of the extracts in question. Although these references disclose some of the assumptions that hinder rather than help Leach in pursuit of a correct historical context, they testify to his honesty and diligence in attempting to understand contemporary educational issues from the perspective of historical precedent.

While Chichester offered the point of departure for Leach's research into the history of the grammar schools, Southwell Minster did the same for his study of the relation of those schools to the ecclesiastical institutions of the Middle Ages. His *Visitations and Memorials of Southwell Minster* was published as a volume for the Camden Society in 1891. In the introduction Leach states that until quite recently he shared a quite general perception of Southwell – "if its name is known at all" – as being the newly-constituted see of the counties of Nottinghamshire and Derbyshire. He shared the perception, that is, until he had the good fortune "to be deputed by the Charity Commission, at the end of 1886, to inquire into the case of Southwell Collegiate Grammar School."[12] In attempting to determine whether the attached grammar school was an integral part of the foundation of the church and, as such, came within section 27 of the Endowed Schools Act, Leach had to undertake research into the early manuscript records of the church as there was little mention of it in print. In this investigation, Leach states, "the unique position occupied by the Minster, the antiquity of the school, and the extreme interest of the two pre-Reformation registers of the church, which are still preserved, at once arrested attention."[13]

In Leach's *English Schools at the Reformation*, published five years after his work on Southwell, early references to that collegiate church include the introductory statement that "some of these colleges were amongst the most ancient and important of ecclesiastical institutions, when ecclesiastical institutions were the most important institutions in the country." He then states that these collegiate churches were, in fact, "the same in constitution, and hardly distinguishable in purpose from Cathedral Churches." He refers those readers interested in their constitution to his *Visitations and Memorials of Southwell Minster* and his recent paper, "The Inmates of Beverley Minster." When he then asserts that it was sufficient for the moment to state that "a primary duty and an essential attribute of these Colleges were the maintenance of a Grammar School," we can see the extent of Leach's concern to disseminate his views regarding the educational function of these secular institutions (*ESR* 11–12).

Leach traces the school to at least the middle of the tenth century, if not earlier. He sketches the church's constitution into Henry VIII's reign, before coming to one of his central points:

Without here recapitulating the facts and arguments which I have adduced in my report on Chichester Prebendal School to show that it was the duty of every College of secular Canons to keep schools ... I may say that the case of Southwell Collegiate Church ... distinctly strengthens those arguments and facts. These are still further strengthened by two recent cases which I have come across; – Howden, in Yorkshire ... and Ledbury in Herefordshire ... in both of which the grammar school buildings, corporally part of the edifice of the church, are still standing, and both of which were till the Reformation collegiate churches. In fine I propound as an absolute rule "Ubi Ecclesia Collegiata ibi Schola Grammaticalis," and that the latter is an "inseparable accident" of the former.[14]

Improving upon the palaeography of Dickinson in his Southwell *Liber Albus*, Leach makes the point that the phrase *regere scholas* meant to "keep" or "teach school," and that *scholae*, used always in the plural, actually referred to a single school. Like that of his predecessor, however, Leach's search through the ancient register has revealed virtually no mention of schools but the additional reference he did find was sufficient, he thinks, to show that "the Grammar School Master was regarded as in some sense a member of the Collegiate body," and the school itself "as a part of the College foundation" (RAC:S 627).

Not content with such slender evidence, Leach has recourse to a *Register of Leases*, extending from 1449 to 1621, and a *Registrum Capituli*, 1470–1537, the only additional sources still at Southwell. Concerning the second of these he observes that it is in a cursive hand "full of abbreviations." Leach mentions that he found this second register "so hard to read" that he appealed for help to the Record Office in connection with some words that he could not decipher, to find that one of the chief officers there experienced similar difficulty. Leach has, however, managed to extract a number of passages, which he then produces to furnish strong proof, he says, that the chapter exercised "general scholastic superintendence" throughout the county of Nottingham, and that the prebendary of Normanton possessed "special scholastic duties" in his capacity as chancellor (RAC:S 627–31). Leach concludes his comments on the reestablishment of Southwell Collegiate Church by act of Parliament in 1543 with the statement that "the school, therefore, became or remained just as much a part of the church after the dissolution as before" (RAC:S 631).

When Leach considers the effect of the Chantry Acts on the institution, his argument for the continuity of the integration of church and school ultimately rests on showing that the collegiate church was never "in point of law dissolved." Paying special attention to the new statutes issued for the church under letters patent in 1585, during the reign of Elizabeth, Leach admits that the text is not conclusive on whether or not the *ludi magister* was included among the *ministri ecclesiae*. He makes the point, though, that "the Grammar School was not, as sometimes is contended in such cases, a mere choristers' school, since there is to be a separate school for choristers." He adds that this grammar school was for "everyone in Southwell and the neighbourhood (*vicinis locis*) who chose to come" (RAC:S 633–5).

Leach then proceeds to outline the series of "sweeping changes" that began in 1836, including the removal of the soke of Southwell from the secular jurisdiction of the archbishop of York to the county of Nottingham.[15] Although the collegiate church itself did not, in Leach's opinion, appear to have been dissolved, the changes did contribute to the dying out of the collegiate body and the beginning of the school's decline. In the Cathedral Commission Report of 1854, for instance, there were only seven day pupils listed and no boarders. As the headmaster expressed it, "without knowing the intention of the Commissioners [i.e. the financial arrangements for the possession of the school-house], I am necessarily unable to judge whether it is desirable for me to continue to hold the mastership of the School or to incur the necessary expenses in having it fairly and properly organized" (RAC:S 637).

The actual progress of the school is not, however, the issue for Leach. Although the school's fortunes revived to some extent in the 1860s and early 1870s, the inevitable question of jurisdiction surfaced once the last canon of the collegiate church died early in 1873. With the county of Nottingham in the diocese of Lincoln since 1837, and the spiritual jurisdiction of the deanery of Southwell part of the archdeaconry of Nottingham since 1841, the then master, the Reverend J. S. Cargill, resigned his mastership into the hands of the bishop of Lincoln, the collegiate chapter now being presumed extinct. When, in 1877, the bishop of Lincoln made a new appointment to the headmastership of Southwell Grammar School, partly, at least, on the strength of an earlier expression of support from the ecclesiastical commissioners, his action appeared to be in line with the transfer to Lincoln in 1841 of the powers of visitation traditionally vested in the archbishop of York. Notwithstanding this, Leach questions the legality of the appointment. Conceding without any question that the patronage of benefices with cure of souls possessed by prebendaries, dignitaries, or non-resident officers had been transferred by the Ecclesiastical Duties and Revenues Act of 1840 to the bishop of the diocese in which such benefices were situated, Leach observes that no such provision had been made with respect to benefices without cure of souls. He states that the prebend of Normanton in the church of Southwell was of this kind, and hence the patronage of the prebendary from which the support of the grammar school was derived was not so transferred. Nor, in Leach's view, did the bishop of Lincoln acquire the patronage of the mastership of the school as the successor to the presumably defunct chapter. He argues that although the previously cited act of 1841 transferred the patronage of benefices with cure of souls to the bishops of Ripon and Manchester, benefices without such cure of souls were not included: "I should submit, therefore, that the Bishop of Lincoln had no legal title to appoint the Grammar School Master in 1877" (RAC:S 638–9).[16]

The import of Leach's challenge to the bishop of Lincoln's action is not evident from his report, since Leach wants the Board of Guardians to determine whether the right of appointment of the master of the grammar school lay with the bishop of Lincoln, the ecclesiastical commissioners, or the Crown. After further discussion this group is extended to include not only the bishop of Southwell, "as the transferee of part of the diocese and rights of the Bishop of Lincoln," but also the "Honorary Canon of Normanton," "the Honorary Chapter of Southwell," or "the Rector of Southwell as representing the ancient Chapter" (RAC:S 640–1).

It is not clear to Leach, then, as he explained to the bishop of Southwell, who, precisely, had the power of appointment. Nor did Leach consider it any more certain, within the terms of the Ecclesiastical Commissioners Act of 1841, whether the grammar school master qualified as an "officer" of the church for whom "competent provision" was to be made by the commissioners. What he does know is that the entire endowment of the schoolmaster was now less than it had been at any previous time (RAC:S 641). Still, Leach is satisfied that he has demonstrated that "the Collegiate Grammar School was an integral part of the old foundation of the Collegiate Church," that it remained a part of the new foundation of Henry VIII and was expressly recognized by the Elizabethan statutes, and so continued at least till 1841. It is, therefore, an educational endowment that in the terms of section 27 of the Endowed Schools Act, 1869, forms or has formed part of the endowment of a cathedral or collegiate church" (RAC:S 642).

Having proved that Southwell's grammar school had traditionally received assistance out of the endowment of the collegiate church, Leach proposes to show that the current endowment is "wholly inadequate" and that the sources of additional funds − church estates − have been transferred to the ecclesiastical commissioners. He then enters upon a lengthy discussion as to whether the grammar school was entitled to scholarships at St John's College, Cambridge, based on an agreement dating back to the reign of Henry VIII but again left unresolved owing to the existing relationship between the grammar school and the Southwell choristers − the original beneficiaries.

The central issue, however, is a particularly difficult one to resolve: "Is the School maintained out of the endowment of any Collegiate Church?" "Does it form part of the foundation of any Collegiate Church?" The answers depend on whether there is still a college at Southwell, as all the canons had now passed away, leaving no successors, and on "whether the Chapter and the College or the Collegiate Church are convertible terms." Although Leach had made good use of his medieval history, the nineteenth-century changes only obscured the main lines of development (RAC:S 648–50). His conclusion, therefore, appears to be an honest, if disappointing one. He thinks that if the collegiate church is still in existence, the grammar school, not having been cut off from it, is still part of the foundation, and that, even if the collegiate church no longer exists, there is still a possibility that the school might have a claim on the endowment (RAC:S 650).

While Chichester and Southwell both reveal the relevance of historical research towards the resolution of difficult legal problems, Beverley provides the fullest details with regard to general procedure. Leach states that on 24 July 1888 the charity commissioners ordered an inquiry to be made, under his direction − specifically under sections 35 and 50 of the Endowed Schools Act, 1869 − with a view to establishing what was called a "scheme," pertaining to the Beverley Foundation School and other charities, the inter-relationship of which had already been worked out in a "draft scheme" dated 29 March 1888. A November date for the inquiry was subsequently set aside in favour of 10 January 1889, at the behest of the town council. The charity commissioners then had to see to the public notice of the inquiry: this they did through notices in the local press, including the *Beverley Guardian* and the *Beverley Recorder* on 15, 22, and 29 December 1888 and the *Beverley Echo* on 14 and 25 December and 1 and 8 January 1889. In addition, posters were placed on the door of the Town Hall and other public places in Beverley.[17]

As will later be revealed from the inquiry proceedings themselves, the disposition of the educational side of the Beverley charities had been regularly postponed for several years. Some of the confidential and unpublished material pertaining to this delay is extant in the charity commission files, including a letter to Leach written early in the year 1888 in which George Young, one of Leach's superiors, informs him that "the Beverley people have been such a puzzle to me throughout, with their unusually unreasonable crankiness, that I hardly know what to write." He goes on to say that no one has so far fathomed the evident hostility the townspeople entertained toward the commissioners. Young is prepared to accept the view that it was caused primarily by the mutual jealousy between the town council and the municipal trustees, but even this, he thinks, "ought not to have hindered us so long." Since Leach is a "new hand" in the matter, he will be in a position to determine the cause of the "misunderstanding" or "irremovable dislike." All that the charity commissioners are trying to do, Young remarks, is, with the grammar school no longer in existence, to find a way of transferring its endowment to some other school "for which the town can derive *more than double* the benefit at present received from it."[18]

In his report Leach gives the names and official status or occupation of all seventeen persons who provided him with information during the inquiry. He remarks that, with two exceptions, no one had earlier given him notice of any intention to give evidence, and that, in fact, no one had stepped forward to conduct the case, either to defend or criticize the scheme. Leach's challenge – and opportunity – can best be appreciated from his remark that, not having the acquaintance of any person in the town, nor having any knowledge ahead of time of either the evidence to be considered or the particular witnesses to be called, he was forced to act as "judge, counsel, solicitor, and reporter" all at the same time.[19]

Leach is not exaggerating his sense of distance from the local Beverley scene. Readers of his Chapter Act Book on Beverley Minster will recall the vivid description of his first visit to the ancient town on "a damp, dismal November evening" and how he at first mistook the parish church across from his hostelry for "the far-famed Beverley Minster." In spite of this unfamiliarity with Beverley, Leach is able to state quite early on that he has been able "to elicit a very considerable body of opinion in favour of the Scheme as a whole," but, understandably enough, "with some modification in matters of detail."[20]

He points out that the case of the Beverley educational endowments had already been before the commissioners for several years, as far back as 1876 in fact. A scheme was then put forward to consolidate the three main endowments deriving from the grammar school, the Foundation School – a fairly recent institution dating from 1854 – and the Blue Coat School, founded early in the eighteenth century for a small group of poorer children. The scheme provided for what was termed a "second grade" grammar school, but, to the dismay of many persons, including Beverley's town council, the venerable grammar school identified for centuries with the community's leading citizens was not selected as the core of the new institution. Instead, the recent Foundation School was chosen. Its master, Mr. Ridgway, was to be the headmaster. With general sentiment in the town for the abolition of the Blue Coat school, in December 1879 the town council virtually agreed to hand over the old grammar school – assuming the consent of the Treasury – as an educational endowment within a scheme for a "second grade" school that involved the removal of Mr. Ridgway. These considerations led Leach to state that it was "a great mistake" not to have implemented the whole plan at that time.

The result of the delay, protracted over the next eight years and sometimes affected by developments beyond any one person's control, was what Leach terms "a complete *volte face*". The municipal charity trustees, along with the Foundation School trustees, objected to the removal of Mr. Ridgway. Nor did they want the Blue Coat School to be abolished. Rather, they believed it required an augmented endowment in the interests of the poor.[21]

After inquiring into the industries and the population growth of Beverley and its relationship with the larger neighbouring city of Hull, Leach directly considers the earlier historical factors that had helped to shape the current educational situation. He is able to prove "beyond a doubt," he states, that the school was "an integral part" of the collegiate church foundation before the Reformation, as had been noted by Poulson in his history of Beverley.[22] In the wake of "the Colleges and Chauntries' Acts" in 1547, however, no school by that name appeared again until 1645, when the corporation's accounts reveal a payment of £20 salary paid to the master by that body. The corporation honoured that together with the upkeep of the school buildings until 1835.[23]

Leach's one major point of dispute relating to the history of the grammar school was the directive to the corporation at the time of the Municipal Reform Acts that it would no longer be in a legal position to pay the master's salary or maintain the school buildings. Leach remarks that this interpretation of 1835 was based on the view that the master's salary was a voluntary payment, an opinion he is inclined not to accept. Since, however, the relevant documentary evidence is not entirely forthcoming, he is satisfied not to dispute the claim. Rather, he is pleased to report that a near unanimous opinion favoured retention of the name "Grammar School" for the school reconstituted under the scheme.[24]

Leach reports that support was also obtained for the restructuring of the Foundation School because it did not answer to the educational needs of any substantial part of the community; and for the elimination of the Blue Coat School because it did not provide for the "absolutely destitute and helpless children" who might be in Beverley. Leach was able to state that there was "a great preponderance" of opinion in Beverley in favour of the scheme, at least on substantial points.[25] After listing the proposed amendments to the scheme, he concludes by expressing the opinion that the delays in the implementation of the scheme have seriously hindered its reception in Beverley. Nevertheless, even if the municipal charity trustees oppose the scheme, as he expects they will, he does not think that they will win over the town to their views, especially if the scheme is "pressed forward" speedily.[26]

The Beverley Independent of 12 January 1889, under the title "The Educational Endowments of Beverley: Proposed New Public School," included a complete and quite factual description of the meeting, not omitting Leach's defense of his superiors with respect to the delay in sanctioning a rearrangement of Beverley's educational funds.[27] *The Guardian* stated that not only was the committee a representative one, but that the members generally favoured "a good commercial and classical school" as the great need of the town and that "if the ancient charities of this ancient town and borough could only be fused," it would result in a "great and lasting benefit."[28] This particular description of the proceedings also affords some evidence of the impact made upon the local people by the assistant charity commissioner. Leach was tendered a vote of thanks for the "courtesy and patience" as well as the ability he had shown in presiding over the inquiry. The committee felt certain, therefore, that regardless of the outcome, their views would be conveyed to the commissioners in London with "fairness."[29]

In marked contrast to Southwell, Leach's investigation of the Beverley scene did not provide him with an opportunity to investigate the relation of the grammar school to the collegiate church. He was apparently not always able to use his official duties to advance his own historical views. Other school inquiries distracted him for a time from his central interest, as, for instance, his assignment to Walsall, in Staffordshire, at the end of 1891. His primary focus there was on the education of girls.[30]

Nevertheless, the ancient collegiate church in Beverley provided Leach with material for several publications, notably his two-volume edition of *Memorials of Beverley Minster*. Although the assignment to Beverley did not provide Leach with the opportunity to pursue his medieval research, he appears to have done so on his own. Leach loved Beverley. In his report to the charity commission he expresses his sympathy for the "hurricane of opposition" from various groups in the town at the threatened extinction of the old grammar school. Leach claims that the school "probably" originated as far back as A.D. 937 with King Athelstan's foundation of the minster as a collegiate church.[31] Beverley, therefore, was pivotal to Leach's emphasis on the educational significance of the early English collegiate institutions. This fact, together with his personal attraction to both church and town, undoubtedly inspired him to pursue Beverley's history independently of its relation to the Endowed Schools Act.

The appointment to conduct the commission's inquiry in the modern town of Walsall came when he was already involved with the ancient ecclesiastical city of York, a more congenial assignment, and one which later bore fruit in his two-volume publication *Early Yorkshire Schools*. He was called upon to deal with two schools in York, that of York Minster and the sixteenth-century foundation of the archbishop, Robert Holgate, named after him. Only the former is described here since, as a cathedral school, its current needs appealed to Leach by virtue of its long and informative history.[32]

Among all of Leach's confidential reports within the purview of the charity commission, the one on St Peter's Grammar School in York is probably as compact and as far-ranging as any he worked on. Unlike the school situation in places like Beverley, for instance, the request of the dean and chapter of York was relatively straightforward: to seek the commission's sanction for the modernising of the school's facilities by the addition of "workshops, gymnasium, and laboratory" (RAC:Y 584).

In the second half of his report Leach provides a fairly detailed summary of the property of both the school and the hospital of St Mary, which had been proposed as a source of money to realize the new facilities. He states quite categorically that the plans of the dean and chapter should be implemented and to this end "the acquisition of additional land adjacent to the school is imperatively required" (RAC:Y 604). His figures show that in the year of his inquiry, 1891, the number of boys attending the school had declined by 23 percent from 1881 with the drop somewhat greater among the boarders than among the day boys. The composition of the student body of 125 had remained fairly constant, the majority of the boys being sons of professional men, especially clergy, and few, if any, sons of tradesmen: "The sons of tradesmen, I was told, are not desired and do not desire to go to the school" (RAC:Y 608).

Leach finds that religious instruction is taught within the framework of Church of England doctrine, but since there is no conscience clause – something which, however, the headmaster would like to see – the religious instruction, as he informed Leach, "is not so distinctively on church lines" as he considered it ought to be in a cathedral school (RAC:Y 609). Leach's inquiry into the quality of education in the classical and modern subjects taught reveals a fairly satisfactory situation. The Latin of the sixth form was "distinguished ... rather for a praiseworthy equality of moderate attainments than for brilliance or a high standard," while a Cambridge examiner spoke "favourably" of the papers in "Euclid and algebra." Leach thinks, though, that their effort at higher mathematics "seems to have been extremely poor for a school with a Cambridge connexion" (RAC:Y 609–11).

The main obstacle to St Peter's receiving the benefit of both modernization and expansion derives from the fact that the school had not been included in any application made to the ecclesiastical commissioners under section 27 of the Endowed Schools Act, 1869, on the grounds that it did not qualify as a cathedral school (RAC:Y 585). This constitutes Leach's challenge and opportunity. He proceeds to show, from the inception of his report, that the cause of the grammar school in question has suffered from misleading as well as erroneous historical statements.

Comparatively recent historical information furnished to two successive cathedral commissions in 1854 and 1879 by the dean and chapter of York had ascribed the foundation of St Peter's to a royal charter of Philip and Mary and its principal endowment to James I. This interpretation was confirmed by the statement of the then headmaster, Rev. William Hey. Hey claimed that there was no cathedral school that drew upon the common funds of the dean and chapter. He went on to state that the grammar school of St Peter, York, possessed a "distinct endowment," of which the dean and chapter were the trustees. He added that the same questions that the cathedral commissioners had sent to him had already been answered by those trustees with his concurrence and approbation (RAC:Y 584). Leach then quotes from the Schools Inquiry Report: "The Royal Grammar School of St Peter ... has always been administered as a separate trust and not incorporated in the general revenue at the disposal of the dean and chapter. It is therefore not strictly a cathedral school" (RAC:Y 585).

Leach argues that, contrary to the above views of the dean and chapter, there was no augmentation of property by James I, whose letters patent clearly show that he was merely confirming what was already there. Moreover, Leach thinks that the present dean and chapter are correct in questioning the assertion of their predecessors that the school was not a cathedral school (RAC:Y 585). Leach concedes the difficulty in making a precise distinction between the terms "endowment" and "foundation" as used in the documents. He nonetheless contends that the ancient "endowments" of England's cathedrals were "granted to and held by the archbishop personally." Only gradually were they separated into the possessions of the dioceses as distinguished from the possessions of the church, that is, of the canons, who eventually developed into a corporation. The final subdivision occurred when there was a separation made between "the common fund of the church held by the chapter as a whole" and "the separate prebends or possessions of the individual canons held by them in severalty *virtute officii*," including the well known prebends attached to the offices of the chancellorship or archdeaconry (RAC:Y 586–7). The problem is that, whereas the foundation charters of the post-Conquest sees are "known and ascertained," those of the cathedrals of the "old foundation," like York, from pre-Conquest days, are not extant. This means, then, as Leach admits, that it is "an extremely difficult question whether the school is either part of the original foundation, or maintained out of the endowment, of York Minster" (RAC:Y 586).

Leach's argument from this point creates a background survey to which he refers throughout his career. He first surveys the very early history of York within the context of St Wilfrid's career (666–710) through Alcuin's mastership of the school of York to the time he was called by Charlemagne (780) to direct the palace school at Aachen. Leach also considers the various decretals of canon law – A.D.

826, 1179, 1215 – enjoining cathedrals and eventually other churches of sufficient means to provide for the maintenance of grammar
schools as essential parts of their educational obligations.

The historical evidence goes far to confirm the continuity of the
grammar school at York in Anglo-Saxon England – even to, from
the practice at Aachen, inferentially supporting the view that "the
cathedral schools were not confined to cathedral boys, but that the
laity and outsiders were admitted." He admits, though, that the proof
of the school's continuation into post-Norman times is lacking. He
claims that "there is every reason" for thinking that it did continue.
Not only did York escape the attacks of the Danes, but also some of
the later Saxon archbishops founded prebends at York, as they did
at Beverley and Southwell. This practice Leach infers to have included the maintenance of the school. He is dependent on the use of
inference and analogy to substantiate the existence of a grammar
school at York for close on to three centuries (RAC:Y 587–9).

The dearth of material is momentarily illuminated in the pages
of Hugh the Chantor's history of the first Norman archbishops,
written in the first quarter or so of the twelfth century. In it a
reference is made to the appointment of the cathedral's schoolmaster
by the first Norman archbishop some time after 1075 (RAC:Y 588–
9). After another two centuries or more, however, Leach is happy
to report that the earliest extant statutes of York Minster – he attributes them to around 1307 – contain the very information he has
been looking for: the chancellor's responsibility of collating to the
grammar schools. Originally referred to as the schoolmaster (*magister
scolarum*), the chancellor was now expected to be a master in theology
and to teach in the vicinity of the church. With specific reference to
the "school of York," the statutes provide that the chancellor present
an acceptable master in arts who would, in conformity with the
ancient custom of the church, hold the preferment for three years,
or, "by grace," for one additional year (RAC:Y 589). From this point
on, Leach is able to produce an increasing number of specific references to the grammar school in York. Before he addresses himself
to these, however, he cannot resist the temptation to fill in – again
by inference – those two hundred years of silence broken by the
York Minster statutes. He takes the reference to "that ancient statute," mentioned in the earliest York Chapter Act Book under 4
February 1290 with respect to the leasing of prebends, as a probable
reference to the statutes of Saint Osmund drawn up for Salisbury
in 1091. He bases his assumption on the fact that the duties of the
chancellor are described "in practically the same terms" in both documents and on the belief that both the Salisbury and contemporary

Lincoln statutes were – on the authority of Mr.Bradshaw, the late librarian of Cambridge University – "probably" drawn up by a committee of which the first Norman archbishop of York, referred to above, was a member. Added to this inferential evidence is Leach's factual claim that the same Thomas of York was one of the witnesses to both the statutes of Salisbury and those of Lincoln. Leach then feels confident in asserting that "as the schoolmaster of York was, as there is good reason to believe, before, and was certainly after, Thomas's reconstitution a part of the foundation, I submit that a grammar school was part of the foundation of the metropolitical and cathedral church of the Blessed Peter of York" (RAC:Y 589–90).

Among the later references to the school is one from 1289 in which "it appears" that the archbishop and chapter assigned the York mansion of the prebend of Donington for the use of the master and scholars (RAC:Y 591). Another from 1343 stems from the archbishop's visitation of the cathedral chapter, in which it is very clear that at least by this time, "the schoolmaster is ... a different person from the chancellor" (RAC:Y 591). Leach is interested in this new kind of schoolmaster. He finds that the documentary entries that bear on the subject, although still relatively infrequent as compared with the post-Reformation period, reveal first, that the mid-fourteenth century catastrophe of the Black Death interfered with the hitherto customary appointment of masters in arts to the headship of the school, and, second, that it was not uncommon for such head masters to be married and therefore "not bound to be in holy orders." Such was the case with Gilbert Pinchbeck, whose appointment in 1426 by the chapter during a vacancy in the chancellorship extended for some twenty-eight years beyond the original three provided for in the agreement (RAC:Y 592–3).

To include the reign of Henry VIII in his account, Leach has to contend with the fact that the roll relating to York Minster is not in the *Valor Ecclesiasticus* of 1535. Fortunately, however, the roll for nearby St Mary's Abbey is. In the entry pertaining to the abbey's distribution of alms to the poor – thereby constituting one of the deductions to be made from the revenues of the institution – there is mention of a house called "Conclave" or "the Clee" assigned for the board and lodging of fifty "poor scholars, ... *studying the art of grammar in the school of the metropolitan church of York.*" Six of these boys were maintained by the abbot, two by the prior, and one by each of the twenty-two senior monks. The maintenance of the total of thirty is a form of charity described as a community responsibility "from old time," along with the maintenance of twenty additional scholars "out of the broken victuals of the convent" (RAC:Y 593).

In view of Leach's opinion of monks and monasteries, it is interesting to read his comment on this contribution of St Mary's Abbey to the grammar school of York. He expresses great satisfaction with St Mary's by ignoring its monastic character completely, focusing, instead, on how it shows without any qualification how erroneous was the generally prevailing view of pre-Reformation schools as "mere chorister schools" or as designed to serve only "junior members of the church or the clergy" (RAC:Y 593).

Finally, he considers the projected source of revenue for the new school facilities – the hospital of St Mary, outside York's Bootham Bar and quite close to the Minster. Founded in 1330, and endowed mainly through the church and rectory or, as Leach explains, "the tithes and glebe," of Stillingfleet in the East Riding of Yorkshire and close to the city of York, the hospital was granted by Philip and Mary under letters patent in 1557 to the dean and chapter of York. The royal license provided for the establishment of "a grammar school in or near the city of York, in such fit place as shall seem best to the dean and chapter, for the education of boys and youths of this our realm, in knowledge of literature (*literarum scientia*) and soundness of morals" (RAC:Y 595–6).

Leach then shows that this grant of the hospital for the endowment of the grammar school was soon followed by a whole series of documents issuing from the dean and chapter. The series culminated in an indenture of 2 July 1557 involving the archbishop of the first part, the dean and chapter of York of the second part, and the patrons – Lord Eure, Thomas Eglesfield, and Richard Marshall – of the third part, stating the intention of the said dean and chapter to "erect, found, and *build* one grammar school within or nigh to the city of York" before the feast of St John the Baptist, 1558. This school was to have a master, an usher, and "a certain convenient nombre of scolars." The boys were to be taught grammar free of charge and provided with sufficient food and drink until such time "as they, or any of them, shall be of age and disposed to be priests, able to serve in the said cathedral church of York and other places within the said diocese, or elsewhere," according to the ordinances and directives, that is, of "the said dean and chapter and their successors" (RAC:Y 598).

Before proceeding to an interpretation of the above documents, Leach cautions that "no statutes were ever made by the dean and chapter for the school," at least, "none ... have been found." He makes the point that the school has never, since the hospital was granted, "been supported by the dean and chapter out of their common fund, nor by the chancellor of the church." The school has,

however, always been governed by the dean and chapter. This governance has included the regular appointment of the schoolmasters
and the vicar of Stillingfleet, the management of the rectory of Stillingfleet and other property, as well as the management of the school
in a general fashion, "applying to its support the endowments of the
late hospital so transferred to them" (RAC:Y 598).

The central question, therefore, is whether the documents show
the school to be a cathedral school or not, or, more precisely, whether
the grant of the hospital endowment constituted "merely a new endowment of the existing and continuing cathedral school," or, in
fact, "a new foundation" (RAC:Y 599). Leach cautions that "no certain
conclusion" can be deduced from the language of the letters patent
of either Philip and Mary or James I. It was "common form," he
remarks, for Tudor and Jacobean monarchs to claim the foundation
of a school or a college that at the most they "abstained from plun-
dering" (RAC:Y 599). His own view of the matter is that the real object
of the grant of St Mary's Hospital was to provide a substitute for
the boarding house at St Mary's, "which has been shown to have
been kept up by St Mary's Abbey, before its dissolution, for boys
attending the cathedral school." As he says, to have made the provision from the abbey resources "would have been mulcting the
Crown or its grantees" (RAC:Y 599). Perhaps even more insightful is
Leach's historical explanation of the changes in responsibility within
the cathedral body itself. He points out, for instance, that the chancellor's school tended increasingly to become the school of the dean
and chapter. This was, he claims, primarily, if not entirely, because
the traditional term of three years for the schoolmaster's office was
no longer practicable and the intervention of the dean and chapter
was required to give a "fixed tenure" on each new appointment,
thereby ensuring to that body "the practical nomination" (RAC:Y 600).

As Leach has intimated throughout his report on St Peter's School,
whether the institution is a continuation of the cathedral school or
a completely new foundation is a moot question. He notes, for instance, that the words of the letters patent do not seem to imply
anything more than that "the dean and chapter are to be the governing body of the school" (RAC:Y 600). He finds several "remarkable" features in the terms employed in the various documents. Not
least is the fact that in connection with the appointment of masters
of the school by the chapter "it is not until 1726 that the school is
described as 'of the foundation of Philip and Mary'" (RAC:Y 601–2).
In view of the lack of any clear-cut explanation deriving from the
documents themselves, therefore, Leach is prepared to submit the
whole question to the decision of the Board. He has, nevertheless,

made up his own mind that the "true construction" of all the documents in question points to a continuance of the old cathedral school, together with a boarding house and a "considerable endowment" for its maintenance (RAC:Y 600).

The above selections from Leach's files in the records and correspondence of the charity commission may be taken as fairly representative, not only of the procedures generally adopted by the commission itself, but of Leach's own special kind of historical inquiry. These selections reveal not only his care for detail in ascertaining the facts of a given situation, but also his patience in bearing up with the politics of local communities. No amount of internal dissension or interminable delay seems to deter him from his objective. By and large, the newspaper accounts of the inquiries over which he presides testify to both his efficiency and fairness.

From our point of view, Leach's outstanding merit, as revealed in these sources, is his ability to relate historical study to contemporary issues. It is interesting to note that Leach treated all four of the examples described above with equal objectivity. While it is clear that Chichester, Southwell, and York afforded him opportunities to engage in his favourite lines of historical inquiry related to cathedral and collegiate institutions in a way that Beverley did not, he did not show less diligence in dealing with Beverley. Leach never lost sight of his duty as a commissioner to find ways of using already existing benefactions in the best interests of new and more extensive educational demands. At the same time he was ever on the alert to enlist the support of historical investigation whenever it was relevant to the situation at hand. In brief, Leach shows how historical research can respond to the analysis of current issues.

CHAPTER FOUR

Analysis of "English Schools at the Reformation, 1546–48" and "The Schools of Medieval England"

Leach's best-known books are separated by some twenty years. *English Schools at the Reformation, 1546–48*, which appeared in 1896, was the author's first attempt to survey for the reading public his research into the schools of pre-Reformation England. *The Schools of Medieval England*, first published in 1915 and intended as a popular compendium of what was known about the subject, followed a remarkably sustained period of research and publication during the intervening years. It is useful to discuss these two works together.

English Schools at the Reformation consists of three parts. The first is a lengthy introductory essay in which the author outlines the various kinds of schools found in medieval England and the fate of some of them under Henry VIII and Edward VI. The second, and by far the most extensive, section consists of documents, including the texts of the Commissions of Inquiry and Continuance associated with the Chantry Acts of Henry VIII and Edward VI, followed by a series of extracts from the chantry certificates and warrants. The third part consists of a chronological list of schools obtained from the information contained in the chantry certificates and the continuance or refoundation warrants printed earlier in the book.

In a short historiographical essay in the introduction, Leach accounts for the widely accepted but completely unfounded opinion that the secondary school system of late Victorian England owed its inception to Edward VI. Several writers, in Leach's view, have lent their support to this mistaken attribution, including an historian of Cambridge, J. Bass Mullinger; two Anglican historians, Canons Perry and Dixon, in their respective histories of the Church of England; and a French writer, Jacques Parmentier, whose *Histoire de L'Education en Angleterre* appeared in the same year as Leach's *English Schools at the Reformation*. The historian J.R. Green, author of the widely read *Short History of the English People*, is singled out for more extended criticism because Leach regards him as "the most brilliant and best known of [the] propagators" (*ESR* 1–3). The weakness of all these writers, Leach claims, is that they have been too prone to quote uncritically from early eighteenth-century works like Knight's *Life of Colet* and Strype's *Ecclesiastical Memorials*, sometimes even misinterpreting what they copied. Instead of a theory based on "hearsay evidence," Leach hopes to provide one "founded on facts placed on record at the time the transaction took place" (*ESR* 7).

At the outset, Leach denies that Edward VI was the founder of England's schools. Although as a teenage boy Edward was not himself the "spoiler" of schools, one or the other of his two protectors, Somerset or Dudley, was (*ESR* 5). Leach contends that records appended to his book reveal the existence of some 200 grammar schools prior to the reign of Edward VI, of which the majority were "abolished or crippled under him." These records, however, are very incomplete and Leach doubts if the destruction and loss of so many others will ever permit the recovery of a full account of all the grammar schools in pre-Reformation England. His own "moderate estimate" is that there were 300 by the year 1535. "The great revolution" then began that saw most of the schools "swept away" under Henry VIII or his son and, if not done away with, "plundered and damaged" (*ESR* 5–6).

Leach states that he will limit himself to discussing the provision for secondary education "as it appears in the official records taken in the last two years of Henry VIII and the first two years of Edward VI." On occasion, though, he will find it necessary to go beyond these limits (*ESR* 6). His main concern is with grammar schools, "not mere monkish Schools, or Choristers' Schools, or Elementary Schools." Since these schools were of "exactly the same type" and performed very much the same functions as the public and grammar schools of his own day, Leach classifies them according to the institutions with which they were connected. He thus identifies seven categories of schools, including those connected with cathedrals, collegiate churches, hospitals, guilds, and chantries. He also makes room for some "independent" schools, and for those associated with monasteries (*ESR* 6–7), although he already has serious reservations concerning the role of the monks in England's educational development (*ESR* 15–19).

This method of distinguishing the various kinds of grammar schools has moved a considerable distance beyond that given by Carlisle. During some ten years of historical research, most of it on a part-time basis, Leach has struggled to understand the underlying principles behind the establishment of schools and in this case has succeeded in identifying the very raison d'être of the medieval grammar school. As might be expected, since Leach is dealing with the impact of the Reformation on education, the chantry school is the object of his special attention. In his opinion, the chantries constitute "the latest and largest class of institutions in connection with Schools" (*ESR* 47).

Leach defines a chantry as "usually confined to an endowment, generally of one or two priests only, to pray for the soul of an individual, his family, and friends." He mentions that if there were more than two priests on the same foundation the institution was often referred to as a "college" (*ESR* 48).[1] Leach does not explain when and how the early chantries began to be connected with grammar schools. As he remarks, the foundation deeds and licenses in mortmain seldom mention a school, even when a school is known to have been intended. Leach provides a good example in the foundation at Durham in 1414 by Bishop Thomas Langley of both a grammar school and a song school, under the direction of the priests entrusted with the chantry of our Lady and Saint Cuthbert, at the west end of the cathedral. Leach points out that neither in the episcopal licence issued in Langley's ecclesiastical capacity as ordinary regulating the services and prayers at the chantry altar, nor in the palatine licence related to his temporal capacity as earl of a county palatine and creating the priests a corporation, is there any mention of schools. Only in a deed attested the day following the issuance of the licences is it disclosed that the main duty of the two priests in question is to keep schools of grammar and song, "teaching gratis the poor ... but charging the rest moderate fees, such as are usually paid in other Grammar or Song Schools" (*ESR* 52–3).

To understand Leach's interpretation of the effect the Reformation had on medieval schools, it is necessary at the outset to appreciate the distinctions that he draws between the Chantries Act of Henry VIII and that of his son, Edward VI. First, Leach is convinced that Henry VIII did not intend any damage to education. On the contrary, he sees in Henry a well-intentioned, if vain and erratic, ruler who eventually was of two minds regarding the chantries. In commenting on Henry's legislation, Leach notes that whereas the effect on learning of the dissolution of the smaller monasteries was probably minimal, the act pertaining to the larger monasteries extended to colleges, hospitals, and institutions designated as "ecclesiastical" or "religious." The result, therefore, was the destruction of many schools, including Higham Ferrers – "a smaller Winchester"

– and Cardinal College at Ipswich. In the wake of further suppression of colleges and chantries by the king's mesne lords, acting on their own, Henry introduced the Chantries Act. Since this statute, Leach remarks, has been the subject of much comment without a corresponding examination of the text, and is found, not in the statutes at large but only in the statutes of the realm, a full account of it will prove useful (*ESR* 59).

After providing the text of the Chantries Act, which, as chapter 4 of 37 Henry VIII, Leach assumes must have been passed quite early in the Parliament that began in November 1545, he observes that the text is in two parts or is two separate acts merged into one. He lists two main reasons for the act: (1) other people have taken upon themselves to appropriate the chantries without licences, and (2) since the king needs money for his wars, the plunder from the chantries might just as well go to his cause as line the pockets of a few. All chantries such as those listed, therefore, are to be given over without any qualification to the king. The other chantries, which have not been suppressed but survive, are put at his disposal to take what he pleases by way of commissions. Leach lists the only known instances of the foundations thus taken over, all but one of them in the last three months of 1546. They are St Edmund's College, Salisbury; the colleges of Tong in Shropshire, Pleshey, and Hastings; the hospital of St Bartholomew the Great; the chantries at Aldwinckle and Lufwick in Northamptonshire and at Bakewell in Derbyshire (*ESR* 59–64, passim). Leach observes that the new Chantries Act passed in the first year of the reign of Edward VI proceeded on a different basis. The Parliament of the Protector Somerset placed the action of the new government on religious grounds, dissolving the chantries because Somerset's regime "condemned the objects of Chantries" (*ESR* 65).

As Leach expands on both the meaning and the intent of the Chantries Act of Edward VI, he concludes that provision for the abolition of the superstitious practices of the chantries and for the maintenance of schools, especially grammar schools, held a promise of true reform. The intent of framers of this legislation, Leach states, was undoubtedly commendable, since there can be little question that if the schools had been treated "beneficially," there would have been no grounds for retaining chantries per se. Leach is convinced, in fact, that no reasonable man, Catholic or Protestant, would be prepared to defend them:

No form of charitable endowment could be less defensible in theory, or less beneficial in practice, than that of the Chantry pure and simple. To set one,

two, or even three or more, priests, educated men, or supposed to be educated, to spend his or their days in singing psalms, or saying masses at a
salary of £5 a year, (say £60 to £100 a year of our money,) for the soul of
some one who had "emigrated from this light" perhaps two or three centuries
before, and was in most cases far better known by his Chantry when dead
than he had ever been by his charity when alive, was perhaps as great a
waste of men and money as could well be conceived. Prayers for the dead
may, or may not, commend themselves as useful or meritorious; but hired
prayers for the dead are surely superstitious. (*ESR* 67–8)

Leach explains that there was, apart from one very important omission, little in the act that threatened schools. The one important
exception to this relates to the song schools – or elementary schools,
as he tends to regard them – since these were not provided for at
all. In Leach's view this was "a grievous omission," even though the
song schools and reading schools, both associated with music in the
churches, may well have been regarded as at least bordering on
superstition. In his opinion, however, it was a fatal omission, and
accounts for the destruction of many schools maintained by chantries
or guilds, whether they were bound by their foundation charters to
maintain such schools or not. As he further observes, "the Act had
it both ways. If the School did not appear in the foundation, it was
suppressed, even if one was in fact kept. On the other hand, though
one ought to have been kept according to the foundation, yet if in
fact it was not kept, it was suppressed" (*ESR* 69–70).

Prepared as he is to give as much credit as possible to those who
formulated the Chantries Act under Edward VI, Leach is acknowledging the degree of discontent the Act provoked. He mentions,
for instance, that Latimer refers to the matter frequently, though
in general terms. In sermons preached before Edward VI in 1550,
Lever, the master of St John's Cambridge, beseeches the king and
his council on behalf of the poor and the godly zeal they had for
"good learning." He exhorts them to reflect on "how many Grammar
Schools be taken, sold, and made away," not only to the "great slan-
der" of the laws, but to the "grievous offence" of the people, the
abandonment of youth to ignorance, and "sore decay of the Universities" (*ESR* 78). Lever mentions a particular school founded in
the north country – identified by Leach as Sedbergh – that had now
come to a miserable end. Leach thinks that it was owing to appeals
such as these in both public and private that the restoration of some
of the grammar schools began. He notes in particular that Sedbergh
School, founded in 1527–28, was ordered to be refounded on 20
February 1551 (*ESR* 78–80, passim).

Whatever the destruction wrought by the process described by Lever, Leach thinks that the central factor is the commission dated 20 June 1548. Two officials of the Crown, Sir Walter Mildmay, the general surveyor of the Court of Augmentations, and Robert Keylwey, surveyor of the Royal Liveries and the Court of Wards, were given responsibility by the government for the implementation of the continuance of the schools. Leach states that "to these two was practically committed the settlement of the whole question of Secondary Education at this crisis." He goes on to show how broad the scope of their commission actually was, including, as it did, not only the continuance of schools and preachers, but also the appointing of vicars and curates, wherever needed, in places where there were colleges or chantries. In addition, Mildmay and Keylwey were to assign money for the poor and pensions for those who were disestablished. About this Leach remarks, "The Schools are made quite a subordinate part of the business they had to do" (*ESR* 75–5).

The royal charge to the two commissioners, as voiced through the king's uncle, Somerset, speaks of the number of grammar schools that should be erected and continued in every county, as well as the actual establishment of "divers and sundry Grammar Schools in every county in England and Wales, for the education and bringing up youth in virtue and learning and godliness" (*ESR* 75–6). Leach understands the weakness in the entire scheme. Tacked on to the above charge was a "fatal addition" whereby whatever money had customarily gone to the maintenance of schools and schoolmasters should continue to be made available until "other order and direction" could be taken. This meant, Leach claims, that Mildmay and Keylwey issued their warrants on the strength of a certificate presented by any surveyor or his deputy. The question of which schools were to be continued, Leach says, "was really settled by the clerk of a person who occupied the same sort of position as a local agent of the Woods and Forests now." Owing to this kind of "fiasco," Leach concludes both Henry's "great promises" to his Parliament and the intent of that body under Edward VI to reform the chantries and promote learning came to an end. With regard to the majority of the schools, further instructions "never came" (*ESR* 76).

Finally, Leach explains what the documents of dissolution tell us and what they do not. He mentions that the documents, as catalogued in the record office, constitute three distinct sets: the certificates under the Chantries Act of Henry VIII, the certificates under the Chantries Act of Edward VI, and the abstracts of the certificates under the act of Edward VI compiled for the assignment of pensions. Leach states that altogether there are about 110 documents classed as chantry certificates, but that they do not include anything like one certificate of each class for each county. On the contrary, many of the documents have nothing to do with colleges and chantries under the act in question, and among those that do only eight counties are fully represented in all three classes: Cornwall, Essex, Gloucester-shire, Northumberland, Staffordshire, Warwickshire, Wiltshire, and the North Riding of Yorkshire. Norfolk, Surrey, Cambridge, and Huntington have virtually no certificates worth mentioning. Only twenty-three certificates remain from those under Henry VIII's act, thirty-one from Edward VI's act, and only twenty from the pension certificates (*ESR* 83–4).

Leach was surprised to find that only the chantry certificates of Lancashire, Somerset, and Yorkshire had been published by the time he came to use them. He states that in the other counties he had gone to the originals and extracted all that he could find relating to schools and exhibition foundations. He hopes that no grammar schools have been omitted, "though it is hardly to be expected that none have been overlooked" (*ESR* 84–5).

Leach is concerned that the extracts from the various certificates show that the schools were treated very unevenly. He is confident, for example, that the commissioners under Edward, at least in a county like Essex, were interested in education. While Henry's com-missioners, headed by Bonner, had singled out only the school at Walden (now Saffron Walden), the commissioners for Essex under Edward presented seventeen places as having schools. In the return for Hereford they listed fifteen schools, the officials recognizing and continuing ten of these, while an eleventh, at Leominster, was, Leach observes, re-endowed and refounded. By contrast, not a single school is recorded for Derbyshire even though a certificate under Henry VIII's Chantries Act was extant. Yet, Leach claims, Chesterfield, with its guild, "must certainly have had a School"; and he thinks that the same would probably hold for places like Ashburn and Bakewell. The list of omissions could be extended. Buckinghamshire, for example, is "almost as scurvily treated." Only two schools are listed for this county in either certificate and none for Buckingham itself, which, Leach states, is absurd, since the school there was that of the chantry of Thomas "the Martyr." In Aylesbury, also unmentioned, there actually was a school as late as 1818 held in the chantry attached to the parish church. Leach concludes: "It must not therefore be assumed that the lists of Schools are exhaustive, even in the 8 counties which are represented in each class of Certificate" (*ESR* 87–90, pas-sim).

Although Leach is not particularly interested in either the song schools or the elementary schools, he laments the loss of so many of these institutions at the time of the Reformation. He is not always consistent, though; on this particular occasion he is not concerned for the song schools but laments the loss of schools such as those in Northallerton and Hemingborough in Yorkshire. In them the teaching of song, reading, and grammar "were combined in one person." Leach makes the point, though, that the song school and grammar school masters were usually quite distinct from each other. The former was always present in the colleges, mainly to teach the choristers, and in this capacity still maintained his position at Winchester College. Other places where the song school master is mentioned include Brecon, Crediton, Fotheringhay, Lincoln, St David's, Pleshey, Southwell, Stoke-by-Clare, Stratford-on-Avon, and Thornton. Leach contends that a "strange measure" failed to keep up these and similar schools, causing "immeasurable" harm (*ESR* 95–6).

Leach concludes that a much larger proportion of the population in medieval England had the opportunity to attend grammar schools than in his own day. He says: "Certainly it was larger than the proportion at the time of the only authoritative statistics on the subject; viz., in 1865–66, as given in the Schools Inquiry Commissioners Report. The Report gives some 830 Secondary Schools of all grades ... That number was no more than one Secondary School for every 23,750 people, among the then population of 19 millions." Leach maintains, moreover, that wherever class size is mentioned, the numbers attending these later medieval schools were "surprising for their magnitude" (*ESR* 97–8). He illustrates this general theme with several examples. There were, for example, 120 scholars at the free grammar school at King's Norton in Worcestershire in the charge of the schoolmaster, Harry Saunders, and his usher, John Peart. There was also a third stipendiary, a curate, who took care of a chapel of ease at Moseley. That grammar school had declined in Carlisle's time to an elementary one of fifteen boys and now, in his own day, Leach says, it had become nothing more than an exhibition fund connected with the elementary school (*ESR* 101–2).

Leach remarks that besides erroneously crediting Edward VI with the foundation of "this once great school," Carlisle had given currency to the "legend" of a choice presented to the inhabitants of King's Norton between having the endowment either in land or in money, their decision being in favour of the money. Not only did the people in question not possess the option of retaining their lands, Leach asserts, but when one realizes that the lands were let "on fixed rents on beneficial leases" and that considerable fines accrued every few years, determined not by the fixed rent but by the improved value, "no one in his senses could have chosen a fixed charge instead of the lands" (*ESR* 101–2).

The focus of *English Schools at the Reformation* is relatively sharp –

an analysis of the chantry certificates to determine the effect of the dissolution on the educational life of the nation. As such the book remains a seminal work on the economic and social dimensions of the Reformation as well as on the more specialized topic of the schools. Leach's thesis that reformers in the reigns of Henry VIII and Edward VI supplanted an earlier Catholic school "system" is, of course, debatable. Leach views the dissolution of the chantries as especially indicative of this process of decline, but only because so many schools attached to these chantries were dissolved or, if continued, were reduced to straitened circumstances. With chantries per se Leach has not the least sympathy. His own interpretation of the chantry certificates is not so much a criticism of the program for Protestant reform as a critical analysis of an unfortunate by-product of that program: the near destruction of a network of grammar schools servicing the country in greater numbers per capita than was the case three centuries later at the time of the *Schools Inquiry Commissioners Report*.

By contrast, *The Schools of Medieval England* surveys almost a thousand years of educational development. The book ranges from a consideration of the educational services provided by Augustine's Christ Church Cathedral in Canterbury to the fate of the schools under Henry VIII. Unlike the earlier work, there is no place for the citation of sources or the inclusion of explanatory footnotes. Yet this survey reveals the author's easy familiarity with complex issues and his ability to work many of the sources into the body of the text itself. As a deceptively simple descriptive and analytic narrative, the book conveys the impression that if we consult the sources as Leach did, we will reach the same conclusions about medieval schools.

Almost from the outset, after establishing that the schools of medieval England derived from the heathen Greco-Roman institutions rather than from the catechetical schools of early Christianity, Leach directs the reader to question any association made in the past between a school and a monastery. In considering, for instance, the well-known schools of Northumbria in the eighth and ninth centuries, Leach casts serious doubts on some of the traditional authorities by using "the unimpeachable evidence of Bede" as a foil for the "unveracious" testimony of the later monastic historian, William of Malmesbury (*SME* 37). In the same vein, Alcuin's biographer is referred to as having shared with later writers "visions of a long chain of monastic schoolmasters"(*SME* 53). By contrast, the church of Ripon, around 925 A.D., since it was presided over by secular canons, had a grammar school attached "as a matter of course" (*SME* 48–9).

The point should be made that in discussing these earlier centuries, Leach is intent on going well beyond the identification of monasteries with schools, the untenability of which he can to some degree advance for the later Middle Ages from the sources themselves. He is disposed to undercut the reputed connection between monks and the world of learning itself in England's earlier missionary period. Only a small minority of the monks were literate, Leach insists; the typical monastery, far from being "a home of learning," was more like "a voluntary workhouse or a penitentiary" (*ESR* 52–3).

Apart from his ability to jolt the reader with such an unusual and sometimes humorous juxtaposition of concepts, Leach has a flair for multiplying examples without obscuring the focus of his argument. Having remarked, for instance, that "one of the worst effects of the Conquest was the foisting of the Italian adventurer Lanfranc into the See of Canterbury" (*ESR* 96), he points out that the abbot's *Constitutions* have little to say about schools or education. When they do, as in the twenty-first chapter, they are "very minute, very stringent, and very monastic, but not at all scholastic," and they assume very little "beyond knowing the psalms and services by heart," (*ESR* 33). If this is not enough to convince his readers, he draws attention to a contemporary writer's treatment of Henry, the youngest son of William the Conqueror. Not without humour, Leach insists that the article by the Rev. William Hunt in the *Dictionary of National Biography* – betraying the "curious *penchant*" the author reveals "for sending people to imaginary schools" – failed to produce a single piece of evidence to support his claim that Henry, any more than the grammarian Aelfric, attended school at Abingdon Abbey (*SME* 103–4).

Leach develops one of his more solid themes in connection with the educational changes of the late eleventh and early twelfth centuries in the period he refers to as "Lanfranc to Becket." He describes how the schoolmaster in the cathedrals and collegiate churches became associated more with "grammar and elementary logic and rhetoric," while the chancellor became increasingly identified with the local school of theology. This development – a move downward on the educational scale for the schoolmaster as Leach sees it – is attributed to the rise of the universities, which "had great influence on the schools everywhere else" (*SME* 106–13, 132).

Not unrelated to the above evolution is the description of the schools in twelfth-century London given by William Fitzstephen, the biographer of Becket, and included in John Stow's *Survey of London*. This evidence helps to confirm in Leach's mind not only that the domain of the grammar schools consisted of the *trivium* – grammar, rhetoric, and logic – but that these grammar schools were giving precisely the same kind of classical education as the great public schools in the sixteenth to the nineteenth centuries. In Leach's view the grammar schools were providing it perhaps even more effectively (*SME* 139–40).

Leach does not miss the chance, however, of ascribing to John Stow responsibility for more than one "legend" that had gone unchallenged for far too long. In his *Survey*, Stow unluckily threw the history of London's schools into "hopeless confusion" by identifying the other two schools besides St Paul's as those of Westminster and Bermondsey. If, instead of lending credence to unfounded tales, Leach continues, Stow had minded his geography – neither monastery was within London's boundaries at the time in question – he would have come to realize that Bermondsey never possessed a school at any time, while the school attached to Westminster had originated only in the fourteenth century. Leach acknowledges that Stow did not have access, as Leach's contemporaries did, to the mid-thirteenth-century statutes of St Paul's by Dean Henry of Cornhill or to those of a generation later by Dean Ralph Baldock. In those statutes the other two "privileged" schools were identified as St Mary-le-Bow and St Martin's-le-Grand (*SME* 141–2).

Without, therefore, showing concern for any deviation from the norm, Leach posits the following as an educational model for the country in the first half of the thirteenth century. Each of the "great churches" had a theological school under the direction of the chancellor, who was usually expected to be a master in theology, that is, a doctor of divinity. His deputy was the grammar schoolmaster, appointed by the chancellor, and "generally required to be an M.A." Finally, there was the song schoolmaster in charge of the song or music school, the deputy of the precentor and appointed by him, but for whom "no special qualification was laid down" (*SME* 158).

Although Leach views the rise of the universities as the main cause in the decline of the status of grammar schools, he appreciates how the universities helped increase the number of such schools. Concentrating for the moment on the establishment of colleges at the universities, including Merton at Oxford in 1274 and Peterhouse at Cambridge in 1285, Leach notes how these were soon followed by "a new crop of colleges or collegiate churches of secular canons all over the country, each with its schools of grammar and song" (*SME* 166). In the absence of any distinction, however, between the later developments and those of the earlier Anglo-Saxon period, Leach manages to imply a close connection between the formation of collegiate bodies and the provision for secondary school education throughout the middle ages, at least into the later thirteenth century.

He is confident that his own research has not exhausted the subject, and that, when more and more people come to examine local records in the interests of "living educational institutions" as opposed to "dead monasteries and chantries," the number of schools ascribed to the thirteenth century or earlier will be "indefinitely increased" (*SME* 178).

Arriving at the fourteenth century, the "era of school statutes," Leach can determine the comparative position of schoolmaster, the records being available for such centres as Canterbury, St Paul's, Beverley, and St Albans (*SME* 182). He is prepared to take issue with the editor of the Rolls series on the meaning of "bachelor" at the St Albans grammar school. Leach asserts that he was not an usher or master, as stated, but an advanced student "who had either taken the degree of bachelor in a university" or was ready to take it "in the school" on due examination (*SME* 186). In the midst of similar observations on the internal development of grammar schools and their extension up to the Black Death around 1349, Leach includes a rare glimpse of his personal involvement in the contemporary educational scene: "At Northallerton, in Yorkshire, is a grammar school, which the present writer assisted to raise from a decadent state to its present flourishing condition as a mixed grammar school for boys and girls with not far short of 200 pupils" (*SME* 197–8).

After establishing a close connection between the foundation of Wykeham's college at Winchester and the evident need for recruitment of clergy following the Black Death, Leach is ready to make his one concession to the monks in the area of lay education: their provision for almonry schools beginning in the early fourteenth century. Even here Leach has his reservations, reminding the reader that in providing "board, lodging, and, eventually, teaching for their choristers," the monasteries were only following the example set by "the great secular churches" a century earlier (*SME* 213).

In the fifteenth century Leach looks for an educational institution with characteristics of the Renaissance; he thinks he has found one in the school foundation of William Sevenoaks, a London grocer. This man gave lands in London to provide for a free grammar school in Sevenoaks, stipulating that the master was to be "sufficiently advanced" in grammar, a bachelor of arts, and – in Leach's translation – "by no means in holy orders." Leach's explanation for this requirement is that the founder might simply have not wanted the schoolmaster to be "wasting his time" in offering Masses for the dead as a chantry priest, or holding a living while neglecting his school. But, he says, "the provision has a distinctly Renaissance ring about it as putting education before religion" (*SME* 244). Leach ties in the above example with that of John Abbott, who on 19 June 1443 founded a free school under the trusteeship of the city company to which he himself belonged, that of the mercers, giving them lands in London for a master to teach *libere et quiete*, that is, free and quit of all charges, at Farthinghoe in Northamptonshire. In Leach's view Abbott's Foundation "thus anticipated by sixty-seven years the supposed innovation of Colet in entrusting his new endowment for St Paul's to the same company, because, in Colet's words, 'while there was no absolute certainty in human affairs, he found less corruption in a body of married laymen like the Mercers, than in any other order or degree of mankind'" (*SME* 244–5).

It may be well at this point to note how Leach interpreted the Renaissance, central as this movement was to his overall evaluation of medieval education:

The very term Renaissance is misleading. There was no new birth of learning wanted, because learning had never died – in schools at all events. The learning of Latin was the whole aim and end of education in schools. The authors read may have differed, though Virgil from first to last formed the staple. Otherwise Horace and Juvenal may have given way to Prudentius and Juvencus, and Cicero to Augustine, and vice versa. But it is by no means clear that the latter were not better stuff for the schoolboy than the former. There may well have been more interest in a poet who believed in the God of whom the boy knew than in Horace's skeptical references in a mythological and antiquarian vein to the dying divinities of Greece and Rome. (*SME* 248–9)

The ideals of the Renaissance, Leach thinks, can best be expressed in the term "humanism." The introduction of Greek or the imitation of Cicero, even the preference for grammar and philology over dialectic and logic, did not make the Renaissance. Rather, "the substitution of humanism for divinity, of this world for the next, as the object of living" distinguished the humanists from those who went before them. For a thousand years "the sole object of education" had been not to prepare for life but "to prepare for death." In his adoption of the dogma "the noblest study of mankind is man," Leach claims that an exponent like Petrarch replaced the Christian writer Lactanctius with Cicero and, in doing so, "substituted political for theological study" (*SME* 248–9).

Leach's concluding chapter is given over to the educational activity in the reign of Henry VIII. While Leach makes no secret of the fact that for many years he had been anxious to disprove the claim of Edward VI as a founder of schools, nevertheless it comes as something of a surprise to learn that he now thinks Henry VIII was the positive influence that Edward was not. He claims that the reign of Henry VIII deserves far more credit than that of his son to be regarded as an era of educational development, "though it has no more title than the latter to be regarded as the starting-point of an entirely new system of schools or of any great educational advance" (*SME* 277). Before providing examples of these school foundations, Leach feels constrained to clarify the position of Colet in the history of education.

As he has already indicated in his appraisal of the Renaissance, Leach does not consider that new courses in a school curriculum signal Renaissance humanism. The curriculum of Colet's "supposed foundation" of St Paul's school is a case in point, including the alleged novelty of Colet's introduction of Greek. Leach thinks that Greek had already formed part of the program at Winchester and Eton. In any event, Greek does not appear to have shared pride of place with Colet's own catechism, Erasmus's *Institute of a Christian*, and a number of traditional Christian authors from the third to fifth centuries. Colet's fame, Leach insists, rests primarily on the "encomiums" of Erasmus, whose praises rang out like those of the later German reformers regarding the "similar re-foundation" of Strassburg School by Sturm. All that Colet did, in fact, was to transfer the government of the cathedral school from the dean and chapter to a city company comprising married laymen which, again, in itself, was nothing new. There had already been a "constant stream" of schools governed by city companies, Leach remarks, for more than half a century. What did happen, though, was that the already famous St Paul's became, in the process, not only the richest but the largest free school in the city of London – 153 boys compared to the twenty-five at the Mercers' own school or the twelve at St Anthony's (*SME* 279–81).

Cautioning that many of the schools credited to Henry VIII's time were, like Colet's, not new foundations but "revivals, augmentations or conversions into free schools of old schools which were not free," Leach summarizes what is known of these sixteenth-century institutions. Among these schools he lists, for example, Wolverhampton Grammar School. Wolverhampton owed its establishment to Sir Stephen Jenyns, merchant tailor and ex-lord mayor, who had obtained a charter in September 1511, having previously bought the ground "for the education of boys and youths in good manners and literature and for the better maintenance of a master and usher of the same." Leach finds it necessary to add that it is impossible to believe that the ancient collegiate church of Wolverhampton of Saxon founda-

tion did not possess, like Warwick and other ancient collegiate churches, a grammar school. He allows, though, that if it did, its
endowment was probably a fixed payment of £2 a year or so and
therefore "inadequate for the sixteenth century and free education"
(*SME* 281).

Another such school is Wimborne Minster, Dorset, founded by
the Lady Margaret Tudor, grandmother of Henry VIII. This was
to be a free grammar school open to all who wished to attend, with
the master to be appointed by the master and fellows of Christ's
College, Cambridge. Although the ordinances for the school were
made by Bishops Fox of Winchester and Fisher of Rochester in the
second year of Henry VIII's reign, 1511, Leach notes that the licence
for the school had been given by Henry VII in 1497 and the endowment granted in 1504: "Nor can we suppose that this ancient
Saxon collegiate church had not always maintained a grammar
school in some form." The Lady Margaret merely created a new
chantry, which is returned in the valuation of 1535 as the "Scole
maisters chauntrey," and "annexed it to the schoolmaster's office
permanently" (*SME* 281–2).

Although the collegiate church of Southwell might seem to have
little to do with the school foundations of Henry VIII, Leach draws
a parallel between what Lady Margaret effected at Wimborne "permanently and by a new foundation" and what the Southwell chapter
did, in the same year, to augment the grammar schoolmaster's pay
of £2 a year which had remained unchanged for at least three centuries. This was to request the senior vicar-choral to waive his customary right to the vacant chantry of St Cuthbert, the richest in the
minster, in favour of the appointment of a fit chaplain, Sir William
Babyngton, to take charge of the grammar school. Leach adds that
Babyngton's agreement to govern the school throughout his tenure
of the chantry was only terminated with the temporary surrender
of the college to Henry VIII in 1540 (*SME* 282).

Guildford Grammar School is, in turn, associated with the history
of Southwell Minster within the area of endowments. Guildford was
founded in 1509 by a citizen and grocer of London, Robert Be-
kyngham, who gave all his lands in Bromley and Newington towards
the establishment of the school. In 1512 the lands in Bromley were
conveyed by deed for this purpose, and the appointment of the
grammar schoolmaster was vested in the mayor and four of his
brethren. When, however, Southwell Minster was again dissolved
under the Chantries Act in 1548 – the school being continued as a
charge on the Crown revenues of Nottinghamshire to the value of
£10 a year – this chantry endowment was in 1553 annexed to Guild-

ford Grammar School. Leach states that Mr. Mullinger, in the *Cambridge Modern History* of 1910, "in teeth of the evidence," refers to Guildford Grammar School as one of Edward VI's creations. Leach states, instead, that Edward VI, by patent of 27 January 1553, refounded the school, giving his own name to it and, by way of endowment, two rent charges deriving from the endowments of a chantry at Stoke d'Abernon and the Southwell chantry mentioned above. Under Queen Mary the chancellor, Archbishop Heath, recovered the Southwell chantry for Southwell Minster. By act of Parliament under Elizabeth, after Heath had been deposed, St Cuthbert's chantry endowment was once again given back to Guildford School. Unfortunately, however, this was a fixed rent charge on the manor of Battersea, not worth much in later times. Guildford's chequered career, Leach contends, is "a striking instance of the Edwardian school foundations, so-called, robbing Peter to pay Paul," and of the looseness of historians in dealing with them (*SME* 283).

Leach contends that Blackburn Grammar School in Lancashire, though commonly attributed to Queen Elizabeth, actually dates from the first year of the reign of Henry VIII, Elizabeth having only given it a new charter. A deed in English of 4 April 1514 asserts that the churchwardens and the parishioners had provided lands for an "honest, seculer prest," not a member of a religious order, sufficiently learned in grammar and plain song, "if any such can be gettyn, that shall kape contenually a Free Gramer Scole." Since the Earl of Derby added a piece of land worth fourteen shillings a year to the lands bought by the parishioners, he was regarded as the founder and patron and given the appointment of the chantry priest schoolmaster. Leach states that a rather remarkable provision in this instance was that if a person able to teach grammar was not to be found, he could be replaced by one who could keep a free song school (*SME* 283–4).

The schools at Berkhampstead and Stamford are other examples of foundations of Henry VIII's reign attributed to the reign of Edward VI. In 1523, Leach explains, the inhabitants of Berkhampstead agreed to devote all the lands of their brotherhood to providing for a school building and finding a schoolmaster to teach their children. The president of their fraternity, the dean of St Paul's, John Incent, gave all his lands there to be united with the brotherhood lands for this purpose. In 1541 Incent obtained a licence to found a chantry and also "one Free Scole within the towne of Berkhampstedde, of one mete man being a scolemaster, and one other mete man being an ussher for the techyng of children in grammer frely, withoute any exaccion or request of money for the teaching of the same children, not exceeding the nombre of one hundreth fourty and four." After the founder died, the king "as principal founder" was to present the chief master and teacher, and the dean of St Paul's was to present the usher. Although Leach does not explain how this came about, the dean, an ex-fellow of All Souls College himself, appointed Richard Rive, a fellow of that college, as master. The example from Berkhampstead affords Leach the opportunity of using some thinly veiled sarcasm in focusing on the mistakes of a well-known historian:

This school has been lately selected for special notice by a Professor of History in the University of London as one of three schools founded by Edward VI, where no school was before, and as thus effectually disproving the wanton assertion, made by the present writer, that none of the Edwardian Grammar Schools were really his creation. Professor Pollard cited as proof an Act of Parliament for Berkhampsted [sic] School passed in 1548. Had the professor, however, looked at the Act he professed to quote he would have seen that it recited Incent's foundation and alleged flaw in the conveyancing of the property, which was therefore claimed by Andrew Incent, the founder's cousin and heir. The Act negatived this claim and corrected the alleged flaw by a re-foundation; Rive and his usher and their succesors being incorporated as "Master and Usher of the Free School of King Edward VI in Berkhampstead", a title which has deceived the unsuspecting professor. (*SME* 290–1).

Similarly, in attempting to prove that Stamford Grammar School was a further example of Edwardian initiative, Professor Pollard "showed even greater abstinence from research and regard for facts." Leach reinforces his criticism by stating that the act of Parliament of Edward VI for this school in 1548 did not pretend to found or refound the school, or even call it Edward VI's grammar school. The act only made the alderman of Stamford ex-officio trustee and governing body of the school, vesting in him the property bequeathed by the founder of the school, a William Radcliff. The act recited that Radcliff's intentions had been fulfilled for the past seventeen or eighteen years since his death by "an honest learned schoolmaster."

Leach asserts that the very book that Pollard was attacking – Leach's *English Schools at the Reformation* – included the printed certificate of Edward VI's commissioners that revealed the "pre-existence" of the Stamford school from 1 June 1532. The endowment by William Radcliff – of a free chantry grammar school under an able secular chaplain empowered to obtain a licence in mortmain for the alderman of the Corpus Christi Guild to hold it – was in part honoured. Although the chantry lands were confiscated, the commissioners directed that the school itself be continued, with the master's salary charged on the Crown revenues (*SME* 291–2). Leach goes on to suggest with some authority that the school's endowment was saved mainly through the influence of one of its old boys, William Cecil, who was MP for Stamford in the Parliament that passed the Chantries Act. Leach also mentions that Ratclif was not the creator of a new school, as there was evidence of the school's existence in 1309, in 1327, and in 1389, "and the Henrician founder was therefore at the best only reviving and probably only refreshing an ancient institution" (*SME* 292–3).

Leach recites many more examples of schools founded during the reign of Henry VIII. The cumulative effect of his account inspires him with the conviction that Henry, not Edward VI, is to be regarded as a true founder of schools. Although Henry's main contribution to education, Leach remarks, consisted not in creating schools but in refounding and improving them, he did this on such a scale that he could be regarded as "the greatest of school founders." The common view that Henry, in abolishing the monasteries, also destroyed a great number of schools, is wide of the mark, since it derives from the "erroneous" notion that monasteries and schools were virtually one and the same thing. As for the admittedly "large number" of schools under the administration and trusteeship of monasteries, Leach claims that "as far as is known," the masters connected with them continued to be paid (*SME* 310–12).

The reader who has followed Leach's main lines of argument throughout will not be surprised that in these concluding pages the author is quite positive about the educational impact of the dissolution of the monasteries. The schools that Henry abolished in this takeover were "the small and insignificant almonry schools of a few charity boys." He more than made up for these in the "great schools" he established in the new cathedral foundations of Bristol, Chester, Gloucester, Peterborough, and Westminster (*SME* 329). The import of the dissolution, however, went well beyond its educational dimension. Leach claims that with the death of Henry early in 1547 the Middle Ages had virtually come to an end "by the swift, wholesale and, on the whole, peaceful dissolution of those fortresses of medievalism, the monasteries" (*SME* 329).

Leach at this point appears to recognize the dichotomy between a positive development – a surprising number of educational institutions, surpassing anything that England had seen almost up to Leach's own day – and the unfortunate development in monastic centres of a spiritual and cultural outlook that was retrograde from the moment it was brought from the continent to England. To what extent he thinks these two aspects can be reconciled is the burden of his final remarks.

In brief, Leach views the results of the proliferation of schools as "disappointing." This was mainly becasue monasticism, furnishing "a safe and easy refuge from the struggle for existence," enforced its own celibacy on the clergy. In forfeiting their right to have families of their own, therefore, the clergy missed out on forming "a cultured middle class," which alone, in Leach's opinion, could promote the advancement of "science and learning." Although the Renaissance was distinguished for its expansion of education to the laity "in the prince, the noble, and the merchant," as in the case of Henry VIII himself, a "sterilized" clergy, in possession of an "ever-increasing proportion of the territory and wealth of the world," remained an obstacle to progress (*SME* 331–2).

By any standard the source material at Leach's disposal for the writing of *The Schools of Medieval England* was extensive. In working some of this material into the body of the text the author intended to acquaint the reading public with the kind of factual history that would dispose once and for all of the "myths" and "legends" that characterized current interpretations of England's educational past. Readers would now be led to realize that the educational contribution of their medieval forebears had been all but obliterated by the triumph of Reformation principles.

Leach's use of documentary evidence lent an air of credibility to his own particular kind of generalization, especially with respect to extolling the educational facilities of collegiate and chantry institutions as opposed to anything of the kind attributed to the monasteries. This thesis might impress with its novelty, as did others, including, for instance, the view that the effects of the Renaissance on educational development were quite minimal. Yet Leach made no distinction between such conclusions ostensibly based on an accumulation of relevant examples and more specific topics, such as the meaning of "free" schools or the incidence of married lay schoolmasters. The net result, therefore, is that *The Schools of Medieval England* impresses one kind of reader as a handbook of educational facts while impressing another as a collection of new "myths" in place of the old.

That *The Schools of Medieval England* could be a potential source of quite another set of myths underlies A.G. Little's review of Leach's work in 1915. While recognizing the need to distinguish between the monastic contribution to learning in general and the actual involvement of the monks in grammar school teaching, Little describes as "astounding" Leach's "refusal" to recognize "the greatness of the debt which Western culture owes to the Irish monks." In a similar way, while appreciating Leach's concern to show that schools, unconnected with monasteries, existed long before the Reformation, Little claims that Leach's assertion that collegiate churches, like cathedrals, invariably maintained schools is a "sweeping statement" that cannot be justified from the extant records. So, too, in regard to the educational responsibility of the chancellor: while it was the general rule for him to teach theology and appoint to schools in the diocese, except when this responsibility devolved upon the bishop in lieu of a secular chapter, there were more exceptions "than Mr. Leach's generalizations would lead one to suppose."[2]

The above review appeared scarcely two months before Leach died at Bolingbroke Hospital in London, 28 September 1915. We do not know if he had the opportunity to read it.[3] We can be quite certain, however, that if he had been able to reflect on Little's criticisms, Leach would not have conceded very much. His *Schools of Medieval England* was, after all, his own compendium of thirty years of research and publication. Whatever its defects, Leach evidently intended his book to convey to as wide a reading public as possible a number of basic truths that would replace the myths which had for so long obscured the history of England's pre-Reformation schools. No one, therefore, would interfere with his larger purpose – least of all a person like Little who, as the historian of the mendicant friars, would have undoubtedly impressed Leach as one more contributor to the "monastic thesis."

CHAPTER FIVE

The Secular Origins of England's Schools

Visitations and Memorials of Southwell Minster, which appeared in 1891, was Leach's first full-length study on the origins and main features of the early English grammar schools. Leach mentions that the later of the two pre-Reformation registers still extant, covering the period from 1469 to 1547, is important because it is "a very full record of the inner life of the place during those critical years." Quite apart from its interest with respect to the persons actually involved in the life of the minster, the register affords a picture "of the whole manner of life and working of a collegiate church." Leach conducted this particular inquiry under several limitations. The writing of the book was long delayed owing to the "multiplicity of legal and other questions" connected with the grammar school itself at Southwell. There were also, he says, heavy official demands not only on his time but on "one's whole brains," so that he had to snatch "scraps of time" from his vacation and the night hours to see the project through.[1]

These opening remarks of Leach are interesting for two reasons. They tell us something of his method of work, testifying to his energy and diligence with this timely volume on Southwell, the fruit of only part-time occupation. More important, Leach emphasizes the central educational role of the collegiate church, a theme to which he returns time and again with greater and greater emphasis.

Leach evidently thinks of himself as a pioneer with reference to these collegiate churches and he makes his point with some humour:

It is remarkable how little was until very lately known of, and how little study was given to, the collegiate churches of secular canons, even to those which were cathedrals, compared with the great amount of research that has been devoted to the conventual establishments. Indeed, the former have

often been confounded with the latter by professed authorities on ecclesiastical history, and the canons of Beverley or Southwell talked of as monks
or friars, or identified with the Augustinian canons; which is very much as
if an Oxford college were confounded with a Jesuit seminary or Salvation
Army barracks. (*MS* xi-xii)

At the outset Leach wishes to establish that these collegiate churches
of secular canons were probably "the most ancient, certainly in historical times the most important, of the ecclesiastical institutions of
the country, when the most important institutions of the country
were ecclesiastical" (*MS* xii). The collegiate churches, since they were
parish churches as well, "were far more living institutions and more
intimately connected with the life of the country than the monasteries" (*MS* xiii). The great ecclesiastical statesmen – men like Becket,
Grosseteste, Wykeham, and Wolsey – came from the ranks of the
secular canons rather than from the ranks of the regulars. He expands further on this by saying that the collegiate churches furnished
"the lawyers and judges, the civil service, and the diplomatic service
of the day." Although he is ready to acknowledge that they did not
provide as many historians as the monasteries did, he is satisfied that
they did supply what is perhaps more important – the makers of
history (*MS* xiii).

The role of the collegiate church in the educational life of pre-
Reformation England is central to Leach's perception of Southwell
Minster. Few interpretations of his would lend themselves so readily
to controversy both in his lifetime and after his death. The sweeping
range of his thought in this regard can be gleaned from his assertion
that the collegiate churches were not only the "direct parents and
models" of the universities, especially of their colleges; they were
also the "direct keepers and founders" of many of the country's
existing grammar schools and the parents – through Winchester and
Eton – of "our great public schools." Moreover, Leach claims,
through the chantries, which turned so many churches into "small
colleges," the collegiate churches were "indirectly" the "nursing mo-
thers" of "by far the largest portion" of England's existing grammar
schools (*MS* xiv).

In this respect, Leach once again finds himself in one of his favourite roles, that of a clarifier of confused or erroneous interpretations of England's history. He relies on Bishop Stubbs to help him
make the necessary distinction between a monastery and a collegiate
church: "The difference between a monastery of monks and a minster of secular priests or canons consisted in the fact that the former
were bound by laws of obedience, poverty, and chastity, but were

not necessarily in holy orders; those of the latter were ordinary clergymen, bound by no particular vows, but living together on common estates, serving a common church, and under common local statutes" (*MS* xxiii). Leach goes on to add, "Essentially, the monk was a person devoted to saving his own soul by severing himself from this world, and devoting himself to the world to come. Essentially the secular canon was a person devoted to saving the souls of others, and endeavouring to improve this world" (*MS* xxiv). It is no secret which of these alternatives Leach favours. He proceeds to enlarge upon the historical development that witnessed the supersession of the collegiate churches by the monasteries.

His interpretation of this important change is that the canons of collegiate churches, like other secular clergy, had the right to marry until about sixty years after the Norman conquest when, under the impact of monasticism, they were enjoined to celibacy. Therefore, in effecting their later "conservative revolution," in reality Henry VIII and Cranmer were merely "restoring" the right of marriage to the canons of the older collegiate churches like Southwell; at the same time the two were ridding England of a narrow and outworn monasticism. If Leach has in mind nothing more than the influence of the wider European monastic reforms, like that of the early twelfth-century Cistercian movement, on the secular clergy generally – and not least in the matter of celibacy – he is on solid historical ground. When, however, he links the actions of Henry VIII and Cranmer with a "general feeling of Christendom" more in sympathy with the "freer character" of the more recently established Augustinian canons, friars, and "new" collegiate churches than with a monasticism that "had been tried and found wanting," he creates the misleading impression that canons and friars were less committed to celibacy than the monks (*MS* xxiv-xxv). Leach, of course, knows better, as he clearly indicates elsewhere, when he speaks of the same Augustinian canons "who eschewed matrimony," but the enthusiasm of the moment not infrequently causes him to make such reckless assertions.[2]

Leach wishes, too, to make the point that at a collegiate church like Southwell the chancellor was historically the earliest dignitary. He says that "the Chancellorship was annexed to one of the first, and most ancient prebends, that of Normanton, a fact which suggests that here, as at York and Waltham, the Magister Scholarum was the earliest dignitary" (*MS* xli). He then claims that "all collegiate churches and cathedrals were bound to keep schools," and that teaching a grammar school in those days was more important for the chancellor than his legal and clerical business (*MS* xli).

Although observations elsewhere in this volume on Southwell reveal that the essential connection of schools with collegiate churches and cathedrals applies only in the earlier medieval centuries (*MS* xiv),[3] Leach wants to show that the pre-Conquest collegiate chapters, being secular rather than monastic, maintained their control over not only the grammar schools attached to their own churches but also all the schools throughout the territory of a chapter's general ecclesiastical administration. This meant that the chancellor was the chief education officer for the entire area in question.

Among the documents that Leach appends to his account of Southwell Minster is one from 1472 that records the peaceful resolution of a dispute between the grammar schoolmaster at Nottingham and a teacher in the village of Wollaton, who promised that he would limit his teaching in grammar to twenty-six boys or men. Since the chapter of Southwell was a party to this agreement, Leach views this document as illustrating the wide jurisdiction enjoyed by the chapter who, as ordinaries, exercised control over all grammar schools in Nottinghamshire (*MS* 13).

When Leach contributed his article on "Schools" to the eleventh edition of the *Encyclopaedia Britannica*, he made a point of clarifying the position of the chancellor with respect to education. Although the chancellor had originally been committed to the teaching of grammar school, in time he came to be directly related only to the school of theology, in which he continued to lecture until the Reformation. Leach does not furnish any precise time period for the development of the chancellor's withdrawal from direct responsibility for the grammar school to his eventual identification with the school of theology. He notes only that at York this change had been effected by at least 1307 and in London by as early as 1205. Inasmuch, however, as in this later period the chancellor continued to be responsible for the collation to grammar schools, that is, the appointment of teachers to their benefices, Leach claims that "he always remained the educational officer of the chapter."[4]

In explaining the historical background to the supplanting of secular canons by monks, Leach emphasizes the triumph of the monastic ideal around the beginning of the twelfth century, specifically with regard to the state of celibacy as opposed to that of matrimony, Leach ascribing to the then secular clergy an insistence on "the liberty to marry." Examples of places where this change took place include Dunwich and Thetford: the schools in both centres were given over to the Cluniacs in the late eleventh century. Other examples are the schools at Gloucester and Derby, confided to the care of the Augustinian canons at Llanthony Abbey and Darley Priory respectively towards the middle of the twelfth century.[5] Leach reiterates, however, that such transfers did not make the schools monastic. They remained, in fact, secular, outside the monastic grounds, attended by both clerical and non-clerical students, and "taught by secular clerks, sometimes in holy orders ... but more often only in minor orders, and not seldom married men."[6]

A careful reading of Leach reveals that one of his objectives is to associate collegiate churches with England in a distinctively cultural way. For example, in his article on collegiate church schools, contributed to *A Cyclopedia of Education*, after remarking on the establishment of collegiate churches both before and after the conquest, he mentions that throughout the century and a half from about 1100 to 1250 few additional collegiate churches were established owing to the greater popularity of the new orders of canons and friars. Around 1260, however, a "revulsion" set in that favoured colleges for secular clergy. From this point until the Reformation, Leach contends, we can observe an almost annual increase in their number, especially if we include the colleges associated with the universities. Although the collegiate churches suffered a more serious loss of their records when they were dissolved in 1547 than the monasteries had earlier, there are enough remaining sources to show that both a grammar school and a song school were normally part of the original foundation. Leach then cites specific examples, including the episcopal foundations of Howden in Yorkshire (*c.* 1266), Auckland in Durham (1283), and St Thomas of Glasney at Penryn in Cornwall (1267), as well as the lay foundations in Suffolk of Mettingham (1344) and Stoke-by-Clare (1419), and Fotheringhay in Northamptonshire (1447).[7]

The inference is that as the later Middle Ages wore on, England was reverting to type. Leach views the collegiate church and its accompanying school, especially the grammar school, as all of a piece with the resurgence of the English language at the initial expense of Norman French. Integral to this development is the secular collegiate church, which for a while must concede to a long-standing monastic climate favoured by the ecclesiastical establishment, if not by the people at large. Ultimately, however, as the English – and lay element – wins out, history comes full circle with the dissolution of the monastic institutions under Henry VIII. The continental influence, with its celibate tendencies, is brought to an end. This is a fitting recompense, in Leach's opinion, for the harmful results of that disastrous watershed, the Norman Conquest.

If Southwell Minster furnished Leach with his basic introduction to collegiate churches and the schools attached to them, there is little doubt that his favourite collegiate church was Beverley Minster. There are few examples in Leach's writing as personal and intimate as his description of his first visit to Beverley Minster, the most beautiful building, he claims, in all of England. "Never shall I forget the first sight of it. It was a damp, dismal November evening, and a dirty-white fog struck chill to the bones as one got out of the train." After the weather had cleared and the moon had come out, however, he strolled through Beverley's streets and markets with their "quaint old-fashioned names," and soon ventured upon what he had come to seek:

Suddenly, at the end of High Gate, appeared in front the beautiful north porch of a great church, while above it rose the splendid clerestory of a stately nave. Coming to the end of the street, the whole length of the lovely minster was spread out before one, with its two transepts and its stately western towers revealed and yet concealed in the soft moonlight. Sir Walter Scott warns us to visit Melrose Abbey by moonlight; but what, even by moonlight, is that mangled fragment of a second-rate church, with its mean surroundings, compared with the vision of Beverley Minster in its entire and perfect beauty? And Beverley Minster only reveals its perfections the more amply in the full light of day.[8]

Between 1898 and 1903 Leach produced his two volume work entitled *Memorials of Beverley Minster: The Chapter Act Book of the Collegiate Church of St. John of Beverley, A.D. 1286 to 1347.* This work includes illustrative documents as well as his usual introduction. Once again, Leach is concerned to separate the church at Beverley from any monastic origin. To do this, he cites the use of the word "minster." He says that "it must be remembered that the word minster itself is peculiarly one used not of monasteries but of secular churches — York, Beverley, Ripon, Southwell, Lincoln, Lichfield, Wimborne, these are the churches to which the title of minster has clung, even to modern days, and they were one and all churches of secular Canons."[9]

To arrive at a fairly precise notion of the composition of Beverley's chapter, Leach has recourse to the Certificate of the Commissioners for Colleges and Chantries, drawn up with the view to the dissolution of the same, under the Colleges and Chantries Act from the second year of Edward VI's reign, 1547. According to this certificate, Leach notes that there should have been in the minster seventy-seven persons: one provost; nine canons or prebendaries, including the archibishop; three dignitaries or officers (precentor, sacrist, chancellor); seven parsons; nine vicars choral; fifteen chantry priests;

two subordinate officers (master of the works, chamberlain); seventeen clerks, called clerks of the second form; four sacristan or sextons; two incense bearers; and eight choristers.[10] No grammar schoolmaster is mentioned in this list, but in the selection of documents included in the second volume of his publication on Beverley are several references both to the school and to the schoolmasters themselves. For instance, in 1322 the chancellor presents Geoffrey of Whitby to Beverley Grammar School, with no term being fixed according to the ancient custom of the church. Geoffrey is admitted to his post by the chapter on an oath to teach school faithfully and to do all that custom required. A second document, from 1335, informs us of the presentation of Master William of Bredon to the rectorship of Beverley Grammar School on the death of Geoffrey; again the presentation is made by the chancellor of the minster.[11]

There are other references in the sources published in these two volumes that, while not directly relating to schools as such, at least imply the necessity of schools for a church of this importance. For example, in 1307 notice was given that clerks who belong to the choir in the chapter of Beverley, according to the customs of the church, have to put in at least a year in the choir before being ordained to the sub-diaconate. They are to stay one year in that state before they present themselves for ordination to the diaconate. They must then put in another year as deacons before being ordained priests.[12] The documents also include a 1339 memorandum to the effect that a number of such candidates have indeed received their promotion. Six are listed by name as advancing to the rank of sub-deacon; three as attaining the diaconate; and William of Scarborough and Peter of Hedon as ordained to the priesthood.[13] Although such examples do not rule out the possibility that the song clerks might have received their education elsewhere, the local nature of educational services would seem to suggest the independence of an important church like Beverley in this regard.

Leach asserts, too, that at least in the twelfth century the cathedrals and collegiate churches probably constituted the sole supply of grammar schools. Since, however, England was unique in Europe in having so many of its cathedral churches in the control of monks, there was no chancellor in several of the main centres, such as Canterbury, Winchester, and Worcester. Leach is bent on showing that even in these places the grammar schools were not within the jurisdiction of the monks but were under "the immediate care" of either the bishop or his archdeacon, that is, the secular clergy.[14]

The earliest and clearest exposition of the connection between education and the secular clergy, as opposed to the monks, comes from the extensive midland diocese of Lincoln. Leach notes, first, that the four principal persons of Lincoln Cathedral were the dean, precentor, chancellor, and treasurer. While the precentor's duty was to rule the choir and look after the singing, Leach finds that the chancellor's responsibilities changed between 1214 and 1236. In the earliest period, as elsewhere apparently, the chancellor's responsibilities included the direction of the school – *regere scolas* – and the correction of the books. He was to hear and determine the lectures, keep the seal of the church, prepare letters and deeds, and enter the readers on the daily schedule. By 1236 his duties apparently related more to the teaching of theology and to preaching than to the responsibilities for the grammar school and its related activities. Leach, however, continues to think of the chancellor as "the Diocesan Inspector and Board of Education for the county." He observes in this connection that the schools over which the chancellor still presided are named from time to time. In 1329, for instance, when the chancellorship was vacant, masters were appointed by the chapter to take over the grammar schools of Partney, Grimsby, Horncastle, Boston, and Grantham, and in the following year Stamford.[15]

Leach is also anxious to clarify the relationship of the choristers' school in Lincoln to the grammar school. He finds, first of all, that the choristers, being only twelve in number, "would not form a real school." He further observes that prior to 1264 they were lodged as charity boys in the houses of the canons or other officers of the church, but from that date on they were all boarded together in what was, in Leach's day, the organist's house. This development, which helps to explain the relationship of grammar to choristers' school at Lincoln, began with the appointment by the chancellor on 23 December 1406 of John Bracebridge, who had been master of Boston Grammar School since 1390, to the position of master of the High School – *Scolas gramaticales generales civitatis Lincoln.* At the same time, a priest, Thomas Prestcot, was appointed the master of the choristers by the precentor. In the summer of the following year, the chapter permitted the choristers' master to admit commoners along with the choristers, as well as to teach relations of the canons in the school of the college gratis (*libere*). Boys from outside who left the general grammar school of Lincoln, whether they were from the city or the surrounding country, were not permitted to go to this school. Leach is interested in the fact that this limited admission of outsiders was apparently resented by both the city and the chancellor as constituting an attack on the privileges of the ancient grammar school. Accordingly, a chapter act of 12 February 1407 records the resolution of this conflict between the chancellor, the mayor, and the citizens on the one side and the precentor and chapter on the other. The details are as follows: the boys attending the grammar school in the close, that is, the choristers, and the commoners boarding with them, as well as relations of the canons or vicars choral of the cathedral or those living with them, were permitted to attend class in the separate school now established, without paying any "collections" or salary to the general or public schoolmaster or having to be under his control. The sole condition was that for one day in each of the three school terms – Michaelmas, Christmas, and Easter – these boys were to go down to the general school of the church of Lincoln to attend the teaching and accept the chastisement of the grammar school master "unless of his own free will some other arrangement was made." It was further stipulated that no one else, "whether living in chantries or inside or outside the close," was to be allowed to attend this new choristers' school.[16]

In commenting on this arrangement, Leach is anxious to show how misleading has been another of the myths that have confused the grammar school and the chorister school. He remarks, for instance, that the terms used in the preceding documents make it clear that the ancient grammar school, like the present one, "connected ... with the Cathedral and the city," was "sharply distinguished" from the "semi-private school" of the choristers. Leach goes on to point out that the two grammar schools enjoyed a continuous existence from 1407 to 1567. Although, he says, the choristers' school was under the tutelage of the Lincoln cathedral chapter and the high school under the corporation, the masters of both schools were appointed by the cathedral chancellor.[17]

The mention in the Lincoln sources of individuals living in chantries provoked Leach to another investigation. He found that more than half a century earlier, in 1345, Sir Bartholomew of Burghershe had founded a chantry in Lincoln for five priests, living under a warden, to celebrate in St Catharine's Chapel on the north side of the choir. A few years after this foundation, the chapter found that it had a surplus of £10 a year and decided to make a foundation in favour of six boys who were to be maintained on the said £10 and taught grammar (*in gramaticalibus instruendi*).

To be admitted to this foundation, a boy was to have completed his seventh year, have mastered his Donatus, and have learned to sing. Those selected were to hold out some genuine hope of progress. They were to remain in the chantry for a maximum of eight years. They would leave after they had completed their fifteenth year or earlier should they have contracted any incurable disease or mental infirmity that precluded their promotion to the priesthood. The boys were to be boarded and lodged in the chantry house. And on every full school day they were expected to attend the grammar school, going and coming as a group, while on feast days they were to attend the parish church at least for matins, mass, and vespers. In his concluding observations on the Burghershe chantry foundation, Leach notes that it was not the first of its kind, having been preceded by the provision for grammar school boys at the two Oxford colleges, Merton and Queen's, in 1264 and 1334 respectively, and by the boarding house at St John's Hospital in Exeter in 1332. Its significance, in Leach's view, lies more in the fact that William of Wykeham, as archdeacon of Lincoln before he became bishop of Winchester, probably used it as one of his models in developing his concept of Winchester college, the progenitor, Leach claims, of the nation's great public schools.[18]

Leach's preoccupation with the collegiate church and the secular clergy was deepened with his research into the largest ecclesiastical centre of all, that of London. Reminding his readers once again of the essentially ecclesiastical character of the grammar schools, he states that the identification of the earliest and principal schools of London follows directly upon the identification of the city's earliest and principal churches, with the proviso that the churches are those of the secular clergy, not those belonging to monasteries and the religious orders. With this in mind, the chief secular churches, in order of importance, were St Paul's cathedral, the church of St Martin's-le-Grand and the London church of the archbishop of Canterbury, St Mary-le-Bow. According to Leach, all three churches had grammar schools attached to them that were already "old" before the first documented reference to them in 1138. They constituted the entire provision for the city's education until the establishment, in 1441, of a fourth grammar school in St Anthony's hospital.[19]

It might be expected that the story of London's medieval schools would be straightforward and comparatively simple. Yet Leach is impressed with the fact that "it has been so obscured and complicated by successive writers that it has been converted into a tangled and twisted texture of guesses and fables, which we must endeavour to unravel." He takes up the challenge with vigour. First, he finds it necessary to determine why there is such a serious discrepancy between Fitzstephen's identification of the twelfth-century schools of London in his life of Becket and Stow's sixteenth-century description. Leach quotes Fitzstephen to the effect that "the three principal churches have famous schools privileged and of ancient pre-eminence, though sometimes through personal favour to some one noted as a philosopher more schools are allowed." When Stow writes of these schools, adds Leach, he ascribes one to St Paul's rightly enough, but the other two to St Peter's at Westminster and the monastery of St Saviour at Bermondsey in Southwark.[20]

Leach was not satisfied until he had examined the manuscript sources. In his attempt to identify the particular manuscript of Fitzstephen that Stow made use of to gain information on the schools, Leach mentions that, of four extant sources, the only one that contains the description of London's twelfth-century schools – the Lansdowne manuscript from the late fifteenth century – fails to mention the churches to which they were attached. This last information, however, does appear in the *Liber Custumarum* of the city of London, a Guildhall manuscript from the first half of the fourteenth century. Leach does not accept the opinion, however, of Mr. Riley, the editor of that work, that this was the source of Stow's account, since otherwise it would be difficult to account for the latter's "bad guess" in naming the churches in question.[21]

Having disposed eventually of the difficulties raised by Stow's identification of London's schools, Leach proceeds to examine the statements of Bishop Stubbs concerning St Paul's school in particular. He draws attention to the fact that Stubbs had not only made a mistake with respect to the school's foundation date in his misreading of two early twelfth-century documents; he had also inferred two schools instead of one from the use of the Latin plural form instead of the singular. Leach explains that, until the middle of the fifteenth century, the word for "school" was not *scola* but *scolae*, a usage that has caused so much misunderstanding of "the whole status and history of medieval schools." The official title of the master of a grammar school – almost universal until the reign of Edward VI, he contends – was *Magister Scolarum Gramaticalium*, that is, he was not "schoolmaster" but "schoolsmaster."[22] Leach is satisfied that the two or three exceptions that he has come across only serve to prove the rule. He insists that the clarification of this point is "important" since the use of the plural, in leading people to look for two or more schools, has also led them into confusion over "two entirely different schools, the Grammar School for the world at large, and the Song School chiefly, if not exclusively, for the choristers."[23]

After this initial clarification. Leach points out how meagre the sources are for the history of London's medieval grammar schools. While, for instance, "very full" documentary evidence is available at Canterbury relative to the important position enjoyed by both its school and schoolmaster in the first half of the fourteenth century, and an "unbroken series" of chapter acts from the cathedrals at York and Lincoln provides continual notices of their respective grammar schools, St Paul's, by contrast, suffers from an "absolute dearth" of such records. He goes on to remark that a single chapter act book of the canons of St Paul's remains from the last quarter of the fifteenth century, but it throws no light at all on the school attached to the cathedral.[24] With regard to the school of St Mary-le-Bow, Leach found only two references, including an order from Archbishop Robert Winchelsea, 25 September 1309, with respect to the right of appointment of the schoolmaster, and a second item, dated 4 October 1399, consisting of Archbishop Arundel's appointment of Thomas Barym, master in grammar, to the control of the grammar school of the Arches of London.[25] With regard to the third school, that of St Martin's-le-Grand, "there seems to be no history recoverable." Leach did find a reference in the city *Letter Books* to the schoolmaster in 1298, and he thought that the entry was sufficient to show that at least the school was in existence and that the master was a man of substance.[26]

In the case of St Anthony's Hospital there is sufficient information, even if not all of it is correct. The hospital itself owes its origin to being a cell of the hospital of St Anthony at Vienne. Stow, followed by other writers such as Lupton in his life of Dean Colet, asserted that the original foundation included provision for a schoolmaster, a central point that Leach is anxious to set straight. He explains that it was only when the hospital had undergone a complete revolution that it provided for a school. He is referring to the fact that the hospital, beginning with its foundation around 1249 and throughout the first century and a half of its existence, did not have a grammar school. It was only when this period under a "foreign and monastic parent" gave way to a "native English" and non-monastic administration in the early fifteenth century that a school was added. St Anthony's school, he claims, went on to enjoy the "highest reputation" for a century or so. It came to an end only in the great fire of London during the reign of Charles II.[27]

Contending that John Carpenter, the future Bishop of Worcester and founder of the college of Westbury-on-Trym (near Bristol), should be regarded as the second founder of the hospital and the actual founder of its school, Leach gives the details of what he considers to be the principal developments in the evolution of the hospital. In 1441 Pope Eugenius IV authorized the conversion of the formerly Augustinian administration into a secular one. At the same time, Robert Gilbert, bishop of London, granted the licence to have the church of St Benet Finck in the city converted from a rectory to a vicarage and appropriated to the hospital. Under this arrangement the revenues of the rectory – sixteen marks a year – could be applied to the maintenance of a master in the faculty of grammar: "To keep a grammar school (*regere scolas gramaticales*) in the precinct of the hospital or some fit house close by, to teach, instruct, and inform gratis all boys and others whatsoever wishing to learn and become scholars (*scolatizare*)."[28]

To return to St Paul's: Leach found that he had his hands full trying to establish the necessary historical facts with reference to two central issues: the relationship of the grammar school at St Paul's to the school for the choristers and the circumstances surrounding the foundation of Dean Colet's school early in the sixteenth century.

Leach begins by pointing out that towards the end of the thirteenth century the choristers of St Paul's were boarded in the almonry, an institution that he is prepared to identify as essential to any early cathedral church. The almoner's register beginning around 1345 states that "if the Almoner does not keep a cleric to teach the choristers grammar, the schoolmaster of St. Paul's claims 5s. a year for teaching them, though he ought to demand nothing for them because he keeps the school for them, as the Treasurer of St. Paul's once alleged before the Dean and Chapter." Leach comments that the assertion that the grammar school was kept for the choristers is "historically untrue," though he admits that probably the choristers ought to have been admitted free to such a school.[29]

Referring to a similar case in Beverley in 1312 in which the succentor took issue with the grammar master for insisting on payment by any chorister seeking instruction in grammar after the quota for "free" students from the choir had been reached, Leach is anxious to show that "the Grammar School was not a choir school or a choirboys' school."[30] Similarly, there was, Leach contends, a grammar school maintained at St Paul's for the benefit of the choristers. This school was quite separate from the choir school in which they were taught singing. Both of these schools were distinct from the cathedral grammar school open to all boys. Leach's reasons for insisting on these distinctions at such length is owing, he explains, to the confusion created by "a certain Miss Hackett" whose interventions on behalf of the St Paul's choir boys in the early nineteenth century were reinforced by the documentary evidence she published in a pamphlet "misnamed" *Correspondence and Evidences respecting the Ancient Collegiate School attached to St. Paul's Cathedral*. Although Leach concedes that she successfully established in chancery the right of the choir boys to share in the revenues of the almonry, "her zeal outran her discretion," so that she mistakenly attributed every reference in the records to a school as invariably denoting a choir school. In this way, he claims, she caused much harm to the grammar schools by popularizing the notion that they were "mere choir-schools."[31]

On a separate but related topic, Leach's article on the history of St Paul's school in *The Journal of Education*, July 1909, considerably clarified the details regarding the dates and acts of the school's foundation. This article involved Leach in a dispute with A.S. Lupton, the son of the biographer of Colet, mainly on the ground of Leach's insistence on the continuity of Colet's foundation with that of the older St Paul's cathedral school. The dispute once again encouraged him to see his immediate task as one of clarification:

Clouds of confusion have gathered about Colet's work, thickened rather than dispelled by the latest writers on the subject. Knight's "Life of Colet," published in 1724, and Miss Hackett's works in 1827 and 1832, are primarily responsible for such statements as that Colet "commenced the work of educational reform in England by establishing a school in London which ... soon became known, probably from the situation of its buildings, as St. Paul's School" – definite statements which are demonstrably wrong. At the same time, so indefinite is the knowledge about it, that its beginning is variously attributed to 1508, 1509, and 1510; the middle year, in which no beginning took place, having been by an evil fate selected as the year to commemorate its beginning.[32]

As Leach then proceeds to show, it was on 10 June 1512 that the three trustees representing the mercers' company conveyed the old and the new schools to Colet and that his will, enrolled in the Hustings Court of the city, conveyed them to the company. One week later Colet exhibited to the Mercers his "Boke of Ordinances of the Scole of Poules." Together, these two facts satisfied Leach that Colet himself must have considered that only in this year, 1512, did he complete the foundation of his school.[33]

While on the subject of Colet's early sixteenth-century foundation at St Paul's, it may be useful to consider a less known foundation from the same period, that of Pocklington Grammar School in the East Riding of Yorkshire. This school, the subject of an extensive article by Leach in *The Transactions of the East Riding Antiquarian Society*, illustrates the trend towards lay responsibility for educational development in the generation preceding the Reformation. Equally, the foundation provides an interesting example of the establishment of a guild for the sole purpose of maintaining the school. Leach's introduction is concerned initially with the documentary sources.

He mentions that Pocklington is one school that, though "having escaped" designation as one of Edward VI's foundations, rightfully belongs to that monarch, as it was re-founded in his reign by an act of Parliament in 1551. There is no extant copy of this act, Leach admits, either on the rolls of Parliament or on the statute rolls in chancery. There is only an exemplification or "office copy" under the great seal from 1552 found among the school records in the care of the governors. With this copy, however, are the original letters patent of Henry VIII from 1514 granting the founder a license to establish and endow a guild for the maintenance of the grammar school. There is also the same founder's deed of endowment of 1525, consisting of a grant of lands to St John's College, Cambridge, for the support of five scholars from the grammar school at that college.[34]

Leach has printed the three documents in full. But before attempting to answer why it was necessary to found a guild to maintain a school, Leach warns us concerning letters patent. Whereas such documents are often equated with foundation charters, they were so, Leach explains, only on the "very rare" occasion when the king himself was the founder. This was the case, for instance, with Eton, the colleges of Windsor and St Stephen's, and the Savoy hospital. These are the only examples Leach can cite between the Conquest and the Reformation. In almost every instance, he says, letters patent were addressed to individual persons, authorizing them to "found and endow" particular institutions. If not implemented, such letters patent became merely "dead" letters. One must not assume, therefore, that the date of letters patent is the date of an actual foundation (FRP 71–2).

While Leach does not pretend to any certain answer with respect to the foundation of the guild, he does think that the main reason for this particular procedure is that "no one hitherto had founded a School as an independent entity, or under a governing body existing *simpliciter ad hoc*" (FRP 67). The founder, John Dowman (or Dolman), was a doctor of laws from Cambridge and a canon of St Paul's, an ecclesiastical office that was merely one among many which he enjoyed as benefices in his capacity as an ecclesiastical lawyer (FRP 65). All that we know is that he founded the guild, presumably because it provided a convenient governing body for his school. Leach leaves it an open question as to whether Dowman was also seeking a lay character for his governing body. The main point that Leach wishes to make is that the movement in which Dowman shared was one not merely to found grammar schools, "but to found Free Grammar Schools; schools, that is, in which all who came, or some favoured class, parishioners, or next of kin, or a limited number, were admitted free, *i.e.*, without payment of tuition fees" (FRP 70).

As would be expected, the Chantries Act of Edward VI, 1548, abolished Dowman's guild and placed the school endowment at the disposition of the Crown. Leach, however, is able to show that owing to the failure to complete all the arrangements, Pocklington School managed to avoid this fate. For one thing, since the property representing the endowment had never been legally conveyed to the guild, the property had not been assumed by the Crown under this Chantries Act but had remained "in the legal seizin of the heir." For another, the estates included in the deed of 1525 that constituted the exhibition endowment, being in the legal possession of St John's college, also survived intact since the university colleges were among those institutions affected by the Chantries Act of Henry VIII but exempted from the similar legislation of Edward VI. It was fortunate, therefore, Leach says, that Thomas Dowman, the founder's heir, was a man "of honour" and a lawyer as well, for he was able to arrange for a private act of Parliament to confirm, not only the school's existence along with its possessions but also the intent of the deed from 1525 with such variations, Leach adds, "as the altered circumstances required" (FRP 81–2).

Among the provisions of this act is that for an usher or second master, whether or not such had been provided for in the original statutes of John Dowman, and procedures to incorporate the schoolmaster and usher, in place of the extinct guild, under the name of "Master and Usher of the Free Grammar School of Pocklington." Another provision requires that the election of scholars from the school be given to "the master, together with the vicar, or curate, and churchwardens of the parish church." Finally, a new provision granting the archbishop of York the right to appoint a master or usher, in default of a proper body, gives to the archbishop of York and the master of St John's the power to make statutes for the governance of the master and usher. The only thing that remained to make the confirmation of the school complete was Thomas Dowman's conveyance of the lands originally intended to be given by the founder. A letter of 12 November 1599 from Robert Dolman, complaining about the state of the school and making the recommendation that a change be made in the condition of the masters' tenure, suggests that the lands had been conveyed (FRP 84–6).

Leach then proceeds to show that the fortunes of Pocklington Grammar School continued to decline, reaching a low point in 1612 when only two children attended the school. There appears to have been no improvement until the period of the Commonwealth when within a single year, 23 September 1650 to 23 September 1651, no fewer than 76 boys were admitted, with another 42 arriving during the ensuing twelve months, making 118 in all, mostly boarders. These figures are vouched for by the register of the school that was started at that time. Leach has no difficulty in ascribing the main cause of the earlier decline to the arrangement under which the master and usher – "the principal persons to be governed" – were made the chief governing body in control of the property (FRP 88–91).

This relatively happy state of affairs did not last long, for with the Restoration – in Leach's opinion, "that period of decay and retrogression" (FRP 63) – the school once again went into decline. With particular reference to its history from 1754 on, and provided with the reports of the commissioners of inquiry concerning charities (commonly referred to as Lord Brougham's Commission), Leach draws a close connection between the evil consequences of Edward's Chantries Act and developments in the early nineteenth century. He refers especially to the fact that the headmaster had to spend much of his time in law suits trying to undo the arrangements of former masters involving "improvident leases for long terms." The relative neglect of the school, therefore, was reflected in sparse attendance, varying from six to thirty pupils between 1817 and 1825 and reaching only forty-four at the time of the visit by the Schools Inquiry Commission in 1865–66 (FRP 94).

In conclusion, Leach is quite satisfied to record that the present flourishing condition of Pocklington Grammar School can be directly attributed to the change in the government of the school made on 13 May 1875 by the Endowed Schools Commissioners, their scheme receiving the approval of the Queen in council. Under this new arrangement the Edwardian corporation of master and usher was abolished. All the powers of management, including the appointment of a headmaster, now reposed in a governing body constituted ad hoc, representing the East Riding, the diocese of York, and the town of Pocklington. The connection with St John's College, which Leach considered on the whole to have been beneficial to the school, was maintained not only by an improved system of university scholarships, but by the fact that the college was granted two representatives on the governing body. The school's present healthy condition, Leach states, "amply vindicates the operation of the Endowed Schools Acts" (FRP 94–5).

Leach published his *History of Winchester College* in 1899. This study, though extensive, was only one of several that he fondly contributed to his Alma Mater and favourite school. For example, in 1893, the year that was taken to be the quincentenary of the foundation of the college, Leach contributed an essay to a compilation of works by old Wykehamists entitled *Winchester College 1393–1893*, and in the *Contemporary Review* for that year published an article under the title "Winchester College, 1393 and 1893." Ten years later his informative and well written contribution with respect to the schools of Winchester appeared in the second *Victoria History of the Counties of England (VCH)* volume on Hampshire. It may be said in general that throughout most of this writing on Winchester, Leach is primarily concerned to show that Wykeham's foundation of Winchester College was not a monastic foundation but a secular one and that it was not a lay institution, but a designedly ecclesiastical one. Before discussing the details of the college itself, however, Leach examines the educational services provided by the city of Winchester to enable his readers to see the college in better perspective.

First, Leach is able to show from documentary evidence that the public grammar school of Winchester apparently had a continuous existence throughout the later Middle Ages. This school, referred to in the late fourteenth century as the high grammar school of the city of Winchester, was located at the junction of the west side of the present Symond's Street and the north side of Little Minster Lane. We also learn that thirteen poor scholars from the school were among the hundred poor people provided with their daily dinner at St Cross Hospital.[35]

The chapter at Winchester being monastic, there is the question of two other schools connected with it – the novices' school and the almonry school. As far as St Swithun's priory is concerned, Leach notes that the greatest number of monks at any time was apparently sixty-five. In 1353, shortly after the Black Death, there were only twenty, while there were forty-four in 1533 on the eve of the dissolution. These figures provide some perspective on the number of younger members being trained for this kind of life. Leach notes in this connection that the high point apparently was in 1459–60, when there is record of nine novices receiving instruction; in 1485 and 1516, for instance, there were none. As to the almonry school, Leach states that we are here talking about two groups: the choristers, who sang in the Lady Chapel, and the charity boys, who provided the menial services and, in a general way, waited on the monks. He notes that in 1402 four choristers are listed and that in 1482 this number has been doubled to eight. His main point, as to be expected, is that "neither the grammar school for the young monks, nor the almonry song school for the choristers, can be regarded as in any real sense constituting a school ... The City Grammar School was the only real school."[36]

William Wykeham became bishop of Winchester in 1366. Shortly afterwards, certainly by 1 September 1373, he was supporting grammar scholars in Winchester.[37] The college itself was founded on 20 October 1382.[38] It is worth noting that throughout the first century and a half of the college's existence the public grammar school of the city continued to function. The school came to an end only around 1529–30, as had been revealed in a recently discovered Obedientiary Roll by the cathedral librarian shortly before Leach contributed his article to the *VCH*.[39]

As to the origin of the college, Leach acknowledges that the two most commonly received opinions ascribe it either to Wykeham's enlargement of the existing cathedral and monastic school or to the bishop's creation.[40] Rejecting both these views, Leach emphasizes that Wykeham's career as a secular cleric is the probable key. Wykeman enjoyed canonries, for instance, at Beverley, Southwell, Salisbury, York, and St Paul's in London; he also held the offices of archdeacon of Lincoln, provost of Wells, and dean of St Martin's-le-Grand. Wykeham, Leach claims, would have found "flourishing schools" connected with all these churches. The specific model, however, was, in Leach's view, the house of the scholars of Merton, founded in 1264, where thirteen boys from among the founder's kin were instructed in grammar.[41]

Leach's reasons for selecting Merton are closely related to the parties involved in the various transactions associated with the foundation. He is impressed, among other things, with the fact that when Wykeham first began to look into the foundation of his new college at Oxford, the people he employed to buy his land were two fellows of Merton, John of Buckingham, canon of York, and John of Campden, canon of Southwell. The same two Merton fellows later witnessed Wykeham's agreement in 1373 with the master of his Winchester school. The fellows also, with the warden of Merton, John of Bloxham, archdeacon of Winchester, witnessed the foundation charter of Winchester College itself in 1382 (in which, incidentally, another fellow of Merton, Thomas of Cranley, was named the first warden). Leach argues that this is "evidence enough" that Merton was Wykeham's model, even if more is not forthcoming in the statutes: there is the name of "warden," the provision for founder's kin, the preference for Winchester diocese and other dioceses in which the college lands were situated, the encouragement given to civil and canon law, and the entire internal economy.[42]

It now remains for Leach to inquire into the origin of Merton College itself. He states quite categorically that this origin is not to be sought, as is commonly supposed, in the monasteries, but in the collegiate churches like Beverley and Howden in Yorkshire and St Martin's-le-Grand in London, among many others.[43] Leach enlarges upon this theme by observing that Merton was "a collegiate church" in Oxford with St John's parish church appropriated to it, in the same way that the church in Howden was made collegiate two years later, with a grammar school attached to it as required "by canon law." The difference, Leach claims, between Merton and the normal collegiate church was that, whereas in the latter, the scholars were an adjunct of the chaplains, at Merton "the chaplains were an adjunct of the scholars."[44]

Leach's history of Winchester College was the first attempt, he tells us, at providing the entire history of the school from its origins to the present day within the compass of a single book. The work was aimed at one question in particular: the place of Winchester in "the great system of Public School education," since, as he remarks, Winchester was commonly regarded as the progenitor of that great system. He did his best, he says, to find first class authorities for his book, "in spite of considerable obstruction in some quarters where it was least expected."[45] Leach acknowledges' his indebtedness to a number of people who have helped him in the preparation of his work. Included among these are the dean of Winchester and the cathedral librarian, as well as the late mayor of Winchester and members of the town council, not omitting the two wardens of New College and Winchester, and the headmaster of the college, Dr Fearon (*HWC* v-vii).

In acknowledging his written sources, Leach singles out *William of Wykeham and His Colleges*, by the late Canon Mackenzie E.C. Walcott, published in 1852. Leach credits Walcott with being the first to use the original documentary sources for the college's history; but since the book took in such a wide scope, including the life of the founder and a history of New College as well as of Winchester, the final result was but a sketch of each of these (*HWC* viii). Leach shows particular indebtedness to the person he regards as the "paramount" authority, the Bursar of Winchester, T.F. Kirby, who in 1888 published *Scholars* and in 1892 *Annals of Winchester College*. Leach adds a note to the effect that in some points his own research has led him to form conclusions at variance with those of Kirby. Finally, Leach praises the 1878 work of the Reverend H.C. Adams, *Wykehamica*, "the most readable of School books" (*HWC* viii-ix).

Leach states that the foundation deed of Winchester College was executed by Wykeham on 20 October 1382 at Southwark, the location in those days of the town house of the see of Winchester.

Wykeham mentions in the deed his recent foundation at New College, Oxford, remarking that "as experience, the mistress of life, already teaches, grammar is the foundation, gate, and source of all other liberal arts, without which they cannot be known, nor can any one arrive at their pursuit" (*HWC* 65). Leach says that the founder then established "a college of poor scholars, clerks, near the City of Winchester," directing that the college was to consist of "seventy poor and needy scholars, clerks, living college-wise in the same, studying and become proficient in grammaticals, or the art and science of grammar" (*HWC* 66).

Leach states that the founder put the finishing touch to his statutes on 11 September 1400. These same statutes, subscribed to by all members of the college above fifteen years of age, were the binding rules of the school until a number of them were repealed by the Oxford University commissioners in 1857 (*HWC* 68). The statutes, Leach notes, provide for a body of 105 people, including the warden, headmaster, ten fellows, three chaplains, an usher, seventy scholars, as well as three chapel clerks and sixteen choristers; not to mention a large staff of servants, not defined, who include a porter-barber, a baker, a brewer, cook, steward, laundress, a warden's clerk, a valet, and boy (*HWC* 68).

As far as understanding the founder's objective in the establishment of New College and Winchester College is concerned, Leach experiences no difficulty. He says that it is best to look at the statutes of the two colleges. Together they reveal that Wykeham is primarily concerned to make up the losses in the clerical order suffered in the Black Death of the mid-fourteenth century and the second pestilence, as it was called, of 1361 (*HWC* 69–71). Leach enlarges upon this interpretation as follows:

The ultimate cause was the wish to have a learned clergy. The whole cast of the statutes is that of a collegiate church. Of forty-six chapters, or rubrics, as they are called, only six deal in any way with scholars and learning. The other forty might belong to any collegiate church. It is significant that the Warden was to be a priest ... All scholars were to have the first tonsure within a year of admission, if not before, except Founder's kin, who might put it off till the age of fifteen. None were to be admitted who had any bodily defect which "would render them unfit to take holy orders." (*HWC* 72–3)

After disposing of many of the claims advanced in favor of the unique position of Winchester College in the later Middle Ages, Leach proceeds to make an analysis of where there was, if any, a new departure. First, the scale of the foundations themselves exceeded anything preceding them, the seventy scholars of New College, for example, being almost equal to the entire number of the scholars in all the other colleges put together. The actual size of the foundation does not in itself, however, impress Leach as much as one might have expected, partly because he sees this as part of a more general trend toward the spending of money on colleges and educational institutions instead of on the monasteries as in earlier days. In this vein he thinks that if Wolsey's foundations had been permitted to continue, they would have exceeded both in size and wealth anything that Wykeham had established (*HWC* 88). He does, however, think that it was an innovation for Wykeham to have restricted his college at Oxford to those who came from his grammar school at Winchester. It is not so much a question of determining whether in the long run this was the best thing for either the college or the school, but it was, as far as Leach is concerned, a good thing for both of them at that particular time in history (*HWC* 89).

What Leach views as the really important new departure was Wykeham's making his school a separate and distinct foundation, independent of New College. This was in sharp contrast to all previous educational establishments. Although the grammar schools kept by "the old Collegiate Churches" had flourished, they were nevertheless accidents, even though "inseparable" accidents. Similarly, the "new Collegiate Churches" at the university, called "colleges," had substituted adult students for priests and study in place of services, but the schoolboys, Leach maintains, remained an accident and a rather unimportant one at that. In Winchester, however, the reverse was true. Within the framework of the collegiate church structure, the fellows replaced the canons, but instead of the boys being subordinate to them, "the Canons were subsidiary to the boys." Winchester College, was, Leach insists, the first school founded as "a sovereign and independent corporation existing by and for itself" (*HWC* 89–90).

Winchester's independence as a separate corporation had to be reconciled with its close ties to New College, one expression of which was the annual "scrutiny." This was conducted by the warden and two fellows of New College along with a "Master Teacher in grammar" of Winchester; they were to elect not only the scholars graduating from Winchester to New College, but also those entering Winchester itself. Leach notes that this election was by examination and was competitive among both present and past scholars of Winchester. With the exception of the founder's kin, who had an absolute right to admission at any age from seven to twenty-five, those selected were to be "poor and needy scholars, of good character and well conditioned, of gentlemanly habits, able for school ... completely learned in reading, plain song and old Donatus." The candidates were to be between eight and twelve years of age, but might be admitted up to sixteen years of age should they be sufficiently advanced in their studies in order to master Latin grammar by eighteen. Preference was to be given, first, to inhabitants of the places where the estates of the two colleges were situated; next, to those born in the diocese of Winchester and then, in the order named, to the inhabitants of the counties of Oxford, Berkshire, Wiltshire, Sommerset, Essex, Middlesex, Dorset, Kent, Sussex, and Cambridge; and, finally, to the inhabitants of the entire realm. All were to have the first tonsure or be tonsured within a year of their admission, except of course the founder's kin, who could put off their tonsure till fifteen. College choristers were also to be eligible for election and to be examined along with the other candidates (*HWC* 90–1).

It has already been noted that, as in the case at Lincoln and other places, Leach was anxious to draw a sharp distinction between the grammar school scholars and the choristers, wherever these happened to appear on the same scene. In the case of Winchester, Leach is concerned to make the same distinction, though in this case it is not on the usual educational ground, as in most of the other instances, but on the level of economic means. He says, in part, that "it is possible that the poor boys of Queen's were really intended to be paupers, as they were of the almonry type, and were to act as choristers; but the scholars of Winchester were certainly not intended to be of that type, a clear distinction being drawn between them and the choristers." He then remarks that the Winchester choristers, sixteen altogether, were to be admitted "by way of charity," and were to wait on the fellows both in their rooms and in hall, eating what was left over from the meals of both the fellows and the scholars. Leach admits, nevertheless, that these same choristers were eligible for scholarships, but whether any of them were ever elected "is another matter" (*HWC* 95).

It is evident, then, that Leach entertains little doubt that by "poor and needy" the founder of Winchester College really meant only the poor of the middle classes, that stratum of society that, in Leach's view, both in the Middle Ages and in his own day, provided the members for the learned professions. What has to be borne in mind is that in medieval England the clerical profession embraced them all (*HWC* 102–3). He concludes by observing that there was nothing novel about Winchester's being a foundation for secular clerks as opposed to monks, nor in its having a grammar school attached to it or serving as a preparatory school for the college of a university. Not even in the numbers it was to provide for, nor in the admission of commoners along with members of the upper classes, did any novelty attach to this particular foundation. What made Winchester a new departure, Leach maintains, was the combination of all the above features on a larger scale than had previously been the case, making this institution "the first of Public Schools, as that term is now understood" (*HWC* 103).

It remains to note some of Leach's observations with respect to the effects of the Reformation on Winchester College. He remarks that Winchester was, like other "spiritual" foundations, included in the *Valor Ecclesiasticus* of 1535. On this score he takes issue, not for the first time, with Kirby, who stated that "the College was not, legally speaking, an ecclesiastical corporation." On the contrary, Leach insists, the frequent visitations by the bishops of Winchester as ordinaries, recorded in the *Annals*, testify to the ecclesiastical basis of the college. He reiterates the point that "all schools and colleges" were ecclesiastical institutions and under ecclesiastical jurisdiction (*HWC* 237–8). He observes in passing that the value of Winchester College, as it appears in the *Valor*, exceeds that of any other ecclesiastical foundation in the county, with the two exceptions of the cathedral monastery itself and Hyde Abbey (*HWC* 241).

As for Edward VI's Chantries Act, since one of the expressed objectives was the erection of grammar schools and the further increase of the universities, it was only to be expected that exemption would be provided for the colleges, hostels, and halls of the universities and chantries at those institutions, including that of St Mary's College of Winchester (*HWC* 258–9). Leach believed that both Winchester and Eton were saved not so much on their own merits, but because they were perceived to be part of the universities. He notes, for instance, that along with the university colleges both institutions were exempted from subsidies in 1496 "when nearly all other ecclesiastical foundations were made subject to them." Likewise, he observes that they had already been exempted from tenths and first fruits along with the university colleges in 1536. In his view, the clearest statement that they were regarded as an essential element of the universities is contained in a letter from the privy council to the commissioners for church goods for Hampshire in 1553. In the letter it is stated that the college at Winchester, as a member of Oxford university, should enjoy the same liberties as the university itself, including the plate and other goods of the college church, provided that the college convert the same from "monuments of superstition" to the "necessary and godly uses" for its own maintenance (*HWC* 260). So, too, in examples drawn from Queen Elizabeth's reign until his own day, Leach concludes that it was not partiality but "precedent" that saved Winchester and Eton from Edward VI, "Spoiler of Schools" (*HWC* 261–2).

The schools selected for consideration in this chapter are broadly representative of the entire network of grammar schools in pre-Reformation England. They all share in the secular as opposed to the monastic tradition. The cathedrals of York, Lincoln, and St Paul's in London, together with the collegiate churches of Southwell and Beverley, are the seminal institutions, designed *ad orandum et studendum*. The last considered – Winchester College – brings us full circle in this development since it is *ad studendum et orandum*. In between are the schools connected with St Anthony's Hospital in London, the Burghershe chantry at Lincoln, and the newly formed guild in Pocklington – a variety of institutional developments associated with the later Middle Ages. Whatever the differences among them, and whether predominantly clerical or lay in their particular foundation, they derive their ultimate inspiration, if not their structure, from an institution already well established in Anglo-Saxon times – a college of secular clerks.

PART TWO

The Strengths and Weaknesses of Leach's Research

CHAPTER SIX

The Grammar Program: The Teaching of Latin

As the previous discussion has made evident, Leach's contributions to the documentary study of England's medieval grammar schools were of a decidedly institutional kind. He did not have the time or the opportunity to investigate what he evidently considered fascinating – the details of the daily curriculum for which the institutions were intended. Under the circumstances, therefore, it is not surprising that he should have assumed, whenever he alluded to the Latin program of the grammar school, that the program was primarily classical, at least to the extent that a few ancient authors, both pagan and Christian, constituted the basis of study. Leach was driven to emphasize this classical background of the medieval schools, if for no other reason than that he wished to counteract the prevailing view of medieval Latin as decadent and possessing little or no cultural value.

Leach was, nevertheless, always on the alert to note specific references to the medieval curriculum. One of the places that served him best in this regard was Warwick. His *History of Warwick School*, published in 1906, confirmed what he had already indicated in his *English Schools at the Reformation*, that the school in that city originated in the union, early in the twelfth century, of Warwick's two main churches – the collegiate church of St Mary of Warwick and the church of All Saints, a college of canons in the castle.[1] Although he was forced to conclude that the documentary sources provided little information on the constitution of the first-named church, it was quite otherwise with the program of the attached grammar school. As elsewhere in the thirteenth century, Warwick was the scene of a dispute arising from the need to distinguish between the secondary and the elementary schools, that is, between the grammar and the song, or reading, schools respectively.

Leach contends at the outset that at Warwick, "as at all collegiate churches," there were two schools: a grammar school under the schoolmaster and a song school under the music or song-schoolmaster. He states that it was the prerogative of the grammar school to provide instruction in grammar, which he defines as "literature, classical literature, dialectic or the art of argument, the beginnings of philosophy, and rhetoric or the art of persuasion, including composition." The song school, on the other hand, besides singing, taught "reading, and, we may suppose, writing."[2]

The source of the dispute was whether the grammar school or the song school should admit the Donatists, that is, those whose learning in grammar was confined to the "accidence" or parts of speech. Leach states that the question as to whether boys learning their Donat were to be considered elementary or secondary pupils was a "vexed" one in many places and admitted of no uniform solution. He cites a similar case from Breslau in 1267, in which the dispute appears to have originated in circumstances not unlike those at Warwick. The decision of the papal legate in the settlement of the respective claims of town and castle was that the younger boys could attend class in the town church of St Mary Magdalen for the purpose of learning their alphabet; the Lord's prayer and the salutation of the Virgin; and the creed, psalter, and the seven psalms as well as singing, "so as to be able to read and sing in the churches to the honour of God." They would also be permitted to learn Donatus, Cato, Theodulus, and the "Boys' Rules," which, as Leach explains, were "versified books of manners." If, however, the boys wished to proceed to more advanced work, they would have to attend the castle school of St John or some other school of their choice.[3] While Leach, in an appended footnote, acknowledges his indebtedness in this respect to Rashdall's *Universities of Europe in the Middle Ages*, he makes the point that here as in other places, Rashdall himself "has not appreciated the distinction between the song, or elementary, and the grammar schools."[4]

Leach further considers that Warwick School is deserving of praise because its grammar and song schools were distinct, and the dean and chapter recognized and enforced this distinction. Moreover, the grammar schoolmaster was entitled to teach dialectic as well as grammar. In this connection Leach explains that the seven sciences of the Middle Ages, derived from the *De artibus ac disciplinis liberalium artium* of Cassiodorus, were divided into the familiar *trivium* and *quadrivium*, the former consisting of grammar, dialectic, and rhetoric, the latter of arithmetic, geometry, music, and astronomy. He says that the *trivium* became the province of the grammar school after separation was effected between grammar school and university. Noting that dialectic meant what his own generation referred to as logic, Leach mentions that the *Etymologies* of Isidore of Seville, "based chiefly on Cassiodorus" and containing material on dialectic and rhetoric, was presented by William of Wykeham to his college at Winchester, "apparently as the text-book for use in the school." It is this book, Leach thinks, that was also in use at Warwick at the time of the dispute cited above. Dialectic, in particular, has for Leach a positive educational value: "The study of dialectic must have been a great relief from eternal gerund-grinding, and the perpetual pious platitudes of the 'Christian poets,' Sedulius, Juvencus, Arator, Prudentius, which had for the most part superseded the classical authors in school curricula. Not, indeed, that even in dialectic you got very far away from pious platitudes. Alcuin's example of a syllogism is 'All virtue is useful, chastity is a virtue, therefore chastity is useful.'"[5]

Leach is disposed to maintain, nevertheless, that with all its shortcomings, particularly those of the text-books, "dialectic was an excellent training for the mind, more especially as it was accompanied by practical work in argument: the boys being set to 'pose' and answer each other, the master 'determining.'"[6] His general assessment, stemming from this predisposition towards the art of logic, is: "No doubt, as in all things medieval, there was a great deal too much formalism, a superabundance of definition and classification, and the letter was apt to kill the spirit. But still the mere introduction to predicables and syllogisms, and learning to detect and name fallacies in argument, was itself a life-giving exercise. It was certainly appreciated by the youth of the day."[7]

Leach's study of Warwick provided him with one of the clearest illustrations of the difference between the elementary and the more advanced study of Latin. That it did not do more than this is attributable to his unwavering belief that the curriculum of the medieval grammar school was in a direct line of descent from the wedding of the Roman and early Christian authors. Although constantly on the lookout for developments within the institutional framework of the same medieval schools, Leach did not allow for any parallel changes in the curriculum itself. The use at Warwick of the ninth-century Theodulus text, for example, might have suggested to Leach the possibility of something different, but his curiosity simply did not extend in that direction. There is, therefore, a dichotomy in Leach's treatment of the medieval grammar schools, a dichotomy between his appreciation of the response of the institutions themselves to social and religious change on the one hand and his presentation of the school curriculum as relatively static on the other.

Several years ago, the late Richard Hunt drew my attention to a number of grammatical manuscripts relevant to the curriculum of the grammar schools. In an attempt to gather more detailed information about the medieval school curriculum, some two dozen manuscripts were selected for examination. They were divided almost equally between two groups, the first containing some manuscripts which had not been properly catalogued, and the second comprising manuscripts whose contents had been adequately described in their respective catalogues for the purpose at hand. The manuscripts of the first group were examined in detail with a view to determining the principal features of the curriculum as well as obtaining some insight into the prevalent methods of teaching. The second group of manuscripts was used mainly as a corrective to determine whether the frequency of particular literary texts already identified among their contents supported the use of the term "readers" for a number of selections found in the first group, which, from their distribution, seemed to warrant this classification.

The first manuscripts, drawn mainly from the British Library in London and the libraries of Oxford and Cambridge, all appear to have been in use in England during the fourteenth and fifteenth centuries and are concerned, in one way or another, with formal instruction in Latin.[8] While an attempt will be made to furnish a general view of the contents of these manuscripts, the basis of the present inquiry, an exception will be made in the case of the Latin readers. Since the latter constitute the basic literary sources of the grammar school curriculum, the import of their distribution may, with some advantage, be left to the end.

MS Trinity o.5.4., in the possession of Trinity College, Cambridge, is a beautiful early fifteenth-century composition ascribed to Battlefield College, a small college founded by Henry IV in 1409 near Shrewsbury in thanksgiving for his victory there, providing for a master and five chaplains, with an almshouse attached. This manuscript is the most comprehensive, containing examples of virtually every aspect of Latin grammar as well as material on arithmetic and solid geometry. Two items are of special interest: the complete text, minus the introduction, of the ubiquitous grammar text in verse, the *Doctrinale*, written around the end of the twelfth century by Alexander Villa Dei of Normandy, and a collection of some forty-six model letters inspired by a severely condensed form of the *Practica Dictaminis* of Lawrence of Aquileia, who is thought to have been teaching at Paris around 1300.[9]

MS Add. 37,075, in the British Library, is a heterogeneous collection of both Latin and English grammatical material from the late fifteenth century, in various hands, but probably the possession of a John Claveryng, whose name appears in three places and who apparently wrote two of the selections of Latin exercises himself. Most of the numerous local references are to life in London, and from a reference to the celebration of the feast of St Anthony the manuscript has been ascribed to the grammar school attached to St Anthony's Hospital in Threadneedle Street. Included are an extensive *nominale* (list of nouns) in Latin and English, including some towns and counties of England and other European countries; exercises in syntax to provide alternate ways of expressing oneself in colloquial Latin, with many allusions to London; and at the end some 180 hymns and 130 prose sequences for both the proper of the season and saints' feast days.[10]

MS Harl. 1002, in the British Library, a collection of several distinct grammatical treatises sewn together at the same time, is quite certainly a teacher's lesson plan from the late fourteenth or early fifteenth century. The collection contains a commentary on the gender of nouns as presented in Alexander's *Doctrinale* and on monosyllabic nouns from the sixth chapter of the other popular grammatical text in verse, the *Grecismus* of Evrard of Béthune, thought to be a Flemish grammarian from around 1200.[11] The collection also includes both a *nominale* and a similar listing of verbs for all four Latin conjugations, called a *verbale*. The material ranges from an extensive tract on orthography through synonyms and accents to figures of speech. In what appear to be exercises for writing practice near the end of the manuscript, there are prayers to Saint Sebastian to ward off the plague, which could refer to any one of several visitations between 1348 and 1400.

MS Harl. 1587, in the possession of the British Library, also contains separate grammatical treatises sewn together at the same time. Although written probably by as many as four different hands between 1483 and 1504, with earlier dates, such as 1396 and 1469, attached to specific treatises, the entire collection belonged to Dom William Ingram, a monk of Christ Church, Canterbury, who was responsible for the education of the boys in the almonry. A close inspection of the handwriting suggests that the first part – some fourteen folios – was his as a student, and that he subsequently added to it and collected other treatises of various dates and sources, arranging everything for his own use some time after 1483, very likely for the instruction of the almonry boys.[12]

In addition to a lengthy tract on Latin cases, with sentences translated from English into Latin, there are *questiones* on predominantly biblical terms and usages, together with proverbs in Latin and English, and the complete text of the second part of the *Grecismus*, chapters nine to twenty-seven, concerning mainly nouns, conjugations and parts of speech, the whole interspersed with interlinear glosses. Finally, the writing exercises at the end contain verses arranged for the most part in four-line stanzas, a series of business letters, and several references to Edward IV of England (1461–83) and the date 1474. Included are letters from such prominent persons as John Carpenter, bishop of Worcester and an educational founder through the middle decades of the 1400s, and William – probably William Waynflete, the second provost of Eton and later bishop of Winchester.

MS Add. 17,724, also in the British Library, is a relatively brief manuscript with all one hundred and twelve folios the product of a single, legible hand, probably around 1400. Included are rules of grammar and versification, a treatise on accents, and a tract on orthography. There are two separate treatises on dictamen: one ascribed to John de Latere and referred to as the "Roman method"; the other identified simply as the "Cistercian method." The emphasis upon prosody and dictamen, together with a book of hymns of the Sarum Use accompanied by explanations of the themes, suggests a monastic origin, a supposition that receives a degree of support from the exclusive employment of Latin throughout the book.

MS Auct. F.3.9., in the possession of the Bodleian Library, is an extensive compilation from the first half of the fifteenth century in a single, legible hand. The compilation belonged to the Benedictine cathedral church of Coventry and was probably intended for the almonry school, not for the town grammar school. The manuscript is noteworthy for its inclusion of the *Speculum Gramaticale* of John of Cornwall, written in 1346, the earliest surviving grammatical treatise in which English was employed rather than French to help the student in the learning of Latin.[13] Of related interest is the extensive work by Thomas Hanney on the four parts of grammar, completed at Lewes in 1313 and entitled *Memoriale iuniorum*.[14] In addition to a treatise on dictamen according to the "Oxford use," a metrical tract on grammar, and a tract on the metre of hymns, there are two other items of note: an amplified version of the *Ars Minor* of Donatus, the Roman grammarian of the mid-fourth century, A.D.; and a classical *florilegia* put together by a Benedictine abbot in the form of nearly 300 extracts of a moral nature from classical Latin writers.

MS Caius 383, in the possession of Gonville and Caius College, Cambridge, is a comparatively short collection of material in Latin and French, very irregularly written in three different hands. Internal evidence points to a date a little before or after 1400 and almost certainly to Oxford as the place of composition. There is also little doubt that the book was intended for the use of clerks proceeding to orders since the scriptural and liturgical sources are very numerous. Two of the longer extracts deal with rules for Latin cases and figures of speech, most of the examples in the latter section being taken from sacred scripture. Of particular interest, however, is the inclusion of a number of model letters in French, especially charters and business letters according to the "modern use," these last containing several references to the abbot and monastery of Oseney on the outskirts of Oxford.[15]

MS Lincoln 88 belongs to the library of the dean and chapter at Lincoln. Although it is written in four different hands, a single hand is responsible for three-quarters of the material, probably from the early fifteenth century, though the hymnal included could be from as early as the thirteenth century. The margins of folios 2–118 are frequently crowded with grammatical notes that form at least two distinct but related tracts, written in 1414 at Oxford and based on the work of John Leland, a grammarian with a national reputation, who taught at Peckwater Inn (now part of Christ Church, Oxford) from at least the last decade of the fourteenth century. Some of the main features of this work include an extensive *medulla gramatice* – a vocabulary in alphabetical order – with both Latin and English used in the definitions. There is an advanced tract on the theory of grammar entitled *Donatus in magno*, and a treatise on accents, *Flores Accentus*, the composition of a Master John Chalurys, a resident of Bridport in Dorset, some time before 1414.[16]

MS Add. 32,425, in the British Library, is a relatively compact little book written in a single, legible script. Although replete with illustrative sentences in both Latin and English, the book affords little ground for a precise ascription other than a probable date of composition in the fifteenth century. The book is a straightforward discussion of the "properties" of the parts of speech, including nouns, verbs, adverbs, participles, conjunctions, even the "nature" of the interjection. Priscian, the grammarian who taught at Constantinople around A.D. 500 and whose text book was of a more advanced nature than that of Donatus, is one of the chief authorities invoked.[17] The general approach is quite philosophical, with the terms "substance" and "accident" employed to make the necessary distinctions in separating one part of speech from another.

MS Edinburgh 136, in the possession of the University of Edinburgh library, includes the compositions of John Seward, a teacher of the elementary program commonly referred to as *primitiva scientia*, at Cornhill, London. As might be expected, there is a heavy emphasis on prosody, with the most extensive tract on this subject, entitled

Metristencheridion, dedicated to the bishop of Norwich, Richard Courtenay. A good deal of the material is of an advanced nature, including
the author's commentary on grammar which is dedicated to Master
John Eyton, canon of the Augustinian monastery at Repton. Classical
material derived from the *Odes* of Horace appears in another tract
on prosody, this one dedicated to Simon Southerey, the prior of St
Albans, and in a moralization of Virgil's harpies, taken from the
third book of the *Aeneid*, and dedicated to Edward, duke of York,
who had been killed at Agincourt. One complete section in the last
quarter of the book is given over to a light-hearted description of
the literary disputes engaged in by Seward's circle in London.[18]

MS Harl. 5751, in the British Library, in an ill-formed, though
legible, hand from the fifteenth century, is the apparent compilation
of an unknown Rochus Sallay. The contents leave little doubt that
it was intended for the instruction of young clerks proceeding to
holy orders. While there are several grammatical notes and summaries among the items, particular interest attaches to an extensive
section on the "distinctions" of logic, a "table" of confession along
with definitions of the sacrament of penance from the early church
fathers, and, at the end, a summary of Catholic doctrine, including
rules for the faithful cleric and definitions of theological terms.
There are moral quotations from classical sources, such as Cato and
Seneca, and extracts from Aesop's *Fables*.

MS Peterhouse 83, in the college library of Peterhouse, Cambridge,
was the property of John Warkeworth, master of St Peter's college
from 1473 to 1500.[19] Entitled *Expositio Verborum Difficilium*, the entire
work is an explanation of difficult words employed in the daily liturgy, including their etymology and correct pronunciation. Everything is systematically arranged, first the hymns associated with the
different liturgical seasons, then both the ordinary and proper of
the Masses, the latter beginning with the first Sunday of Advent,
and, for the saints, with the feast of St Andrew on 30 November.
There is also explanation of difficult words found in the psalter and,
near the end, an index of the words previously explained.

MS Lambeth 78, in the library of Lambeth Palace, London, is entitled *Speculum Parvulorum*. It is a beautifully written work, arranged
in double columns and divided into five books with a preface and
table of contents. Written shortly before 1448, the book is the composition of Dom William Chartham of Christ Church, Canterbury,
who entered the community in 1403 and died in 1448. Book I consists of a catechism of the Mass, based on the teachings of Pope
Innocent III (1198–1216). Book II is a collection of moral tales, or
exempla, with explicit reference to topics such as sin and confession
and incidents in the life of the archbishop of Canterbury, St Edmund

Rich (c.1175–1240). There are additional *exempla* in the third book, largely drawn from the *Gesta Romanorum*, with the narrative often followed by a *reductio* or moral application. Book IV is similar to Book II. Book V, while similar to the fourth book, also contains descriptions of contemporary events at Canterbury.[20]

Chartham's work, while related to the educational program presently under consideration, will be best left for separate discussion. The twelve manuscripts in the second group – for the most part in the possession of the university and college libraries of Cambridge and Oxford and known to some extent from their catalogue descriptions – were, with only one or two possible exceptions, composed in the second half of the fifteenth century. Particular interest attaches to *MS Cambridge Add. 2830* since this book belonged to Master John Drury and was compiled by him around 1434 when he was teaching at the grammar school of Beccles in Suffolk.[21] Most of the material in these manuscripts, however, will be used to place the contents of the first group, described above, in a broader context. Re-arranging the main items according to subject matter and keeping as closely as possible to the medieval order, consideration will be given to the various parts of the grammar program under the following headings: orthography, prosody, the parts of speech, syntax, figures of speech, dictamen, vocabularies, theory of grammar, and, in a more extended fashion, the reading "texts."

Tracts on orthography are included in five of the manuscripts described above. No two of them, however, are similar, nor is any one of them to be found in the second group of manuscripts included for purposes of comparison. There is one tract on orthography, nevertheless, that is common to four manuscripts of this second group. It begins with the words *Apud Latinos viginti sunt litere* and appears to be the closest we have to a text.[22]

Prosody in some form appears in two-thirds of the manuscripts and accounts for some twenty items, exclusive of the hymnals. *MS Trin. o.5.4.* contains no fewer than six separate tracts on prosody, including lines 1550–2360 of the *Doctrinale* treating of metre and accent. Mention has already been made of the contributions of John Seward and John Chalurys in this regard. To this we can add the tract on prosody that Thomas Hanney includes in his *Memoriale iuniorum*.[23] The most striking feature of the above material on prosody is that none of the tracts makes any use of English. Moreover, with one partial exception, no single tract appears to have enjoyed a wide distribution: the exception, entitled *Que non ponuntur hic omnia corripiuntur*, treating of quantities, in addition to being included in *Trin. o.5.4.*, is also found in three manuscripts of the second group.[24]

Three of the manuscripts containing tracts on prosody also include

Latin hymnals, but the extent to which these hymnals figured in the Latin program is hard to determine.[25] It may be observed, for instance, that whereas the psalms and other biblical sources are used frequently to illustrate various aspects of Latin grammar, no use at all is made of the hymns for such a purpose. The evidence suggests that these Latin hymns, at least by the fifteenth century, were intended for young clerks and religious in different stages of formation on the way to the priesthood and not for the school population as a whole.

With respect to the parts of speech, five manuscripts of the first group contain complete tracts on the subject, as do three manuscripts from the second group; the basic source of all of these is the *Ars minor* of Donatus.[26] They vary quite considerably in treatment, from an elementary tract in English to an advanced treatise entirely in Latin. *MS Add. 32,425*, described above, may be considered as a "Donat" throughout, with the definitions of the parts of speech by Donatus compared with those put forward by Priscian.

As the descriptions of the manuscripts indicate, there is an abundance of material relating to syntax, or the construction of Latin sentences. In addition to the *Doctrinale* and tracts containing rules for construction, there are several exercises in the composition of Latin sentences.[27] In general, the illustrative sentences are either moral exhortations, quotations from the Bible, or references to contemporary events. Although no two sets of sentences are completely identical, three tracts used for teaching purposes extended beyond strictly local usage. One of these, mainly, though not entirely, in English, begins with the question, "In how many maners schalt thou begynne to make Latyn?" and constitutes the third item in *Trin. o.5.4.* and the opening tract in *Peniarth 356*. The untitled second tract, with the opening sentence *Ego sum creatura Dei*, is included in three manuscripts – *Add. 37,075*, *Harl. 1002* and *Corpus Christi 233*. English is employed in the discussion of the Latin sentences.

The third tract, the most advanced of the three, is entirely in Latin. Although no title is given, it is referred to as *tractatus de partibus octo probatus*. It is identified by its opening sentence *Iesus Christus, filius beate Marie, iuvet et expediat Laurencium de Londoniis* and is found in *Harl. 1002* and *Peniarth 356*. Mention should also be made of a fourth tract that is as much an exercise in elementary disputation as it is in written Latin. This consists of a *questio* beginning with the question *Es tu clericus?* or *Domine, estis vos clericus?* and the reply *Non sum clericus sed sum aliqualiter litteratus*. Found in two of the manuscripts, *Harl. 1587* and *Peniarth 356*, the *questio* then continues to develop the definition of *clericus* through a series of "distinctions."

Figures of speech, evidently considered an integral part of the course in Latin grammar, are treated in five of the manuscripts. In a tract on the "colours of rhetoric" in *Trin. o.5.4.* the writer states that these particular figures were not considered by Donatus or Priscian but are employed in theology. Although the writer does not say so, this section is an abridgement of the *Catholicon*, the combined grammar and dictionary of a Dominican friar, John Balbus of Genoa, of the late thirteenth century.[28] In *Add. 37,075* the treatment of figures of speech is based on the twelfth chapter of Alexander's *Doctrinale*, while in *Harl. 1002*, although Evrard's *Grecismus* is cited as the source, there is little or no resemblance between the author's treatment of the subject and that found in the *Grecismus*. In both *Harl. 5751* and *Caius 383* the figures of speech derive mainly from the literature of sacred scripture.

While no one tract on the figures of speech is repeated elsewhere, two standard works, the *Catholicon* and the *Doctrinale*, provide some of this material directly, suggesting a more extensive use of these sources for the subject than strictly vouched for by the manuscript evidence.[29] Moreover, the tracts in question derive largely, though not entirely, from biblical literature, giving this section on figures of speech a unity of purpose and method that at first sight it might not seem to possess.

Treatises on dictamen, which in this context refers to the composition of Latin letters according to standard forms, are included in one third of the manuscripts considered in detail. No single treatise predominates as a standard text. The contents of other manuscripts only confirm this note of diversity: *Peniarth 356, Rawl. G.60*, and *Shrewsbury School IV*, from the second group, each contains a different treatise on the same subject. Nevertheless, it would be misleading to infer from this evidence that teachers of the subject were left to their own devices since, as we have seen above, no fewer than three of the treatises are based on the "use" of the Roman curia, the Cistercian order, and the University of Oxford respectively. The treatise based on the Oxford "use" in the Bodleian manuscript associated with John of Cornwall and Thomas Hanney (*Auct. F.3.9.*), although like the others written throughout in Latin and implying a relatively advanced stage of instruction, is, nonetheless, expressly stated to be for "the benefit of young people."[30]

The vocabularies constitute one of the most common features of the grammatical manuscripts. Reference has already been made to those designated as *nominale* or *verbale*. Most of the *nominale* begin with terms relating to God and divine things, but no two of them are identical. The *verbale* generally are arranged in the order in which the conjugations are learned, but even these have several minor differences among them and no single *verbale* appears to be the source for any others. Nor is there much in common between two examples of quite extensive alphabetical vocabularies. The same may be said for lists of synonyms that are sometimes made to serve in lieu of vocabularies.

It is quite otherwise, however, with vocabularies in verse. One of these, beginning with the parts of the human body and usually referred to as "Os, facies, mentum," is included in five of the manuscripts and appears in a sixth as the basis of a *nominale*, though not in verse.[31] Two others of this kind of verse vocabulary include that called *Liber Caballus*, or *Bursa Latini*, found in four manuscripts,[32] and no fewer than five examples of what is referred to as *Distigium*, attributed to John of Garland, the well-known English grammarian who taught at Paris and Toulouse around the middle of the twelfth century.[33] There is also the poem beginning with the words *Deus nichil fecerat frustra* which, in describing the occupations of various classes of society, includes the vocabulary associated with each class activity. It is found in three of the manuscripts and is entitled in one of them *Liber Ricardini*.[34] In conclusion, however, it is to be noted that the metrical tract enjoying the widest circulation of all is the *Synonyma*, which begins with the words *Ad mare ne videar latices*, and its closely associated *Equivoca*. Both of these appear in eight of the manuscripts under consideration and are attributed to John of Garland.[35]

The theory of grammar, that is, Latin considered as a speculative science rather than a language to be learned, does not, strictly speaking, come within the framework of the program examined in these pages. Yet it would be misleading to ignore the subject, appearing as it does in four of the manuscripts. It arises so naturally at times, especially from the study of the parts of speech, that it is difficult to see how some teachers could altogether avoid this kind of discussion.[36] Although treatises such as John of Montpellier's *Donatus in Magno* and John of Cornwall's treatment of the subject in his *Speculum gramaticale* are evidently for advanced students, attention will be given below to the more pedagogical aspects of their presentations. The author of *Add. 32,425*, which is an interesting work on the parts of speech with an abundance of illustrative sentences, cannot refrain from branching off into logical analysis and philosophical concepts of grammar. Finally, even John Seward, whose main preoccupation is prosody, begins his work with a commentary on the nature of grammar.

A first reading of the manuscripts examined above is sufficient to identify the sources of most of this material. Such reference books can broadly be classified into general grammars covering nearly all aspects of the subject, treatises dealing with the specific subjects of prosody or etymology, and specialized dictionaries. The majority belong to the first category. In addition to the works mentioned above, belonging to such authors as Donatus, Priscian, Alexander, John of Garland, and John Balbus of Genoa (Ianuensis), there are the *Etymologia* of Isidore of Seville (c. 570–636), which is an encyclopedia of the different branches of knowledge, and the *Summa* of Peter Helias, which is a modernization of Priscian by a teacher in Paris towards the middle of the twelfth century.[37]

The second group is represented by the *De arte metrica* of the venerable Bede (673–735), the monk of Jarrow in England, whose educational manuscripts enjoyed a remarkably wide circulation throughout medieval Europe, and by the *Derivationes* and *De dubio accentu*, composed some time before 1210 by Hugutio of Pisa, bishop of Ferrara.[38] The third group includes the dictionary *Elementarium*, composed by Papias from Pavia around the middle of the eleventh century, and the dictionary entitled *Summa* or *Vocabularius Biblie* by William Brito, a French Franciscan friar, completed some time before 1272.[39]

From the pedagogical point of view, probably the most noticeable feature of these sources as a whole is the emphasis upon etymology. Nearly all the authors named above, particularly Isidore, Hugutio, and Brito, are called upon to supply information on this topic. Although a partial exception to this, the *Elementarium* of Papias evidently justified its persistence throughout the later medieval period by its inclusion of a large number of geographical and historical names for quick and easy reference.

From the historical point of view, however, the outstanding feature of the entire group of reference works mentioned above is that the learning of Latin in later medieval England involved a dependence upon authors whose careers span almost nine centuries, from Donatus in the middle of the fourth century to Brito in the thirteenth. No fewer than five of the eleven authors produced their work within the period from 1200 to 1275. If we include Peter Helias, the greater amount of this grammatical material circulating in later medieval England dates from a period roughly between 1150 and 1275. Moreover, the manuscripts clearly show that much of the work of Donatus and Priscian is brought to the fourteenth and fifteenth centuries through this later group of writers, with Peter Helias serving as a bridge between them. Comparisons are not uncommonly made in the manuscripts between the "ancient" and "modern" authorities. There is little doubt as to whom these later medieval teachers and commentators mean by "modern." For the writer of the early fifteenth-century manuscript, *Trin. o.5.4.*, for instance, "modern" works include John of Genoa's *Catholicon* and Alexander's *Doctrinale*.

A second feature is no less interesting. The writers of the "modern" reference books are either Italians or Frenchmen, and the one known exception – the Englishman, John of Garland – produced his works in France. It is scarcely an exaggeration, therefore, to state that the basic educational influence at work in later medieval England had its source for the most part in the schools of thirteenth-century France and Italy. It seems extraordinary at first sight that the teachers of Latin in fifteenthcentury England were dependent upon grammatical material written outside their own country some two centuries earlier. In explanation, it should prove helpful to consider the teachers mentioned in the manuscripts together with their treatises.

Richard of Hanbury's tract on metre dates from the late thirteenth century,[40] followed by John of Cornwall's important work from 1346 and John Harford's *Regule utiles* of about a generation later, if he is the John de Hereford who studied at Oxford from 1388. From the first generation or so of the fifteenth century we have no fewer than five authors of educational treatises, all with the baptismal name of John: Chalurys and Seward, with their tracts on prosody; Boryngton, with his treatises entitled *Regimina* and *Communis versus*, if he is correctly identified as the person of that name who was granted a licence to study at Oxford in 1438; and Leland and Drury, authors of various grammatical tracts and commentaries. To these may be added Thomas Syltone, about whom nothing is known except that his treatise on accentuation appears to be from the fifteenth century.

All those listed above are *magistri* and three of them – Richard of Hambury, John Cornwall, and John Leland – are comparatively well-known Oxford men. No single master, however, appears to have dominated the field. While some of John Seward's tracts on prosody, for example, have been located in three different manuscripts, he is not mentioned elsewhere, much less referred to as an authority. The one possible exception to this might be John Leland, who was held in such regard by John Seward and was, in the opinion of John Drury's scribe at Beccles, *flos grammaticorum*. While the total manuscript evidence as cited above does not, in itself, support this reputation, Thomson's recent study of English treatises on grammar goes far to suggest this pride of place for Leland, based on a number of anonymous publications of the fifteenth century that derive in whole or in part from his teaching.[41]

One significant point that emerges from the above survey is the predominance of Oxford men. As far as can be learned, John Drury may well have been the only one who might have attended Cambridge. The implication is that the University of Oxford was not only one important centre among others for grammatical studies, but that it probably continued to provide leadership in this field through at least the first half of the fifteenth century.

In his examination of vocabularies current among teachers in the fifteenth century, Thomas Wright drew attention to the differences they revealed "both in their general arrangement and in the words introduced under each head," leading him to conclude that "each schoolmaster compiled his own book."[42] The same observation may be made with respect to the entire Latin program in general: there appear to be as many treatises as there are masters. The procedure appears to have consisted, first, of the master copying out an authoritative tract, in whole or in part, or commissioning a scribe to do so; second, adding to it his own commentary or inter-linear gloss and, on occasion, even tracts of his own devising. We are informed, for example, that the author of the *Memoriale iuniorum*, Thomas Hanney, began to compile a detailed list of chapter headings for a course in grammar in the month of May, 1313, while he was in Toulouse, and that he completed it the following December at Lewes "at the instance of Master John of Chertsey," the rector of the schools in that town.[43] At Beccles, in 1434, the scribe, Hardgrave, identifies some of the grammatical pieces he is copying out as the work of the local schoolmaster, John Drury. The inference is that the other items not so assigned, if they are not Drury's own tracts, are his personal adaptations of those of someone else.[44]

If the procedure suggested above is indicative of the way in which most of the manuscripts considered in the present study were compiled, it remains to explain why the grammar masters of later medieval England followed the course that they did. In this connéction the texts described above prove especially relevant. Their most pronounced feature is the predominance of verse. All the selections are in verse, except those dealing with syntax. This is significant, for it shows at once the task which confronted these English masters. They were the beneficiaries of a complete program of Latin studies, didactic in tone and suited to "modern" conditions. This program was "new" as contrasted with that of antiquity, although it had taken at least a century in the making. Preserved in Latin verse, the program was brief and generally appealing, and had only to be memorized to be learned. There was no need to add anything substantial to this program: it had only to be absorbed and then transmitted to others.

The manuscripts themselves illustrate very clearly, though, how difficult this twofold task could be. Originating for the most part in France and Italy, this grammatical material required varying degrees of revision and adaptation before it could be used effectively in England. Hence the frequent English glosses that accompany the vocabularies in verse, as well as the commentaries and paraphrases employed to give meaning to standard texts or works of reference. The masters' use of Alexander's *Doctrinale* is a case in point. The one manuscript that includes the complete text, *Trin. o.5.4.*, also contains a prose paraphrase while *Add. 37,075*, containing the section of the *Doctrinale* treating of figures of speech, includes a commentary in Latin. Of the three manuscripts that include the verses pertaining to the gender of nouns, only *Caius 383* provides the text by itself. *Harl. 1002* has a commentary in Latin along with it, while *Add. 37,075* includes both a commentary in prose and the English meaning of the words in the *Doctrinale*. Paetow's assertion, then, that "in the fourteenth and fifteenth centuries the *Doctrinale* was the universal grammar of nearly all Europe" appears to be more limited in its application to England.[45]

As already observed, the tracts on syntax are the only "texts" not in verse. What may be termed a "verse" curriculum had been extended and consolidated at a time when England still shared a predominantly French culture. To teach Latin to English youths through the medium of their native tongue in the changing climate of the Hundred Years' War required, however, a different pedagogical method of syntax from that of the standard versified texts. It is interesting, then, to note that these texts on syntax in prose are readily identified as the work of the later medieval English grammar masters.

Whatever their pedagogical suitability, these tracts on syntax reveal the poverty of the Latin language in fifteenth-century England. Pagan Latin modes of thought and expression have given way to more modern, Christian ones. This, in itself, is understandable, for as long as Latin was retained as the living universal language of western Europe, it had to adapt to changing conditions and local differences. Surveying the educational scene of fifteenth-century England, however, forces one to conclude that the price paid was very high. The liberties taken with Latin construction and the inconsistencies in the spelling render the language almost unrecognizable to a person brought up on classical Latin. The principal reason for this can be seen in the sentences employed in lessons on syntax: except for a number of quotations from sacred scripture, which are often related to the liturgy of Sundays and feast days, the sentences are divorced from any body of literature, and therefore from models of style. Sooner or later there would have to be a return to the sources. This, in turn, would entail an important change in the curriculum of the nation's grammar schools. While this development would have its own special rationale and need not detain us here, it is pertinent at this point to look at the selections that provided whatever literary background there was for the generations immediately preceding the Renaissance.

The contents of *Trin. o.5.4.* and *Add. 37,075* reveal a number of selections in verse evidently employed as reading material for students of Latin. Since the first-named manuscript contains most of these selections, it can serve as a convenient point of departure for the entire survey. The first "reader" of this kind in the manuscript from Battlefield College is *Catonis disticha*, the Distichs of Cato. Appearing in *Add. 37,075* and *Harl. 1002*, as well as in seven of the manuscripts in the second group, it enjoys a relatively high frequency, owing perhaps to the didactic character by which it sets the tone for most of the other selections. The complete text, however, consisting of a prologue in prose with some fifty-seven brief *sententie*, together with four books of distichs, is found in only one-third of the manuscripts. What appears more often is a considerably abbreviated form consisting either of a few of the distichs only or the prologue with the *sententie*, in either case usually entitled *Liber Parvi Catonis*.[46]

Liber urbanitatis, beginning with the well-known line *stans puer ad mensam*, is concerned with rules of politeness and is attributed to Robert Grosseteste, bishop of Lincoln from 1235 to 1253. In addition to its appearance in *Trin. o.5.4.*, *Add. 37,075*, and *Harl. 1002*, it is included in three manuscripts of the second group.

The third item of this kind in *Trin. o.5.4.* is *Liber cartule*, a series of reflections on the vanity of this earthly life. It has often been attributed to St Bernard of Clairvaux (1091–1153) or John of Garland, but its authorship is still in doubt. It is included in three manuscripts from the second group.

Liber penitencialis, more often referred to as *Peniteas cito* from the opening words, summarizes in verse the doctrine of the sacrament of penance. The *Liber penitencialis* appears to have enjoyed a wide circulation as a mode of instruction particularly suitable for inclusion in a program of Latin grammar and, in addition to its inclusion in *Trin. o.5.4.*, appears in seven manuscripts of the second group. For a long time associated with the published work, though not exclusively, of John of Garland, this material has more recently been identified with William de Montibus, a lecturer in theology and chancellor at Lincoln in the early thirteenth century.[47]

Facetus, or *Liber facetie*, is a didactic poem of some 290 verses instructing youth in Christian living. Included in *Trin. o.5.4.* and *Add. 37,075*, the poem also appears in four of the manuscripts from the second group. Very little is known about the poem's origins except that it seems to have been in circulation near the end of the twelfth century.

Liber parabulorum of Alanus de Insulis, a French poet of the early thirteenth century, is a relatively lengthy didactic poem of 642 hexameters. It is also called *Proverbia* or *Doctrinale minus*. It, too, appears to have been a well known reader in England in the later middle ages, for it is included in seven of the manuscripts under consideration, including *Trin. o.5.4.* and *Add. 37,075*.

The *Eclogue of Theodulus* comprising 352 lines of verse, provides younger students with an appreciation of famous persons and events connected with both classical and sacred history. The poem consists of a pastoral disputation between an Athenian shepherd and a Hebrew shepherdess. Included in *Trin. o.5.4.* and *Add. 37,075*, the poem is also found in three manuscripts from the second group. Although its origin has not been established with any certainty, the *Eclogue* appears to have been composed by a northern author as early as the ninth century.

Mention should be made of another poem entitled *O Magnatum filii nostri commensales*. Comprising some 150 goliardic lines characterized throughout by an end rhyme, it is an essay on the manners proper to noble households; in this respect it resembles *Liber urbanitatis*. Although it is included in only two of the manuscripts in question, *Harl. 1587* and *Peniarth 356*, its appearance in such widely separated places as Christ Church, Canterbury, and a school in Wales merits its inclusion with the preceding readers.[48]

The above reading selections are didactic. They are predominantly moral, as in Cato, *Facetus*, and the Parabolae; or religious and instructional, as in Theodulus, Cartula, and the *Liber penitencialis*; or primarily concerned with good manners, as in the case of the *Liber urbanitatis* and the *O Magnatum filii*. As such these Latin readers offer a broad educational program, not just instruction in the learning of Latin.

Yet there is almost nothing of classical antiquity in the readings. As Nicholas Orme has described it, the *Sex Auctores* of the thirteenth century – Cato, Theodulus, Avianus, Maximian, Claudian, and Statius – with their "not inconsiderable fragment of classical culture," gave way to the *Auctores Octo* of the fourteenth and fifteenth centuries in which only Cato and Theodulus remained to link up with the culture of the ancient world.[49] With regard to Cato, moreover, it is interesting to observe how a highly abbreviated edition circulated in its own right. Even the morality expounded in the distichs is no longer distinctively pagan but has been Christianized. As for the *Eclogue of Theodulus*, a student would obtain from it some degree of classical mythology, but only in comparison with important events in the history of the chosen people. In other words, whatever these two books contain of antiquity is made to serve specifically Christian purposes. The classical element, as the basis of an educational program, is almost totally absent.

Following this summary description of their contents, it remains to examine some of the grammatical manuscripts more closely to discover what they reveal of the purpose and method of the Latin program. The treatises used for illustration will be arranged in a topical order according to the various divisions of a grammar course. With this in mind, it will be helpful to begin by defining the terms used to describe the principal parts of grammar.

Grammar is defined as the art of speaking, writing, and expressing oneself correctly, and it consists of the letter, the syllable, the word, and the clause.[50] In keeping with this definition, the four principal parts of grammar are orthography, prosody, etymology, and syntax.[51] Orthography teaches a person to write correctly and prosody, to read correctly, while syntax includes both the rules and the actual construction of sentences.[52] The term *ethimologia* has a considerably wider application than what we normally mean by etymology. It is defined as that which teaches a person to know each part of speech by itself as distinguished from the relation of one part to another in discourse.[53] That is to say, etymology as a division of grammar comprises what we would call morphology; in this sense it has a very wide connotation. The entire learning process can thus be summed up as follows:

Recte *scribere*	to write correctly
Recte scripta *pronunciare*	to pronounce correctly what is written
Recte pronunciata *intelligere*	to understand correctly what is pronounced
Intellecta *exponere*	to express what is understood.[54]

ORTHOGRAPHY

Orthography was essentially the learning of the Latin alphabet and included formation of the letters, distinguishing vowels from consonants, and construction of Latin words. A tract on the subject observes that the letters A, E, I, O, and U are called vowels (*vocales*), for without them no sound (*vox*) of the letter can be expressed. Again: the letter Y is not classed as a vowel but is used in Greek works such as *eleyson*.[55] When important rules are stated or cases of doubtful usage discussed, reference is made to previous authorities, including John of Garland and Hugutio.

At the beginning of one tract the author remarks on the necessity of learning some of the fundamentals of the subject, especially as few people really know these points well. He has therefore set out briefly for the reader's convenience some of the essentials. When writing is poor, the voice sounds uncertain. The reader is then confused and the writer is blamed, so attention should be paid to the ways in which poor writing can cause a person to make mistakes. The author then launches into his subject, explaining that a syllable can have as few as one letter and as many as six and that two vowels coming together have the force of a diphthong.[56]

As can be seen from the foregoing, orthography in later medieval England meant what we mean today by writing and spelling. The important difference is that it consisted of the written expression of Latin rather than one's native tongue. Orthography was the first stage in the process of becoming *litteratus*, of being able to employ the then universal language of learning with some degree of facility.

PROSODY

This second part of grammar is concerned with metre and accentuation. In contrast with the order of the parts of grammar given above, the author of the *Catholicon* begins his book by dividing grammar into orthography, etymology, syntax, and prosody. Nevertheless he discusses prosody immediately after orthography because prosody is his main concern and orthography is a necessary introduction to it. He then deals briefly with etymology and syntax together, not because they follow prosody, but simply because he wishes to give them some consideration.

Positioning prosody as the fourth and last part of grammar, instead of the second, would seem to be more reasonable as otherwise the young student would be introduced to a study of metres before he knew the parts of speech. Yet this is precisely what appears to have been the practice in England. For one of the grammarians, John Seward, an early fifteenth-century London schoolmaster, prosody is the main preoccupation. One of his treatises on this subject, the *Hisagoga*, is intended for beginners. He assures the child who has learned his letters and syllables that he will teach him to recognize the various metres.[57] Remarking that his authorities include Augustine, Servius, Bede, Papias, Brislegh, and Malleus, Seward then enumerates in some detail the various kinds of metres, his examples, for the most part, being taken from Greek authors. Drawings of the human hand are included as a kind of visual aid, each finger representing a metre.[58]

It is clear, therefore, that at least some aspects of prosody were learned quite early in the grammar program. In his longest and most advanced tract, the *Metristenchiridion*, Seward considers the Latin liturgical hymns, though he mentions them only to afford examples of the metres employed by classical poets.[59] His efforts are not confined to students, for he carries on literary disputes with Master William Sheffield – all in mock seriousness – about the correct scansion of the line in Boethius' hymn *O stelliferi conditor orbis*.[60]

In another tract, metre is defined as "the correct measurement of feet divided into lines of verse." Various kinds of metre are then given with examples, based primarily on Bede with reference also to John of Garland. The method of presentation is illustrated in the following:

The iambic tetrameter metre allows for an iambus in every foot, but a spondee only in the uneven feet, as in the composition of the hymn of Sedulius, *A solis ortus cardine*, and in the *Iam surgit hora tercia*, the *Splendor paterne glorie*, the *Eterne rerum conditor*, and the hymn of the blessed martyrs where, throughout its entire length, there is an alternate spondee and iambus in both the uneven and even feet, and which begins as follows:

Eterna Christi munera
Et martirum victorie
Laudes canentes debitas
Letis canamus mentibus.[61]

This consideration of metre is followed by a collection of hymns, *liber ympnorum*, which can be sung and understood from the preceding rules. The author remarks that although metre is not maintained throughout all the hymns, nevertheless "metrical cadence" is preserved. This is sufficient, he says, "since Holy Mother Church rejoices in freedom and does not submit to the rules of Priscian's books."[62]

These hymns appear to be so closely related to the art of prosody that they deserve some attention. A hymn is defined as *Laus Deo cum cantica facta* – "praise given to God in song." The composition of the hymns is credited to Gregory, Prudentius, Ambrose, and Sedulius; the collecting of them into a single volume to Hilary.[63] The *liber ympnorum*, where it is found in the above manuscripts, is a closely written book of Latin liturgical hymns of the Sarum Use, with or without an accompanying analysis or commentary. One example is a book in which each stanza is paraphrased; the following hymn sung at the office of compline will serve as an illustration:

> Te lucis ante terminum
> Rerum creator poscimus
> Ut solita clemencia
> Sis presul ad custodiam.

The theme of this hymn is the appeal to God in the coming on of night to protect us from all evil, just as we beseech God at the dawn of each day to protect us throughout the entire day. In the beginning of night we call upon him to protect us all through the night from every evil, that is, from the snares of the devil; *O creator omnium rerum poscimus*, that is, we entreat you before day draws to its close, meaning, before we depart this life or before day leaves us; *ut sis presul*, that is, our guardian or overseer; *ad custodiam*, that is, the keeping watch over our souls; *solita clemencia*, or with your accustomed mercy.[64]

Accentuation is the other topic considered at some length in the tracts on prosody. One writer begins his discussion of the subject by defining accentuation as "the modulation of the voice in signifying by pronunciation."[65] He distinguishes three kinds of accent: grave, acute, and moderate. He remarks that the "old" grammarians also used a circumflex accent, still in use among some religious. He observes that in "modern" usage only a moderate accent can be predominant on the first or middle syllable and only an acute accent on the final syllable. He then proceeds to show how a common accent can be interfered with, summarizing this material from Priscian, Peter Helias, and Hugutio. A question, for example, interferes with the accentuation, since in an interrogative word the accent falls on the final syllable. If, however, the interrogative word is connected with other words in a sentence, then the accent is placed on the last word of the sentence, as in the question *Quid existis videre?*[66] He next draws attention to three ways by which interrogation loses its force. The first of these is in narration, as in the Gospel of St John: "Peter, turning, saw that disciple whom Jesus loved following him, and who, leaning on his breast at table, said, Lord, who is to betray thee?"[67] The second way is by transition, as in the book of Job: *Indica mihi cur me ita iudices.*[68] The third way is by continuation, as when "Nobody dared to ask him, who art thou, knowing that he was God."[69]

The relatively large number of tracts on prosody testify to its important place in the program of Latin studies. It was closely associated with the Latin liturgical hymns and many of the school texts that were in verse. Not the least of its aims was the correct pronunciation of the divine office, as is stated by Master John Chalurys. His *Flores accentus* offers an improved method of pronunciation, "readers thereby commanding greater esteem."[70]

ETYMOLOGY

The third element of grammar is etymology. As pointed out above, the term had a much wider meaning than it now has. It included everything that had to be known about the parts of speech considered by themselves, as opposed to their relation with each other in sentences. Much attention was necessarily paid to the learning of the regular conjugations and declensions. The more irregular features of the language, such as deponent verbs and heteroclite nouns, formed the subject of special tracts. Donatus' *Ars Minor*, the *Doctrinale*, and the *Catholicon* were all drawn on to help reduce this varied material to a systematic order.

In this connection the work of John Cornwall is of special interest. Cornwall taught grammar at Oxford from 1344 to 1349 and was the first master to use English instead of French in the teaching of Latin. In 1346 he wrote a treatise entitled *Speculum Gramaticale*, which includes a tract on the teaching of the parts of speech.[71] An extract from it will serve to illustrate this part of the grammar program:

How many moods in the verb? The answer is five, namely, indicative, imperative, optative, conjunctive and infinitive.
It should then be asked, "What is the function of the indicative?," to which the reply is, "It always points out, as *Amo*, I love, *amas*, thou lovyst, *amat*, he loveth, *amamus*, we loven," and so forth, covering, in this manner, all the tenses of the indicative mood of each conjugation.
The imperative always gives a command, and has two tenses, present and future, as *ama* or *amato*, love thou, *amet* or *amato*, love he, *amemus*, love we, *amate* or *amatote*, love ye, *ament*, *amanto* or *amatote*, love thei.
The optative, however, expresses a longing, as *utinam amarem*, wolde God I schulde love, *amares*, thou schuldst love, *amaret*, he schulde love, and so on.
The conjunctive mood joins one clause to another, as *si amem te, tu amabis me*.

But the infinitive, as one treatise puts it, lacks both number and person, that is, it does not distinguish in number or person, as *amare*, in English, love, *amavisse*, in English, hadde lovyd, *amatum iri*, in English, go to love, or *amaturum esse*, other to be to love, and so on, continuing through all the conjugations.[72]

The pedagogical method of John Cornwall can thus be seen to involve three essential steps: question, answer, and illustration. It is characterized chiefly by its conciseness of expression. He continues as follows:

It should further be asked, "How many tenses are there in the verb?" to which the reply is, "five"; *presens*, the tyme that is now, as *doceo*, I teche; *preteritum imperfectum*, the tyme that is litil agon as, *docebam*, I taught; *preteritum perfectum*, the tyme that is fulli agon, as *docui*, I have taught; *preteritum plusquam perfectum*, the tyme that is longe agon, as *docueram*, I hadde taught; *futurum*, the tyme that is to come, as *docebo*, I schal teche. This is the way to teach boys all the conjugations.[73]

The above passage evidently illustrates the teaching procedure of the writer based on his own experience. The replacement of French by English as the medium of instruction in Latin represents an important change in teaching methods. The fact that it was brought about by a grammar master at Oxford provides a further indication of the central position held by that university in the grammar studies of the fourteenth century.

SYNTAX

The teaching of the fourth part of grammar comprised two fairly distinct exercises: the explanation of rules governing sentence structure and the writing of Latin sentences. (The more advanced stage of composition – the writing of continuous prose – is comprised under dictamen and will be treated below in that section.) An example of the first kind of exercise, employing both Latin and English, begins with the method derived, it is stated, from the "new grammar":

EGO SUM CREATURA DEI.
This verbe *Sum* is the syngler nombyr and the fyrst person, for so is his nominative case, *Ego*; and every verbe schall accord with his nominatyf case in nombyr and yn person ...

BONUS VIR AMAT DEUM SUPER OMNIA.
This adiectif *Bonus* is the nominatyf case, masculyn gendyr and syngler nombyr, for so is his substantyf *Vir*; and every adiectif shall accord with his substantyf in gendyr, nombyr and person.[74]

This treatise is a departure from the more usual question-and-answer method. Also, the sentences have evidently been selected to allow the child to reflect on the presence and reality of God without any interruption of the lesson.

By way of contrast, a second treatise is entirely in Latin and of a more advanced nature. The first part of it is as follows:

Iesus Christus, filius beate Marie, iuvet et expediat Laurencium de Londoniis, qui coram rege Anglie vel Anglicorum et archiepiscopo Cantuariensi dimicabit infra licias cum quodam homine de Beverlaco se falso proditore accusante.[75]

What case is "beate Marie" in the above Latin? It is the genitive, governed by "filius" by virtue of the possessor or the thing possessed. Why? Because every term signifying possessor or possession can govern the genitive case of the possession or of the possessor respectively, as *rex Anglie, equus regis*.

Versus:

Possessor vel possessivi substans quoque nomen
Post se constructum semper poscit genitivum
Sum dominus ville, sed equus regis fuit ille.

The various steps in the learning process are here clearly indicated: a question followed by the answer; a general statement or rule, followed by examples; Latin verses recapitulating the lesson and assisting its retention in the memory. The lesson continues as follows:

What case is "Londoniis" in the Latin above? It is in the ablative, depending on the preposition "de." Why? Because according to the rule, proper nouns do not govern genitive cases, but ablatives, in dependence upon the preposition "de." They may on occasion govern the genitive in the case of an appellative noun understood, as "Katerina Laurenci," that is, Katherine, the wife of Lawrence; whence in the Gospel, *Maria Iacobi et Maria Salome emerunt aromata* et cetera; "Maria Iacobi," that is, Mary, who was the mother of James.

What case is "Anglie" or "Anglicorum" in the Latin above? It is the genitive.

Why? Because when the name of a temporal dignity or office has to be determined through the name of the place, then the genitive of the proper name of the place is to be used, or the genitive plural of its possessor, as *imperator Rome* vel *Romanorum, rex Anglie* vel *Anglicorum.*

What case is "Cantuariensi" in the above Latin? It is in the ablative. Why? Because of the rule, when the name of a spiritual office or dignity has to be determined through the name of the place, then, instead of the proper noun of the place, the possessive form of the proper noun of the place must be used, and put in the same case as the noun of the spiritual office or dignity, as *papa Romanus, archiepiscopus Cantuariensis, archidiaconus Florentinus.*

Another aspect of syntax is the learning of the usual order of words in a Latin sentence. The attention of the student is drawn from time to time to a consideration of the occasions on which the usual order may not be followed. The following tract, in Latin and English, is an illustration:

In how many maners is the ryghtful order of construccyon lette?[76] By fyve.
By askyng, as "Whom lovest thou?" *Quem diligis tu?*
By relacion, as "My lorde comyng to contre hys bondemen gretlych dred-yth": *Dominum meum venientem ad istas partes sui servi vehementer formidant.*
By negacyon, as "No man I love but God": *Neminem diligo preter Deum.*
By infuirtacion, as "Whomever thou lovest, hym followe in goodnesse": *Quemcumque diligis, illum sequaris in bono.*[77]
By prolemps, as "Maystres disputyng in scole, on is connyngg, a nothyr ys a fole": *Magistrorum disputancium in scola, unus est sapiens, alter stultus.*[78]

Most of the exercises involving the application of the rules of syntax consist of the composition of Latin sentences. A number of these refer to local customs or current events, such as the following:

QUOMODO DICITUR IN LATINIS:
Pilgryms ar gone to Canturbery to worshyppe the shryn of Seynt Thomas.
The kyng of Inglond shal wed the emperowes doghter of Almayn.
The kyng of Inglond somtym soiorns, somtyme at London and somtyme at Lyncolne.
My fadir owtlawd et for to be owtlawyd wo is me his eyre.
I am rede Cato, thou art red Virgil.[79]
Ther gooth a grete company of knyghtes welaparelled out of Englonde into hethenes.[80]

Other sentences are given in both English and Latin, probably to be memorized by the student, especially if the particular construction is unusual or difficult. An example is afforded by exercises on the use of the impersonal verb:

I have no house to wonne in.
Non est mihi domus manendi.

I have no pen to wrytt my lattyng with.
Deest mihi pena sermonem scribendum latinum.

I have no boke to say my mattyns on.
Non est mihi liber dicendum matutinas.[81]

The emphasis on memorization is evident in the quite frequent use of proverbs for the same purpose, as the following illustrate:

A gode be gynnyng makyth a gode endyng.
Felix principium finem facit esse beatum.

The nerer the chyrch the further fro God.
Quanto propinquior vir sit [ad]ç ecclesiam, tanto remociorius a Deo.[82]

Better is a byrd in hond than iv owt.
Plus valet in dextera volucris quam quatuor extra.[83]

It will be noted that the above sentences, which are fairly typical, either are drawn from current events and customs or are designed to have the young student reflect upon some aspect of God or the moral life. They do not derive from any body of literature; except for the proverbs and moral quotations from both pagan and Christian writers, they are the invention of the grammar master. The one exception to this is provided by sacred scripture, especially the book of psalms and the gospels. Biblical quotations furnish a never-ending supply of sentences easily memorized and illustrating the parts of speech or Latin word order, such as the following:

Et exultabit lingua mea iusticia tua.[84]
Iudica me Deus et discerne causam meam.[85]
Euge serve bone et fidelis, intra in gaudium domini tui.[86]
Domine labia mea aperies.[87]
Beati qui audiunt verbum Dei et custodient illud.[88]

The final item to be considered is a series of Latin sentences illustrating two different ways of expressing the same thought.[89] In at least one instance the aim is to teach the boy how to abbreviate by contraction and suspension.[90] The teacher apparently dictated these Latin exercises, or at least the first one in each group, and the student set down what he heard. The content, rather than the method, is of interest here, for these exercises reveal many aspects of school life in London in the fifteenth century. Accordingly, a selection of the more interesting items follows.[91]

We are gathering roses every day as they are now in bloom, setting some aside to wear in procession on the feast of St Anthony, and the water distilled from the others we shall use to relieve afflictions of the eyes.[92]

Since the oftener we get permission to play the less we apply ourselves to study, we are given few opportunities for games until, after many corrections, we know our Donat perfectly.[93]

After spending many years in London learning grammar, it will be to my advantage in the future to stay in Cambridge or Oxford where I can study in faculties which are not to be had so easily in other parts of the kingdom.[94]

In future we shall bless our parents and friends who are making provision for our instruction and behaviour; they deserve kindness who have put up with the insolence of youth which insists on playing games; anxious for us to advance, they have not considered themselves worth half the expense they assume in maintaining us at school rather than setting us to mechanical arts or common everyday jobs.[95]

If boys are inclined to be annoyed while speaking English, they will surely be so when the master questions them and harps on their difficulties since everything they say then has to be in Latin.[96]

It is a fact that those boys who do not serve God by saying Matins of the Blessed Virgin Mary every day lack the grace to recite their Donat without a mistake, and therefore they get a caning every day from the master.[97]

In several parts of Christendom the books of heretics were being burned so that no error or heresy might touch the faithful through heretical notions; some of these heretics were recently burned to ashes.[98]

To the extent that men are honoured in the present life on account of their temporal wealth, to that extent will they receive no honour in heaven; the most wretched of this world will enjoy more happiness than those with the greatest amount of gold or silver.[99]

Although attending school with some discomfort is a sad and dreary prospect, yet most students like walking through the city and its suburbs looking for lodgings, so impressed are they with the abundance of wealth and goods.[100]

For scholars to acquire knowledge by which they can understand what they read is better than going after gold and silver like misers who, because of such greed, are more likely to be damned than saved.[101]

Those scholars who display an ill will towards learning should by all means be encouraged with the master's cane. This they fear more than any weapon, even the ordeal by hot iron and the sword, and that proverb is to be remembered, "he who spares the rod spoils the child."[102]

If, therefore, I could in some way get some money to buy a book which my companion has, it seems to me that I would become a clerk like those who have books, for, as the proverb has it, "a sieve draws water as a clerk does books."[103]

The region in which I was brought up is quite a distance from London; I had the idea that it would be a long time before I would see my friends or at least receive permission to go home; a boy who is far from his friends is missing a good part of his comfort. I do not need to be reminded about not speaking in English; the penalty for those who do not use Latin, which cannot be learned without much practice, is very deserved.[104]

The "toga" which I wear on feast days suits me much better than the one I have for the vigils, which, nevertheless, as you know, I like well enough when I am sitting in school learning grammar.[105]

It is more becoming for scholars to occupy whatever recreation time they get at bows and arrows than to be wildly running around playing ball, quoits or similar games.[106]

There is a good deal of money to be earned pleading cases at Westminster Hall; it seems sometimes that little scruple attends the getting of it as the one who is more skilful usually gets his way, right or no right.[107]

All the Latin exercises, for the most part, will be written before the feast of Pentecost. Questions on them will be asked in the master's examination at the end of term; in this way they can be known perfectly and all the parts answered.[108]

I have spent many years learning grammar, but as I have been unable to get it into my head my friends have wisely arranged for me to take up a mechanical art or some ordinary job by which I can earn my living.[109]

Scarcely a single one in the whole school can be found who is accustomed to saying Matins of the Blessed Virgin of his own free will, or from that devotion without which a boy lacks the grace to acquire knowledge.[110]

FIGURES OF SPEECH

Figures of speech are a form of irregular syntax. They constitute the one section of the Latin program based almost entirely on sacred scripture. The relevant parts of the *Doctrinale* and the *Catholicon* also provide material, but these works are likewise dependent upon the Bible for some of their examples.

A verse from the psalter furnishes an example of metonymy: *Iubilate Deo, et omnis terra.* We construe this, the writer says, as if it were, *vos omnes terra iubilate Deo,* that is, "all you on earth, rejoice in God," thus illustrating metonymy, since He who contains all stands for what is contained, and earth for men on the earth.[111]

The distinction between a paradigm and a parable is made by definition and example. A paradigm, the writer says, is present when one first draws a comparison and afterwards assigns a similitude. He selects for illustration the man in the Gospel who "went out to sow his seed on good soil, some among thorns and some among rocks." The seed is the word of God, continues the writer, the thorns are riches and the rock is the parched soul. Herein lies the difference, then, between a parable and a paradigm. A parable expresses a comparison of dissimilar things without any subsequent explanation; if there is an explanation, the figure is a paradigm.[112] On another occasion the parable is defined simply as "the comparison of dissimilar things," such as the kingdom of heaven compared with a mustard seed, or the Son of Man raised up as Moses raised the serpent in the desert, or the man who went out to sow his seed.[113] A paradigm is an exhortation in the form of an example – a moral tale, as "Elias was a man, passible like us, and he prayed that it would not rain, and it did not."[114]

An extremely detailed classification of figures of speech, known as the "colours of rhetoric," follows this last consideration of the parable and paradigm. The author remarks in a brief introduction that although these particular colours of rhetoric and figures of speech received no attention from Donatus or Priscian, yet they are esteemed in theology. A few examples will serve to indicate the contents. *Antropaspatos* occurs when a human passion is attributed to God, as *Domine ne in furore tua arguas me*; it is derived from *antropos*, which is man, and *patos*, passion. *Climax* is the gradual ascent of one word into another (*de uno verbo in verbis fit gradacio*), as *ex innocencia nascitur dignitas, ex dignitate honor, ex honore imperium*. *Conniunccio* occurs when two distinct parts are connected by a single word placed between them, as *Aut etas forme decus atterit aut valetudo, id est, infirmitas*. *Fantasia* is the imaginary speech of an animated creature attributed to something inanimate, as *seges loquitur*.[115]

It may be noted in passing, as one writer points out, that solecisms and barbarisms are not to be included among the figures of speech, since they are really grammatical faults. He refers to the author of the *Doctrinale*, who defines a barbarism as a pronunciation of Latin speech lacking concordance.[116]

The more common figures of speech were probably included in the usual program of Latin grammar. More detailed studies, such as the colours of rhetoric, were likely intended to serve in the preparation of sermons for, as one writer said above, they had their place in theology. In this case they would for the most part be learned by students preparing for the orders of the priesthood.

VOCABULARIES

The vocabularies present much variety in both their arrangement and content. To simplify matters, they may be considered under two general headings: those arranged according to topics and those following an alphabetical order. The first group, called a *nominale*, usually consists of a list of nouns associated with the various classes of society. This kind of vocabulary usually begins with terms relating to God and His Blessed Mother. One such vocabulary is preceded by a statement of the compiler's aim. It has been made up, he says, in honour of the Blessed Trinity, the source of all good, the Blessed Virgin and all the saints. He has in mind especially young boys who know only English; this vocabulary should help them to know God all the sooner and love and honour him above everything else. He has listed nouns, adjectives, and adverbs, which he has collected from learned sources, but as his knowledge leaves much to be desired these should be corrected by competent people wherever necessary. Special attention should be paid to learning the principal parts of the verb *amo* and the others that follow it in *Donatus*. In this way children will come to know and understand what they hear and read; in particular, they will know how to speak of God, the most worthy object of knowledge.[117]

The vocabulary begins with a series of Latin synonyms for the English word "God," including *Hic Deus, hic creator, Pater et Filius et Spiritus Sanctus.* The terms *Hic Iesus, hic Christus, hic redemptor* are equivalent to "God hede." These are followed by those describing God, such as *hoc omnipotens.* The thought behind this arrangement then leads quite naturally to terms denoting "angel," "heaven," "holyness," and "forgeveness," followed by the terms for "swettnesse," "comfort," and "swete song," and issuing finally in the names of musical instruments.[118]

Another vocabulary, after beginning in a manner similar to the one above with terms relating to God and heaven, proceeds directly to the human body, listing the parts of the body in great detail and the various kinds of sickness and disease. Then come names of ecclesiastical and secular dignitaries, followed by terms relating to municipal affairs, punishments, craftsmen, and metals. Church feasts and customs are then listed together. The last few groups of terms are concerned with domestic topics, including the articles associated with inns, hospitals, halls, rooms, cellars, taverns, stables, farms, woods, and the like, concluding with a list of both domestic and wild animals.[119]

Alphabetical vocabularies appear to vary considerably in both purpose and arrangement. In one instance a topical *nominale* similar to those described above is arranged according to the first letter only of each word: for example, *cathesis* precedes *cathecuminus* and *clerimonius* appears before *clerimonia.*[120] Another vocabulary, entirely in Latin, is characterized by its alphabetical arrangement of all parts of speech, not merely with regard to initial letters but all the letters of the word. The few exceptions to this do not conceal the writer's aim.[121] For the most part, however, the deliberate arrangement of words according to the alphabet is connected with the verb list known as *verbale.* In this case what really matters are the first letters of the verb, so the *verbale* is therefore arranged in groups usually beginning with verbs having the letter B before O and followed by those with C before O and so on. When verbs with the letter B before EO are at length grouped together, the pedagogical aim of this arrangement becomes apparent, that is, the distinguishing of the verbs of one conjugation from those of another.

Closely associated with vocabularies are synonyms, usually consisting of several Latin terms grouped around a single English word. The word "booke," for example, is *liber, codex, carta, libellus,* and *cartula;*[122] "cherle" is *rusticus, rudis, agrestis, villanus, agricola,* and *ru[s]cticula;*[123] "techyng" is equivalent to *doctrina, doctrinacio, dogma, documentum, instructio, informacio,* and *erudicio.*[124] The grouping of synonyms in this manner would be a convenient teaching procedure.

Generally speaking, the vocabularies described above are little more than word lists. Very little attention is paid to etymology. Only occasionally is there an attempt to define terms with accuracy. The vocabularies resemble some of our modern pocket dictionaries. One exception is provided by the most extensive of the vocabularies included in the above manuscripts, that associated with Battlefield College.[125] In it, for example, we find under *scola* "from the Greek, termed *vacacio* in Latin. When we say *scola* we mean the place; when we speak of *scole* we refer to the scholars."[126]

As was pointed out above, some of the texts in general use consisted of vocabularies in verse. The one beginning *Os, facies, mentum* is a detailed list of the parts of the human body. The *Distigium* and the vocabulary beginning *Equus caballus* both contain a rather large number of words adopted from the Greek; they are usually heavily glossed with English meanings. The latter vocabulary is arranged in topical order, beginning with the animal kingdom and concluding with the ranks of human society. Together with the *Synonyma* and the *Equivoca*, these vocabularies furnished a ready supply of useful as well as relatively uncommon words not included in most of the vocabularies compiled by the English grammar masters. It was therefore an obvious advantage to retain them in their verse form to facilitate their memorization.

All the above examples are either Latin-English vocabularies or Latin only. A notable exception is the work compiled in 1440 by Galfridus, a Dominican friar of Lynn. Entitled *Promptorium Parvulorum*, and including in its list of sources, among others, the *Catholicon*, Hugutio, Brito, and John of Garland, this book is an English-Latin dictionary comprising a *nominale* and a *verbale*. The author remarks in an introduction that it is intended for young students and others with insufficient training in Latin, at a time when so many clerks are resorting to barbarous language since they have almost, if not entirely, lost the practice and theory of Latin speech.[127]

By way of conclusion, attention will now be given to a vocabulary that combines several of the features possessed by the vocabularies considered above. This is the selection beginning with the words *Deus nichil fecerat frustra dum creavit*. It is arranged according to topics, has an implicit religious and moral purpose, and is in verse with an end rhyme to facilitate its memorization. The theme is struck in the opening line: God created nothing in vain. Commencing with a consideration of the parts of the human body, this vocabulary then passes to the animal kingdom – the leopard, for instance, is the emblem of the king of England. The work then turns to the various classes of human society. The pope maintains the faith, condemns heresies, consults the cardinals when in doubt, grants bulls to those who seek them, brings enemies together in unity, and loosens penitents from their sins. Included are the duties of cardinals and of the bishop who "anoints children on the forehead with oil," the secular clergy, the monks, friars, hermits, and the "Hospitallers who wear the cross." The beneficed clerk tolls the bell for the dead, lights the candles, frequently sings the epistle, and blesses homes with holy water. Germany has provided an emperor who is the established ruler of the whole world and whose authority, confirmed by the supreme pontiff, sustains the commonweal. The king rules his people while the knights defend both ruler and subjects against their adversaries. The humble artisan, too, has his place in the scheme of things: some twelve lines of verse describing the building of a house tell how the carpenter takes over where the joiner leaves off, squaring the timber with his hand-axe, seeing that the planks are correctly placed, and making sure that the different sections of the house are constructed to provide sturdy comfort and sufficient light.[128]

The immediate object of the entire description is to provide a useful vocabulary in an interesting manner, somewhat after the fashion of John of Garland's dictionary based on everyday life in Paris.[129] The vocabulary was evidently also intended to impress upon the young student that all walks of life, both exalted and humble, are essential to society. As the very order in which the topics are treated suggests, this society is hierarchical. As God has ordained, each person has been endowed with some talent to contribute to the general welfare.

READING TEXTS

It has been shown above that, contrary to wide belief, the literature of the later medieval grammar program in England did not consist of excerpts from classical authors. Rather the literature consisted of a number of didactic poems originating in or modified by a later Christian Europe. Some of the selections, notably *Cato* (an example of pagan moral precepts adapted to a Christian classroom) and *Facetus*, are concerned with moral precepts, which have only to be read to be understood. For instance, the prologue and short maxims that sometimes precede *Cato's Distichs*, or sometimes stand alone, provide a summary of the conduct that one associates with the Christian gentleman. This prologue is in prose although in one instance the prose is accompanied by an edition in verse, evidently intended for easy memorization.[130] The theme is comprised in the words: "Now, my dearest son, I shall teach you under what conditions you shall dispose the conduct of your soul."[131]

By contrast, the *Eclogue of Theodulus* is a narrative, the only one among these selections. It consists of a series of steps in a pastoral disputation between Pseustis, an Athenian shepherd boy, and Alithia, a virgin shepherdess of the race of David. As first Pseustis, then Alithia, describes some major event in the story of his or her people, the young reader learns in a direct, attractive way some of the principal events in classical mythology and sacred history. Pseustis recalls, for example, how a sacrifice of propitiation was first offered to the illustrious Cecrops, how the bull was slaughtered, and how Pallas, the founder of Athens, decreed this sacrifice for posterity. Alithia counters this with the story of the sacrifices made to God by Cain and Abel, how Abel's was accepted, how the lamb is a figure of Christ as a victim, and how Cain slew his brother.[132]

The *Liber Cartule* and the *Liber Parabolarum* provide examples of moral poems more strictly religious in nature than *Cato*. A paraphrase of some thirty-five lines of the former, beginning with the words *Vox divina sonat*, is sufficient to indicate its content:

God admonishes men not to place their trust in themselves nor in things of the world which eventually perish. The person who loves Christ is not taken up with this world, but spurns the love of it as he would something rotten. The joys of this world are doomed to perish; it is the amenities of Paradise that are worth longing for. Take care, then, to please Christ while you are on earth. Death may come at any moment – tomorrow perhaps? Why should the flesh rejoice when it is destined to decay? Here and now is the opportunity to be sorry for your sins: those who weep now will merit the greatest happiness. The joys of the foolish serve but to increase future grief. Death is no respecter of persons: the mighty and the humble, dukes and princes, young and old – all fall victim to its merciless ways, this death whose approach strikes fear into every creature as it stalks through the world. The strong character, humbly contrite, is prepared to meet it. Why, then, you who are doomed to die, why do you wish to be magnified and seek to store up riches?[133]

Two of the poems have to do with rules of politeness, the relatively short *Liber Urbanitatis* treating especially of table manners, and the *O Magnatum filii nostri commensales* concerned with the manners proper to the households of the nobility. The first fifteen lines of the latter poem may be paraphrased as follows:

Be careful to act courteously in your duties. On entering the guest chamber look for the proper time to speak and then bend the knee; do not sit down, but remain standing in the correct order, neither leaning on your elbow nor hanging on to the door. Keep your attention fixed on the person speaking, and refrain from turning your head this way and that. Do not touch anything in the room. Keep your gaze steady and your head raised. Do not use your hand without using the fingers. Do not cross your legs. Bend your knee when you make a reply. Should someone greater than yourself enter, give him your place; let honour be given to all for the honour of God.[134]

All students would stand to profit from poems like the above, which provided for instruction in good manners, but especially those destined to be set to work in noble households in accordance with what appears to have been a well established custom.[135]

Finally, there is the more strictly doctrinal content of the poem *Liber Penitencialis*, beginning *Peniteas cito peccator*. The first four lines advise the sinner to repent now while the judge extends mercy. Five things remain to the sinner: hope of pardon, a contrite heart, confession of sins, satisfaction through penance, and flight from evil. These five points correspond to the five divisions of the sacrament of penance; this is, therefore, a good example of the use of verse to teach religious doctrine in summary form.[136]

So much for the content of the Latin readers. It remains to consider how they were used in the classroom. The shorter pieces, such as the *Liber Urbanitatis*, were probably used as selections to be memorized. All of the readers would be expected to provide ready material for parsing and other exercises in grammar. This is precisely what John Drury did at Beccles, using the *Facetus* and the *Liber Parabolarum* to illustrate rules of grammar. Occasionally one or more of the readers is glossed or accompanied by a commentary, but for the most part the Latin readers appear "clean." This is rather puzzling, for it would seem to be the accepted pedagogical procedure to make use of them as John Drury did – to illustrate grammatical rules and Latin construction. It may be remarked in passing that judging from the early printed editions on the continent, normal practice in the fifteenth century was for the readers to be accompanied by extensive commentaries.[137]

DICTAMEN

Dictamen is a special study in its own right and represents an advanced stage of Latin composition. A few examples of its use will be set out to illustrate its relation to the present study. One writer expresses its purpose and content in the following words:

Those who wish to learn the common method of composition have but to take note of the following rules which the compiler has collected in summary form for young people. He has arranged these in a more simple manner, to comply with teachers and as little as possible to oppose their assertion that we have to proceed to more difficult matters through easier ones. The contrary method might perhaps result in boys and young men giving up their studies, to the extent that these appear to be too much in comparison with what they have been taught.[138]

Dictamen consists in the art of writing letters. The principal divisions of the letter form the subject of the writer's first lesson:

The first point to be learned is that in a full and perfect letter there are five distinct parts. The first of these is the salutation, the second the narration, the third the petition, the fourth the conclusion, and the fifth the sub-salutation. Of course, so many parts are not always required and, hence, with some authorities the above names are changed: the first is termed the introduction, the second part narration, the third petition and rhetorical division, the fourth confirmation with the conclusion, and the fifth the sub-salutation, which stems from the conclusion.[139]

A second writer defines *ars dictandi* as "the arrangement of phrases so as to produce gracefulness."[140] He then outlines two methods of composition, one called Roman (*stilus Romanus*) and the other Cistercian (*modus Cisterciencis*). In his introduction to the second of these methods, the writer explains that he has composed this treatise for two groups of people: those who wanted him to provide a number of standard letter forms that could serve them as models, and those who wanted some instruction in devising letters for themselves as necessity demanded. According as God grants him the ability to do this, therefore, he hopes to satisfy the desires of both classes of persons. After a brief explanation of dictamen, he will proceed to the actual composition of letters, particularly after the Cistercian method. He expresses confidence that even mediocre writers and younger people who are rather slow at this task will profit.[141]

One of the distinctive features of this method is the use of proverbs. The procedure is explained as: "Having considered salutations in general, let us now give our attention to proverbs. First of all, then, we should note what a proverb is, why it is so called, in what kinds of letters it is conveniently introduced, and how it should be adapted. Now, we call that a proverb which in rhetoric is known as an introduction, and in Tully's definition, an introduction is that form of speech which properly prepares or attunes the mind of the hearer for a forthcoming delight." The writer then proceeds to show how a proverb is suitably named. Since its function in speech recalls its derivation from *prothos*, the Greek word for the Latin *primum*, a proverb is a protoword with respect to the narration. In conclusion, he remarks on the truth of Bede's observation at the beginning of his commentary on the Proverbs of Solomon that the effect of the proverb depends mainly upon the respect entertained by the hearer for the speaker.[142]

A few examples of the actual use of proverbs in letters follow. The first would suit a man entering the religious life: "Now that nearly all flesh has corrupted its way through sin, which the flood has begun to cleanse, salvation seems to be better assured in the ark of Noe than in the ocean of iniquity which engulfs a pleasure-filled world."[143] A second example is suitable when extending congratulations: "If one member glories, as the Apostle says, the other members are wont to rejoice together, from which example we are bound to rejoice in another's good fortune, regarding it as our own."[144] Still another example is by way of reproof for disgraceful behaviour: "Just as a little yeast will corrupt the whole mass, as the Apostle says, or as a disease infects an entire flock, so do the evil manners of one contaminate the conduct of many, and give scandal to those beholding them."[145]

A third treatise provides a considerable number of model letters to be employed in the various ranks of society; it also includes a detailed schematic device summarizing the different forms of address. Each letter is followed by a *responsio*. The first letter is that of the pope to the king, followed by such examples as a letter from a prince to the rulers of Denmark, one from the Duke of Lancaster to the Earl of Arundel, another from the Archbishop of Canterbury to the Bishop of Lincoln. Then come letters from one abbot to another, a letter between knights, one between friends, another between two companions, a letter from a subject to his master, a father to his son, another from a son to his mother.[146] Included among these is a homily by Brother John de Waldeby, professor of sacred theology, on the Apostle's Creed.[147]

The second part of the summary is a series of *tabule* giving the correct forms of the several parts of the letter for whatever rank of society it is intended.[148] A letter has four parts, namely, the salutation, the body of the letter, the petition, and the conclusion. The first *tabula* includes the form of salutation when addressing the supreme pontiff. The second *tabula* addresses itself to cardinals, patriarchs, archbishops, and other superiors; the third to educated men such as priors, archdeacons, canons, judges, chaplains, masters (*magistri*), friars, teachers (*doctores*), monks, and scholars. The fourth *tabula* is concerned with the emperor, kings, princes, dukes, counts, barons, margraves, those in authority (*potestates*), justiciars, knights, chaplains, learned men, and other lesser laymen. The fifth *tabula* addresses itself to friends, colleagues, brothers, relatives, notaries, scholars, and other equals; the sixth to inferior clergy and laity, while the seventh is taken up with Saracens, Jews, heretics, traitors, enemies, rebels, slaves, and others not of the faith.

In conclusion, the sections on dictamen in the rather heterogeneous collection of material comprising *MS Caius* 383 contain, first, the now familiar collection of model letters in use among the various ranks of society. These include the correspondence of one prince with another, a count with a baron, a father with his son at school, and a lord with his bailiff.[149]

The second treatise is of a more specialized character. It consists of some twenty pages on the correct method of drawing up charters. The writer first sets down some general principles:

And it should be observed that in the drawing up of charters, the clerk has first of all to inquire into all the circumstances, so that no loss of goods should be suffered by any party as a result of his neglect or ignorance, in order that he might be reckoned among the honest instead of the untrustworthy. The first thing that should be known, then, is what a charter is. A charter is a certain feoffment or sealed writing in regard to immoveable goods, granted in peaceful seisin without any intermediate condition in the transferring from one person to another.[150]

A quotation from a well-known statute, *Quia emptores*, is then used as an illustration. The writer proceeds to consider briefly the defects in a charter, as, for instance, the alienation of land or tenements by one who is under age, for on attaining the required age that person is free to revoke such gift or alienation. Finally, the charter is divided into six principal parts, as, for example, the opening sentence *Sciant presentes et futuri quod ego.*[151]

In view of the above, it is not surprising to find a series of model letters of a distinctively business nature, including such topics as manumission, presentation to a church, and letters dimissory, together with documents and charters of a more general kind (*carte generalie*).[152] This business correspondence is of a more specialized nature than the usual letter forms appearing in these treatises on dictamen. It belongs to that kind of dictamen closely connected with legal procedure and has been the subject of several studies by H.G. Richardson.[153]

It has already been shown that Leach stopped short of an inquiry into the curriculum of the medieval grammar school. Even though he was quick to note any reference in the sources that threw any

light on the topic, such a reference, being marginal to his main
institutional thrust, served only to reinforce his preconceived notion
of what such a curriculum must have entailed. His overall view of
the grammar school program may be reduced to three main points:
first, that instruction tended to be dialectical or argumentative in its
method, reflecting the prevailing climate of scholasticism; second,
that it inculcated basic Christian beliefs; and, third, that whatever
literature might serve on occasion as its source of inspiration was
selected from the classical writers of Roman antiquity.

So Leach could say, with particular reference to the schools of
medieval London, that "so powerful during the twelfth and thirteenth centuries did dialectic become, that not only did theology
become almost a branch of logic but grammar itself was taught and
practised 'dialectically.'"[154] Equally, he could assert that throughout
the entire medieval period, though some authors might be substituted for others – as, for instance, Prudentius and Juvencus, the
fourth-century Christian poets, for writers like Horace and Juvenal
– "Virgil from first to last formed the staple of all."[155] Leach was
prepared, in fact, even to state that "alike in title and substance the
schools of England before the Reformation were very much the same
as those after it up to 1860."[156]

This last generalization points up the basic flaw in Leach's interpretation of medieval education: while he correctly allows for change
and development on the institutional side, he does not allow for such
on the curricular side. He thinks of medieval teachers as essentially
committed to preserving the Roman heritage, albeit in the more
Christianized form of the later empire rather than that of pagan
antiquity. When, therefore, Leach notes that the curriculum of the
school at Warwick included Cato and Theodulus, that in twelfth-
century London a writer like William Fitzstephen could quote the
classical author Persius as a matter of course, or that in Colet's early
sixteenth-century school at St Paul's, Roman Christian writers were
selected very much as they had been by Alcuin of York in the eighth
century, Leach is providing examples that support his conviction
that the medieval program in Latin – a product of both Roman
culture and early Christianity – had only to be preserved to be made
viable for centuries to come.

While the manuscript sources described above testify to the soundness of Leach's instinctive grasp of the theological nature of medieval
education and, in a more limited way, to its "dialectical" nature as
well, they seriously undermine his view of the continuity of classical
influence in the school curriculum. Leach completely missed the
importance and significance of the newer educational developments

of the thirteenth century that grew out of European Christendom rather than Roman Christianity. Equally important, having missed this central development in its more positive aspects, he also failed to appreciate the extent to which this Christian European curriculum had strayed from its Latin cultural roots. This led him in turn to underestimate the potential of Renaissance humanism to help redress the educational balance and even to question the necessity of such a movement. Understandable as this progression of ideas may be, Leach's view of the Renaissance could serve only to undermine his overall credibility.

CHAPTER SEVEN

The Grammar Program: Related Topics

Included in the grammatical material previously examined are a number of treatises and notes pertaining to topics related to the learning of Latin. One of these is philosophical grammar. Though it is not certain to what extent this subject entered the grammar program, it appears to have engrossed the attention of several of the grammar masters. The inference is that, owing to the development of faculties of grammar in the universities of the thirteenth century, the scholastic method had in this later period filtered down into the advanced classes of the grammar schools. It is, of course, the method and subject matter, not the philosophical conclusions, that are of interest to the present study.

First, there are a few exercises in logical method that might very well form part of any advanced grammar lesson. These are termed *questiones*. One of them arises from a passage in the gospel, the beginning of Christ's discourse to his apostles before the Last Supper: "Amen, I say to you, in my Father's house, there are many mansions. If not, I would have told you, because I go to prepare a place for you."[1]

The master proceeds to enlarge upon this as follows:

That is, I tell you the truth, since there are many mansions in my Father's house; *minus* is used for *non*; if there had not been many mansions in my Father's house I would have told you; *quo*, that is, *aliquo modo*, I go to prepare a place for you.

My question is, is this sentence correct or not, I go to prepare a place for you?

Objection: when actions in a sentence coincide and the first of them signifies motion towards a place, then the second will be the first supine, but here it is not so. Therefore, I say that this is consonant with sacred scripture, since sacred scripture is so worthy and noble in itself that it does not have to conform to grammatical rules:

Utitur ecclesia contra vim grammaticorum
Dic alio, cape sal, dic multus murmur eorum.[2]

The conflict between ecclesiastical Latin and the rules of grammar as illustrated in this *questio* is explained by recourse to the general principle that the church possesses criteria independent of grammatical authorities. In another instance a writer attempts to explain this contradiction. He observes how the church, in the common opinion of both educated and uneducated, has often seen fit to contradict the rules of grammar. The writer then examines the different instances in which ecclesiastical usage violates the laws of grammar; in doing so he explains the verses at the end of the *questio* above.[3] He enumerates three violations: first, in the baptism of children when the words *Accipe sal sapiencie* are pronounced, according to the rules of grammar the person baptising should say to the child, *Accipe salem sapiencie*, since, although all nouns ending in *al*, as *tribunal*, are neuter and retain that ending, monosyllables are expressly excepted. Second, in the gospel it is said, "Amen, I say to one, go, and he goeth, to another (alio) come, and he cometh:" *alio* is not correct grammatical usage.[4] Third, the occurrence of an adjective not agreeing with its substantive, as in the sentence *multus murmur erat in populo*: here *multus* is put for *multum*.[5]

A somewhat different kind of problem is presented in the examination of another biblical passage, the description of the water changed into wine at the marriage feast of Cana. The clause in question is *Ut gustasset architriclinus aquam factum vinum*.[6] The teacher asks whether it is better to say *factum* or *factam*, since the past participle modifies both *aquam* and *vinum*. He asserts that it makes no difference which kind of agreement is used between two substances of different kinds, since one of them signifies matter and the other what has been made from matter with a "signifying substance."[7]

As this last discussion touches upon a metaphysical question, it provides a suitable opportunity to introduce the commentaries on the nature of grammar itself, a grammar that can be reduced to scientific rules. A treatise on the parts of speech forms a useful introduction to the subject. In this work, each part of speech is introduced by a commentary on its nature. For example, in the discussion of the verb: "What is a verb? A part of speech with time and person, but no case, signifying action or passion, or neither."[8] This definition is taken verbatim from Donatus.[9] The writer is not content with this and immediately inquires how Priscian defines the verb: "According to Priscian, in his eighth book of the *Maior*, a verb is a part of speech with moods and tenses, but no case, signifying action or passion. In saying 'moods' and 'tenses' he excludes participles: in referring to 'time' he excludes nouns which signify 'time.'"[10]

As the foregoing examples indicate, the writer is not so much intent upon the exercise of his dialectical skill as he is concerned to obtain the best possible definition of the verb. Things become somewhat more involved, however, when he turns to a consideration of the pronoun:

What is the property of a pronoun according to Peter Helias? To be used for a proper noun.

Objection: if a pronoun can be used for a proper noun, the pronoun can be removed and be replaced by a proper noun, for the philosopher says, 'That thing is greater for which another exists.' But the pronoun can not be removed and a proper noun used in its place, since, when you say, 'Ego, Petrus, lego,' if the 'Ego' be removed you can not say, 'Petrus, lego,' owing to the lack of concordance; therefore, it is not the property of a pronoun to be used for a proper noun.

Solution: one thing can be used for another in two ways, namely, because of signification and function, or because of signification alone. It should be said that pronouns of the third person are used for proper nouns because of signification and function; whereas pronouns of the first and second persons are used for proper nouns because of signification only, since they have the same signification though not the same function. Accordingly, it does not follow that wherever a pronoun is employed a proper noun can replace it.[11]

The above passage illustrates the procedure of the writer: he begins with a question, states an authoritative answer, raises an objection, furnishes a solution, and finally states a brief conclusion. The main outline of this method is also illustrated in the writer's discussion of the interjection. Unlike the pronoun, the interjection cannot readily be classified as a part of speech, so in his efforts to define an interjection, the writer's dialectical training is afforded some scope. What is an interjection? he asks. According to Donatus, it is a part of speech signifying a movement of the mind produced by an inarticulate voice. Considering this inadequate, he recalls Priscian's definition that an interjection is an indeclinable part of speech injected between other parts of speech to indicate various emotions of the soul. He proceeds as follows:

What is the property of an interjection? It is the movement of the mind, that is, an affection of the soul uttered by an inarticulate voice, signifying something imperfectly. I object as follows to the description of the interjection given by Donatus: every part of speech, as Priscian says, signifies a mental concept, whereas Donatus says, a movement of the mind; therefore, an interjection is not a part of speech. To this one should reply that although an interjection signifies an emotion of the mind in the person uttering the interjection, nevertheless, in the hearer it signifies a mental concept, for the hearer conceives what the soul of the one uttering the interjection exclaims, whether it be from sorrow, joy, fear or admiration.[12]

The writer of the foregoing introduces these dialectical problems quite incidentally in the course of a detailed treatment of the parts of speech, for his main object is to put these definitions to practical use in the classroom. In other places, however, the writers appear to be concerned primarily with logical and metaphysical aspects, incorporating their opinions in introductory commentaries. One example of this is John Cornwall's discussion of the interjection near the end of his treatise *Speculum Gramaticale*. Cornwall first recalls the definition of Donatus, a movement of the mind uttered by an inarticulate voice. He observes that some books speak of an "unrecognised" or "unpremeditated" voice (*vox incognita ... non deliberata*), noting that Remigius thinks of an interjection in this sense, as when in using other parts of speech in discourse an interjection is uttered unexpectedly.[13] Cornwall continues: "From this it is to be noted what the commentator says, that some parts of speech, when spoken suddenly, are considered interjections, as *pro dolor*, *pro nephas*, *Deo gratias*, *verbi gratia*; *ite missa est* is of this class, as will clearly be seen later on. Furthermore, observe how some wished this member to be classed with adverbs, whereas Donatus did not agree with this, since it possesses its own proper nature as do the other parts of speech, namely, to indicate a movement of the mind."[14]

Three further questions are now raised: whether an interjection is truly a part of speech and, if so, what makes it such; whether or not, assuming that an interjection is a part of speech, it should be distinguished from an adverb; and whether or not an emotion can be attributed to the sound made by an interjection. The writer's approach to these questions is illustrated by his treatment of the first of them:

[W]ith regard to the first I proceed as follows and prove that the interjection is not a part of speech since nothing else is a part of speech unless it signifies a mental concept, as Priscian states in the *Maior*. An interjection, however,

does not signify a mental concept but, as Donatus says, an emotion; therefore, the only alternative is that
an interjection is not a part of speech. Moreover, every part of speech
signifies an intention to apply a name to a thing, whereas some interjections
seem to signify an impulse and not an intention. The same thing, moreover,
may be observed in Priscian's reference to it, where in regard to the order
of parsing in book VI of the *Minor,* he disposes of it in a single line, which
he would not have done if it had been a part of speech.[15]

Even more than the previous writer, Cornwall is at great pains to
distinguish the nature of each part of speech. His method is characterized by a careful examination of several recognized authorities,
balancing one against the other. His main interest lies not in Latin
grammar as such, much less in its literature, but in a speculative
grammar that lends itself to deduction from scientific principles.[16]

The introductory commentary of a third writer is concerned with
the nature of a part of speech. Known as *Donatus in Magno,* the
commentary begins as follows: "What is a part of speech? A voice
indicating a mental concept, as Priscian says in his treatise on participles. Objection: letters and syllables are parts of speech and yet
they do not indicate a mental concept; the above definition, therefore, is not adequate. This definition, however, is adequate for words
that are almost parts of speech. Letters and syllables, indeed, are
distinct from these and this definition does not apply to them."

There is an objection to this definition of a part of speech and it
is furnished by the interjection:

An interjection is close to being a part of speech and in that case indicates
a mental concept. Donatus denies this, since it signifies a movement of the
mind. If an interjection signifies a movement of the mind or passion of the
soul with respect to the person uttering it, then with respect to the hearer
it indicates a mental concept. For when 'alas.' (heu) is exclaimed, the person
exclaiming it reveals the emotion of his soul, and the hearer naturally re-
cognises the presence of that emotion in the one so exclaiming; thus, the
interjection gives rise in the second person to a concept of the mind even
if at first it signifies a movement of the mind. It is through such signification
that it is distinguished from the other parts of speech.

The author now brings forward a further objection, so intent is he
on formulating an accurate definition: "Objection: the verbs *letor,*
doleo, miror, metuo, and the nouns derived from these, *leticia, dolor,*
miracio, and *metus* signify a movement of the mind, that is, an emotion
of the soul; accordingly, this is not the proper signification of the

interjection by which it is distinguished from the other parts of speech." [17]

As mentioned above, the conclusions of these grammarians are not of immediate concern to this study. Of concern are the kinds of problems that preoccupy the grammarians and the methods they employ to deal with them. This last illustration affords an insight into the mind of a teacher bent on formulating precise definitions. His efforts to define the verb even more clearly reveal the dialectical and metaphysical background of his training. After stating Priscian's definition of the verb, he proceeds:

It is first of all asked whether two parts 'with time and person' may be placed congruently in the definition of a verb. It seems not, since when one part of a definition is removed, the defined thing itself is removed from it. But it is clear that that part 'with person' is removed from impersonal verbs and infinitives: therefore, these are not verbs. It is asked, in this connection, what it is that Donatus denies in the negative, 'neither,' when he states that the verb signifies action or passion, or neither. If it be said that he denies the action or the passion this does not appear to be true, since it is impossible for a verb to be without action or passion. Therefore, he denies the signifying.

The writer now suggests a plausible interpretation of Donatus' definition of the verb: "If, rather, it be said that the verb should be understood in the sense of signifying action transitively, or passion transitively, or neither, that is to say (signifying) neither action transitively nor passion transitively, but without qualification, this explanation appears to be made rationally enough."

Though this interpretation suggests a way out of the difficulty, the writer cannot accept this interpretation, so he now enters upon a metaphysical analysis of the problem: "This, however, (i.e., explanation) can not be maintained, since, as Peter Helias and (the Catholicon?) state, 'neither' denies the substance, though not the accident. The action and passion, nevertheless, may well be the substantial forms of the verb, notwithstanding that transitive action and transitive passion are accidental forms. Accordingly, it (i.e. 'neither') is not used in the sense of denying them." [18]

By way of conclusion, consider an introductory commentary of John Seward. Dedicated to Master John Eyton, canon of the Augustinian monastery at Repton, this opening treatise is entitled *Compendium Seward super modis significandi essentialibus et speciebus partium singularium*. [19] Seward begins with a consideration of substance and accidents. When he has satisfied himself as to the philosophical foundation of his treatise, he proceeds to discuss the parts of speech. In common with the other grammarians so far considered, Seward is concerned primarily with the scientific aspects of grammar. The noun, for instance, is said to signify quality, that is, the noun signifies the thing it stands for or the concept of that thing in such a way as to distinguish that thing from any other thing. This is the way of signifying by quality and by distinguishing. This way is similar, he says, to determining the apprehension in the mind (*per modum determinate apprehencionis in anima*), since quality determines and distinguishes things from their opposites.[20]

In the latter part of his treatise Seward applies this principle of definition to each of the parts of speech. As Boethius expressed this principle, every part of speech signifies by way of habit (*habitus*) or by way of becoming (*fieri*). In the first instance it is by way of something distinguished, that is, a noun; in the second it is by way of something not distinguished but capable of being so, namely, a pronoun. In Aristotle's words, in definitions of things that can be defined, the accidents should not enter into the description. Only the essentials that pertain to the nature and species of the thing in question should enter.[21]

The author is now ready to define each part of speech according to kind and essential differences. A noun, for example, is a part of speech signifying a mental concept by way of habit already distinguished, whereas a pronoun signifies a mental concept by way of habit that can be distinguished by relation or derivation. A verb signifies a mental concept by way of change and becoming originating from another (*per modum fluxus et fieri dicibilis de alio*). A conjunction likewise signifies a mental concept by connecting what are different. The author also includes the interjection among the parts of speech, since it signifies a mental concept by way of affecting (the mind). He concludes this summary by observing that these definitions correctly include the kind (*genus*) as well as the essential differences. On the other hand, they exclude those accidentals which have found their way into definitions of Priscian, Donatus and other grammarians.[22]

The foregoing commentaries of a few grammarians have been dwelt upon because they clearly reveal the pre-occupation of their authors with logical and metaphysical questions. It is difficult for them not to regard Latin grammar as a speculative subject, a science that can be deduced from principles. The grammarians are not primarily interested in the Latin usages that an authority such as Priscian furnishes in abundance, but the extent to which his definitions can stand up to their dialectical and metaphysical analysis.

It is not the art of letters that commands their attention but philosophy itself.

While the search for accurate definitions evidently attracted a number of grammarians, it did not necessarily involve the kind of philosophical questions considered above. The search sometimes consisted of the distinguishing of terms; an example is provided by one writer's efforts to distinguish the three Latin words, *inter*, *intra*, and *infra*:

In what respect do *inter*, *intra*, *infra* differ? *Inter*, as Papias says, signifies distance of place or time between two extremes, as 'between the temple and the altar,' 'between the Pasch and Pentecost.' *Intra*, however, signifies an included place as opposed to *extra*, which signifies an excluded place, as 'the citizens live within the walls, but the scholars outside.' *Infra*, on the other hand, signifies a place beneath, as opposed to *supra* which signifies a place above, as 'the sun rotates above the moon but the moon beneath the sun.' No one then should say, *Sum infra muros civitatis* unless he lies buried within or under the very walls, as Hugutio says in the verse:

Inter significat tempus spaciumve locale
Temporibusve locis proprie stabit sociale
Nos edes intra stamus vos luditis extra
Sol currit supra lunam que currit et infra.[23]

A second example is a catechetical device, beginning with the question *Es tu clericus?*, which deals with the difference between the terms *clericus*, *litteratus*, and *liber vir*. A man may not be a clerk and yet be literate; a free man becomes literate from the imposition of hands; another is truly literate because of his learning. What, then, is a clerk? A clerk is one who is literate, morally good, and both constituted and consecrated in holy orders.[24]

This preoccupation with the precise meaning of terms is nowhere better illustrated than in the interesting collection of material contained in *MS Harl. 5751*. The grammatical parts are so closely interwoven with what may be termed an elementary course in moral theology and philosophy that it is difficult to classify the book exclusively under one heading. The definition of terms receives a detailed treatment in the form of *distinctiones*, comprising the various ways in which a single term can signify.[25] The following are a few examples.

Light (*lux*) can be posited (*ponere*) in four ways (*modis*): first, it is spoken of as Christ, as in the words, "I am the light of the world"; second, it is identified with the apostle, "you are the light of the world"; third, it is life, as "light descended upon them"; and fourth, it means brightness (*claritas*), as "let perpetual light shine upon them."²⁶ So, too, with fire (*ignis*), which is employed in three ways. There is celestial fire, the fire of hell, and material fire. Celestial fire illuminates but does not burn, the fire of hell burns but does not illuminate, while material fire both illuminates and burns.²⁷

The word king (*rex*) can also be used in three different ways: first of all, in the sense of prince (*princeps*), as "Richard, by the grace of God, king of England, is the prince"; second, the term is equivalent to king (*prelatus*), as in the case of David and the kings; while third, it refers to one who is his own master, as over many kings and prophets: "I see what you do not see."²⁸

A school term is also considered in this collection of *distinctiones*. Disputation (*disputacio*) is defined as "a contest between two clerks." It can be posited in three ways: for the purpose of putting questions, obtaining instruction, and for the sake of learning.²⁹ Finally, the word bread (*panis*) can be employed in no less than seven different ways: first, in the sense of material bread (*panis corporalis*), as in the words, "our daily bread"; second, as spiritual bread, as "man shall eat the bread of angels"; third, as an equivalent to teaching (*doctrina*), "He gave them the bread of life"; fourth, in the sense of repentance (*penitencia*), as "in my bread of tears day and night"; fifth, in reference to the body of Christ, "the bread which I will give you is My flesh"; sixth, referring to Christ himself, "I am the living bread which came down from heaven"; and finally *panis* is equivalent to a word, as in the Gospel, "Not on bread alone does man live but on every word that proceeds from the mouth of God."³⁰

The *distinctio* usually finishes with a verse or two to facilitate the memory; that for *panis*, for example, is as follows:

Panis corporis est panis spiritualis
Panis doctrina panis penitencia fertur
Est verbum Christus sic eucharistia panis.³¹

With sacred scripture forming the principal source of most of these *distinctiones*, it is not surprising that the different ways of interpreting the Bible are also discussed. The writer enumerates four ways in which sacred scripture can be construed, namely, historically, allegorically, tropologically, and anagogically. The historical sense narrates something as actually taking place, as, for instance, the noun "Jerusalem," which refers to an actual city. Allegorically, Jerusalem is spoken of as one thing but understood as another, as our crossing over to it as a haven or refuge; in this case Jerusalem is a figure of the church militant. The tropological sense signifies behaviour for whatever is said or done, as Jerusalem as a type of the faithful soul. We are speaking in an anagogical mode when for the thing said or done we signify heavenly things; Jerusalem is thus considered as a likeness of the church triumphant.

The four-fold sense of scripture is illustrated in a similar manner by the word "temple." Historically, this is the house that Solomon built. Allegorically, the term refers to the body of our Lord, as when in the Gospel of St John our Lord says, "destroy this temple," that is, this living church (*ecclesiam presentem*); moreover, the apostle says, "The temple of the Lord is holy, which you are." Tropologically, the term refers to whosoever is faithful, for the apostle says to such as these, "Do you not know that your bodies are the temple of the Holy Spirit?" Anagogically, the term is used with reference to the fatherland of heaven, where, as it is said, there is a holy temple like to Jerusalem.[32]

It remains to explain the names of these four senses. "History," the writer continues, is, according to Isidore, "the narration of an event by means of which those things that have taken place are deduced by interpretation, and the word itself derives from *hesteron*, to perceive on all sides." According to Donatus, allegory is "a likeness or mystery by which one thing is said and something else understood," the term deriving from *alleon*, "another," and *gore*, "to speak." Tropology is a saying that has been altered to edify the soul, from *tripos*, a "change in speech." Anagogy, according to Brito, is an expression treating of earthly matters in order to convey an understanding of that Jerusalem that is our mother; from *ana*, "on high," and *goge*, "a giving."[33]

The most noteworthy feature of the entire book is the economy of words. Short, pointed definitions and moral maxims abound. "Study," says Boethius in his *Consolation of Philosophy*, "is the earnest application to the performance of something with good will." Learning, according to Sallust, is "an incorruptible treasure, the ornament of virtue, and the purifier of defects." St Paul says that "life is love; therefore, death is hatred."[34]

Probably the best example of this brevity of expression is a kind of theological summary that is quite extensive and may be illustrated by the following examples: In enumerating the clerical orders the writer briefly relates each of them to a historical incident related in the Gospels:

Hostiarius:	when He (Our Saviour) broke the gates of hell
Lector:	when He read the book of Isaias

Exorcist:	when He drove the demon into the sea
Acolitus:	when He said, 'I am the light of the world.'
Subdiaconus:	when He changed water into wine
Diaconus:	when He washed the feet of His disciples
Sacerdos:	when He blessed and broke the five loaves of bread.[35]

The daily round of duties of the young clerk is similarly arranged under the title of *opera clericorum*. He is to rise in the morning, wash his hands, sing the hours, keep to his studies, refrain from gorging himself, put up with hunger, and be reserved with women. The whole program is comprised in the following:

surgere mane
manus lavare
horas cantare
studium frequentare
ventrem non implere
famem sustinere
mulierem timere.[36]

Four signs (*signa*) distinguish the clerk: the performance of good, the avoidance of evil, his saying what he knows and asking what he does not know:

ut impleret bona
ut prohiberet mala
ut diceret quod sciret
ut interrogaret quod nesciret.[37]

Four virtues are proper to him as a clerk: chastity of the flesh, humility of heart, kindness in speech, stability in God:

Castitas in carne
Humilitas in corde
Benignitas in ore
Stabilitas in Deo.[38]

Several topics pertaining to the Christian life are summarized in like manner. The *Pater Noster* is divided into seven petitions following St Augustine:

sanctificetur nomen tuum
adveniat regnum tuum

fiat voluntas tua
panem nostrum cotidianum da nobis hodie
et dimitte nobis debita nostra
et ne nos inducas in temptacione
sed libera nos a malo.

Each of these petitions corresponds to the request for a gift. These gifts are properly known as the gifts of the Holy Spirit that are bestowed on the recipient of the sacrament of confirmation. They are *donum sapiencie, intellectus, consilii, fortitudinis, sciencie, pietatis, timoris*. To these are added three more gifts: forgiveness of the penitent, mercy to the suppliant, and eternal rewards for the faithful servant.

The number seven is pursued still further. Seven virtues are implanted in the heart of one reciting the Lord's Prayer: the virtues of sobriety and temperance, chastity, mercy, honesty, equity (*equitas*), friendship, and humility. There are also seven merits to be derived from the recitation of this prayer: beatific vision, apotheosis (*deificacio*), merciful disposition (*misericordia passiva*), abundance, consolation, possession of the earth, and inheritance of the kingdom of heaven.[39]

Near the end of the manuscript are a number of theological terms that the writer is content to leave variously defined. Confession, for instance, is defined by St Augustine as "a declaration (*sermo*) through which a hidden disease is made manifest in the hope of forgiveness." Gregory defines it as "a detection of sins," while "other authorities" speak of it as "a very satisfactory declaration of sins before a priest."[40] Hope is "the certain expectation of future happiness resulting from the grace of God and personal merit," or it is "the boldness of mind arising from the liberality of God in granting eternal life for faithful service."[41] Virtue is considered "the firm habit of the soul," "a profound respect for nature," "a love of good conduct," "the veneration of divinity or honesty," "honour towards men," or "the reward of everlasting happiness."[42]

From the foregoing it can be seen that *MS. Harl. 5751* is a handbook displaying everywhere that brevity and systematic arrangement so convenient for the memory. While a large number of the authorities quoted are from the classical period, there is no evidence that they have been studied at first hand. What has been extracted from these authors is intended primarily to cultivate discretion and exactitude in the employment of terms, together with the inculcation of moral and religious principles. Even the Bible, extensively quoted, need not have been studied at first hand to produce this kind of summary.[43] Scripture, the classics, and the Fathers all contribute to this compilation, but the net result is a textbook of elementary theology that is a practical application of grammatical principles.

There are several miscellaneous items included in the grammatical manuscripts noted above; those items need not be considered here. One of these, however, may have served as a vocabulary of geographical centres. It is given below because it may reflect the places familiar to a schoolboy in fifteenth century London:[44]

Amiens	Britain	Lombardy
Orleans	Burgundy	Shaftesbury
Dublin	Scotland	Leicester
St Albans	Cornwall	Essex
Worcester	Athens	Sussex
Verona	Wales	Middlesex
Ely	Salisbury	Norfolk
Lynne	York	Malmesbury
Gloucester	Sandwich	Peterborough
Warwick	Dover	Bury St Edmunds
Bath	Winchester	St Neots
Ireland	Gascony	

The final item that deserves attention is a specialized application of grammar to the understanding of the divine office: a work entitled *Exposicio verborum difficilium* which belonged to John Warkeworth, master of St Peter's College, Cambridge, in the late fifteenth century.[45] A brief introduction sets forth clearly the purpose of the entire book:

The Reader (Lector) is to blame if the Lesson is not prepared beforehand; if you first read over your lesson you will easily see that it presents little difficulty.

Here begins the explanation of difficult words pertaining to the hymns proper to the season; and also the shortening and lengthening of doubtful accents, which can be a cause of laughter to those hearing them, or embarrassment to the readers, even a source of disturbance.[46]

The author is referring to the public recitation of the canonical hours by the college of St Peter. His first explanation is naturally enough that of the first Sunday of Advent, the beginning of the liturgical year. He begins as follows: "The vision of Isaias the prophet, the son of Amos. *Isaias* is to be understood in the sense of 'saviour,' and rightly so, since by his prophesying, he preached the salvation of the world and the sacraments of the Lord more than did the other prophets. *Juda* here stands for the land of the Jews, and is accented on the last syllable."[47] What is worth noting here is the identification of the prophet's name with a particular historical fact. The etymology, in other words, has an historical basis. Another example is the name of Job, which is understood to mean "sorrowing" (*dolens*) because of that prophet's tribulation of body and spirit.[48]

Not all the terms are explained so concisely in a historical setting. Names of saints, for instance, are sometimes credited with several possible etymological interpretations. The writer evinces no desire to accept one at the expense of the others. The word *Thomas*, for example, is explained in the sense of being cut off from others by his words, example, and suffering, or of displaying outstanding manliness in resisting the king. This last is intended as a historical etymology, but five other possible meanings are also included, such as the derivation of the name from *thomos*, that is, a "division," since Thomas "was set aside from the vanities of the world."[49] Similarly, the expression of praise in the Mass, *Alleluia*, "is interpreted in many ways." After relating its first recorded use in the New Testament, that by St John in the Apocalypse with reference to the angels praising God, the author proceeds to discuss the various interpretations of the term that have been given it by Saints Jerome, Ambrose, and Gregory.[50]

The grammatical approach to these liturgical terms may be illustrated by the exposition of the opening verse of the gospel of Holy Saturday, which describes Mary Magdalen's visit to the tomb of her Lord. The verse is: *Vespere autem Sabbati que lucescit in prima sabbati: venit Maria Magdalene et altera Maria videre sepulcrum*:[51] "This 'Vespere,' indeclinable, is the hour between day and night. The relative 'que' does not refer to 'vespere' but to the hour which is understood in 'vespere,' since 'vespere' is here used adverbially and does not retain its force as a noun. *In prima sabbati*, that is, on the first day of the week." This is straight syntax and could find its way into any grammar lesson. Since the author is explaining this passage primarily for the benefit of clerks who will be called upon to read it aloud in choir, he now explains the stress which should be given to the syllables: "'Vespere autem Sabbati,' that is, the festival day. *Magdalene* is shortened here, and is always shortened when it is substantive. Thus, in saying *Maria Magdalena* it is shortened, but as an adjective it is long and so in the other oblique cases. According to Hugutio and Papias, *Magdalenum* is a certain town from which Mary takes her name, Magdalen. Consequently, it is declined as *Magdalenus, a, um*, and is a possessive noun whose penultimate syllable should be accented in the manner of barbaric words."[52] The author concludes this part of his explanation with some verse to recapitulate the lesson and help the reader to retain it in his memory.

The main purpose of the entire work is referred to from time to time. One footnote expresses the hope that readers "will read better and understand" the lessons so explained.[53] This hope is even more clearly expressed in his remarks concerning the use of non-Latin terms: "On every double feast throughout the year in the Sarum Use, *Kyrie eleison* and *Christe eleison* are said with versicles. The more difficult words of these, as of all the sequences of the Sarum Use which are read in church, are explained, so that both readers and celebrants will be moved with greater devotion towards God."[54]

In the grammatical material so far described, one feature that is never entirely absent is the effort to have the learner reflect in some way upon God's presence or the moral life. This intention is sometimes explicitly stated. One author, for example, explains in a short introduction the various classifications of books, including sacred writings, authentic works, hagiography, and apocryphal books. He remarks that some of the last-mentioned kind contain heresy, whereas others are not only not harmful to one's faith but actually increase it. He assures his readers that he has confined himself to authentic works in compiling his book, and requests the reader to give him no other thought than to beseech God to be merciful to him.[55] The conviction that it is the author's humble duty to be careful to put before his readers only what is consonant with the faith and morally edifying is observed time and again throughout these grammatical treatises.

So much for the details of the Latin program itself. Our notion of the educational theory that underlies the later medieval grammar school can only be determined from a study of the grammar program and the institutions themselves. Apart from a few brief introductions and commentaries on specific treatises, we do not possess anything resembling an educational essay. One interesting and partial exception to this, however, is the compilation of the Benedictine monk, Dom William Chartham of Christ Church, Canterbury, entitled *Speculum Parvulorum*.[56] Since his introduction comes as close as anything we possess to the statement of an educational theory, it is worth paraphrasing.

When Chartham was very young both in years and in wisdom, he tried, with the help of supernatural grace, to fulfill the admonition of the psalmist to refrain from evil and to do good. He took up reading since it enriches a man's mind and draws him away from the world's trifles to the love of God. As to his studies, Chartham continues, he made no attempt to reach the heights of theological speculation, nor did he waste time with either the doubtful assertions of philosophers or those foolish comedies that tend to narrow the mind. He spent his time, on the contrary, in the perusal of devout narratives, including the lives and achievements of the early Fathers, the deeds of the Romans (*Gesta Romanorum*), chronicles, and other works calculated to help a person towards the good life and the salvation of his soul. He has, therefore, put together a number of his favourite selections in this present volume.

Some people, no doubt, in common with those who have no desire to lead young people to God, will question the utility of a book like this by an unknown author. His reply will be that it is an encouragement of goodness and a defence against evil. The actual arrangement of the work is not important, nor does it need a title, which, after all, is only "a distinguishing of diversities," but since the book for that very reason might appear to have little value, he will entitle it *The Mirror of the Poor*. No matter how deficient it may appear to more important and able people, the book will provide examples for the young and ignorant. The author begs his readers, therefore, not to disparage a work intended as a force for good among young people. If any of them should be familiar with its contents, may they not, on that account, despise the small and humble, for it is the Lord himself who protects the young and has regard for the lowly.

Chartham is addressing his book, then, to the child, the child young in wrong-doing, whose tongue speaks wisdom and whose heart is steadfast in patience, who stands to be enlightened by the words of wise men handed down to us for our instruction. Should, however, the child find anything in the book that does not meet with his approval, he is to attribute it to the author's simplicity and commend at least the latter's good will. Let all together thank the Lord, therefore, who conceals his gifts from the wise and prudent and reveals them to little ones.

To make his book easier to read, the author has thought it best to divide it into several sections, each preceded by a table of contents. It has been divided into five parts in honour of the five wounds of Our Saviour suffered upon the cross to make merciful reparation for the sins of our five senses.[57]

Chartham's first book is largely devoted to a doctrinal exposition of the Blessed Sacrament, deriving from the teaching of Pope Innocent III. This discussion is closely bound up with discussion of the Mass itself, in addition to several ecclesiastical institutions, such as the clerical orders, which cannot be divorced from it. Among other matters, the author discusses the historical institution of the Eucharist by Christ himself, the four principal parts of the Mass, whether St Peter first celebrated mass at Antioch, the significance of Christ's words *hoc est enim corpus meum* at the Last Supper, and whether Judas received Holy Communion together with the other apostles.[58] Some questions concerning the Holy Eucharist border on the metaphysical, such as whether the Body of Christ when in one particular place "creates a local difference."[59] Others are theological, as whether bread can be consecrated without the wine or the wine without the bread. He also includes in this part an explanation of the Lord's Prayer,[60] as well as a note exhorting beneficed clerks to perform the obligations of their benefice in the church to which their benefice is attached.[61]

The most striking feature of this first section is the freedom with which such serious and important matters are discussed. Remembering that the author addresses himself mainly to boys, it is remarkable how he raises questions of theological and philosophical content, especially concerning the Mass and the Holy Eucharist. What is characteristic of his approach to these matters is the historical setting in which he considers them. As he has explained in his introduction, he never made any effort at speculation in the higher reaches of theology. He is, however, immersed in sacred scripture, at least in the Gospel narratives. A typical example of his method is his exposition of the very last part of the Mass:

Communion being completed, the celebrant proceeding with his ministers to the altar, bends over to kiss it. Then, raising his hands, he pronounces the last prayer, signifying that final blessing which, it is written, Christ gave to his apostles at his ascension into heaven. For, as Luke recalls, he led them out as far as Bethania, and lifting up his hands, he blessed them. And while he blessed them, it came to pass that he departed from them, and was carried up into heaven. After the priest has given this last greeting to the people, the deacon, in a loud voice, pronounces the *Ite missa est*, in memory of the words to the apostles, 'this Jesus who has been taken up from you into heaven.' The choir responds with a hymn of praise, *Deo gratias*. This recalls the apostles who, adoring the Word, returned to Jerusalem with great joy, praising and blessing God. Take note of this on those days when *Benedicamus Domino, Deo gratias* is said, when a hymn immediately follows and afterwards they are said to bless and praise, etc.[62]

As the author has previously intimated, his divisions of the rest of the work are quite arbitrary. The third part is the one which most resembles the *Gesta Romanorum*, since each narrative is followed by a *reductio*, or moral application. All four of the remaining "books," however, are primarily concerned with affording examples of moral edification; members of the clerical and religious states are quite frequently the subjects of moral narratives. There is the story of a dean who aspired to be bishop of Lyons and afterwards repented;[63] a monk who was spirited away from the dormitory by devils;[64] and a clerk who had a special devotion to the Virgin Mary.[65]

Some of the examples are, on the other hand, moral exhortations rather than narratives. One of these is addressed to preachers, exhorting them to preach the word of God "boldly and devoutly,"[66] while another explains why clerks should not participate in unseemly games.[67] Still others range over a wide variety of topics, such as the dimensions of Noah's Ark,[68] and the question of whether the devil knows the thoughts of men.[69]

Several of the moral examples possess a more local colour. It is related, for instance, how St. Dunstan performed a miracle with two knights,[70] and how St. Bernard was stabbed.[71] Two lepers involved in the life of St Brigid are described,[72] as well as St Patrick's purgatory in Ireland,[73] and several incidents in the life of St Edmund.[74] There is an account of the death of King William Rufus,[75] of a man in London in the throes of despair,[76] a sinful woman in Berkeley,[77] and how the devil went to confession to the bishop of Lincoln, Robert Grosseteste.[78]

Though Chartham's book has little direct relation to the grammatical treatises described above, his underlying educational thought is similar in that his main concern is the moral life. His sources, moreover, show quite clearly how little of antiquity enters into his educational background. What he has really compiled is not another version of the *Gesta Romanorum*, but what may correctly be called *Gesta Christianorum*. Like the grammarians, he has gone mainly to medieval Christendom for the basis of his work.

The foregoing material, however marginal it may be regarded with respect to the Latin program of the grammar schools, at least lends no support to Leach's emphasis on the use of classical sources in the curriculum. Several of the excerpts do testify, nevertheless, to one feature that Leach recognized – the underlying religious and moral philosophy that gave ordinary class exercises a distinctive tone. Leach would have noticed, too, that whereas some of the treatises were evidently intended for "clerical" students preparing for the diocesan priesthood or the religious life, others were the shared experience of many whose clerical status might be construed in the widest possible sense. As such, the treatises provided the latter with the only kind of learning that Leach believed the proper basis for a "school." It is, nonetheless, the dominant argumentative aspect of the material in question that does most to validate Leach's opinion that medieval education was mainly a training in logic. While Leach might not have given his stamp of approval unreservedly to the more speculative features of Priscian and Helias, he would certainly have applauded the efforts of teachers and at least the more senior students in the grammar schools to master what he regarded as especially useful – dialectical skill. Much of this material, therefore, would likely have struck Leach as all of a piece with a passage he was always fond of quoting – Fitzstephen's description of the scholastic exercises in the schools of twelfth century London.

CHAPTER EIGHT

Educational Institutions: The Religious Orders and the Diocesan Clergy

Having described the program of Latin grammar, it remains to consider the educational institutions for which this program was intended. It has been noted above that while some of the grammatical material was apparently intended expressly for clerks proceeding to holy orders or aspirants to the religious life, much of it is of a more general nature and was included in the curriculum of urban grammar schools. What characterizes the entire program is its predominantly clerical nature. One is left with the impression that most, if not all, grammar students shared in a common training, irrespective of the particular professions they intended to follow. In the following pages I will attempt to determine how far this impression is correct.

Leach's insistence on the importance of a "real public grammar school," to the exclusion of any educational institution connected with the monastic orders, confuses the nature and purpose of the study of Latin grammar. For one thing, Leach was inclined to minimize, if not altogether ignore, the considerable numbers of young men who learned Latin precisely because they were preparing to enter the religious state with either the monks or the friars. Moreover, he created the impression that since the monks were not teachers in the grammar schools, they played no part at all in the conduct of "public" education. The first point, therefore, to be considered is the role of the religious orders in the promotion of Latin studies on the grammar school level.

No survey of the educational institutions of England in the fourteenth and fifteenth centuries that did not include the religious orders could be considered adequate. Every aspirant to the religious life had to possess some knowledge of Latin, the language employed in the daily liturgy and in the constitutions of his respective order.

The immediate problem is to determine from the scattered evidence available what standards in Latin training were expected of the prospective candidate before his reception, and what provisions, if any, were made by the order to develop and continue this instruction after the candidate's admission.

For the purpose of this survey, the religious can be classified broadly into the monks, the canons, and the friars. Only the largest groups will be considered, that is, the Benedictine monks, the Augustinian canons, and the Franciscan and Dominican friars. The statistical evidence we possess establishes the total number of male religious in England in the period of the poll tax, 1377–81, as around 8,500, including approximately 2,000 Benedictine monks, 1,600 Augustinian canons, 1,150 Franciscan friars, and 950 Dominicans. The one feature that characterizes all these orders of religious is that they had attained their greatest numbers before the fourteenth century. The Benedictines and Augustinians appear to have experienced a decline before the Great Plague of the mid-century. Between the poll tax and the dissolution, the orders of friars either showed little increase or declined, while the general population appears to have increased by about fifty per cent. Some idea of what happened may be obtained from observing the foundation of new houses: of some 240 friaries in medieval England, only about 31 were founded in the half century preceding the Great Plague, 8 between 1350 and 1400, and 1 between 1400 and 1476.[1] The religious orders, therefore, included an impressive number of young religious who received training in Latin – however narrowly professional it might be. In the period under consideration, however, this kind of life was attracting a smaller number of young men than had been the case in the thirteenth century.

With regard to the Benedictine monks, it is clear that, quite apart from any tradition of humanist learning, instruction in Latin would have been directed towards the public recitation and understanding of the divine office. In 1324 a young candidate was refused admission to the monastery of Christ Church, Canterbury, because he lacked skill in singing and reading, that is, the ability to participate intelligently in the daily round of liturgy. He was promised further consideration, provided he undertook to learn Latin grammar and the essential skills.[2] The prior and convent of Worcester even found it necessary to refuse a young clerk recommended by the Bishop of Worcester: "After examining him in literature and other things, as is our custom, we have found him incompetent to discharge the usual duties due to our church in divine service. Therefore, to our regret, we cannot in this instance comply with your appeal; we are prevented by the insufficient qualifications of him for whom the request is made."[3]

Whatever training in Latin these two large monasteries provided for their younger members, it is clear that they expected the more elementary part of it to be learned outside the monastery before admission. That such standards were not enforced, at least for a time, may be seen from the visitation of Hyde Abbey in February 1386 by William Wykeham, bishop of Winchester. In his injunctions to the abbot, the bishop points out that some of the monks do not understand what they read and sing in the divine office. He observes that they do not even read aloud correctly, mistaking short accents for long ones, and so forth. Such lack of understanding of sacred scripture, he remarks, easily leads to violations of its precepts. The abbot is ordered, therefore, to arrange for a competent master to instruct the unlearned monks in *primitivae scientiae*, to the end that they might better contemplate the mysteries of sacred scripture.[4] By *primitivae scientiae* the bishop evidently means Latin grammar and especially prosody.

Instruction in Latin grammar was provided for in the educational reforms included in the constitutions for the Benedictine monks drawn up by Pope Benedict XII in the summer of 1336. Several monastic cathedrals had already experienced the advantage of having some of their members trained at the university and it was training in Latin grammar that laid the foundation for these higher studies. A master was to be appointed, therefore, in every monastic establishment to teach the resident monks the *primitivae scientiae*. These "elementary sciences" were defined as grammar, logic, and philosophy. It was strictly enjoined, moreover, that these studies were to be conducted within the monastery, and that secular persons were not to be admitted to these classes.[5]

The fact that seculars were to be excluded from the classes of monks learning the elementary sciences raises the question of the extent to which the monks were involved in the education of seculars. The monastic almonry schools had made their appearance at least by the fourteenth century. The register of Abbot John Whethamstede contains a short list of the statutes of the almonry school attached to the monastery of St Albans. Drawn up on the feast of St Ambrose, 4 April 1339, these are entitled "the manner of life of the poor scholars of the almonry." They prescribe that a scholar's residence in the almonry is not to exceed the five years considered sufficient for the learning of Latin grammar. On their admission to the school, the scholars are to receive the broad tonsure of the choristers, and thereafter their hair is to be cut after the manner of clerks.

Every day each scholar is to say matins of Our Lady for his own intentions and every feast day the seven psalms for the monastery and its founders.[6] These few provisions reveal the essential nature of this kind of establishment: the almonry school is designed to provide food and lodging, together with suitable moral training, for a poor boy capable of profiting from study. The manner in which a boy could obtain a place in an almonry school is illustrated by a letter written in 1332 by Richard, prior of Christ Church, Canterbury, to Queen Philippa:

Very dear Lady, I received your letters on the 22nd of February, by one Richard of Bedingfield, [asking] that I and my Convent, out of respect and charity, would receive him into our Almonry, and that he might be supported as are other poor scholars of his condition. Know, Madame, that I have willingly received him into our said Almonry, and if he will but apply himself diligently to learning, he will, out of love to you, be the more respected.[7]

The kind of testimonial that a boy could earn through diligent application to learning is seen in the letter from the prior of Worcester to the abbot of Westminster in 1324, regarding the application of a young clerk, Robert de Henleye, to be received into the Benedictine Order at Westminster Abbey. The prior writes that Robert, the bearer of the letter, has been found "during his stay at Worcester at an earlier date, to be well mannered, peaceful, quiet." The prior has no doubt that "starting from so virtuous a beginning, his character will justify the hopes we form of him."[8]

The reference to "scholars of the almonry," or the almonry school, does not necessarily mean that the grammar master taught these boys within the almonry or that his teaching duties were confined to them. Such an arrangement existed in some monasteries, as at Westminster Abbey and possibly at Christ Church, Canterbury.[9] In 1448 a John Downham was licensed by the prior of Ely to teach grammar to five poor boys in a proper schoolroom "within the Grammar School of the Monastery;" and in a room within the monastery he was to teach the "junior brethren," an arrangement evidently in keeping with the insistence on separation of young monks and seculars.[10] In many places, however, the almonry scholars attended the city grammar school, as they did at York and Worcester.[11] The duties of the almoner of St Albans included the provision of a fit grammar master for the town school with the consent of the archdeacon, and also the payment of 26s. 8d. to the same master for teaching the boys of the almonry.[12] The numbers of boys maintained in a monastic almonry as grammar scholars varied quite considerably. As mentioned above, Ely had five boys in 1448, Reading maintained ten in 1345–46, while Westminster had twenty-eight in 1385–86.[13]

There is no known instance of a monk teaching grammar to almonry scholars in the fourteenth and fifteenth centuries in England. Invariably a secular clerk appears to have been employed. Possibly owing to this circumstance, it seems that outsiders were sometimes admitted to the classes of the almonry school. In 1439 the mayor and six councillors were deputed by the Coventry city council to discuss the problem of schools with the prior of Coventry Cathedral. They agreed to the prior conducting a school of grammar "to teach his brethren and children of the almonry." They wanted him to understand, though, that every man of the city of Coventry was free to send his child to whatever grammar teacher he pleased. The implication is that the prior had attempted to enforce, or at least to encourage, the attendance at his school of boys living within the city, to the exclusion of whatever other schools might be set up within Coventry.[14]

In 1431 the abbot of St Augustine's monastery in Canterbury obtained papal licence to build within the monastic grounds, or in some place close by, a school for the teaching of grammar. The licence granted the monks' request that several groups of students be provided for: the poor boys nourished with the alms of the monastery, students at the almonry school properly so-called; "lay" scholars who wished to attend, presumably boys living in the city of Canterbury and vicinity; and other "very poor people," probably adults, who desired this instruction. A suitable salary was to be provided for the master or rector of the school from the goods of the monastery.[15]

The only other official connection commonly existing between the monks and the grammar schools derived from the obligation incumbent upon some monasteries to appoint the masters and maintain their jurisdiction and privileges. Such a responsibility existed in those schools where the episcopal and archidiaconal jurisdiction had been transferred to the abbot, as at St Albans, or to some monastic obedientiary, as at Beccles, where the school was in the collation of the chamberlain of Bury St Edmunds.[16] This kind of educational responsibility was not, of course, restricted to the black Benedictine monks. The patronage of the school at Melton Mowbray, to cite one instance, belonged to the Cluniac and alien priory of Lewes.[17]

Like the Benedictines, the Augustinian canons were the subject of constitutions issued in 1339 under Pope Benedict XII. They provided for each group of young religious to be placed under a suitable master who would teach the "elementary sciences." A century later, in 1434, the Augustinian canons met in chapter at Northampton. The delegates noted that "in these days in several monastic centres our young religious are extremely lazy, flighty and very dissolute." To effect a remedy, the chapter ordained that, in keeping with the constitutions of 1339, their youthful members be put to "honest study" by their superiors. This chapter ordained, too, that a master be appointed to teach each group of young religious the "elementary sciences," especially grammar.[18]

Some indication of how such legislation worked in practice is afforded by a study of the visitation records of religious houses in the diocese of Lincoln only a few years after the Northampton chapter. Bishop Gray began his visitations of the houses in 1440. In that year his injunctions at the Augustinian priory of Newnham quite expressly stipulated that there be maintained in the priory a teacher "who shall instruct and inform the canons in the elementary branches of knowledge." Moreover, four "teachable children" were to be maintained by the alms of the priory and taught along with the canons. This arrangement, incidentally, seems to have permitted that mingling of the young religious with almonry boys forbidden in Benedictine monasteries.[19]

In the same year, the bishop visited the monastery at Thornton. A Brother John Hulle confided to him that "there were aforetime in the almonry twelve or fourteen poor clerks nurtured therein, who served the canons at the celebration of masses; and now, by reason of the lack of such boys very many masses are omitted, even a hundred in the year."[20] This testimony confirmed that of Brother Thomas Gartone, who had stated that whereas there used to be a man responsible "for teaching the clerks and young canons in the elementary branches of knowledge, now there was no such person."[21]

In the same year, at the Augustinian priory of Kyme, the prior stated that the young canons were instructed in the "elementary forms of knowledge" in the parish church, which at Kyme was in the nave of the priory church.[22] Even here, however, the educational arrangements were not entirely satisfactory, since a Brother John Sotertone stated that Master Thomas Kyngtone would not instruct the novices in grammar unless "he may have more for his pains than the resources of the same novices can supply."[23] In December 1440, at the monastery of Blessed Mary of the Meadow in Leicester, the abbot acknowledged that no teacher of grammar was being maintained, either in the monastery for the instruction of the novices and younger canons, nor in the town of Leicester itself, "for the instruction both of the clerks of the almonry and of others of the country round."[24] At the priory of Dunstable, the prior admitted that no teacher was kept to instruct the canons in grammar and as a consequence "they do not understand what they read."[25]

There is, finally, the instructive entry from Newnham Priory, which in 1442 underwent its second visitation in two years. On the first occasion, Bishop Gray had ordered the priory to engage a teacher for the instruction of the young canons in the "elementary branches of knowledge." At this second visitation, Bishop Alnwick singled out a Brother John Kempstone as being "almost unlettered," remarking that he "understands not what he reads, nor does he work to acquire knowledge." Another member of the house, Brother William Wolastone, stated that there was no teacher in grammar to instruct the canons, and, as a result, "they are almost nothing but laymen, and because of this they pay no attention to books."[26] In his injunctions to the prior, the bishop pointed out that "certain canons ... are so unlettered and almost witless that they barely read, and what they read they do not understand, and so are rendered profitless and unfit for study and contemplation." Before the next feast of Easter, then, and under pain of specific penalties, the prior was to provide a serviceable teacher to instruct and inform such canons in grammar. The teacher was to receive his food and stipend from the house and from his pupils.[27]

It appears, then, that the arrangements for the scholars of almonries in the houses of the Augustinian canons were for the most part not unlike those obtaining among the Benedictine monks. Where there was a public grammar school, as at Leicester, the almonry boys went to class along with the boys of the city. Where there was no such school or where a parish school would not provide all the grades of Latin instruction, as at Newnham, Thornton, or Kyme, the almonry scholars were taught in a school of their own or along with the young canons. It is also clear that promising almonry scholars could and did become canons. In giving evidence of the decline of the almonry school at Thornton, Brother Thomas Gartone stated that he himself had been one of the boys maintained out of the monastic alms.[28] At the visitation of Leicester, Bishop Gray, recalling the custom of boys being bred and nourished from the monastic alms, observed that the more deserving among them ordinarily were chosen to be canons of the same monastery. He, therefore, commanded the abbot to see to it that boys were admitted to the almonry at once. The abbot was not to receive any presents or goods from them, however freely offered, and was to select them without any undue favouritism. There were to be at least sixteen of these boys.

They were to be "capable, serviceable and teachable," and were to mind nothing else but "their learning and their service in church."[29] In this connection, Dom David Knowles points out that, whatever the limitations on their numbers, a fairly large group of almonry boys was needed to serve the private masses of the monks, and these clerks probably became monks far more often than the records suggest.[30]

Like the black monks, the canons held the collation of some of the urban grammar schools, such as the one in Leicester, while the school of Derby was under the jurisdiction of Darley Abbey.[31] The Augustinians were not the only canons to possess such collation of schools. The school of Gloucester, for example, was in the patronage of the Premonstratensian canons of Llanthony Abbey.[32] Between 1221 and 1290 the four principal orders of friars – the Dominicans, Franciscans, Carmelites, and Augustinians – had established houses of study at both Oxford and Cambridge. This fact alone would assume quite an extensive system of Latin instruction, at least for some of the younger members of the order destined to specialize later in theology. Moreover, the Augustinian chapter held at Venice in 1332 appears to assume the presence in the order of young friars not sufficiently instructed in Latin to proceed directly to a *studium grammaticale*. This being so, the order had to undertake responsibility for their more rudimentary as well as advanced Latin training. This raises the question of the recruiting system of the friars. Some parliamentary legislation in England has a bearing on this subject.

In 1402 Parliament legislated against the recruiting practices of the friars in England. It was henceforth forbidden to the Friars Minor, the Augustinians, the Friars Preachers, and the Carmelites to receive into their respective orders any boy who had not begun his fourteenth year without the consent of the boy's parents, relatives, responsible friends, or tutors.[33] This piece of legislation directed against the friars is not an isolated one but it serves to focus attention on the extent to which they provided instruction in Latin grammar. The fact that the friars are accused of receiving into their ranks boys younger than fourteen years of age without regard to the wishes of their relatives may imply that the friars conducted grammar schools for prospective members of their order. (Despite the tenor of the legislation, it is to be observed that with the consent of the responsible people the friars might continue to receive these younger boys into their ranks.) Beyond this probability, the evidence does not go. There is no record of a friar actually teaching in a grammar school of a town, parish, or monastery. Whatever evidence there is for secular students having been admitted to a grammar school intended primarily for young friars comes from places other than England.[34]

It is of interest to note, however, that some friars did undertake to conduct schools but were unable to realize their plans. In 1349 the Friars of the Holy Cross obtained a licence to acquire a residence and property in Wotton-Under-Edge to be held, not only for celebrating divine service, but also for maintaining free schools in the town. Probably the Great Plague interfered with this arrangement, since no more is heard about it.[35]

The relation of the religious orders to education in later medieval England has been briefly summarized to help correct a few of the misleading impressions that resulted from Leach's efforts to stamp out the tradition that the medieval schools were monastic. Leach tended to ignore the educational aspect of the regular clergy, and, in the case of the Benedictine monks, also underestimated the rôle of the almonry schools. More justifiable, as we have seen, is his main contention that the secular clergy were the principal agents in education and the only ones deserving of any serious attention. It is this role of the secular clergy in education that will now be considered.

It must be observed at the outset that, as in the case of the religious orders, Leach is not especially interested in the training of the young man who was specifically preparing for the different orders of the priesthood per se. What he is concerned with is the extent to which training in Latin helped to provide a much broader group of persons with the essential skills to assume a range of "clerical" positions in both church and state. In this connection Leach finds that two institutions in particular made adequate provision for this – cathedrals and collegiate churches. There has been no basic disagreement over Leach's survey of the educational activity of the cathedrals. His contention that all collegiate churches maintained grammar schools has, however, come in for serious criticism.

In his review of *The Schools of Medieval England*, A.G. Little pointed out that Leach did not furnish a sufficient number of examples to justify his conclusion that the establishment of a collegiate church always included provision for a school. Moreover, as Little observed, the foundation charters of such churches often make no mention of schools.[36] More recently, in a study of the effects on education of the dissolution of the monasteries and the suppression of the chantries, Joan Simon has also refused to accept Leach's view on this point. In reference to the period 1286–1548, Leach stated that "scarcely a year passed without witnessing the foundation of a college at the university or a collegiate church with its grammar school attached."[37] Like Little, Simon thinks that the evidence adduced is insufficient. She also disagrees on the ground that Leach's arguments "fail to take into account the decline of the Church in the Later Middle Ages."[38] Finally, W.K. Jordan in his study of philanthropy in England adopts the view, though without furnishing details, that the provision for "lay" education in the later Middle Ages was inadequate and that Leach's arguments to the contrary are quite unconvincing.[39]

Both Simon and Jordan are primarily concerned with the extent to which the laity were provided with educational facilities. The principal aim of the next part of the present study is not to assess the actual extent of such provision but to explain why, in order to describe the education of the laity, one must first consider that of the secular clergy.

During the fourteenth and fifteenth centuries the secular clergy of England were the subject of widespread reorganization. About 120 secular colleges were founded between 1300 and 1475, amounting to one and one half times the number of houses established by all the regular orders combined during the same period. This development was fairly consistent, with some forty-four colleges founded in the half century preceding the Great Plague, thirty-five in the second half of the century, and about forty between 1400 and 1475.[40] To what extent this activity represents an actual increase in the number of secular clergy is not known. It is mainly the number and nature of the collegiate foundations that are of importance in the history of education at this period.[41]

The educational aspect of this development can first be seen in the canonical legislation of the fourth Lateran Council of 1215. This legislation provided for a more comprehensive system of teaching than had hitherto obtained. Confirming the aims of previous councils, that of 1215 takes for granted that every cathedral church will provide a competent benefice for a master to teach the cathedral clerks and other poor scholars free of charge. In addition, however, the Council expects as many other churches as can afford to do so to provide for instruction in the faculty of grammar. The masters are to be elected by the bishop and chapter or by the senior and more learned members of the chapter. Finally, each metropolitan church is to provide in a similar manner for a theologian to teach sacred scripture to priests as well as others, and especially that scripture which relates to the cure of souls.[42]

It is not the purpose of this enquiry to determine to what extent this canonical legislation increased educational activity in England, or merely gave expression to existing custom. It has been noted, however, that in those cathedrals that had secular chapters – eight out of seventeen in England – the grammar schools had been established institutions for a long time, while a *theologus* was normally supported not only in the metropolitan centres of Canterbury and

York, but in the secular cathedrals generally. The evidence seems to support the view that the canonical decree of 1215 had scarcely any effect on England, because the English secular cathedrals, at least, had already more than fulfilled the decree.[43]

The most important work of a cathedral or collegiate church was the faithful performance of the divine office. To participate in the office intelligently a clerk had to acquire a knowledge of Latin, the language of the liturgy. It would be difficult to determine with what diligence the study of Latin grammar was pursued among the clerks of a cathedral or collegiate church over a period of time, but the scattered evidence makes it quite clear that all ranks of clerks had their duties to perform in this regard.[44]

The young choristers required special attention. In 1314 at Salisbury, Bishop Simon of Ghent gave rents and tenements to maintain fourteen choristers and a master to teach them grammar.[45] At the collegiate church of Ottery St Mary, in 1342, the choristers were to have a master to teach them grammar within the church precincts.[46] In the visitation of Chichester Cathedral by Bishop Reade in 1403, the cathedral chancellor was singled out for not providing a diligent master to instruct the choristers in grammar.[47]

The promotion of young clerks to the second form is the subject of a series of entries from a chapter act book of Exeter Cathedral.[48] In the latter part of 1390 four clerks were examined in plain chant and reading – *in cantu et lectura* – and one, in addition, in Latin construction. All were promoted by the cathedral chapter, although one was enjoined to give more attention to his singing.[49]

The York chapter acts record the examination in Latin grammar of eleven young clerks of the cathedral by some of the canons in February, 1421. Three are accounted satisfactory and each is described as *competenter literatus*. Two others are also found to be satisfactory in as much as they attend school regularly. Three are described as *mediocriter literatus* and two of them are ordered to attend class. The remaining three are found to be *illiteratus* and are enjoined to start learning. All, including apparently those described as satisfactory, are instructed by the examiners to attend classes. They are also to take part in the cathedral processions and in those held in the city, and to be present in choir on Sundays and feast days for matins, the capitular mass, and vespers.[50]

Two further examples of capitular examinations at York may also be cited. In 1413 four members of the cathedral chapter were singled out for not making any attempt to understand the lessons of the daily office which they would be called upon to read aloud in choir.[51] Similarly in 1472 some members of the chapter were reported for not learning these lessons by heart as they were bound to do, while many of the vicars were not beyond absenting themselves from choir on a feast that demanded special preparation.[52]

Whatever their precise rank in the cathedral or collegiate church, all the clerks were expected to attend one or other of the schools. In his injunctions to the dean and chapter of Lincoln in 1432, Bishop Gray ordered the poor clerks, or ministers of the church, to attend the schools of either song or grammar on any day which was not a feast day, immediately after they had finished their ministry in the church. In this way they would bring their knowledge of Latin to perfection and deserve to advance to higher studies.[53] At the visitation of the collegiate church of Ripon in 1439, the commissioners of Archbishop Kemp stipulated that "deacons, subdeacons, choristers and clerks" were to attend the schools. If, on being examined with a view to promotion to higher orders, any one was rejected for lack of learning, he was to leave the choir until he had attained the required standard in general deportment and learning.[54]

This brief description of some of the scholastic activities of cathedral and collegiate churches is sufficient to show how a number of boys and young men received training in Latin grammar precisely because their clerical duties required it. This much is fairly obvious. What is not so obvious is the arrangement under which the educational facilities provided for the clerks were shared with other boys and young men who did not perform any ministerial function in the church. This is the point that will now be considered.

In 1384 Lady Katherine Berkeley, showing concern for the study of grammar, which is "the foundation of all the liberal arts" but "daily diminished and brought to naught by want of means," gave lands and tenements to two chaplains to build a school house for a master and two poor grammar scholars at Wotton-Under-Edge in Gloucestershire.[55] The master and the two scholars are to live together as a college. Admission requirements specify that no candidate is to be more than ten years old, though an exception may be made in the case of one who has an evident ability to learn Latin. If accepted, the young scholar may remain in the school for a maximum of six years without being required to pay anything for his board and instruction. The master's teaching, however, is not to be restricted to the two scholars living on the premises. The master is to teach all scholars coming to the school to learn, without demanding any remuneration for his services. It is to be noted that the two clerks are not only students, but, as Leach points out, apparently pupil teachers as well.[56]

In 1410, in the diocese of Coventry and Lichfield, a Dame Isabel bought the perpetual advowson of the parish church of St Bartholomew in Tong and made it into a college. The college was to include a warden, four chaplains, an almshouse for thirteen pour people, and two clerks who were to have at least the first tonsure. One of the chaplains or one of the clerks, if such a chaplain could not be obtained, was to be skilled in reading, plain chant, and grammar. He was to teach Latin to "the clerks and other ministers of the college." As at Wotton-under-Edge, his teaching duties were not to be confined to members of the college; he was to teach "poor youths" from the town of Tong and the neighbouring settlements.[57]

One more example will suffice. In 1463 Bishop John Carpenter of Worcester appropriated the parish church of Clifton to the college at Westbury-on-Trym on the understanding that the dean and chapter of the college would maintain a grammar master on the premises. While the master was to educate and instruct the clerks ministering in the church, his teaching duties also extended to any others who came to him for instruction. As in the instances cited above, he was not to require anything from them in payment for his work.[58]

It is quite clear that in all three of these colleges the teaching of Latin grammar is provided first for the clerks of the colleges. Once the provision is made, however, the same training is extended to any others who wish to benefit from it. In other words, the clerks of the church have to be taught Latin, and in those places where the college itself has to provide the school – presumably where there is no other conveniently near by – the college school is open to "outsiders."

Pertinent to the theme of the reorganization of the secular clergy and the educational developments resulting from it is the institution known as the chantry. The chantry has been called "the most characteristic foundation of the later Middle Ages,"[59] but its educational features, though important, must not be exaggerated.[60] There were a number of parish schools attached to chantries that maintained a chaplain to teach grammar. A few examples will suffice to illustrate their relevance to the present study. In 1432, for instance, John Kemp, Archbishop of York, founded a chantry on his own land in the parish of Wye, county Kent. The chaplains of this new chantry of St Gregory were charged with the sustenance of some choristers and the exhibition of a master in grammar, who was to teach free of charge all those repairing to him and his schools.[61] In 1446 royal licence was granted to Henry, Earl of Northumberland, and William Alnwick, together with Henry Percy, knight, and John Lematon, lawyer, to found a chantry of two chaplains in the chapel of St Michael, Alnwick. One of the chaplains was to teach poor boys in grammar without requiring fees. The cost of the exhibition was to be met by lands and rents that the chaplains could acquire in mortmain to the value of £40 a year, provided they were not held of the king by knight service.[62]

In 1450 royal licence was granted for the foundation of a guild, that of the Holy Trinity in the parish church of St Mary, Chipping Norton, in Oxfordshire. Lands, rents, and possessions were granted in mortmain to provide for the maintenance of two chaplains and a suitable teacher who would instruct in the rudiments of grammar, free of charge, the poor boys and scholars coming to Chipping Norton.[63] In 1451 Thomas Gloucestre, esquire, bequeathed lands in several counties towards the foundation of two chantries, one in London, the other in Gloucester. The latter was in the church of St Nicholas; there the chaplain's obligations included instructing "all persons coming thither, and so desiring, in the faculty of grammar, gratis and without reward." The chaplain was to have a suitable house and a salary of 20 marks.[64]

To consider one further example in more detail, there is the foundation in 1446 by Robert Grayndoore, at Newland, Gloucestershire, of a perpetual chantry in the church of All Saints at the altar of SS John the Baptist and Nicholas.[65] The chantry was to consist of a perpetual chaplain "skilled in the art or science of grammar," together with a clerk of similar qualifications who would teach grammar to all scholars coming to Newland for such instruction.[66] Four pennies were to be charged to each boy learning the alphabet, matins, and the psalter, and eight pennies to each boy learning grammar; the amounts in each case were the maximum allowed to the teacher per term.[67] Classes were to be held continuously from the octave of Easter until the vigil of Pentecost, from the second day after Trinity Sunday to the feast of St Peter in Chains, from the feast of the exaltation of the Holy Cross to the feast of St Thomas, and from the day after Epiphany to Palm Sunday. On one day each week, before breakfast at nine o'clock, all the scholars were to recite the psalm *Deus misereatur nostri*, the *Pater Noster,* and the *Salutacio Angelica* for the soul of the founder, his good estate during his lifetime, and the souls of all the faithful departed. Likewise, on one day at the fifth hour after None and before leaving for supper, the scholars were to say on bended knee the antiphon *Sancta Maria, virgo, intercede*, together with the psalm *De profundis*, and the collect *Inclina aurem tuam*, for the soul of Robert.[68]

It may be noted that the Newland chantry school forms an exception to the principle of gratuitous instruction which is evidently one of the aims of the founders of these chantries. A second feature of these schools is the lack of any specific conditions for admittance, whether of age, locality, or commitment to any particular profession.

In this sense they were truly public schools. It will be useful at this point, therefore, to consider the hospital, another kind of institution in which the educational arrangements were designed for a select group of scholars. The educational aspect is clearly illustrated at the hospital of St John the Baptist in Exeter.

Dated 18 November 1332, the lengthy entry in Bishop John Grandisson's register begins with a tribute to the bishop's predecessor, Walter de Stapledon, who had given such careful attention, Grandisson says, to those weaknesses that bring about widespread and serious losses, chief among them that sickness which had become all too common – the insufficient learning of priests. Rectors of parishes, those exercising cure of souls, and other priests are unfit for higher studies unless they possess a solid foundation in grammar. Grandisson recalls his predecessor's foundation at Oxford, Stapledon Hall, for scholars studying logic. He recalls, too, his provision for the maintenance of boys studying grammar while receiving instruction in morals and in manners (*vita*). For this last, Bishop Stapledon had set aside property near Ernescombe together with the advowson of the local church, the king consigning all this to the master and brethren of the hospital of St John in Exeter.[69]

His predecessor's death having cut short the implementation of this program, Bishop Grandisson now sets about to complete it. He stipulates that the master and brethren of the hospital are to provide accommodation within the hospital precincts for boys learning grammar and for their grammar master. Food, drink, and material for their beds are to be supplied them and each scholar and the master are to receive 5d. every week. On Sundays and feast days the master and his scholars are to be present in the hospital for the canonical hours. Since the work of the grammar master in educating boys in good manners and learning is more exacting than the work of others, he is to be given half a mark in addition to his commons at each of the four terms annually.[70]

The bishop then addresses the selection of the scholars. Two are to be chosen from the archdeaconry of Barnstaple, one of them to be from Ernescombe parish, both if they are thought suitable; one or two will come from the archdeaconry of Totnes, two from Exeter archdeaconry, and one or two from the archdeaconry of Cornwall. Three boys are to be selected from Exeter Cathedral itself, that is, from among the more proficient choristers who either cannot continue in the cathedral choir or do not wish to do so, owing to their change of voice or some other sufficient reason.

With regard to training in Latin, a skilled grammarian – a priest, if he can be obtained – is to be the general master and teacher of the school, taking charge of the boys within the hospital and during class. When the present scholars, on account of their age, on completion of their studies, or for some other good reason, are to be replaced by others, the manner of selecting them shall be as follows: the head master of the Exeter city school shall choose from each of the four archdeaconries four poor boys of upright character who are free, legitimate, and capable of learning Latin grammar. These boys should already know their psalter, as much as can be expected of boys, and plain chant, at least the singing of it for divine service. The master of the city school shall present these boys to the warden of the hospital, who shall admit as many of the more capable ones as he has room for. The scholars shall remain in the hospital for five years while they attend the city grammar schools, unless they complete their studies before that time and are capable of advancing to other liberal sciences, or they decide to enter religion – whatever seems best to them and their friends.[71]

The emphasis by the bishop upon provision for poor boys – poor in the sense that their parents are not able to maintain them away from home for the five years necessary for the complete course in Latin grammar – is unmistakable. Furthermore, these candidates must be worth the trouble – "teachable" and willing to learn. Finally, the stipulation that they be free and legitimate leaves no doubt as to the founder's expectation with regard to at least some of them – promotion to holy orders.[72] It is worth noting that although the scholars are to have their own grammar master, the master of the Exeter city schools exercises jurisdiction. The lessons, even if given by the former, must be supervised by the latter.[73]

The hospital of St Leonard in York also had its educational side. On 2 March 1365, in connection with his visitation of this hospital the previous year, Archbishop Simon Langham, as its chancellor, published an ordinance that, among other matters, dealt with formal instruction in grammar. Choristers ministering in the church and living off the alms of the hospital are to learn grammar during their free time "that they may be an asset to the church."[74] There were no fewer than thirty such choristers in 1376. Although the above source does not itself contain the evidence, it has recently been established that the classes, in both grammar and song, were held at the hospital itself, and were open to others besides choristers, including orphans living on the hospital grounds.[75] This, however, did not apply to the teaching of theology, since the same ordinance goes on to recommend that all hospital chaplains who can profit from it are to attend theological schools in the city.[76]

In 1370 David de Wollore, canon of York and an important royal clerk, made a bequest to the hospital of St John in Ripon, a dependency of Ripon collegiate church. A former warden of the hospital, de Wollore was aware of its poverty. In providing the hospital with cattle and other goods to help restore its former state, he wished to maintain two services that the hospital had been able to render in earlier and better times – the celebration of mass by the master of the hospital or a chaplain in the hospital chapel, and the accommodation of poor boys studying grammar. The provision for these boys consists of their board and lodging, which had apparently come to an end with the onset of the hospital's financial difficulties.[77] The teaching of grammar does not appear to be carried out within the hospital precincts. It is probable that the scholars so provided for are to attend the grammar school of the collegiate church of SS Peter and Wilfrid in Ripon. There is no specific reference to these poor scholars being candidates for an ecclesiastical career. In the context of the preceding examples, though, this is very likely the case. It is quite probable that they were poor clerks of Ripon college.

These few examples are sufficient to show the concern expressed for the proper moral and literary training of candidates for the priesthood. Since, strictly speaking, all boys are eligible for the priesthood unless it is proven otherwise in a particular case, owing to some impediment or simply the boy's own wish, arrangements have to be made to give deserving boys an opportunity to learn Latin. With regard to relieving a particular kind of poverty, the educational endowments in chantries and hospitals were not very different from those in the monastic almonry schools.

It was one thing to provide for the learning of the clergy but quite another to prevent insufficiently instructed candidates from receiving clerical appointments. In 1317, for example, in the diocese of Exeter, Robert de Umfraville, clerk, was instituted to the rectorship of Lapford by his patron, Henry de Umfraville. Bishop Stapledon took exception to Robert's lack of learning and stipulated that he was to attend a grammar school and to appear before him once a year to give an account of his progress, a fine of one hundred shillings to be levied in the event of non-compliance.[78] Another clerk, William Fitzstephen, was presented to the rectorship of Kentisbury, also in Exeter diocese, in 1323. Once again Bishop Stapledon considered the patron's choice insufficiently "literate" to hold a benefice. On the representation of some of Fitzstephen's friends, the bishop was persuaded to give William a chance. William was to attend a grammar school until at least the feast of the Ascension; if found competent at that time, he would be admitted to the benefice, which his patron was to reserve for him in the meantime.[79] To cite one more example from a much later date, in 1444 a Sir John Gernesey, chaplain, was instituted perpetual vicar of the church of Banwell in the diocese of Bath and Wells on the presentation of the prior and convent of St Mary, Bruton. Bishop Bekynton ordered Sir John to study for an entire year so that he could understand the divine office at least literally and grammatically. In addition, he was to maintain in his house at his own expense a young man proficient in grammar to instruct him.[80]

It is against this background, then, of solicitude on the part of at least a few of the bishops for a better educated clergy that attention will now be directed towards the scholastic foundations of Winchester and Eton. In 1373 William of Wykeham, Bishop of Winchester, entered into an agreement with a Richard of Herton, *grammaticus*, whereby for a period of ten years the latter was to undertake to teach Latin grammar to poor scholars maintained at the bishop's expense. Richard was to teach no one else without the bishop's permission. Although no further details are given, this scholastic foundation, for such it was, may have led directly to what followed at Winchester nine years later.[81]

The charter of foundation of the College of St Mary at Winchester, issued in 1382, includes provision for seventy poor scholars, living in the college and studying in the faculty of grammar.[82] The conditions of admission deserve close inspection.[83] Those elected are to be the very poor, of sound morals and good behaviour, capable of study, and already instructed in plain chant and the elementary grammar of Donatus.[84] The boys must have completed their eighth year and no more than their twelfth year. However, a boy can be admitted up to sixteen years of age, provided that he is far enough on in Latin grammar to complete the course by the end of his seventeenth year, the age at which he must be replaced by another candidate.[85] Any person suffering from an incurable disease, a serious and noticeable mutilation of a limb, or other bodily defect – anything that renders him incapable of receiving holy orders – is to be refused admission to the college.[86] Scholars are permitted to remain in the college until they are twenty-five years old, except for those who are nominated to a place at New College, Oxford; these are to leave the college by the end of their eighteenth year.[87]

Two things are abundantly clear from these statutes: the educational facilities are designed primarily to prepare candidates for the priesthood, and the grammar program includes studies of an advanced nature. Two grades of clergy are envisaged: those candidates for holy orders who will receive their grammatical and theological training within the college – these may remain until they are twenty-five years of age, the usual age for ordination;[88] and a special group who will be selected to proceed to Oxford to attain academic degrees.

In reality, it is mainly in its provision for this second group of scholars destined for the university that Winchester College differs from the larger collegiate churches. As Leach observed, the basic aim of the college was to provide "a learned clergy," and no fewer than forty out of a total of forty-six chapters might belong to any collegiate church.[89] This is confirmed by Walsingham's comment, on Wykeham's death in 1404, that the bishop's munificence and industry in founding his grammar college at Winchester and house for advanced studies at Oxford had brought about an increase in the clergy of England.[90]

Every scholar at Winchester was to have the first clerical tonsure within a year of his admission, if he had not received it before. This did not apply to the founder's kin, who might put it off until they were fifteen years of age.[91] This exception was probably made to extend the educational facilities of the college to the bishop's relatives without requiring them to commit themselves, at least for the duration of the grammar school program, to an ecclesiastical career.[92] The academic services of the college, however, extended well beyond this provision. Apart from the founder's condition that four boys be elected from each of the parishes of Broughton and Downton whenever practicable, Winchester College was open to boys from all over England who had learned the rudiments of Latin in their parish schools or by some other means.[93] Once more, training in Latin, primarily directed towards a group of young candidates for the orders of the priesthood, was extended to any other students who wished to avail themselves of the opportunity.

As at Winchester, so at Eton: the grammar faculty was only one of several groups provided for in the college. The papal bull of foundation in 1440 refers in order to a provost, ten priest fellows, four clerks, six boy choristers, twenty-five poor grammar scholars, and twenty-five poor and feeble men, as well as a master, or *informator*, in grammar.[94] The essential nature of the foundation is evident from what actually took place – the parish church of Eton was converted into a collegiate church governed by a provost and fellows.[95] A revised code of Henry VI, put into statute form, increased the personnel considerably, making provision for ten clerks, sixteen choristers, and seventy-five scholars, together with an usher to assist the grammar master.[96]

As archdeacon of Buckinghamshire, Thomas Bekynton exempted Eton from his own jurisdiction and that of his successors. This archidiaconal jurisdiction over the entire parish of Eton was assumed by the college provost and confirmed by the bishop of Lincoln.[97] The head master and the usher, appointed by the provost and fellows, were to be unmarried, the latter a layman and if possible a bachelor of arts, the former if possible a master of arts.[98] The head master was to instruct free of charge not only the scholars and the choristers, but any other boys coming to Eton, no matter from what part of the country, who wanted at least an elementary knowledge of Latin.[99] Moreover, as many as twenty sons of noblemen and of special friends of the college were permitted to live and board in the college, provided that no expense was involved beyond that of their instruction in grammar.[100]

All scholars and choristers were to receive the first tonsure; those who did not have it on their admission were to receive it within the year or suffer expulsion from the college.[101] No one was to be admitted to membership in the college who was a serf, illegitimate, or afflicted with an incurable disease or some serious physical defect, since such a person would thereby be prevented from proceeding to holy orders.[102] Every scholar was to leave the college on completing his eighteenth year; if, however, his name was on the indenture for King's College, Cambridge, he might stay on until the completion of his nineteenth year. Scholars could be elected from the realm of England generally, except that preference would be given to the choristers of Eton and King's colleges who came from parishes in which either college owned property or who were natives of the counties of Buckingham and Cambridge.[103]

As with Winchester College, the close relationship set up between the college at Eton and the university college marks off Eton College from any number of collegiate churches. The close relationship of Winchester and Eton with their parent universities calls for some consideration of those grammar schools conducted in Oxford and Cambridge. Several colleges in the university centres provided for boys learning Latin in preparation for their more advanced studies. This is not surprising in view of the fluency in Latin, both written and spoken, required of any student who seriously contemplated a university course of studies, whether it was in arts, law, medicine, or theology.

College entrance requirements are set forth in the statutes of King's Hall, Cambridge, founded in 1337. The prospective candidate is to be of "cultured and upright conversation," at least fourteen years of age, and sufficiently instructed in the rules of Latin grammar, an essential requirement for the study of dialectic or whatever other course of study he is assigned to.[104] Individual applications often specify that the candidate has attained the required standard in Latin. Archbishop John Stafford of Canterbury, for instance, in appointing a poor scholar to Canterbury College, assures those concerned that William Appleton is "free, legitimate, and sufficiently instructed in grammar."[105]

In order, then, to make sure that their prospective members were sufficiently fluent in Latin to enter upon their university courses, some colleges provided for training in pre-university subjects. Merton College, Oxford, founded in 1262, maintained twelve grammar students and an instructor who was to devote all his time to the teaching of Latin.[106] Similarly, grammar students were included among the *pauperes pueri* maintained at Queen's College, founded in 1341.[107] In the foundation of Magdalen College by Bishop Waynflete in 1448, the grammar students are singled out for special attention. They are among the thirty "demies," or poor scholars, on the foundation. Great care is to be taken with their progress in Latin, so that no scholar will be promoted prematurely to the study of logic or any other more advanced course of studies. A grammar master, maintained by the college, is to teach Latin to anyone coming to him for that purpose, without requiring any fee for his work.[108] Moreover, the responsibility of the college does not stop with the grammar school at Oxford but is to extend to the grammar school recently established by the bishop in his native town of Waynflete.[109]

The statutes of Clare Hall, which was established at Cambridge in 1326, provided for the maintenance of ten poor boys who were to be educated at the expense of the college in *cantu, grammatica,* and *dialectica.* The average age of admission was to be thirteen to fifteen years. Preference was to be given to those boys who came from parishes in which the master and fellows of the college were rectors.[110] In common with the three Oxford colleges mentioned above, Clare Hall made provision for poor scholars who wanted to proceed eventually to holy orders, "clerical" students in the strict sense of the term. In this respect, these Oxford and Cambridge colleges – those, that is, which provided for such pre-university Latin training – bear close affinity to the colleges of Winchester and Eton.

There was, however, another kind of grammar school at the university centres. Such a school consisted of fee-paying students and was conducted by a master who normally rented a "hall" to serve both as a school and as a residence. These schools provided what was essentially "remedial grammatical instruction."[111] Relatively little is known about these grammar masters or their schools. Those associated with Oxford fared better than those connected with Cambridge, partly owing, no doubt, to the fact that the Oxford grammar schools, being under the jurisdiction of the university, were the subject of university statutes, whereas at Cambridge the grammar schools came under the jurisdiction of the archdeacon of Ely.[112]

Several grammar schools in Oxford came to be associated with particular halls or inns. It is chiefly in the records of the rents paid for such premises that individual grammar masters can be traced. Some of these, like John Cornwall and John Leland, are important figures in English educational history and have been considered above. Master Richard Pencriche, who popularized John Cornwall's teaching methods, lived in Pencriche Hall on Kybald Street from 1365–76.[113] In some cases these grammar masters taught Latin to the poor scholars of the colleges: Walter of Cat Street, for instance, taught the boys of both Merton and Queen's between 1353–59.[114]

Probably owing to the increasing provision for free instruction in Latin grammar, notably in the statutes of Magdalen College School, founded in 1479, the grammar halls of Oxford were on the decline by the middle of the fifteenth century, if not before.[115] By mid-century there were only about six of these schools left, including Ing Hall, Lyon Hall, and Tackley's Inn, all in St Mary's parish; and Boster Hall, White Hall, and St Hugh Hall in the parish of St Peter in the East.[116] St Hugh Hall was connected with St Edmund Hall, in that its students would pass on to the latter hall as undergraduates, but St Hugh fell into decay around 1487.[117] Probably it is in this context of the decline of the grammar halls for fee-paying students that a statute of the university of 10 April 1478 is to be interpreted. By this legislation the traditional payment by teachers of grammar to the university was not to be required of those who took up teaching posts in grammar schools in which the founders had made provision for free instruction in Latin for all those desiring it.[118]

Such, in brief outline, are the various arrangements under which the teaching of grammar was conducted in later medieval England. Three points in particular require further comment: the gratuity of the instruction, the status of the grammar teachers, and the program itself. As to the first point, while it is quite apparent that gratuitous instruction was the ideal and was frequently realized, it was by no means taken for granted. In addition to the fee-paying schools referred to above, several other examples of payment for instruction could be cited. In the foundation statutes for the school at St Albans in 1309, sixteen poor scholars were to be given free tuition, but any others who wished to avail themselves of the educational facilities were to be accepted by the master as fee-paying students.[119] In 1394–95 a chaplain brought a man to court for his failure to pay him for instructing his son during five terms and the chaplain eventually won his case.[120] In 1400 Robert Rede, a clerk from the diocese of Bath and Wells, obtained a papal licence to keep a boys' school "in any honest place he pleases in the realm of England" to teach grammar there, and to receive fees from the boys by way of salary "according to the custom of the country."[121] Finally, on being given charge of the grammar school at Wisbech in 1446, Jacob Creffen was granted leave by the bishop of Ely to accept an "adequate salary" from each scholar in every term, according to the "praiseworthy, ancient and approved custom."[122]

As to the grammar masters, there is no reason to question Leach's conclusion that they were invariably seculars, both clerical and lay. Their qualifications, however, appear to have varied considerably.[123] In the cathedrals and in the more important collegiate churches that possessed grammar schools, the master was ordinarily a master in arts. The evidence for this is consistent as far as it goes, though the loss of life in the Great Plague of the mid-fourteenth century made such a standard impossible of attainment for some time.[124] Among a group of some seventeen grammar masters discussed by Leach, only one is certainly a master in arts, the priest John Stone, who was the first master of Lady Katherine's foundation at Wotton-Under-Edge in 1384.[125] Two others have the title of "master" and are therefore presumably university graduates: the priest William Broune, entrusted with the chantry grammar school at Durham in 1414, and Master Reginald, appointed to the school at Beccles in 1396, who is also called *lector capellanus*.[126] Two have the title of *magister grammaticorum*: Thomas Baryn, appointed in 1399 to the school of St Mary-le-Bow in London, and Roger Fabell, appointed in 1463 by Bishop Carpenter to his college at Westbury.[127] As mentioned above, Richard of Herton, the teacher of Bishop Wykeham's scholars, is styled *grammaticus*.[128] Two are chaplains; they are Robert of Brougham, appointed to the school of Penrith in 1361, and John of Langham, appointed to Canterbury grammar school in 1375 and referred to as "chaplain in the faculty of grammar."[129] Two are priests without any other title, including John Caton, entrusted with the school of Hadleigh in 1382, and Richard Garbald, appointed to the school at Shipden in 1455.[130] One master, John Eluede, who was placed in charge of the school at Shouldham in 1462, is a bachelor of law.[131] Finally, many of the grammar teachers are referred to simply as "clerks," including all six appointees in 1329 to various schools in the diocese of Lincoln.[132]

With regard to the program, the foregoing evidence makes it quite clear that there is only one kind of school involved, and it is invariably termed the "grammar school." In other words, the evidence points to a common program in Latin for both clerks and laymen, for those intending to proceed to holy orders as well as for those aiming at positions that required a knowledge of Latin but were not restricted to the clergy. This deduction is confirmed by the recorded agreement, or "composition," which terminated a dispute over the relation of the cathedral choristers' grammar school to the city grammar school of Lincoln. Dated 12 February 1406–07, the "composition" informs us that in the choristers' grammar school in the cathedral close grammar was to be taught to the following: the choristers themselves; "commoners," or sons of nobles and important people, and special friends of the church or college; relations of the canons and vicars of the cathedral; and, finally, students supported by the canons and vicars or living in their families. It is evident from this that even in such a "clerical" school as that of the cathedral choristers, lay youths had their place, since there was no stipulation that the non-choristers were expected to have the clerical state in mind, though probably some of them did take up an ecclesiastical career.

In the general school of "the Church of Lincoln in the City," grammar was to be taught to everyone not included in any of the above groups, not excepting those living in chantries. According to this arrangement, the six boys of the Burghersh chantry, though living within the close and future candidates for holy orders, were to attend the general city school along with the boys and young men from the city of Lincoln and surrounding district. The stipulation requiring those attending the choristers' school to attend the general school once in each of three terms – Michaelmas, Christmas, and Easter – did not interfere with this arrangement. Moreover, the concluding note to the effect that others could attend the choristers' school only with permission of the chancellor and the *principalis magister* clearly implies that the program of studies prevailing in the choristers' school was equally useful to all those intent on learning Latin irrespective of their ultimate purpose.[133]

Apparently it was not unusual for adults to attend grammar schools along with boys and young men. This can be inferred from the arrangements existing in a number of the schools described above, where no particular age is stipulated as a necessary condition of admittance. On occasion the evidence is more explicit. When Bishop Welton, in 1362, appoints Master John of Burdon to conduct a grammar school in the city of Carlisle, he specifies that the instruction is to extend to "boys, adults and any others" wishing to learn grammar.[134] The inference would also be that many adults, as well as younger people, would attend a grammar school for only a relatively short time, long enough to acquire whatever fundamentals of Latin they needed for their employment.

Evidence for both these points appears in the "proofs of age" taken in various parts of the kingdom. On 31 July 1329, at York, John

Dounyour stated that he had been at the school of Hovyngham eighteen years previously, that is, when he was twenty years of age.[135] On 4 March 1361, in a proof of age taken at Sandhurst, Walter Brounyng stated that he had left for school at Cirencester twenty-one years before, that is, when he was in his twenty-first year.[136] At a proof of age around Christmas, 1328, at Derby, John de Burton testified that he had left the school at Nottingham in 1307, making him twenty-one years of age at the time, as he was now forty-two.[137] Finally, on 28 April 1345, Geoffrey Corunner, aged fifty, said that he had gone to school at Norwalsham twenty-one years previously and that he had stayed there "a whole year."[138]

As was mentioned above, the present study is not concerned with the question as to whether the educational facilities of later medieval England were considered by contemporaries to be adequate to existing needs. It will be useful, nonetheless, to give some attention to the situation in London around the middle of the fifteenth century. In March, 1445, Bishop Gilbert of London issued an ordinance recognizing only five grammar schools within the city: those of St Paul's Cathedral, the church of St Mary-le-Bow, the collegiate church of St Martin's-le-Grand, the church of St Dunstan in the East, and the Hospital of St Anthony.[139] It may be noted here that St Anthony's School was the latest one to be officially recognized. At its foundation in 1245 the Hospital was to maintain a grammar master, but at that time there was apparently no endowment.[140] In 1440, during the mastership of John Carpenter, the future bishop of Worcester, this provision was made. The nearby church of St Benedict Fynke was appropriated to the Hospital for the express purpose of maintaining a master to teach grammar in or near the Hospital precincts, free of charge to any persons desiring such instruction.[141] The bishop makes it clear that no school apart from these five can be conducted. Nevertheless, some people have set up grammar schools in various parts of the city without undergoing any examination or obtaining authorization. The bishop remarks that such people are defrauding both the students and their friends who maintain them. If illegal teachers do not cease such teaching within twelve days, they will be excommunicated.[142]

Despite this ordinance, only two years later four parish priests in London petitioned parliament to increase the number of grammar schools in the city, alleging the comparatively small number of such schools compared with the number they had formerly. The pastors request that in their respective parishes of All Hallows the Great, St Andrew in Holborn, St Peter in Cornhill, and Our Lady of Colchurch, Parliament "may ordain, create, establish and set, a person sufficiently learned in grammar, to hold and exercise a school in the same science of grammar, and to teach it there to all that will learn."[143] As far as is known, only Our Lady of Colchurch was granted a school.[144] We are not told how the problem was eventually solved. While the bishop is mainly concerned with the questions of qualifications and authorization, the city pastors are equally convinced that the teaching licence should be granted more liberally.

This problem raises the question of another kind of teaching arrangement, that of private teaching, or tutoring. From Bishop Gilbert's ordinance it would appear that illegal schools were common in London, but it is to be observed that the term "illegal" refers to the conducting of "public" schools. To instruct a person privately did not constitute an "illegal" school. In this connection Lynn Thorndike points out that a man could employ a tutor for his children to teach them in his own home, but children of other families could not be admitted to such lessons.[145] This is supported by a letter from the prior of Worcester to the prior of Coventry in 1318 on behalf of a James de Lyndeworthe, who was instructing some boys in their own house. The *rector scolarum* of Coventry was meditating court action against this tutor, but the prior of Worcester regards such action as unjust on the ground that in teaching the boys in their father's house he was within the law.[146] There are a number of scattered references to the practice of tutoring in England. Although it is difficult to form any clear idea of the extent to which it entered into the educational life of the kingdom, it must always be kept in mind in any discussion of educational facilities.[147]

When the four London pastors petition for the establishment of grammar schools in their respective parishes, they speak of the necessity of such learning not only for the proper conduct of the spiritual ministration of the church but for the more general temporal administration of the clergy. The teaching of Latin grammar in fifteenth-century London, though still designed primarily for those proceeding to holy orders, is also essential to all those engaged in "clerical" work in the widest sense of that term. It was to be expected, therefore, as has been noted above, that many youths and young men would acquire some facility in Latin without proceeding to the priesthood, even the lesser orders, and this appears to have been the case. In Hereford diocese in 1350, for instance, Roger de Walford, admitted to first tonsure by letters dimissory and a candidate for holy orders, is referred to as "literate," a term that evidently connotes a non-cleric versed in Latin.[148] In 1408 the Bishop of Durham was commissioned by Bishop Clyfford of London to confer the first tonsure on "literates and other regular and secular clerks."[149] In his mandate of 1445 with reference to the illegal teaching of grammar in London, Bishop Gilbert addressed himself to rectors, vicars, chaplains, public notaries, clerks, and *litterati*, an obvious reference to persons versed in Latin but distinct from the clerical order.[150] Finally, *litterati* are often found performing official duties where a knowledge of Latin, but not necessarily clerical status, was required. They appear as witnesses to institutions of benefices and the probates of wills and they act as proctors to the clergy.[151]

In addition to those who were *litterati* but were always laymen in the canonical sense, there were probably many more who were *clerici* for a time and who then reverted to lay status.[152] The term *clericus* did not necessarily imply the possession of even minor orders, but only the first tonsure, *prima tonsura clericalis*. First tonsure could be received by a boy on attaining the age of reason, that is, seven years, though many received it only much later.[153] Socially the possession of the clerical tonsure could have important consequences, since in principle it freed a man from serfdom and its obligations.[154]

All the examples of teaching and learning so far considered have taken no account of the education of girls. The central point of this part of the present study − that "lay" education was essentially a participation in "clerical" education − virtually excludes it. The Statute of Labourers of 1405 did provide that girls as well as boys could be sent to any school of their parent's choice. In the context, though, this probably means that in addition to the practice of young girls being placed in convents or in private homes, they might also be enrolled in any reading or elementary school available.[155]

This "clerical" and consequent masculine aspect of the education provided in the grammar schools of England during the fourteenth and fifteenth centuries contrasts with conditions in some countries on the continent. When, in 1354, for example, Reginald of Acyaco, advocate, protests to the Holy See against the University of Paris for suspending the teaching in grammar schools along with the four university faculties, he includes among the injured parties women teachers, both lay and religious.[156] On 6 May 1380, Master William of Salvarvilla, the precentor of Paris, lists the names of all those teaching in the grammar schools of Paris and suburbs. There are sixty-two names in all, and they include forty-one *magistri*, both clerical and lay, together with twenty-one *rectrices*, addressed as *honestes mulieres*.[157] Although these women were probably teaching girls in the elementary parish schools, there is nothing comparable to this in London, even a century later.

The city of Brussels furnishes another interesting comparison. In Brussels, as in Paris, there are women teaching in the city grammar schools, for on 15 January 1414 two women are among the twelve teachers who go to the chapter in the cathedral of St Gudule and in the presence of Jean Marchand, the chancellor, promise to conform to the existing legislation for grammar schools.[158] A much clearer picture of the city's schools, however, comes from the preceding century.

In 1320, *ab antique consuetudine*, Brussels had one *grande école* for boys and two *petites écoles*, one of these being for girls. In that year the Duke of Brabant, Jean III, promulgated what might be termed an educational decree, which provided for the extension of the city's educational facilities. In addition to the *grande école* for boys (corresponding to the advanced grammar schools of fifteenth-century London), there was to be *"un institut spéciale"* for girls learning grammar, music, and deportment. This school was never realized, but the fact that it was contemplated at all is revealing. Second, in addition to the two existing elementary schools, or *petites écoles*, five more were to be established for boys, including one outside the city at Molenbeck, and no less than four were to be set up for girls, making five schools in all for the girls of the city.[159] These arrangements form a striking contrast to those in England. Yet, despite this multiplication of elementary schools in fourteenth-century Brussels, the chapter school, or the *grande école*, remained the only one of its kind in the city throughout the later Middle Ages.[160]

In England, it is not until the second half of the fifteenth century that there is any definite indication of a departure from the traditional framework of the nation's schools. First at Acaster, Yorkshire, around 1460, and then at Rotherham in 1483, a master is appointed to teach writing and accounting along with the other masters entrusted with the teaching of song and grammar.[161] At the foundation of Jesus College in the latter centre, the archbishop of York, Thomas Rotherham, states that writing and accounting are intended for the many local youths who, though quick to learn, have no desire to attain to the dignity of the priesthood.[162] Even at this late date, the founder of such an educational institution in England still testifies to the virtual identification of the grammar school program with a preparation for clerical orders.

Significant as the above developments at Acaster and Rotherham might have been, the brief mention of the new subjects of study without any further description of them in the relevant documents reminds us that we do not possess anything of a syllabus, not only for any innovations or evidence of a new educational trend, but even for the Latin program of the traditional grammar schools. In concluding this survey of institutions, therefore, it will be useful to consider a few of the educational statutes and other documents of the period to see what light they throw on this question.

Early in the fourteenth century, at Oxford, statutes known as "regulations to be observed by regents in grammar," that is, by those who could fairly be described as teachers-in-training were drawn up. For one thing, special attention was to be given to the younger students. As elementary grammatical instruction involved a good deal of drill on Donatus, provision for this is now made at Oxford. These young students are to be questioned on the various parts of speech: they will first parse the word and then give the different inflections of that part in correct order. In this manner the students can learn Latin accidence (*partes*) by themselves.[163] The more advanced students are to be given verses and letters to compose, with the emphasis on clear, elegant phrasing. If possible, these assignments are to be written on parchment the following day. On the third day the students will hand their written exercises to the master and repeat them to him by heart.[164] As to the teachers-in-training, no regent master is to teach without the chancellor's licence. This licence is to be conferred only after the candidate has been examined in four divisions of the Latin program: the writing of Latin verse, the composition of letters, knowledge of the authors, and Latin accidence.[165]

There are explicit directives concerning the conduct of lessons. In giving "cursory" lectures, some teachers have departed from "ancient and approved custom." In contempt of the regulations, "unmindful of their salvation and interested only in money," they have been content to lecture to the scholars.[166] To ensure that the students' time, especially that of the younger boys, is not wasted in this fashion, no grammar master is henceforth to employ this manner of teaching, under penalty of dismissal from his post, and even imprisonment at the chancellor's discretion. Instead, all teachers are to set about the careful instruction of their scholars.[167] The term "cursory" as applied to lectures has been the subject of some discussion, but its meaning in this context is clear enough. It evidently refers to the practice of merely talking to students in the form of a set lecture without sufficiently questioning or drilling them on their lessons.

The status of bachelor was primarily connected with the scholastic act known as "determination," which in the faculty of arts consisted essentially in participating in a number of disputations throughout most of the Lenten term. On completion of his "determination" a student became a bachelor. If the bachelor is considered essentially as a kind of junior and assistant teacher, then there were probably several teacher training centres for grammar teachers outside of the universities.[168] The statutes drawn up for St Albans school in 1309 make specific provision for those scholars proceeding to the bachelor's degree.[169] In 1314 the rector of the Canterbury schools had an enquiry made concerning "some bachelors and others in the schools."[170] In the description of a graduation ceremony at Beverley Collegiate Church in 1338 mention is made of the "newly created Bachelors of the grammar school."[171]

The St Albans school statutes are the only ones that have so far come down to us. They probably are indicative, however, of what would be found elsewhere. The program of the advanced students corresponds fairly closely, though not entirely, to that in force at Oxford. The scholar aiming at the bachelor's degree will receive from the master a proverb, from which he will compose verses, letters, and a hymn. In other words, he must prove his competence in the art of *versificandi, dictandi, et metrificandi.*[172] This program may also be compared with that planned for those proceeding to the degree of master in grammar at God's House, Cambridge, nearly one and a half centuries later. At least two years were to be devoted to *sophistria*, that is, the discussing and disputing of grammatical problems, together with logic. Only then would the scholar be prepared to study the most advanced Latin as it is found in Priscian, the Latin poets, and *sciencia metrificandi et versificandi.*[173]

On completing his Latin compositions in prose and verse, the intending bachelor at St Albans must then dispute publicly in the schools, unless the master sees fit to exempt him from this or any other requirement.[174] As at Oxford, the grammar master is not to allow anybody to teach in the schools, even a bachelor, without a licence. To qualify for the teaching licence the candidate must first be examined on the rules of Latin grammar by those appointed by the master to do so, and then dispute the rules publicly in the schools, refuting the objections raised against him.[175]

The pedagogical method of the disputation, then, appears to have been a recognized scholastic procedure in grammar schools, at least in the more advanced classes.[176] The method could lead to abuse, however. Because it actually did so on occasion, some record of its operation has come down to us. In 1377, for instance, some two months after John Wyclif had been summoned to defend his views at St Paul's – to recall but one of the episodes of this period – Walter Cotel, vicar of Elerky in Cornwall, was instructed to proceed to Crediton within two weeks to take charge of the public grammar school there. This appointment by the bishop was inspired by the disorder which had characterized the school for some time, caused mainly by students engaging in useless arguments with the masters and showing them open disrespect. The context of the bishop's letter to Cotel makes it quite clear that unqualified persons had been employing the method of disputation merely for the sake of argument.[177]

Serious doctrinal controversies were the occasion of Archbishop Arundel's constitutions of January 1408. The Lollard movement had not been completely stifled and, in his efforts to provide safeguards against doctrinal error, the archbishop included prohibitions specifically aimed at school teachers. No one instructing boys in arts or in grammar is to teach anything concerning the faith and the sacraments – especially the Holy Eucharist – or theology generally that is not in harmony with Catholic thought and practice. There is to be no explanation of sacred scripture apart from textual analysis, the usual method employed. No scholars are to be allowed to conduct public or private disputations on the Catholic faith or on the sacraments of the church. It is quite clear that there is no question of forbidding disputations in themselves, but only such as involve theological questions outside the accepted grammatical exposition of sacred scripture. The mention of the sacraments, particularly the Blessed Sacrament, recalls the theological controversies associated with Wyclif in the previous generation, and indicates how the method of the disputation could be abused and get out of control. These articles of the archbishop's constitutions also seem to imply that, for good or ill, the practice of the disputation was quite general throughout the country.[178]

Notwithstanding the evidence adduced above for the general use of the disputation in grammar schools and, by implication, the large number of advanced students aiming at the degrees of bachelor and master, references to degrees in grammar in later medieval England are actually quite infrequent. When the founder of a grammar school states the academic qualification expected of the school master, he invariably specifies the master or bachelor of arts degree or employs some such phrase as "skilled in the art or science of grammar." The teachers credited with a master's degree in grammar are few and far between, while no instances at all have been forthcoming of a bachelor in grammar before the sixteenth century.[179]

The conclusion to be drawn from this is that during at least the latter half of the fourteenth century and most of the fifteenth, though there existed at both Oxford and Cambridge a faculty of grammar distinct from that of arts, it had comparatively few students.[180] When, therefore, in 1439 the London priest, William Bingham, set about the establishing of God's House at Cambridge to ensure a constant supply of qualified masters for the nation's grammar schools, it was his material provision for the scholars, not the academic arrangements, that was to break fresh ground.[181] The very fact that his program of Latin studies leading to the degree of master of grammar did not apparently provoke any questions at the university indicates that a distinct grammar program was already in existence. In 1446 Bingham's foundation was re-established and to some extent diverted from its original purpose when scholars from other faculties besides that of grammar were admitted. Precisely why this occurred has not been determined, but the reason for the change would probably go far to explain this obscure phase of English educational history.[182]

Confusing as much of the foregoing still remains, some light has recently been thrown on the faculties of grammar at both Oxford and Cambridge during the fifteenth and early sixteenth centuries. At Oxford the grammar faculty was under the supervision of the arts faculty, and at Cambridge it was under the archdeacon of Ely. Yet the requirements for the master of grammar degree were quite similar in both centres, the degree in question being "more a licence to practice than a degree," comparable, for instance, to a licence to preach. Although the required course of study for the master's degree normally took three to four years, some grammar teachers had their bachelor's degree accepted as the equivalent of the master of grammar, while there was an increasing trend at both universities to confer the degree in grammar as *de iure* recognition of its recipients being *de facto* grammar teachers."[183]

At this point some mention should be made of the status of French in England during the later medieval period.[184] The decline in French in the second half of the fourteenth century is reflected in the occasional university statute. According to the early fourteenth-century Oxford statutes, for example, it is required to teach the meaning of terms, first in English, then in French, so that the latter tongue might be kept alive.[185] In 1432 both oral and written French are expressly recognized: since the university of Oxford does not provide ordinary lectures in French, scholars learning the subject will attend the ordinary lectures of artists reading grammar or rhetoric, the two subjects considered most akin to their own study. The close connection between the learning of French and preparation for the practice of law is to be observed in the other subjects that are also included in this arrangement: the drawing up of charters, holding lay courts, and pleading "after the English fashion"; in other words, the procedure associated with English common law.[186]

To what extent such a course of study was maintained is not known, but one instance of it is furnished by the will of Robert Gerveys, rector of the parish church of Pentelowe in the diocese of London. In 1392 he left one of his relatives forty shillings to enable him to attend school for the purpose of "reading, writing and drawing up charters and indentures in both French and Latin."[187] This is one example of that specialized legal aspect of dictamen that has already been noted.[188]

It may be useful at this point to refer to a set of school ordinances from fifteenth-century France that provide some points of comparison and contrast with the educational life of later medieval England. Issued by Bishop Jean Leguise for the schools of Troyes in 1436, these ordinances are concerned with secondary schools, that is, grammar schools proper as distinct from the elementary song schools.[189] As in England, the mastering of Donatus marks off the senior grammar student from the beginner: in Troyes and its adjoining district the pupil who has mastered Donatus must attend the senior school. Teachers include in their oath of office the promise to see that this long-established custom is carried out.[190] The next step, or class, consists of mastering *principia grammaticalia*. Only when the student has learned the fundamental grammatical rules of Latin is he to proceed to the usual authors, Cato, Facetus, Theodolus, and others – an indication that this part of the program, too, corresponds closely with that generally current in England.[191] For the next and more advanced grade of study it is stipulated that Alexander's *Doctrinale* is the basic text of instruction but that, if the master should think fit, Eberhard's *Grecismus* may be used, though it is implied that both texts require skilful handling.[192]

We also have Georg Altenstein's description of the curriculum at his grammar school attached to the Hospital of the Holy Spirit in Nuremberg shortly before the city council introduced measures of reform in all four of Nuremberg's grammar schools in 1485. Referring to himself as "bachelor of the young clerks," Altenstein specifies four hours altogether in class work, two in the morning and two in the afternoon, with a third hour in the morning given over to divine service and a third in the afternoon to choir practice. Three stages of instruction are distinguished. While the elementary pupils busy themselves in the morning with exercises in orthography, a middle group concentrates on definitions from Donatus and the declensions in Alexander's *Doctrinale*. Simultaneously, the more advanced students employ their time with syntax, using for their exercises a wide range of choices from among a gospel text, a poet, a

moral from Cato, or one of the two didactic poems, the *Facetus* or
Alanus. The afternoon classes are much the same, except that the
senior students spend the first hour in exercises in logic based on
the *Summulae logicales* of Peter of Spain, the second on the more
difficult sections of the *Doctrinale*.[193]

It is clear enough, therefore, that the language of the liturgy, of
learning, and of most business correspondence in later medieval
England was Latin. The learning of Latin grammar was the common
task of the members of religious orders, the secular clergy, and
laymen preparing for clerical work that required a knowledge of
Latin but not necessarily clerical status. In this later medieval period
England thus witnessed the growth of a body of lettered laymen.
All these groups contributed to the educational life of the people:
the monks by providing almonry schools and holding the patronage
of some of the urban grammar schools; the friars by producing,
from time to time, standard texts and works of reference; the seculars, both clerical and lay, by compiling treatises for use in the
classroom and performing the most taxing duty of all – the actual
teaching.

Although some of the schooling was done on a fee-paying basis,
including the instruction by private tutors, free public education
remained the ideal. This ideal was realized to a large extent, inspired
by the effort to provide for a learned clergy, especially in cathedral
cities, in the vicinity of some collegiate churches, and in a few of the
university colleges. In a number of centres some institutions, like
chantries and hospitals, though not primarily educational, provided
either free instruction in grammar or board and lodging for grammar scholars. Whatever the particular arrangement under which a
school was conducted there was only one kind of secondary school
– the grammar school. Boys, young men, and adults, whether clerical
or lay, received a common basic training in Latin.

While Leach, therefore, rightly emphasized the central position
of the diocesan clergy in the educational life of medieval England,
he virtually ignored the contributions of the various communities of
friars that were established throughout most of Europe in the later
Middle Ages. His attitude is to some extent understandable. There
was, for instance, scarcely more evidence for the friars teaching in
the public schools of cities and towns than there was for the monks
themselves. Leach was not concerned, moreover, with the training
in Latin provided by religious orders for their own candidates. It is
fair to state, nonetheless, that this was a restricted view of education.
In adopting it, Leach forfeited the chance to examine the impact on
society not only of those acquiring proficiency in Latin as a requisite

for membership in this form of religious life, but also of others who, having obtained such instruction at the hands of the friars, decided to return to lay society in some professional capacity.

More important, Leach's static view of the grammar school curriculum blinded him to the direct participation of the friars in the designing of a new program of studies, reflecting the confidence and maturity of European Christendom. The lack of acknowledgment of the composition of school texts by two Dominicans, John of Genoa and Galfridus of Lynn, and a Franciscan, William Brito, is, in itself, a good illustration of Leach's failure to perceive the broader educational forces at work in later medieval Europe. Not only did Leach remain unaware of the significance of such publications – even, in some cases, of their very existence – but, perhaps, more to the point, he failed to appreciate the leadership exercised by a number of friars in the teaching and learning of the universities, and, by extension, their interest in pre-university training in Latin. In brief, Leach missed the opportunity to integrate his overall assessment of the grammar schools with the educational thrust of the mendicant orders, by any standard one of the more important agents in the formulation of a Christian culture during the later medieval centuries.

CHAPTER NINE

Leach in Historiographical Context: Contemporary Criticism and Recent Scholarship

Discussions and controversies with contemporary writers as well as those of earlier generations are one of the more interesting features of Leach's research and publication on the schools of medieval England. After close to thirty years of single-minded pursuit of the subject, Leach explained the sorry state of educational history in England in his address to the British Academy in 1913:

My researches have led me first to doubt, then to deny, and finally to disprove the authorized version, and to revise, recast, or perhaps rather to create *de novo* the history of English education, through that of the schools in which it was given. These researches were not in the first instance undertaken through any doubt of the traditional creed, if traditional it can be properly called, when it is no older than the end of the seventeenth century. It is due chiefly to two authors, the Rev. John Strype in his *Ecclesiastical Memorials* and his edition of Stow's *Survey of London*, and Knight in his *Life of Colet*, published in 1724; who founded themselves on the reckless assertions of the reactionary antiquaries and church historians of the Restoration – Fuller, Heylyn, Dugdale, and Aubrey. I must admit that I was fully imbued with it, when my researches began, in a strictly official way for a directly practical object connected with one particular school.[1]

What helped to make these "reckless assertions" even more formidable, however, was their acceptance, at least in part, by the well-known historian John Richard Green. His work *A Short History of the English People* had appeared only a decade before Leach's appointment in 1884 as an assistant commissioner under the Endowed Schools Act. Leach found it necessary to challenge Green's authority with respect to Dean Colet's place in the history of education and Edward VI's reputation as a school founder. Yet it is evident that

Leach shared in the high opinion of the historian whose aim was to eschew the traditional emphasis on war, diplomacy, and court intrigue in favour of "that constitutional, intellectual, and social advance in which we read the history of the nation itself."[2] This was despite the fact that, as Leach noted, education "was barely mentioned" in the new history and, when it was, "the old superstitions were repeated."[3]

Leach's criticism is particularly directed at Green's emphasis on the originality of the foundation of St Paul's School by Dean Colet, and the related assertion that "more grammar schools, it has been said, were founded in the latter years of Henry than in the three centuries before," a movement which in Green's view gained momentum under Edward VI and Elizabeth.[4] In his attempt to unravel the source of such misleading information, Leach contends that Green misunderstood what was apparently his main source: Knight's *Life of Colet*. When Knight mentioned the great proliferation of grammar schools in the thirty years preceding the Reformation, he meant by "Reformation" the whole series of changes introduced by the dissolution of the monasteries in 1535, not those in the mid-1540s associated with Henry VIII's last years. In Leach's view, Knight's statement is of "questionable accuracy," but as "altered by Green" is even more inaccurate. Moreover, Leach insists, there is nothing in Knight's account to warrant the consideration of Colet as an originator in the foundation of schools. On the contrary, Leach believes "that he was himself following, if also improving on, the examples of others, and partaking in a general movement already begun."[5]

Leach remarks that while Green was wrong in his estimate of Edward VI as well as of Colet, he was "not alone in his error," but has been selected for censure "because he is the most brilliant and best known of its propagators."[6] While Leach's attitude towards Green is one of mingled respect and disappointment, it is the latter that dominates his view of other of his contemporaries who have added their authority to the perpetuation of "the authorized version." Commenting on J. Bass Mullinger's book *Schools of Charles the Great*, published in 1877, in which the author speaks of boys being taught reading in order to study the Bible and understand the church services and arithmetic to determine the times of Easter and the festivals, Leach remarks that Mullinger was once again giving expression to the traditional opinion "that there were no schools in England before the Reformation except in monasteries," and that these were "merely elementary."[7]

So, too, in regard to Hastings Rashdall, whose account of the foreign universities – Salerno, Bologna, Paris – was, in Leach's view, "most fully and interestingly retold." Unfortunately for Oxford, however, "the greatest of existing universities," Rashdall left its origin still unascertained. Without supplying any new facts, he had merely added to the "many fables" of earlier historians, wasting "the unrivalled opportunity" such a work gave him of at least placing Oxford's origin "on an authentic basis of uncertainty," if he could not determine it "on a basis of ascertained fact."[8] While the details of Leach's criticism of Rashdall are not of moment here, the implication is that the history of education in England had been ill served with respect not only to the grammar schools but to virtually all educational institutions.

When Leach focuses on specific statements by historians such as those mentioned above, his background knowledge, at least for the later medieval period, usually stands him in good stead. This could have been a saving feature of his controversy with J.E.G. de Montmorency, the author of *State Intervention in English Education*, published in 1902. De Montmorency's argument that there was a close relationship between medieval nunneries and the education of girls of every social class formed the ground of that author's debate with G.C. Coulton. Leach states that there is little evidence concerning this specific question but what little there is indicates fairly clearly that de Montmorency's conclusions "are not justified." Leach was not content, however, with demolishing de Montmorency's thesis. His argumentative approach led him to castigate the well-known Alexander Savine as well.

In Leach's view, de Montmorency is yet another victim of the authority wielded by "the second-hand anti-Puritan writers, Dugdale, Fuller, and Tanner," whose personal knowledge of the matter was no greater than that possessed by Leach's generation and whose documentary evidence was "very much less." Leach says that when Coulton pressed his opponent on the evidence for his claim, de Montmorency invoked the authority of Savine in support of his own position. His tribute to Savine as "the greatest living authority on the dissolution of the monasteries" affords Leach the opportunity to expand on the limitations inherent in the study of English culture by a foreigner.

In Leach's opinion, the value of the professor's authority in support of de Montmorency's argument is quite minimal – a paper, included in Professor Vinogradoff's volume of *Oxford Studies in Social and Legal History* on the *Valor Ecclesiasticus* of 1535, which assessed all ecclesiastical property with regard to the tenths of income that, formerly paid to the pope, now had to be paid to the king. Not only does the paper deal with the use of "an obscure historical document" by one whose "acquaintance" with England is "fugitive," but its bearing on monastic education is marginal, concerned, as it is, only with the deductions allowable for "compulsory charitable payments." Leach's most evident satisfaction, however, derives from the professor's "appalling blunder" in confusing Winchester College with a monastic institution and, even more, with the latter's additional comment that the scholars of those days were little more than beggars. This last provokes Leach to inquire how a number of the well-known county families who contributed "scions" to Winchester College at that time would have appreciated this description of their sons.

Leach goes on to remark that Savine's further expressions of surprise at the commissioner's refusal to recognize the expenditure of alms on "schoolboys" at such monastic centres as Gloucester, Coventry, and Tewkesbury only serve to show that he does not appreciate the fact that these "schoolboys" are in reality the almonry boys. These boys, as Leach explains, "acted as page-boys to the monks and also as choristers in their Lady chapel"; they received education "incidentally." While Savine could have learned all about these almonry boys, Leach remarks, from "the articles on Westminster and Durham Schools in these columns, from the 'History of Winchester College,' and from the 'Victorian County Histories' for Gloucestershire, Warwickshire, and other counties," such a study could not reasonably be expected "for a few incidental paragraphs in a long paper." It is all the more, then, a cause for surprise that de Montmorency should hold up Savine as an authority on the subject of monastic girls' schools, especially since Savine makes no mention at all of girls in connection with monasteries, for the simple reason, Leach says, "that they do not occur at all in the Valor."[9]

Leach's critical appraisal of both de Montmorency and Savine, however forcefully expressed, reveals his weakness for needlessly extending the grounds of an issue. He thus leaves himself open to a charge of irrelevancy, as when he remarks that the question under discussion cannot be resolved by "the incidental *ipse dixit* of Russian professors" or by "modern monks" whose regard for their cloisters is like that of Chaucer's "'fair prelats.'"[10]

The above examples of Leach's method of argument show what may be termed the general tenor of his approach to writers with whom he disagrees. But even if Leach occasionally takes undue advantage of the person's lack of knowledge with respect to specific educational matters, he is usually fair and satisfied with nothing more than getting at the truth of things. It is not always easy, however, to account for Leach's approach in specific instances. A case in point is that of Frederick James Furnivall, the founder of the Early English

Text Society, whom Leach considered "the author of the best historical account of education and schools of England." When, Leach says, he had requested that author's help in 1892 in his research into the history of grammar schools, Furnivall had stated that England had not possessed grammar schools until the reign of Edward VI. "Soon convinced to the contrary," remarks Leach, "he was always ready to impart instances of earlier schools which he came across in his wide reading in ancient manuscripts and books."[11]

The respect shown to Furnivall for his evident honesty of purpose was not extended to the critic of Leach's first volume on the chapter act book of Beverley Minster, published in 1898. In his introduction to the second volume five years later, Leach refers to the earlier criticisms as "both captious and incorrect," including the one aimed at his designation of "provost" of Beverley as a foreign title, and his description of the precentor, treasurer, and chancellor as "dignitaries." The tone of Leach's rejoinder is quite negative throughout. Quoting his critic's charge against him, that he was apparently ignorant of the distinction between an "office" and a "dignity" in reference to a secular chapter, Leach insists that such officers were described as dignitaries "at most cathedral or ancient collegiate churches." He explains that the term was specifically used to designate the officers of Beverley collegiate church by a town jury in 1425. He goes on to remark that the men of Beverley and the bailiffs of the archbishop who were responsible for the inquisition should be given at least as much credence in what concerned the constitution of the "then living" church of Beverley as the critic "who discourses a priori on the subject 400 years after its decease."[12]

In concluding this brief overview of Leach's critical and argumentative approach to writers who strayed into his area of educational history, it might be useful to look at an issue that was central to the political and social climate in which the history of the grammar schools took on an immediate and practical dimension and exercised Leach throughout his publishing career. This was the dispute over the meaning of "free schools," a question that illustrated Leach's concern for the exact use of terms in historical documents. In his article on "free schools" published in the American *Cyclopedia of Education* in 1911, Leach makes the point at the outset that the obvious meaning of a "free school" is that of a school free from tuition fees; he enlists the support of Dr Johnson's dictionary for this purpose. He goes on, however, to explain how other meanings have crept in and now hold the stage to the detriment of both true learning and common sense. Since 1865, Leach explains, the term has become increasingly identified with freedom from ecclesiastical authority, a "wholly unhistorical and untrue" explanation founded on the assertion of "a great classical scholar and producer of classical scholars," Benjamin Hall Kennedy, the headmaster of Shrewsbury School from 1836 to 1866. At the time of the Public Schools Commission in 1862, Leach says, it was a "burning" question whether public schools, founded as "free grammar schools," were justified in charging fees, and whether the poor residents of towns like Harrow, Rugby, and Shrewsbury were not being discriminated against "in favour of the rich from a distance."[13]

After explaining that Harrow and Rugby were at that time not much larger than villages, and that in Shrewsbury, a town of some size, the question was of most immediate concern, Kennedy wrote a paper which was, as Leach says, "practically endorsed by the Commission." In the paper Kennedy asserted, or at least implied, that the term "free school" was due to the numerous foundations under that name attributed to Edward VI – *Libera Schola Grammaticalis Edwardi Sexti* – and that *libera* never meant "gratuitous" in classical or medieval Latin; moreover, that the word could not mean "gratuitous" in the days of Edward VI simply because all schools at that time were gratuitous. Leach then states that Kennedy asserted that *libera* meant free from jurisdiction of a superior corporation, in this case of ecclesiastical corporations. Leach's rejoinder is that "every one of his dicta can be shown to be absolutely false." After citing instances from Livy to show the derivation of the words *libertas*, *libera*, and *libere* and their passage into medieval usage, including the well-known one of a liberty (*libertas*) as a district free of toll. Leach then provides a number of specific historical examples to support his argument. One such example is that of Abbot Sampson in twelfth-century Bury St Edmunds who bought a stone house for the local school on condition that four clerks should be admitted free "as every scholar whether able or not had before this to pay 1d. or 1 1/2d. twice a year."[14]

Leach's first full-length study of this question appeared in the *National Observer* in 1896 in two successive articles.[15] Many of the same points mentioned in the later American *Cyclopedia* article are present in this first extended review of the topic, but with reference to the classical use of the term *libera* Leach is not nearly as emphatic as he is in the later article. His attempt to strengthen his own position in this argument includes a criticism of Kennedy's carelessness in his use of Ducange's multi-volume dictionary of medieval Latin. Kennedy had assumed the name Dufresne to be that of a different person from Ducange himself, and Leach notes that the term "liber" is not in the dictionary at all.[16]

The argument produced in Kennedy's paper in the Public Schools Commission report was echoed in a letter to the *Manchester Guardian* by H.J. Roby, formerly an Endowed Schools Commissioner. Leach quotes the pertinent part of Roby's argument: "Free school no more meant a school to be used by the scholars without payment than a Free Chapel like St George's, Windsor, meant a chapel without pew rents, or a 'free man' meant a man whose services any one could have for nothing, or a 'free city' meant one whose inhabitants paid no rates or municipal taxes, or a 'freehold' meant a piece of land or an office which anyone could take who chose." In Roby's view, the nearest contemporary equivalent would be privileged or authorized; that is, the freedom consisted of a franchise or immunity for the school or its governors, not for the scholars. A free scholar, therefore, is a scholar of such privileged or authorized school.

Leach's reply to the arguments of both Kennedy and Roby takes the form of a quotation from *Piers Plowman* and examples from "more solemn sources," such as early fourteenth-century Beverley, to show that the basis of their argument – that school masters before the reign of Edward VI did not teach for profit – is a "gratuitous" assumption. The practice of ecclesiastical courts to inhibit the holding of an "adulterine" school within the educational jurisdiction of a licensed school master is in itself proof that the rival teacher was taking away fees from the recognized teaching authority. Moreover, Leach asserts, the term used in one of the disputes involving the teaching of grammar to the Beverley church choristers – *libere* – happens to be the very word that Kennedy asserted was unused in medieval Latin in that sense!

In the second of his two contributions to the *National Observer*, Leach expresses the view that Winchester College had "a stimulating effect in starting other free schools." He notes that all seventy scholars on the foundation were to be free scholars, that is, "lodged, boarded, clothed, and educated at the expense of the foundation." Although the word "free" is not used, and the freedom was limited to the seventy foundationers, Winchester was, in his view, "the greatest of all Free Schools at that time."[17]

One example of such imitation is the well-known chantry at Wotton-under-Edge, the foundation of the first woman on the medieval educational scene, Lady Catherine Berkley. Leach notes that it was precisely two years after Wykeham's foundation charter that her Ladyship, on 20 October 1384, directed that the foundation should be for "a master and two poor scholars, clerks, for ever, living college-wise therein," the very same terms, Leach states, as those used by Wykeham himself, "and not apparently used by any of his predecessors." Leach notes that the document states that the master is to "kindly receive all scholars whatsoever, whensoever, and whencesoever coming, for instruction in the said art of grammar, and to duly instruct them in the same art, without any benefit or gain for his pains."[18]

As Leach was later to discover, he had not written the last word on the subject of free schools, however logical his statement had appeared to be in the pages of the *National Observer*. In 1908, in two similar contributions to the *Journal of Education*,[19] he was forced to enlarge upon his earlier arguments: Berkhamstead School had become another "Shrewsbury." Here, as in so many other instances related to his research into the documentary sources, Leach ponders over "the difficulty of stopping the currency of false coin." Leach first recounts the main features of this particular court case, in which it was once again contended that *libera* did not mean "gratuitous" either in classical or medieval Latin, and, consequently, since the people of Berkhamstead did not enjoy any historical right to free education for their sons in the school, neither could they have any ground of complaint at any increase in the fees which they paid.

Leach then proceeds to draw the reader back to the Shrewsbury school case and Kennedy's argument. The central point he wishes to make is that times and circumstances had changed. What had been considered sufficient in Elizabeth's reign, for instance, to support an unmarried schoolmaster and usher was now "wholly inadequate" to support schoolmasters who were married men supporting families and providing boys with instruction not only in classics, but also "in mathematics, French, English, science, and history," to say nothing of such amenities as well-lighted and well-kept school rooms and laboratories and the ample sports fields taken for granted in the days of Queen Victoria. "Instead, however, of adopting the obvious argument from change of circumstances and the impossibility of applying old laws to modern instances in the rigour of the letter, Kennedy hit on the unhappy expedient of denying the undeniable and asserting that a free school did not mean a fee-free school."[20]

The debate over the meaning of "free schools" is a good illustration of the several talents that Leach brought to bear on a topic of current interest: his legal method of argumentation, his philological sense, and his practical turn of mind. This controversy also testifies to Leach's long-suffering patience with educated people who had either ignored his published work or had taken issue with him without having taken the trouble, as he had so carefully done, to verify their statements. Leach, however, was responsible for the ongoing nature of a number of these debates. We see this even in the reviews of his major works, a few of which, though for the most part anonymous, provide us with another side of the major controversies in which Leach readily engaged.

Within a few months of its publication, Leach's *English Schools at the Reformation* was the subject of an unsigned review in the *Athenaeum*.[21] The writer thinks that Leach has established the claim he made earlier in his *Contemporary Review* article of 1892 that the number of schools in pre-Reformation England was "far larger" than common opinion had it, and that the importance of "that part of the material which is here for the first time printed" must be acknowledged on all sides.[22] He qualifies his praise midway through his review, however, with the following comment: "It is unfortunate, however, that the tone which the author has chosen to adopt in speaking of the work of his distinguished predecessors and contemporaries is generally ungracious, and sometimes violent."[23]

The writer goes on to question three points in particular: Leach's statement that schoolboys (at Ipswich) were reading "Valla and other ancient authors"; Leach's definition of secular canons as "ordinary clergyman who, like the canons of our cathedrals now, married and gave in marriage"; and his designation of Richard Fox, later bishop of Winchester, as headmaster of the grammar school at Stratford-on-Avon. The remainder of the review is generally critical of Leach, with special emphasis on his unfair, unnecessary attacks on Edward VI as a school founder as well as on his parallel attempts to minimize the educational efforts of the government under Somerset on the one hand and of the whole monastic order on the other. Although the reviewer agrees with Leach's contention that the exchange of landed endowment under the Chantries Act of Edward VI "did so much in the end to impoverish schools," he is equally certain that the transfer was not deliberately planned with this result in view.[24]

In the last paragraph of his review, the writer chooses to emphasize Leach's lack of background knowledge. Rather than the historian "who weighs his judgments," Leach's tone in the introduction betrays "the ready writer whose depth of ... historic insight" may be gauged from his description of the tenth-century revival of monasticism as a "craze" for "celibacy, fastings, floggings, and other forms of torture" not unlike "the fanatical performances" of contemporary "fakirs."[25]

Leach lost no time in reacting to the above criticism, sending his criticism of the reviewer to the *Athenaeum* a fortnight later. Leach was especially irked by the last paragraph, but ready to waive "such generalities" in the interests of specific points, an area in which he thinks the reviewer "cuts a sorry figure." In reply to Leach's comments on the three topics under discussion, the reviewer accepts his information with regard to Fox's headship of the Stratford-on-Avon grammar school but thinks that Leach has misunderstood the point about Valla being read at Wolsey's Ipswich school; it was the imputation of Valla being considered as an ancient author, with the word "other" as the culprit, that was in the mind of the reviewer. As for Leach's definition of secular canons, the writer stands by his criticism "because it is inapplicable to the whole of the period" during which the canonical prescriptions regarding sacerdotal celibacy "were accepted or enforced."[26]

Within a matter of days Leach had forwarded yet another rejoinder, in the form of a letter, to the same journal. The manner in which the reviewer regarded Leach at this time is revealed in the caption heading the correspondence: "Mr. Leach returns to the attack." On this occasion, while denying that he had given any "definition" of secular canons, Leach contended that he certainly had made a distinction between the collegiate churches of pre-Norman times and those founded after the middle of the thirteenth century in which the secular clergy were "enforced celibates like the monks." Leach concludes by insisting that his reviewer had either "deliberately misrepresented" what he had said, or had been "grossly careless" in his criticism. The reviewer, nevertheless, had the final word: "No indication is given that the explanation of the technical term 'secular canon' is intended to hold good only of pre-Norman times."[27]

In 1899 Leach's labour of love on his Alma Mater, *A History of Winchester College*, was the subject of a quite favourable review in the columns of *The Athenaeum*.[28] The anonymous writer, who mentions that he had already "had occasion to differ" from the author, identifies Leach as that kind of person whose "happy combination of sound learning with technical information" is joined to "a pleasing and unaffected style." Leach's qualifications, in fact, are likened to those of Sir Henry Maxwell-Lyte, the historian of Eton, and the end result of his undertaking is deemed as fortunate as that of the latter.[29]

Although the reviewer expresses some misgivings with Leach's discussion of two or three of the earlier aspects of educational development in Winchester, he thinks that the distinction drawn between the priory school with its "little nursery of novices" and the children of the almonry school is "particularly lucid and interesting." He also thinks that Leach's claim to have thrown new light upon Wykeham's connection with both Winchester and Oxford is justified from the documentary sources he has presented, not least of which is Leach's "useful insistence on the importance of the constitution of New College, Oxford, as bearing upon the new foundation of Winchester College itself." It is, however, in his chapters on "the site, buildings, and internal economy" of Winchester that Leach is "in his element." The reviewer is not sure, though, that Leach is at his best when treating of the political philosophy associated with "the worthies" of the Elizabethan era who were educated at the college, but he gives Leach credit for "most effectively" disposing of "several unfounded traditions" connected with the position of the school during the civil war period of the seventeenth century. While the reviewer has some suggestions for a new edition of the book, including a revision of the index and the omission of some irrelevant material, he thinks that many of the author's passages "are lightened by a quiet humour" that is "far more effective" than any "heroics" in which Leach, from an evident loyalty to his college, might have indulged.[30]

There are three reviews of Leach's *Educational Charters and Documents, 598 to 1909* that may be considered for purposes of comparison and contrast. The earliest of these, from September 1911, is an unsigned review in *The Athenaeum.* The writer is very favourably impressed with Leach's selection of the documents, which is matched by his "lucid and excellently planned Introduction" and by "the judiciously chosen headlines and headings." Particular pleasure is expressed at the author's material treating of the origins and growth of the universities and the body of statutes framed for St Albans School in 1309. Among the very few negative criticisms are those relating to Leach's lack of sympathy with the monasteries and his occasional translations of Latin texts which should be "somewhat amended" in a future reprint of the book. The translation, remarks the writer, is, in many places, "rather needlessly bald and awkward," and in more than one instance, "it slips into actual verbal error."[31]

The second of these reviews, also anonymous, appeared a few days later in the *Educational Supplement* of the London *Times.*[32] This review, a much more detailed appraisal than the one mentioned above, begins with the double observation that "there can be few men who know more" about the history of education in England than Mr. Leach while, at the same time, in this as well as in some of his other writings, there is "a certain asperity in reference to those who differ from him." The entire review is, however, much more descriptive than analytical. The writer occasionally raises a question of fact, pointing out an obvious error or looking for additional information, such as, for example, "the ground of the exemption from the jurisdiction of the school-master of St Paul's of the Schools of St Martin-le-Grand and St Mary de Arcubus." While the reviewer thinks that Leach has done "full justice" to the maintenance of schools under the Commonwealth, the material for the seventeenth and eighteenth centuries is "rather bare." Virtually the only item that he enlarges upon in a negative fashion is Leach's document describing the directive of Bishop Grandisson of Exeter that boys be taught to understand their basic Latin prayers before passing on to other school books: he says that Leach's caption – "Episcopal attack on the Classics in the Diocese of Exeter. 1357" – is "considerably less than just."[33]

The third review of *Educational Charters and Documents* is that of Hastings Rashdall, the well-known author of the three-volume work *The Universities of Europe in the Middle Ages*.[34] Beginning with his recognition of Leach's entire contribution to educational history as "the most thorough and systematic" investigation of the subject, he quickly moves to describe Leach as "so controversial a writer," given to denying any acknowledgment of previous writers who had contributed to his subject, "either in regard to the schools or to the Universities." Although Rashdall is obviously anxious to discuss Leach's criticism of his own explanation of the origin of Oxford university, he credits Leach with dissipating "two obstinate popular misconceptions," namely, that grammar schools originated with the Renaissance and that such pre-university schools as did exist were taught by monks. He does not credit Leach with being the first to single out these errors, however, since the late Thorold Rogers, among others, recognized that "there were more grammar schools in mediaeval England than there have ever been since." Leach has, furthermore, shown that "the real schoolmasters of the Middle Ages" were the chantry priests and, in the particular volume under review, that only some thirty of the 300 or more schools "destroyed by the suppression of the Chantries at the Reformation" were refounded by Edward VI.[35]

Rashdall questions Leach's well-known rendering regarding the master of the Sevenoaks grammar school in 1432 – the translation of *infra sacros ordines minime constitutus* as "shall by no means be in holy orders." His main concern, though, is Leach's crossing over into the territory of university history where, unlike his situation with respect to the grammar schools, Rashdall asserts, Leach displays an "amateurish knowledge" of the Middle Ages. In particular, Rashdall takes Leach to task for his misrepresentation of the argument put forward by the Dominican friar, Heinrich Denifle, to account for the role of both pope and emperor in the origin and development of the universities as *studia generalia*, and Rashdall's own conjecture of Oxford University as having originated in the migration to Oxford of English masters and students from Paris under edicts of Henry II in 1167. When, in this connection, Rashdall draws attention to Leach's statement that "university students were not as a rule beneficed," he remarks that such a statement could not possibly come from a person "really well acquainted with the habits and ideas of the Middle Ages."[36] While Rashdall is prepared to give Leach credit where credit is due, he is not happy to see him "going out of his way" to take on other writers in regard to subjects which he "imperfectly understands."[37]

As might be expected, Leach could not let this criticism go unanswered. In a lengthy letter to the editor of *The Oxford Magazine* two months later, he described Rashdall's review as consisting "almost entirely of a tirade against one page out of the 619 pages which form the book."[38] It is clear that Leach was touched to the quick by Rashdall's relegating him to the history of grammar schools as his "proper subject." Leach begins with an exposure of his reviewer's error in supposing that *infra* would be better translated as "under" or "below" in the Sevenoaks case, thus changing the translation to the requirement that the master was not to be "below holy orders," that is, that he be at least a deacon.[39] Leach then quickly centered his main criticism on Rashdall's theory of the origin of the university at Oxford. For this purpose Leach had evidently gone to the basic documents, for he quotes from Denifle's *Chartulary of the University of Paris*, the relevant volumes of the Rolls series, and the Pipe Rolls of 1169–70. In his closely worded argument, based on these in comparison with Rashdall's own use of documentary sources, Leach concludes in part that Rashdall's assertion regarding the number of English beneficed clergy at Paris in 1167 is "as unproved as it is improbable." While Leach acknowledges having overlooked a key reference supplied by Rashdall in his original history of Oxford, he is confident that Rashdall's attempt to make a direct connection between Henry II's recall of English beneficed clerks from Paris and their conjectured subsequent settlement at Oxford as an incipient university community is little more than a guess, tied in one instance to "several pages of wholly ineffective special pleading."[40] Leach's conclusion is that "it is about time that the learned Canon withdrew and apologized for the false pedigree he has tried to force on his Alma Mater, instead of vituperating those who expose its falsity."[41]

The next review to be considered is that by Foster Watson, a well-respected contemporary of Leach in educational circles and himself an author of repute, having published, among other works, *The English Grammar Schools to 1660: their Curriculum and Practice*. Watson's review of Leach's *Documents Illustrating Early Education in Wor-*

cester, 685 to 1700 A.D. appeared in *The English Historical Review* in the spring of 1914.[42] The review is a very objective assessment; its author's main concern is Leach's disposition to infer, at times, too much from the evidence before him. While this is especially the case with Leach's treatment of the early Anglo-Saxon period, it tends to spill over even into the later medieval period.

It is clear once again that part of Leach's problem with respect to the earlier period of pre-Norman times is his concern to show that education was identified with secular clergy rather than with a monastic community. Watson points out that not only does Leach attempt to link the erection of an episcopal see at Worcester with the establishment of a school, but his use of Bede's *Ecclesiastical History* to connect such a school with a secular cathedral chapter at Worcester from 685 A.D. misses fire because "there is not in Bede or elsewhere any documentary evidence of a school at Worcester so early."[43] Nor do Leach's attempts to show the existence of a school in that city two centuries later in the reign of Alfred the Great fare any better. The truth is, Watson contends, that it is not until 1291 "that Mr. Leach gets well under way in the history of Worcester schools by citing the first document directly dealing with the Grammar School." Watson also remarks, however, that this date is a relatively early one if we consider "the old idea" that tended to rule out grammar schools before the Reformation. He thinks it only fair to state that "no man has done as much as Mr. Leach to show the wide extension of schools in England in pre-Reformation times."[44]

In a survey of Leach's material as it relates to the evolution of Worcester's grammar school into the Royal Grammar School, Watson mentions in particular the importance of the Worcester Cathedral statutes of 1544 for the history of school curricula, as well as Leach's identification of the Guild of the Trinity at Worcester with the "real Grammar School" deriving from the Middle Ages. In addition, he says, Leach lays open for his readers a wide variety of educational topics, including school customs associated with Maundy Thursday, medieval public libraries, monastic students at Oxford, and schools under the Commonwealth. Watson concludes by stating that while Leach would be the last person "to wish every one to adopt all his conclusions," it must be acknowledged that "no one can study the history of English schools without constantly referring to his writings and collections of documents," and that this debt "will be recognized more and more."[45]

The last book to be reviewed was Leach's *The Schools of Medieval England*. We have two assessments of this work, the first of these an unsigned one in the *Athenaeum*.[46] The writer expresses his reservations at the outset, noting that Leach's bibliography, impressive as it is, "does not provide any list of other works than his own on mediaeval education." Moreover, although Leach himself had explained that the plan of the series in which his book appeared excluded references to the sources, the reviewer does not think highly of the option that the author's "multitudinous facts" could only be traced by a careful search, assuming even that the reader "could secure all his writings, and had the requisite time for the hunt."[47]

On the more positive side, Leach's work is to be considered a valuable compendium "of all his previous contributions" to the subject of schools in medieval England, and Leach himself a *"facile princeps* of the investigators in his knowledge of original documents." In particular the reviewer singles out Leach's studies of individual schools, including those of Winchester, Warwick, Stratford-on-Avon, Southwell, and Beverley, as well as his accounts of schools in the *Victoria History of the Counties of England (VCH)*. Moreover, in the area of school organization and finance, "Mr. Leach writes with the decisiveness won by long and close investigation." The reviewer applauds Leach for covering such a wide variety of topics, including the salaries of schoolmasters, their conditions of appointment, and the gradual introduction of lay teachers, as well as providing statistical information on endowments and foundations. If Leach's views on the availability of schools in the later Middle Ages do not win universal acceptance, his suggestions, nevertheless, are a "stimulus to the search for further material." The writer also feels that Leach did well to stress the scholastic achievements of the fifteenth century, since this kind of continuity takes away "much of the abruptness which marks many accounts of the Renaissance."[48]

Laudatory as the above remarks are, the reviewer takes issue with Leach at some length for what he thinks is a too ready disposition to censure persons who do not agree with him. He cites historians such as William Stubbs and A.F. Pollard as having been the objects of such criticism, as well as Erasmus for his praise of Colet.[49] He dwells at somewhat greater length, however, on the attack on Savine, well-known to the English-speaking world for his studies on bondage and copyhold tenure. For Leach to say of the Russian professor's volume on the English monasteries – mainly because of the author's confusion of Winchester College with a local monastery – that "it is to be regretted that it did not remain in its original language" is to create a needless dilemma: the choice between the acceptance of Leach's opinion and that of the editor of the Oxford series in question with respect to the value of Savine's work as a whole is "a problem that need never have arisen, and one irrelevant to the history of the schools of Mediaeval England."[50]

The final review to be considered, that of A.G. Little, the historian of the Franciscans, is by far the best known.[51] After initially commending Leach for explaining the "mystery" surrounding the ability of so many persons who "could copy, understand, and even draw up documents in Latin,"[52] Little expresses his concern with Leach's forays into early monastic history, in part, as follows:

> Mr. Leach is a pioneer, and, like most pioneers, is prone to exaggerations and prejudices; but it is a pity that in a book so full of fresh information he should have adopted such a controversial tone. Fighting, and fighting successfully, against the deep-rooted and carefully nurtured tradition that the medieval schools were monastic, he sees in monasticism the enemy, regards the Inquisition as 'its most formidable development' (p.332), and minimizes its services to education ... He translates Bede's description of James the deacon, *virum utique ecclesiasticum et sanctum*, as 'who though an ecclesiastic was a saint', and adds the comment: 'Bede, writing as a monk, thought none but monks really holy.'[53]

Little is prepared to recognize Leach as a "safer guide" at the conclusion of the missionary period of the monks and even more when records became more plentiful. He admits that from the twelfth century onwards monks did relatively little in a direct way for the education of the laity.[54] Yet, he cannot accept Leach's claim that a school was the normal adjunct of a collegiate church, not only because the number of such documented collegiate churches with schools attached does not support Leach's contention, but also because there is no reason for supposing that with particular reference to the decree of the Lateran Council of 1215, there was not "a long gap between a rule and the observance of it."[55]

Little is also skeptical of Leach's figure of approximately 400 grammar schools scattered over medieval England. The only way in which he can reconcile this availability of schools with "the frequent complaints of the decay and disappearance of schools" in the later Middle Ages is to suppose that many of these institutions had "a short or intermittent life." Little remarks that Leach does not discuss this point, although the lack of continuity is clear from the author's articles in the *VCH*.[56]

The reviewer notes that most of Leach's book is concerned with the evidence for "the foundation, continued existence, and numbers of the schools at various periods between the mission of St Augustine and the death of Henry VIII." His wish, therefore, is that Leach, from his "unrivalled knowledge," will in the future supply his readers with "a more systematic study of the schools from the inside," and reconstruct for them, "so far as it can be done from the somewhat fragmentary materials now extant," the life of both the schoolmaster and the schoolboy in medieval times.[57]

Apart from some of the historians and writers who engaged in controversy with Leach and those who reviewed his major publications, there were at least two other persons who contributed to the history of education in Leach's day. The first of these was Foster Watson, professor of education in the University College of Wales, whose review of Leach's work on the schools of Worcester has been considered above and whose own major work on the schools of the early modern period has already been noted.[58] The extent to which Watson agreed or disagreed with Leach is of special interest in view of the criticism levelled at Leach in more recent years by the historian of Tudor education, Joan Simon. Commenting on Leach's tendency to ignore his indebtedness to other scholars, she mentions in particular his failure in *The Schools of Medieval England* to cite Watson's important *English Grammar Schools,* which had appeared seven years earlier and which contained "some modifications" of Leach's views.[59]

Being primarily interested in the educational aspects of the Renaissance, Watson is understandably concerned with the school curriculum in a way that Leach is not. From his special perspective he thinks that the medieval grammar schools should have been more aptly termed "logic" schools, since their chief purpose was to provide not a literary training but a kind of technical education. Not only were Roman and Greek authors generally not read, Watson claims, but the Latin that was learned was "decadent and barbarous."[60] This was, of course, a view of medieval education that revealed the gulf between Watson and Leach with respect to the school curriculum. Yet it would be a mistake to infer from this a total lack of sympathy between the two writers, since in so many other respects Watson agrees with Leach.

For one thing, Watson shares Leach's conviction that grammar schools in England were especially flourishing in the seventeenth century. In this connection he goes beyond Leach in describing this early modern experience as the most successful of all – the fruit of "the living force of an intensive ideal" – to be contrasted, once more in line with Leach, with "the decadence of the grammar schools from 1660 onwards."[61] Again, with reference to the Schools Inquiry Commission of 1864–68, he quotes with approval the statement of Sir Joshua Fitch that not only was the number of students learning Latin and Greek constantly diminishing, but instruction in other subjects was found to be "very worthless," and the continued omission of modern subjects from the curriculum was justified by "the very existence of statutes prescribing the ancient learning."[62]

In his brief survey of the pre-Reformation period, Watson shares Leach's emphasis on the ecclesiastical domination of the nation's schools as the "central feature" of medieval times.[63] Moreover, he classifies the various kinds of grammar schools in the same way that Leach does, and ascribes educational responsibilities to the collegiate churches "in their typical organisation."[64] He also agrees with Leach's estimate of the number of chantries dissolved by the Act of 1547 and notes that the schools attached to chantries could be either grammar schools or song schools, Watson identifying the latter generally with elementary education.[65] Finally, in his bibliography, along with writers like de Montmorency, Mullinger, Lyte and J.H. Lupton, he includes Leach's *Educational Charters*, his *Early Yorkshire Schools* and *Winchester College*, and his *VCH* articles "in progress."[66] In short, apart from his obvious differences with Leach in respect to the superior worth of the Renaissance Latin culture to medieval Latin literacy, Watson displays a marked agreement with Leach on the more institutional side of medieval education.

The second of these two educational historians, A.W. Parry, principal of the Training College at Carmarthen, obtained a Doctor of Science degree at the University of London for a thesis on medieval education that he subsequently published in 1920 under the title of *Education in England in the Middle Ages*.[67] Parry's research and writing was apparently protracted over several years, so that his investigation of the subject was virtually coterminous with Leach's preparation of *The Schools of Medieval England*. His use of Leach is quite extensive and on the whole analytical. In his bibliography Parry cites *English Schools at the Reformation*, Leach's histories of Southwell Minster, Winchester College, and Warwick School, *Early Yorkshire Schools*, *Early Education in Worcester*, and *Educational Charters*, while in his text and footnotes he makes use of Leach's *VCH* chapters and his entries in the *Cyclopedia of Education*.[68]

Parry is at pains to clarify the terminology relating to medieval schools, noting that some of the confusion over terms has arisen from the views advanced by Leach himself. Parry interprets a "free school," for instance, not necessarily as one that did not charge fees, but as one open to all comers without any restriction in respect to social class, particular professions, or the locality of the candidate.[69] In many instances he would prefer to use the term "class" rather than "school" to denote the gathering of a teacher and his students.[70]

While he sees the utility of the term "elementary" in relation to instruction in a grammar school – elementary classes learn Donatus and the more advanced ones Priscian[71] – he cannot accept Leach's tendency to equate an elementary school with a song school. Observing that the only apparent evidence for this opinion was Leach's interpretation of the misunderstanding between the masters of the grammar and song schools at Warwick, Parry further notes that it was not uncommon for one and the same master to be responsible for the instruction in both grammar and song.[72] He enlarges upon one aspect of this question by remarking that the distinction drawn by Leach between 193 "grammar schools" and the remainder of his 259 chantry schools, which he classifies as "song ... or ... elementary schools," is "quite unnecessary." In Parry's view, the chantry schools were in reality the parochial church schools now supported by a "separate endowment" and taught by a priest who, unlike the parish priest, could attend to his classes on a full-time basis.[73]

The above remarks are in keeping with one of Parry's main contentions, namely, that terms such as "song school," "reading school," and "writing school" all denote separate and distinctive skills, as does "grammar school" itself. They must not be confused with "elementary" education. Although the precise nature of these distinctive kinds of instruction is not always clear, – even the documentary sources for "reading schools," for example, are quite ambivalent – Parry is of the opinion that none of these medieval schools was an elementary institution in any modern sense, and that the elementary school "cannot be traced further back in England than to the establishment of the charity schools of the seventeenth century."[74]

While Parry gives full credit to Leach for being "the first writer to realise fully the significance of the chantries in relation to the provision of facilities for education,"[75] he does not accord him the same credit for his assessment of monastic education. To the contrary, Parry sees something positive in the way the monasteries either founded some of the grammar schools or acted as trustees for their real founders.[76] Parry views the monastic almonry schools, at least with respect to most of the leading monasteries, as providing education as well as board and residence for a number of young boys "who would otherwise be unable to obtain any education," cognizant though he is of Coulton's warning that the temptation was great for monastic authorities to neglect such provision.[77]

After the work of Watson and Parry, it would be a full generation before educational historians were drawn into another ongoing assessment of Leach. Meanwhile, some of his major publications entered, however uneasily, into the wider world of historical scholarship. In her brief survey of medieval schools to c.1300 for the volumes of the *Cambridge Medieval History*, Margaret Deanesly included Leach's *Educational Charters and Documents* in her bibliography under "Original Authorities." Under "Modern Works," she includes Leach's article "Schools" from the *Encyclopaedia Britannica*; his address to the British Academy, "Results of Research"; and *The Schools of Medieval England* – this last, however, with the notation "To be read with reserve for pre-Conquest schools," the reader being directed to Little's review. This was in 1926.[78] Ten years later, in a further volume of the same standard work of reference, G.R. Potter's chapter entitled "Education in the Fourteenth and Fifteenth Centuries" gave considerable prominence to Leach in the section of the bibliography called "Particular Counties and Schools." In addition to *English Schools at the Reformation*, *The Schools of Medieval England*, *Educational Charters and Documents*, the British Academy lecture on "Results of Research," and a list of Leach's articles in the *VCH*, Potter included *Early Yorkshire Schools* and *Early Education in Worcester*, along with Leach's volumes on Southwell, Beverley, Warwick, and Winchester.[79]

Although Sir Maurice Powicke's broad sympathies extended to religious and cultural history as much as to political and administrative topics, the impressive bibliography that appeared in his volume on the thirteenth century for the Oxford History of England series had room for only a footnote: "On A.F. Leach, *The Schools of Medieval England* (1915), see A.G. Little in E.H.R. xxx (1915), 525–9." This footnote remained in the 1954 reprint, with corrections, as well as in the second edition of the work, 1962.[80] In her volume on the fourteenth century for the same series, however, May McKisack, in the section of her bibliography entitled "Ecclesiastical History," refers the reader to Potter's chapter in the *Cambridge Medieval History* "for a good sketch of education in the later Middle Ages," and she directs attention to Potter's list of "the numerous studies of medieval schools by A.F. Leach."[81] Finally, E.F. Jacob, in his volume devoted to the fifteenth century, includes two of Leach's works in his bibliographical section, "The Universities and Education" – *The Schools of Medieval England* and *Educational Charters and Documents*.[82]

It was in the mid-1950s that Joan Simon ushered in the modern criticism of Leach with two articles in the *British Journal of Educational Studies*.[83] In view of the fact that her own studies would eventually result in a major publication on educational developments within the social context of Tudor England,[84] it is not surprising that she initiated the debate with a fresh look at the impact of the Chantries

Act of 1547 on English education. There is no stronger testimony to Leach's influence over the previous forty years or so than her assessment of the state of the question in 1955. Adverting to Pollard's opinion that an adequate study of Protector Somerset's educational policy in the first part of Edward VI's reign had yet to be written, Simon contends that, notwithstanding, no topic continued to be so glibly dealt with as the chief instrument of that policy – the Chantries Act of 1547.[85] Noting that the authority for the prevalent interpretation of the legislation as "a fatal point in English education" was the author of *English Schools at the Reformation*, she goes on to mention that it was precisely "Leach's methods of investigation and findings" that Pollard was challenging when he pointed out the need for further research. Since Pollard failed to make his point, Leach's conclusions gained acceptance among "most historians" of the period, including those primarily concerned with educational history.[86]

Although in Simon's view Leach's emphasis on the role of the secular clergy in medieval education constituted the main ground of his case against the Chantries Act, she cites Little's review of *The Schools of Medieval England* in support of her contention that this was all of a piece with Leach's "deep-rooted prejudice" against the monastic order. It was above all this attitude of mind that led to his "mishandling of facts" and "unsubstantiated conclusions" for the early medieval centuries.[87] It is quite clear, nevertheless, that it is not the anti-monastic bias in Leach, nor the early medieval period in general, that is Simon's main concern. What matters most are Leach's arguments that pre-Reformation England had been well supplied with schools. These she cannot accept, "if only because they rest on formal evidence and fail to take into account the decline of the Church in the later Middle Ages."[88] What exactly she means by "the decline of the Church" becomes clear from a later statement in the same article when she remarks that "from the early fifteenth century, lay initiative in the founding of schools had been increasing, and the interest of the Church in sponsoring education had progressively declined."[89]

Closely related to this question of school supply is Leach's repeated emphasis on the central role of the collegiate church in pre-Reformation England, a view that Simon finds untenable not only because she thinks Leach depends too much on an unverifiable acceptance of the educational provisions of the Lateran decree of 1215 by English churchmen but also because Leach had failed to provide more than a handful of specific examples of early collegiate churches maintaining schools. She points out that when he cites later examples he relies too much on inference, and in the case of five new collegiate churches established in the thirteenth century, he fails to provide any evidence of a school master on the foundation in any of them, "either at their inception or in 1548." She is certain, in fact, that Leach's claim for 200 collegiate schools at the time of the Reformation cannot stand against "the concrete information" contained in the chantry certificates, which allows for only twenty-two collegiate foundations responsible for some degree of educational service.[90]

In the second of her two articles, concentrating on the chantry certificates as well as Leach's interpretation of them, Simon summarizes Leach's case against the Chantries Act as resting on two main assumptions. The first was that the endowed schools lost their lands and received only a fixed stipend in return; as this stipend declined in value, so the schools deteriorated or disappeared. The second assumption was that the unendowed schools lost their lands and received no recognition; having been deprived of financial support, these schools were all done away with in 1548. She cannot accept his first point, simply because Leach did not classify schools at any time "according to this criterion."[91] As for his second point, she maintains that unendowed schools were not swept away but were accorded a definite status "because they received recognition, as schools, from the Crown" and henceforth were regarded as "endowed foundations."[92]

As to the precise number of schools that deteriorated or disappeared altogether, Simon finds little in Leach's figures to warrant any safe generalization. She states that his whole analysis is based on two assumptions: first, that every reference in 1548 to the teaching of "grammar" implies the existence of an established school regardless, among other things, of the size of the place, the qualifications of the master, or the stipend he received; and, second, that if these schools were not in a flourishing condition as "modern" secondary institutions three and a half centuries later, their failure could be traced to the Chantries Act.[93] On the contrary, she is satisfied that the dissolution of the chantries, like the earlier dissolution of the monasteries, was a matter of serious concern for the commissioners, and that it resulted in a kind of "national survey of schools, the first of its kind."[94] Remarking that the incidence of schools had formerly been uneven, owing mainly to the custom of benefactors to settle endowments in their native village "regardless of local demand," she justifies the removal of some schools – "apparently, the only schools swept away" – as the effort of county gentry, as commissioners, to rationalize educational services. She adds that in the other cases schools were given a stipend by the Crown that was the equivalent of the school's former income from lands. The school in question, therefore, operated "exactly as before," with the one difference being that "the masters, relieved of duties in the church, could give their whole attention to teaching."[95]

The three main issues introduced above by Simon – Leach's estimates of the extension and distribution of pre-Reformation schools, his virtual identification of grammar schools with the secular clergy of the collegiate churches, and his interpretation of the Chantries Act of 1547 as disastrous for education – were kept alive in the 1960s by a series of exchanges in the *British Journal of Educational Studies.*[96] What had become an issue in its own right was Leach's general reliability for future students of educational history. In her final comment on Leach and his methods, Simon revealed her concern that a sharp distinction be made between Leach's basic source material and the way in which he was prone to interpret it:

Nor – though I recognize that Leach successfully challenged a prevailing view in his own day – can I muster admiration for one who so resolutely cornered a field and, while trampling on colleagues if the smallest opportunity offered, hindered the advance of scholarly understanding by covering up his own errors. It is because these, which are very material, have never been corrected that it is impossible to reprint Leach's books, even as a makeshift until new supervene. In this respect he was his own worst enemy and it ultimately became necessary to explode the 'Leach legend' before there could be any advance. There remain the materials which, carefully sifted and decisively extracted from the framework in which Leach embedded them, will undoubtedly be fruitfully exploited in the rewriting of educational history.[97]

At the same time that the latest debate on Leach was coming to a halt in the pages of the *British Journal of Educational Studies*, W.E. Tate, in the St Anthony's Hall Publications, produced a pamphlet on Leach as a historian of education in Yorkshire.[98] This pamphlet was essentially an attempt to provide a "critical appreciation" of all the references to Yorkshire schools contained in Leach's works, especially in the *VCH*, together with some additions and corrections made since Leach's death by Tate and other students. On the whole, Leach comes off quite well in his identification of most, if not all, of the Yorkshire grammar schools. This may be contrasted with his obvious neglect of the Nonconformist academies as well as the charity schools of the seventeenth and eighteenth centuries, not to mention his continuing indifference to developments in elementary education. Tate believes Leach "is not particularly interested in the schools which do not follow, and which never have followed, the classical tradition."[99] While Tate advances criticisms of Leach shared by other writers – for example, Leach's claims for the existence of a number of ancient schools in the absence of written evidence to the contrary, and his lack of consistency regarding dates of school foundations[100] – he can still speak in general of "the scholarly accuracy which characterizes his writing."[101] In a restricted and detailed work of this kind, it is understandable that the author is especially indebted to Leach for his *Educational Charters and Documents* and his *Early Yorkshire Schools*, the first as "Leach's basic study" for educational history, the second as "one of the two detailed source-books of education for specific county areas."[102]

Also in 1963, John Lawson published a study of Hull Grammar School from its origin in the late fifteenth century to late Victorian times.[103] Reflecting something of the recent interest in the investigation of local history, Lawson's work may be considered as a microcosm of Leach's published work, revealing within a single urban community very much the same ebb and flow of educational development that Leach discerned on the national scene. There are, for instance, statistics to show how the "free grammar school" of Hull declined perceptibly in numbers between 1677 and 1726;[104] how its "classical" curriculum was considerably broadened in the early nineteenth century to include subjects like English, mathematics, and geography;[105] that from 1838 the traditional "church connection" was broken, with detrimental effects on the finances of the institution;[106] and, finally, that in the early 1860s, in a city of over 100,000, the sole publicly endowed grammar school, with only some sixty boys, was in the same "depressed and decayed" state as most of the other endowed grammar schools in the country.[107]

It is the earliest chapter in the history of Hull grammar School, however, that is of particular relevance to the study of Leach. Lawson makes the point that without any great church, as at nearby Beverley, to support a school, the responsibility for education fell on the shoulders of the mayor and burgesses of Hull, and that in the fifteenth century the schoolhouse was maintained as town property at public expense.[108] Since the master depended on fees for his livelihood, so that the school was faced with an intermittent existence, a fresh start was welcomed in 1479 when John Alcock, bishop of Rochester, offered to provide a chantry in Hull to help support the existing school. Under this agreement the corporation conveyed the schoolhouse to the new foundation, while the bishop, through the chantry, granted a stipend to the schoolmaster so that boys could now be taught free of charge.[109]

The endowment, however, in the form given to it by Alcock in 1479, lasted barely two generations, since in 1548 the chantry was suppressed and the property confiscated. Lawson states that although the school suffered "no immediate ill-effects," its survival was tied to the substitution by the Crown of a fixed money payment in place of the expropriated lands, bringing about, he says, "the progressive impoverishment of the school as prices rose."[110]

In 1967 Lawson followed up his work on Hull with a condensed descriptive survey of medieval education in general, including the Reformation, that relies to some extent on Leach's *Educational Charters and Documents*, his *Schools of Medieval England*, and a number of his *VCH* articles.[111] Lawson's treatment of Leach is even-handed. He endorses Leach's emphasis on the dependence of medieval schools "on some ecclesiastical institution of one kind or another," and further agrees that it is the absence of this characteristic at the foundation of Winchester College in 1382 that makes it so "important."[112] In common with Leach, Lawson stresses the function of the chantry in later medieval education, asserting that the majority of both grammar and elementary schools, at least by the fifteenth century, were taught by chantry priests.[113] He also credits Leach with doing much to explode the "once popular notion" that medieval education was mainly the work of the monasteries, but although "no scholar would now admit the monks to have been a great educational force in later mediaeval England," their exact role in education is still often "misunderstood."[114]

Lawson offers some interpretations of his own. He regards the medieval social order as "relatively static." When it began to be less so in the later Middle Ages, "growing prosperity" brought into being "reading and writing schools" to serve the needs of the urban trading classes.[115] In the majority of schools, however, Latin continued to hold sway, with the *trivium* – comprising grammar, rhetoric, and logic – constituting the substance of grammar school education.[116] Finally, Lawson thinks that from the middle of the sixteenth century the school was in reality a means of securing the new Anglican establishment, an achievement of only some three or four decades, "a part seldom acknowledged by historians of the period." For this reason, Lawson remarks, the Church of England, conscious of its historic responsibility as "guardian of education," jealously took its stand against both the state and Nonconformity in the nineteenth century when national education once again became "a political concern."[117]

Lawson has at least two major points of disagreement with Leach. First, he cannot accept Leach's pronouncement that "there can be no manner of doubt ... that all the cathedral and collegiate churches kept schools." To state, Lawson says, that a grammar school was the "invariable concomitant" of every collegiate church is "only an inference."[118] Even less, however, can Lawson agree with Leach's tendency to take for granted the continuity of schools, a matter that had probably exercised Lawson from his research into the grammar school at Hull. Leach's tendency to ascribe continuity to a particular school mentioned "two or three times in as many centuries" is, in Lawson's opinion, "a rash supposition." It is also an "astonishing" one in view of Leach's personal experience of the decay and death of so many small grammar schools in his own lifetime and the "numerous complaints" with respect to the disappearance of schools in the fifteenth century.[119]

For this and related reasons, Lawson suggests, "we ought not to overrate the amount of schooling available before the Reformation, as Leach does," but, at the same time, keep in mind what must have been "considerable private or unendowed teaching" of which we do not have any record and which it is virtually impossible to assess.[120]

On the central question of Leach's thesis – the disastrous effects of the Reformation on education in Edward VI's reign – we have seen that Lawson's study of Hull tended to confirm Leach's views. Lawson does not, nevertheless, see the larger national picture in the same way. At the end of his discussion of this subject, he concludes that "in the absence of definitive evidence" it is not unreasonable to state that the action of Edward VI "at most ... caused some brief dislocation of schools, but no wholesale closures." While he admits that the awarding of fixed stipends "soon injured many schools," once ex-chantry property had been sold to stave off bankruptcy, "it is difficult to see what could have been done to repair the damage by a government living from hand to mouth in an inflationary economy."[121] Lawson's book, then, may be considered to have its own place in an era of revisionism. With particular reference to Leach's overthrow of the Protestant view of pre-Reformation England as "submerged in ignorance and superstition," Lawson makes the observation that for Leach the Reformation was, indeed, a "disaster," but that it fell in Edward VI's reign, not Henry VIII's. Lawson makes the further point that historians are now denying the existence of any school system before the Reformation for Edward VI to destroy, quoting G.R. Elton to the effect that, although the "old legend" of Edward VI's educational patronage was now dead, the "newer legend" linking "a great system of education" to the old chantry schools still awaited its "overthrow."[122]

Before considering the publications of Nicholas Orme, some of the most important contributions to the study of medieval education, it might prove helpful to note a few of the more recent studies that, though somewhat marginal to the specific research of Leach on the grammar schools, have something useful to say on particular aspects of his work. Margaret Spufford, in a study of English villagers in the sixteenth and seventeenth centuries, has drawn attention to the sporadic nature of the documentary evidence relating to the existence of schools. This could argue for a more plentiful supply of schools just as easily as for their intermittent character, since, as she points out, the evidence in college admission registers indicates that boys were prepared for college in some villages in which, from the episcopal records, "there had never been a schoolmaster, or there was not a schoolmaster at the right time, or there was only a schoolmaster who taught the 'vulgar tongue.'"[123] Moreover, although the author is not directly concerned with any debate over Leach's findings, it is interesting to note her comment that "it will always be impossible to know, for lack of documentation, whether the ordinary villager was better educated in the sixteenth and seventeenth centuries than before the reformation."[124]

In his study of the parish clergy shortly before the Reformation, Peter Heath stresses that the capacity to read Latin fluently was essential "to the priest's moral and spiritual development" and that this was not lost upon some of the leading churchmen of the day.[125] Heath notes that in the two generations immediately prior to the Reformation, university graduates among the clergy ranged from 17 per cent in Norwich to 20 per cent in Canterbury and 33 per cent in London.[126] Heath contends that schools were "varied, widespread, increasing in number and diminishing in fees," with the endowment of both masters and students "fashionable and frequent."[127] In this connection Heath is in agreement with Spufford since it is his observation that evidence of priests involved in teaching is of a sporadic nature, sometimes coming to light only through court records bearing on a very different topic, as in the case he cites of an aged London priest responsible for some thirty pupils.[128]

Heath also mentions the criticism that Simon directed against the chantries and their priests, observing that she was more concerned with and "more successful in" showing their relatively small importance than in establishing them as a "negligible" quantity altogether. He goes on to mention that in the Staffordshire of the early sixteenth century, which he has especially investigated, "schools were kept at ten out of eighty-five chantries."[129]

The most thorough study of the English chantry, however, is that by Alan Kreider. Kreider's investigation centres on, but is not confined to, four "sample" counties: Essex, a Home county; Warwickshire, for the Midlands; Wiltshire, a southwestern county; and Yorkshire, a vast northern county.[130] His conclusions are basically that chantry priests in general were "not a highly educated group of men,"[131] and "relatively few of the chantry priests were also schoolmasters."[132] With regard to the first point, he concedes that this situation varied from one part of the country to the other, noting for instance that in London – and to a lesser extent in Essex – even unbeneficed priests were "frequently well educated."[133]

Kreider states that even Leach, "who tended to overstress the part played by the chantry schools in the medieval educational system," acknowledged that the "great majority" of the "cantarists" were not schoolmasters.[134] Explaining that the "primary motive" in the founding of a chantry was to secure relief, by means of prayers, for the souls of the founder and others whom he might name who were suffering in purgatory,[135] the author notes that the cantarist-school-masters were normally required to offer daily mass and other liturgical services for the souls of their benefactors, to participate in choir, and, on occasion, to perform pastoral duties in connection with their parishes. Kreider views such obligations as a "quite serious drawback" to the efficient conduct of a school.[136] He also mentions that, in addition to their limitations "in scale and in quality of instruction," chantry schools were "casual and uninstitutionalized," with a number of them dependent on meagre endowments and therefore in a continuously precarious position.[137]

Kreider's opinion of the debate in the *British Journal of Educational Studies* recounted above – at least as it involved responses to Simon's "forceful criticisms of Leach" – is that it had led to some "not very illuminating controversy."[138] Noting that the best treatment of the chantry schools at the dissolution is to be found in Orme's work, Kreider states that the latter's treatment, like Simon's in her study of Tudor education, is based mainly on secondary sources as well as printed primary sources. He claims that any final supersession of Leach's writings on the dissolution will have to take the form of "an equally assiduous examination *de novo* of the manuscripts in the P.R.O."[139]

Since Leach's research touched upon so many aspects of the social and religious life of medieval England, it may well be that for some time to come studies of specific topics connected with but not central to Leach's main educational interest will contribute to a better understanding of how pre-university education was related to the mainstream of social and religious developments. In this context the work of writers like Spufford, Heath, and Kreider may well be typical of at least one route that the history of medieval education will follow.

If, however, we turn to the general historians of English life and its institutions, all one can say is that to date there is little evidence that educational history, let alone the published work of Leach, is being integrated into the larger picture. Elton, for instance, has been content to refer his readers to K. Charlton and to Simon, who "between them provide a fairly full picture of the scene – universities, schools, private tuition."[140] A.R. Myers, Anthony Goodman, and M.H. Keen have all produced recent histories of later medieval England or have revised their earlier work, but no summary of medieval schools appears in their pages. Goodman does not have any section on education in his bibliography, but for his chapter entitled "Devotional Trends" includes Nicholas Orme's *English Schools in the Middle Ages*.[141] Keen refers his readers to both Parry's work and Leach's *Schools of Medieval England*,[142] while Myers, under the heading of "Religious and Educational Movements," is satisfied with citing Parry.[143] Even when historians of English history do venture into educational developments, as L.C.B. Seaman does, for instance, in a recent survey from 410 A.D. to 1975, the treatment of the schools that so fascinated Leach is likely to suffer from the far greater attention reserved for the universities of Oxford and Cambridge.[144] It is, perhaps, not an exaggeration to say that English historians in the present generation, as in Leach's own, may be characterized in this matter of pre-university schools as "donnish," the term that Tate used above to describe Leach with his tendency to regard any school that taught no Latin as "hardly a school at all."[145]

Orme's *English Schools in the Middle Ages*, published in 1973, was the first attempt since Leach's day to encompass everything known about secondary and elementary education within the confines of a single volume. In a strictly narrative way, this work replaces Leach's *The Schools of Medieval England*, and, with a criticial apparatus covering all his major themes, the author has been able to establish the subject as a serious line of investigation in its own right, deserving of integration into the more general accounts of the social, religious, and institutional life of medieval and early Reformation England.

While Orme speaks with sympathy of Leach's failure to go into the question of the medieval school curriculum – it is a subject that "leads down unfrequented corridors that few have ventured to explore" – he singles this failure out, nevertheless, as "a limitation which any successor must try to overcome."[146] Orme faces the challenge squarely and, even though his descriptive analysis of the grammar curriculum includes topics that he might have dwelt upon at greater length, provides the English-speaking reader with a short but useful description of the grammatical and literary sources of the new and relatively non-classical educational program that entered England from twelfth- and thirteenth-century France and Italy.[147] In the same chapter Orme includes a particularly lucid survey of the educational changes brought about by the classical emphasis of the Italian Renaissance, beginning in the late fifteenth century.[148] In this context he views Colet's scheme of reform in the 1518 statutes of St Paul's, with their inclusion of fourth- and fifth-century Christian poets together with selections from carefully chosen contemporaries, as "an attempt to retain the Christian tone of the medieval school readers while moving nearer to the type of classical literature now in fashion."[149]

Orme's book embraces three broad areas of educational development. In addition to the inner life of the medieval school, of which the curriculum noted above is a major part, he tries to show the links between educational institutions and the wider society that these institutions reflect, as well as to provide a chronological sketch of the main lines of educational development from the twelfth century to the reign of Elizabeth. Three subjects in particular are of more than usual interest: the "clerical" features of both church and state that encouraged boys and young men to become proficient in Latin; the patronage and supervision of grammar schools; and the increasingly lay participation in educational foundations through the fifteenth and early sixteenth centuries.

In regard to the first subject, Orme observes that to the end of the fourteenth century, literacy, in the traditional sense of being trained in Latin, was virtually the preserve of the ordained clergy, but after this time the records of the secular courts contain numerous cases of merchants and craftsmen, among others, who claimed the status of clerks by means of a literacy test. As Orme remarks, this must mean that either clerks in possession of the first tonsure and the ability to read had taken up secular employment, or literate laymen were anxious to share in a privilege originally restricted to the clergy alone. In either case, he says, "it argues a significant extension of lay literacy."[150]

Emphasising, at least as much as Leach, that medieval education came under spiritual and not secular jurisdiction, Orme notes that the view that assumes that the medieval church exercised a direct control over both the teachers and the curriculum of the schools is not borne out by the available evidence. It was only after the Reformation was well advanced, he claims, that the licensing and supervision of schoolmasters similar to that to which the parish clergy had been accustomed was introduced. On the contrary, he finds that the English bishops seldom, if ever, insisted on their right to "a monopoly of educational appointments," and that the occasions on which their subordinates, the cathedral chancellors and the diocesan archdeacons, did so appear to have been "exceptional rather than normal." He contends, therefore, that the conclusion is inescapable: while the English ecclesiastical authorities had "a certain amount" of ecclesiastical patronage in their possession, "they did not monopolize it to the exclusion of others." In the majority of cases, Orme states, the right to appoint schoolmasters was actually in "private hands" and belonged to "a wide variety of people."[151]

As to the increasing number of lay persons involved in the foundation of schools, Orme identifies this movement as a "major development" in the history of England. He links this development, at least in part, with the increasing urbanization of society, especially with the necessity for the chief officers in the towns to have a knowledge of Latin as well as French and English.[152] He cautions, however, against any disposition to view this greater involvement of the laity from the early fifteenth century as necessarily anticlerical or "at the expense of the ancient clerical interest in education." In his view, "the clergy shared in what was a general growth of interest."[153] Orme explains the wider significance of the movement by noting that as the interest in monasticism declined, that in the schools increased, and that a time was to come when education replaced the monastic life "as a major charitable preoccupation of the pious and wealthy."[154]

Orme followed up his major work with the publication three years later of a study entitled *Education in the West of England 1066–1548*.[155] This is a very informative and factual book on a reduced geographical scale, confined, as it is, to the counties of Cornwall, Devon, Dorset, Gloucestershire, Somerset, and Wiltshire. The author presents sufficient data on the schools of the cathedral cities of Exeter, Salisbury, and Wells to provide some comparison of the ways in which instruction in Latin grammar was made available to both the choristers and secondary clerks of the cathedrals themselves as well as to the wider population of the cities, including adults.[156] The precise relationship, however, between medieval cities generally and their schools is, in Orme's view, "still a mystery."[157]

One of the more interesting as well as more useful lines of inquiry is that connected with school patronage. In his survey of a number of the villages and smaller towns in the six counties mentioned above, the author has uncovered a variety of patrons, extending from the patronage of the grammar school at Crediton by the Collegiate church of that town[158] to that of Lady Katherine Berkeley's foundation at Wotton-under-Edge in Gloucestershire. Orme sees this latter school as occupying "an important place in the constitutional

development" of such institutions. He points out that, in providing
for a schoolmaster to teach free of charge as well as for two scholars
to receive the cost of their board and lodging, Wotton managed to
combine the two major school endowments from the thirteenth and
fourteenth centuries respectively.[159]

At Bruton, Milton Abbas, and Winchcombe, schools were established in the early sixteenth century by groups of people that included abbots of nearby monasteries as well as members of the secular
clergy and laity.[160] Orme contends that all three foundations sig-
nalled a new chapter in educational benefactions in which schools
were now being founded "for their own sake and not, as hitherto,
in association with chantries."[161] While most of the early patrons,
he observes, were clerics, there were exceptions, as in the case of
Plympton, which belonged to the earl of Devon in the later thirteenth
century, and Wotton-under-Edge, which probably was in the patronage of the Berkely family. Orme also remarks that the effective use
of patronage in medieval English towns seems to have varied a great
deal: Bristol, for example, eventually had more than a single school,
owing, apparently, to "a lack of control" in that centre from the
thirteenth century on, whereas in Exeter and Gloucester the patrons
were still trying to make good their claims early in the sixteenth
century.[162]

As regards one of the larger issues that was bound to appear in
a study of this kind – whether the Reformation exercised a beneficial
or harmful effect upon English education – Orme thinks that the
truth probably rests midway between the older "Reformation" view
and the one propounded by Leach in 1896 with the publication of
his *English Schools at the Reformation*.[163] As far as the south-west is
concerned, Orme has identified three monastic houses involved in
public education in their capacity as trustees of endowments, their
responsibility for the appointment of schoolmasters, and their payment of the masters' salaries. These houses included the Augustinians at Bruton, the Benedictines with respect to the schools of
Winchcombe and Cirencester, and the Carthusians of Hinton, who
appointed the master at Bradford-on-Avon. Since no general arrangement had been made by Henry VIII's regime "for extricating
them from the ruin of the monasteries," three of the schools, though
they survived in the long term, experienced periods of "temporary
dislocation," the one fortunate exception throughout being that of
Bradford.[164] The schools of the secular colleges here, as elsewhere
in England, Orme observes, escaped "the consequences of the dis-
solutions" more easily than those of the monasteries had done. The
school at Ottery, for instance, was apparently refounded without

being closed, while that at Crediton was re-opened within two years, leaving only the school at Westbury-on-Trym to die, evidently because of the king's new cathedral school at nearby Bristol.[165]

As for the dissolution of the chantries, Orme has found that, as promised by the Chantry Act of 1548, grammar schools attached to chantries were allowed to continue. This was the case in regard to seven grammar schools reportedly founded in the region in connection with chantries before the 1540s. Nine other school foundations were also spared that, though not originally attached to chantries, had come to be maintained by them in recent years. The one exception to this treatment, Launceston, is explained by the petition of the local inhabitants that the grammar school of Week St Mary be transferred to their town.[166] As to the four chantry schools that were not allowed to continue – those of Enford, Malmesbury, St Briavels, and Truro – the author attributes their termination to the fact that none of them was listed in the chantry certificates as a grammar school. As elementary schools probably confined to "reading or song," they did not qualify under the act for continuance, evidently owing to the view that such instruction was "easily available from other sources." Orme notes, in this connection, that the two "undoubtedly elementary schools" at Launceston and Penryn were dissolved for the same reason.[167] In summation, therefore, he can state that, whereas the fact of the chantry grammar schools surviving the dissolution of the chantries themselves in 1548 "is not in doubt," their survival "in the longer term" is the question.[168] Only four schools in the south-west managed to retain their lands, and this because they had not proved to be chantries: Chipping Camden, Crewkerne, Netherbury, and Wotton-under-Edge. While the other twelve continued to receive their stipends during Edward VI's reign, confusion set in with a financial re-arrangement under Mary Tudor. With the accession of Elizabeth in 1558, most, but not all, received their payments regularly after suing for their rights in court. Finally, as to the promise in the Chantry Act of 1547 that new schools would be endowed out of the confiscated chantry properties wherever they were needed, both the commissioners and the local inhabitants made suggestions along this line in the survey of 1548. In the region under review, however, Orme can report that only two new schools were founded in Edward VI's reign – those at Bath and Sherborne – and that, with the exception of Bruton, where the endowments confiscated in 1539 were restored in 1550, no activity in this direction was forthcoming in the reigns of Mary and Elizabeth.[169]

As implied in the discussion of some of the major themes in both of his studies, Orme's work as a whole is a corrective of Leach. There is no difficulty in recognizing where he differs from the man who "created the modern study of the subject."[170] In Orme's view, Leach's treatment of the religious orders in the educational life of the country is one of his "more serious" deficiencies. Orme notes that, quite apart from his bias against the monastic order, Leach is "wholly silent" in regard to the friars who, as Orme states, were the orders "most committed to the pursuit of education."[171] Another related deficiency is, of course, Leach's "overestimation of the educational role of the collegiate churches." Orme remarks, agreeing with Little, that "no early collegiate church ... ought to be credited with a school without specific information to that effect."[172] Orme recognizes, nevertheless, that with respect to the later Middle Ages Leach appreciated that some collegiate churches had schools attached to them while others did not. The fact that more claims in regard to these collegiate schools have been ascribed to Leach than he ever intended is owing, Orme maintains, to Leach's "own failure to observe clarity and precision" in the statements he made about them.[173]

As for the chantries and their subsequent dissolution, Orme contends that Leach "consistently overrated" their educational importance. He is ready to concede, though, that Leach was right in pointing out the adverse results for education stemming from the dissolution of the chantries, including the extinction of such schools as were elementary and of those grammar schools that had their lands converted into fixed stipends and so were especially vulnerable in an inflationary age. Leach's reassessment of the educational work of the reign of Edward VI, while "necessary," was also accompanied by "too strong" a reaction, resulting, as Orme says, in giving to this one episode an undue importance in the history of Tudor education, "a subject which he never indeed considered as a whole."[174]

Orme's appraisal of Leach's published work is mainly related to his book-length publications and his contributions to the *VCH*. With regard to the former, he thinks that Leach's best work is to be identified with his editions of local, documentary studies, such as his *Early Yorkshire Schools* and *Documents Illustrating Early Education in Worcester*, together with his detailed studies of schools like Winchester, Warwick, and St Paul's, all of these "small, manageable subjects which he researched thoroughly and described on the whole judiciously."[175] As for the *VCH* volumes, they are of variable quality, Orme claims, ranging from a volume like that on Worcestershire, where he had "some good local assistance," to the one on Gloucestershire, in which the treatment "is often sketchy and unreliable." Profitable though Leach's contributions to the *VCH* are, they can no longer be viewed as definitive, with material from the past sixty years having added a good deal to what Leach himself had missed.[176] Finally, in connection with his two more general and ambitious works, *English Schools at the Reformation* and *The Schools of Medieval England*, Orme's opinion is that, although they reveal "an unequalled knowledge of the sources," they also disclose Leach's defects as a historian more than any of his other publications, chiefly for three reasons: the author's failure to discuss topics in which he was not interested, the "extravagance" he displayed in extolling his own theories as contrasted with the denunciation of those of his opponents, and his careless regard for accuracy in relation to dates and facts. In fine, these general studies of Leach, far from crowning his reputation, "clouded" it, bringing the rest of his work under "suspicion," and thus weakening the effectiveness of his entire achievement.[177]

In concluding this survey of Leach's achievement in its wider historiographical context, it remains to take a further look at one of his more far-reaching claims: that England enjoyed a relatively liberal supply of schools in pre-Reformation times. The strictures of Little, Simon, and Jordan in regard to Leach's statistical estimates have all tended to convey the notion that, in his exaggeration of the numbers of documented schools, Leach had, in reality, illustrated the very reverse of what he had intended to show. Until very recently, therefore, there has been a tendency in some quarters to keep Leach at arm's length for reason of his inability to substantiate his favourable picture of medieval England's educational development.

The issue of "school supply," as Leach termed it, has been one of the central questions addressed by Jo Ann Hoeppner Moran. Her studies of lay and clerical education in the city and diocese of York have recently culminated in a major work that for the first time gives due prominence to the role of the elementary schools in the general extension of school facilities. The evidence is mainly drawn from an examination of some 15,000 wills in the diocese of York from the mid-fourteenth century to 1548, the year of the chantry certificates.[178]

One important conclusion from this research is that the proliferation of schools is especially evident in the immediate pre-Reformation generation. Moran, in this instance, is in agreement with Orme, not with Simon and Jordan. Another important point of agreement with Orme, again in opposition to Leach's modern critics, is her finding that schools were more plentiful in later medieval England than has generally been accepted by writers who, like Law-

rence Stone, Simon, and Jordan, have identified the rapid increase
of schools in sixteenth-century England with the distinctively Protestant and lay orientation of the reigns of Edward VI and Elizabeth I.[179]

What is, nevertheless, particularly striking about Moran's educational statistics is that her figures are well in excess of anything put
forward by either Leach or Orme. In a separate index the author
identifies a total of some 250 elementary and grammar schools for
the city and diocese of York.[180] Since Leach's mention of some 300
grammar schools and Orme's list of 253 grammar and elementary
schools apply to all of England, which consisted then of sixteen
dioceses in addition to that of York, it will readily be appreciated
how startling this evidence really is. There are, it is true, other major
areas of interest explored in this study, including, for instance, the
growth of lay literacy and, on the more clerical side, the rapid increase in ordinations during the half century prior to the Reformation. While the educational significance of these and related
issues, however, may have to wait upon the integration of Orme's
results with those of Moran, there can be no question that on the
particular subject of school supply in later medieval England, Moran
has already set to rest any fears that Leach over-estimated the number of pre-Reformation schools.

On the strictly statistical level, therefore, Leach has been more
than vindicated. The price that he paid for his repeated neglect of
the elementary schools is, however, equally important. What Moran
is at pains to show is that Leach failed to appreciate the special
contribution of the elementary schools to the important issues of lay
literacy and clerical training. In this way, Moran is challenging both
critics and defenders of Leach to find a fresh approach to our
understanding of the religious and cultural forces at work in pre-
Reformation England.

Conclusion

From Leach's lifetime until the present, an element of controversy has attended his efforts to delineate the role of the grammar school in the social fabric of medieval England. It now remains, in light of the preceding pages, to present a final assessment of his strengths and weaknesses. This, in itself, may not completely remove the grounds for doubt that, in some quarters, still paralyzes serious effort to build upon his work, but it should help toward a better appreciation of his aims and achievements.

It is clear, for instance, that Leach laid bare the essential features of the medieval grammar school. This was an institution – designed primarily for training in Latin, oral and written – that ordinarily served as entrance to university. The grammar school also provided, of course, for a much more extensive range of the literate population than would proceed to university. Leach showed that such an institution was originally intended to ensure a constant source of supply for the clerical state, but that all grammar school students, whatever their aims in life, shared a common learning experience. The majority of these students would either revert to lay status after attending such a school or avail themselves of at least some of the training offered for positions in such areas as estate management, business, or, more rarely, government service. The grammar school, in short, was the common ground, at least in England, for both church and state.

That Leach was able to show this so cogently was due, for the most part, to his early conviction that the key to medieval education was the church itself – not the monastic life, but the whole ecclesiastical structure based on the diocesan system. Leach never tired of emphasizing the central role of the bishop in the total picture of learning associated with the grammar schools. He saw that role substantiated every time he went to an episcopal register to cite the confirmation of a teacher's appointment or a general mandate to clergy and faithful respecting the conduct of particular schools under the bishop's jurisdiction. While Nicholas Orme, for one, has correctly modified this notion of the almost exclusive role of the bishop in the patronage and supervision of schools, Leach's exaggeration was understandable in his day. It was his mission to destroy the myth that identified very little education with the medieval church.

This investigation into the ecclesiastical context of the nation's schools furnished Leach with many opportunities to delineate the various functions of the ecclesiastical officers. Although Leach showed little interest in the ubiquitous elementary parish schools – and, therefore, in the parishes themselves – he was keenly interested in the greater institutions, especially the cathedrals and the collegiate churches. To assess the degree of responsibility that the chancellor of the later Middle Ages, for instance, still exercised toward the maintenance of grammar schools under his jurisdiction, Leach was led to inquire into the respective rights and duties of the principal officers of the chapters of cathedrals and collegiate churches. Much of this was but imperfectly understood in Leach's day, and some of his publications, such as those on Beverley and Southwell, are a mine of information in this regard. It was in this context, moreover, that Leach was able to distinguish so clearly between a grammar school and a choristers' school, one of the many sources of confusion that bedevilled the whole subject of medieval education when Leach first set to work upon it.

Not the least of Leach's achievements in his efforts to unravel the institutional side of ecclesiastical life was his early ability to make the correct distinctions among the various kinds of grammar schools that appeared in the documentary sources. Fastening on the grammar (Latin) school as the pivot for his entire investigation, Leach succeeded in showing that such terms as "guild school," "hospital school," or even "almonry school" were essentially administrative titles for one and the same kind of institution, the pre-university Latin school. In this connection Leach managed to show that chantry schools, for instance, were not that different in purpose from the great city grammar schools, and that no matter what the actual provisions might be in any given situation, the intent in each case was very much the same: to provide instruction in Latin for boys and young men as well as adults – for all those, in other words, who considered a knowledge of Latin beneficial to their careers. When one compares and contrasts Leach's method of classifying such schools with the state of knowledge that existed on the subject in the first half of the nineteenth century – as is revealed in Carlisle's work on the schools, for instance – one can appreciate the relatively high quality of Leach's achievement in this regard.

There are several more specific topics that Leach's research did much to clarify, even if some of them still remain open to question. These include the widely debated subject of what was meant by a "free" school; the significance of the medieval practice of speaking of "schools" in the plural rather than in the singular; the fact that the teachers of grammar schools were normally persons in clerical orders but could be lay persons as well; and the related fact that monks seldom, if ever, taught in any public school as distinct from classes intended for their own novices. Over and above a further number of other related topics is the very basic one of the antiquity of England's educational institutions, centuries before their common ecclesiastical origins are revealed in the more abundant historical sources of the twelfth to the sixteenth centuries.

Impressive as the above achievements may be, however, it is only fair to observe that Leach's soundness of understanding with respect to them stands or falls on the very extensive body of documentation that he unearthed and made his own. There can be little doubt that this is his most lasting contribution. As Orme himself has expressed it, Leach "created the modern study of the subject and his writings remain indispensable for its pursuit." A.G. Little observed in his now well-known review that Leach is a "safer guide" when records become more numerous. By any standard, these documents constitute the greatest single collection of contemporary source material that we possess today for any future investigation into the development of grammar school learning in England's medieval past. Leach's editions of records pertaining to the grammar schools of Yorkshire and of Worcester; his special studies of the documents pertaining to St Paul's, London, to Sherborne, and to Pocklington, not to mention his own college of Winchester; even his widely distributed volume *Charters and Documents* – these, and several studies like them, place all modern students of the subject heavily in his debt. When, in addition to the more specifically educational collections of source material, there are included the volumes dedicated to the wider ecclesiastical framework of later medieval education, Leach's place in the world of historical scholarship is secure for some time to come. Until more modern critical methods are brought to bear on his method of editing as well as on his translations of some of the more debatable terms and phrases in medieval Latin, Leach's editions of local records, in particular, will remain indispensable for any serious investigation of England's medieval educational development.

In this connection there is equally little room for doubt as to the line of demarcation between Leach's contributions to historical scholarship and his related weaknesses, which tend to negate far too much of his more positive achievements. This was detected very early by Frederic William Maitland, particularly with respect to Leach's projected volume on the town of Beverley for the Selden Society. Maitland, it will be recalled, found little to criticize in Leach's work on the main body of the textual material, but Leach's perorations in his introduction were another matter. This is his Achilles heel; persons of diverse background and outlook – from A.G. Little to Joan Simon – have to some degree echoed Maitland's stricture that while, when working within the limits of textual material relevant to his single-minded pursuits within his own definition of "educational," Leach is at ease and tends to control his evidence, in moving outside this relatively tidy area, however, as he frequently did, he did not have the time and opportunity for the wider reading essential to understanding that more complex world of which educational institutions were but a part. It is here that Leach is often imprudent. In the heat of the moment he rushes into generalizations that do not derive from his facts and in the eyes of his critics detract seriously from his work as a whole.

We must first recognize that Leach's research and publications were to a considerable extent the fruit of hours stolen from his leisure throughout the busy career of a charity commissioner. For instance, he attributed a mistaken reading of the *Durham Almoner's Register* to the circumstance that "utilizing the only time I had for perusing the Register, I read it in bed at midnight." We may attribute his occasional asperity and abruptness of tone to the circumstances in which his work was done. It is evident, nonetheless, that there must have been some deeper reasons for Leach's more controversial statements.

In the first place, in almost every aspect of pre-university education in the medieval period, Leach was justifiably conscious from the first chapters in his research that he was breaking fresh ground. It is difficult from our vantage point today to appreciate some of the implications of this. It was a source of disappointment for him, not infrequently of confessed annoyance, that particular topics such as the distinction between a regular grammar school and a choristers' school, for example, or the meaning of a "free" school, or the relatively limited role of the monasteries in the total scheme of later medieval education – to cite but a few instances out of many – should have continued for so long to be misunderstood or even ignored. All this, despite his clarification of them from unimpeachable sources and his subsequent publication of their salient features.

Leach was not a member of England's academic community in the sense of the university establishment. He did not, therefore, possess the patience and degree of realism of the academic historian, who perceives the inevitability of a time lag between the end product of disciplined research and its ultimate communication to a wider literate public. It may be said with some justice that Leach wanted to write positively about medieval society – but on his own terms. His somewhat peculiar position, therefore, helped to compound other problems. He found himself, for instance, moving against at least two mainstreams of social consciousness. One of these was the air of optimism that characterized much of the outlook of later Victorian England, an optimism related to a fundamentally linear concept of development. It was both a civilized and a civilizing age, and for a person like Leach, with no standing in a recognizable academic community, to pronounce so decisively on questions related to the educational developments of that time was an unmistakable challenge to the guardians of progress.

When the preceding consideration is related to the other stream of social consciousness, it is clear that Leach would eventually be revealed as the destroyer of a myth. This second stream was the heritage of the Reformation, the considered view that nineteenth-century progress had originated in a distinctively Protestant turn of events in the sixteenth century. To suggest, not to mention publicize, the existence of a praiseworthy educational "system" antedating the Reformation, which not only compared favourably with post-Reformation educational developments but appeared in some ways to be superior to them, makes Leach appear at first sight as both a perceptive and a courageous person, who did not hesitate to challenge the very basis of the Reformation tradition.

There is, of course, much in Leach's writing to sustain this view of him. Such an assessment is complicated but not contradicted by Leach's denigration of the monks and the religious and cultural contributions of the monastic order to English society. Leach's earliest known critics – Rose Graham, A.L. Poole and A.G. Little – were by and large monastic historians, and they had little difficulty in exposing Leach's relative unfamiliarity with the known details of monastic history, especially from the earlier centuries. So intent was he in exorcising his fellow Englishmen of a wholesale fiction – that monks and monasteries were as central to virtually all educational activity in the later medieval centuries as they may have been in earlier, more missionary periods – that he left himself open to the charge that he had quite deliberately misrepresented the monastic contribution in very much the same way that he had made the young Edward VI into "the spoiler of schools."

It is now clear that the main and underlying reason for Leach's well-publicized opinion of the monks stemmed from his more general understanding of English history as a whole. He believed that the Norman Conquest was not only a very "foreign" episode, but that its deleterious effects on England extended beyond political and social developments to religious ones as well. Foreign and celibate clergy eventually replaced English and marriageable clergy. This was, for Leach, the real tragedy. There are a number of places in his writings where the reader might conclude that Leach was preoccupied with the problematic nature of celibacy itself. Nevertheless, Leach's overriding concern seems to have been with the place of the Conquest in the history of his country.

This historiographical issue helps to explain in turn a related phenomenon of Leach's history of education – that of the central role he assigns to the collegiate churches. No other major topic, except perhaps that of the dissolution of the chantries, embroiled Leach in more controversy than his contention that St Paul's, London – as one example from among many – precisely because it was "a collegiate church of secular canons" had as one of its responsibilities the maintenance of a grammar school "as part of its foundation." It is only fair to state, nevertheless, that even Leach acknowledged on more than one occasion that this would not necessarily be true in every case – the vagaries of geography alone would affect such distribution of educational services – and that this note of caution was especially relevant to the spate of new collegiate foundations in the fourteenth and fifteenth centuries.

It is a fact, however, that it was Leach's repeated assertion of an essential link between a collegiate church and a grammar school that reached the reading public. This interpretation of pre-Reformation schools not only helped to convey the notion of an actual educational system in later medieval times but also contributed to his conviction that the general public of those earlier days enjoyed a greater abundance of educational facilities than did their descendants in nineteenth-century industrial England.

An analysis of Leach's writing in its entirety reveals at least two reasons for this consistent emphasis on the educational role of the collegiate church. First, Leach is basically sympathetic to the pre-Reformation schools. He has no hesitation in identifying this positive achievement with the early period of his country's development that most appeals to him – pre-Conquest England, characterized by the kind of homespun mentality that he recognizes in the person of Oliver Cromwell. Second, the earliest investigations that he conducted as a charity commissioner into the historical background of schools included the famous pre-Conquest foundations of Beverley and Southwell, a circumstance that tended to foster in Leach the notion that such foundations were the models for virtually all later similar institutions.

While, therefore, the strictures of Little and Simon are well taken, it is equally true that Leach's broad claims on behalf of the educational importance of collegiate churches per se should not be dismissed out of hand. His close study of some of these early collegiate institutions furnishes us with the wider ecclesiastical context in which grammar schools had their origins. The fact that several of the collegiate churches of the fourteenth and fifteenth centuries did not maintain such schools – which can be inferred, at least, from the lack of supporting evidence – does not, in itself, weaken Leach's initial premise in their regard but, rather, raises the question as to why they did not. Until this question is investigated more thoroughly, it appears that the typical collegiate church of later medieval England was intended to play a more local and more restricted role in the social fabric of the nation than the earlier churches investigated by Leach.

Leach's openly expressed bias against the monastic tradition and his equally evident bias in favour of the secular collegiate churches constitute only the more far-reaching deductions that go beyond the evidence cited to support them. There were some minor irritants as well and collectively these helped to weaken his general credibility. In learning from the Lincoln sources, for example, that a friar had been paid in the early fifteenth century as a kind of head music-master for the secular canons, Leach rushed into the position that "the friars seem at this time to have aimed at monopolising the teaching profession," a totally unfounded and even ludicrous suggestion – not lost on Little, the historian of the mendicants. Again, noting the legal context in which particular grammar school teachers appeared in the records of Worcester and Lewes, Leach, in what must have been a moment of wishful thinking, stated that "the schoolmasters of the Middle Ages were generally lawyers as well." A careful reader would, perhaps, overlook these and similar statements as at least out of context.

One instance, however, with more seeming credibility, is worth mentioning. This was Leach's reiterated mention of the donation of William Sevenoaks, an alderman of London, who in 1432 gave lands to his ancestral parish of that name to maintain a grammar teacher with the condition that he be – at least in Leach's translation – "by no means in holy orders." Even assuming that Leach captured the intent of the gift with his translation, he not only interpreted this single document as an indication of a new, lay-oriented social force at work but connected it with the legacy of Wyclif in the context of early Protestantism. For the reader who perseveres in the appointments of grammar masters throughout the rest of the century, no similar condition has so far been found in any of the grants. Once again, then, the conclusion is forced upon one that Leach was prone to undercut his otherwise useful contribution to the source material by making these tendentious statements.

On the other hand, Leach must at least be partly absolved of the assertion of some of his critics that he did not acknowledge the contributions of others. It may well be true that in particular cases he did not make clear the relation of his own research to that of previous writers. Nicholas Carlisle's volumes from the early part of the century, for instance, were part of Leach's starting point for his own investigations. That it is only on occasion that Leach mentions Carlisle can be explained simply by the fact that this early publication, however well intended, is filled with misinformation and helps to consolidate the myth both of the monks' direct involvement with medieval public grammar schools and the spate of "new" foundations under Edward VI.

There are, however, numerous instances in which Leach expresses his indebtedness to others. In his study of the grammar school at Nottingham, for example, Leach thanks the second master of the high school in that city, a Mr Corner, "to whose researches into the history of the school this history is deeply indebted." He expresses a special word of thanks to Bishop Gore of Worcester for giving him "the exceptional opportunities" of studying the episcopal registers at home, a procedure which Leach wishes other "custodians of ancient MSS. would more widely follow." Another example, this one from his *English Schools at the Reformation*, is Leach's expression of gratitude to Edith Salisbury, who took such great care in preparing the transcripts of the chantry certificates for him. Leach remarked that whenever he entertained some doubt about her rendering, a reference to the original had invariably proved that "if there was an error, it was not hers."

These and many other similar acknowledgments reveal a Leach who was generally fair and considerate with others who shared his educational and ecclesiastical interests. One notable exception could be the well-known contemporary of Leach, Foster Watson. That Leach virtually ignores his friend – Watson wrote Leach's biograph-

ical notice for the *Dictionary of National Biography* – may appear ungracious and no specific defense of Leach's attitude is presently
forthcoming. Watson's main interest was schools and learning in
England associated with the Renaissance, and this raises one of the
more interesting points connected with Leach's view of this important development.

That Leach was not able to gain much insight into the curriculum
of the medieval grammar school appears to be directly related to his
assessment of Renaissance humanism. His position, as we have seen,
was that the humanist contribution to education was essentially a
misplaced effort. The Latin language, for one thing, was not really
in the sorry state that the devotees of classical literature claimed.
Moreover, the humanist philosophy – in Leach's view, the emphasis
on temporal life rather than preparation for the life to come – could
not, of itself, earn the commendation of a Christian society. Leach
never tires of reiterating the point that persons like Colet have been
given far too much praise for the relatively little that, in his opinion,
they actually contributed to fifteenth- and sixteenth-century learning. What is from his vantage point even more annoying is that
the whole Erasmian outlook was too self-congratulating.

Leach's evident minimizing of the change of emphasis which Renaissance humanism brought to educational circles underscores his
own perception of what he was in the process of contributing to the
history of education. It could be argued, for instance, that his somewhat erratic approach to humanist learning is all of a piece with both
his own experience of the classics at Winchester and All Souls
and his apparent ignoring of the studies of Watson. Judging from
the reports of the inquiries he conducted in various places as a charity
commissioner, there is ground for thinking that Leach was very taken
up with the new developments in education, especially the effort to
channel funds into schemes for the expansion of more "modern"
and "practical" facilities, not excluding better provision for the education of girls and young women. Leach evinces relatively little concern for the extension of classical education. It seems, in fact, that
the more deeply he delved into England's remote educational background, the further he could see into the needs and aspirations of
the future. Leach is conscious, in short, that his own generation was
making an important break with England's past. It is, however, at
least equally clear that he saw the uniqueness of his own research
as identified with the Latin culture of the Middle Ages, an area of
social experience of which most of his contemporaries, particularly
those brought up on classical Greek and Latin, were quite ignorant.
In fine, Leach perceived himself as a pioneer in medieval studies.

That Leach also perceived that he was not always or everywhere appreciated as such was not lost on him. This helps to explain the circumstances surrounding his relationship to the academic community, especially the historians. These persons were in a position, as Maitland was for example, to observe the deficiencies in Leach's broad reading background, deficiencies that led him to indulge in generalizations that were often unconnected with the more specific evidence that he did know and was able to control. Nonetheless, it must equally be conceded that none of these academic historians had taken the trouble to investigate pre-university education on its own merits, to integrate this aspect of England's development into their own areas of interest. There was thus really no common ground for a dialogue on medieval education between Leach and, say, A.F. Pollard. This may well be the weakest point of all in the Leach legacy, the fact that during his own career Leach found himself producing a whole mine of information on the historical background of several related contemporary issues without the direct involvement of the academic community.

This particular weakness also appears to be a contributing factor in one final observation that should be made about Leach's research. This is the fact that Leach reveals little appreciation of the comparative approach. He does on occasion show that he was aware, even painfully so, of the way in which German writers especially had been able to urge their own version of the development of culture on the English public. Scattered references indicate that Leach was not entirely unaware of the occasional relevant contribution to educational history from France. But he evidently remained quite un aware of similar and parallel investigations going on in more than one area of the continent. Clerval's volume on education in medieval Chartres, for instance, appeared in 1895, while the important work of Giuseppe Manacorda on the schools and the curricula of medieval Italy, published shortly before Leach's *Schools of Medieval England*, contains a good deal of documentary source material that Leach would have appreciated.

If these last two observations point to a lost opportunity in Leach's day, it is even more to the point that they are still relevant. The history of pre-university education has been all but neglected by historians. Apart from Orme's publications it has been customary for writers who include a chapter or so on intellectual history to depend on one or more of Leach's three more popular books. This situation has recently shown signs of change, perhaps under the impact of studies in the various fields of social history, and, in any case, as has been shown above, Leach has been to a large extent superseded by Orme.

Whatever the full significance of Leach's research and publications for the contemporary and future study of medieval education, it can at least be said of him that he made historical study relevant to contemporary concerns. The subject of education takes on life with his pen, and the verve and insight characteristic of virtually all his writing has impressed on the total body of his material a style that is *sui generis*. Alone, it seems, among his fellow charity commissioners, Leach possessed the mode of inquiry that we call historical. It is something of a paradox that one of the communities that Leach did not stimulate in his own day was that of the academic historians, and that in today's world his service to historical study is only now being given some attention when the academic historian himself is being challenged to state his purpose anew.

Appendices

Charity Commission Report (in manuscript) on Chichester, 27 July 1886, by A.F. Leach

MS ED 27/4713 (pp. 37–43)

26. With a view to clearing up the question of the origin of the Prebendal School and specially whether or not it represents the old School of the Chancellor of the Cathedral I thought it necessary to search the Episcopal Registers preserved in the Bishop's Library which has been indexed by the late Prebendary Walcot ... As the bishop of Chichester did not see his way to sending the Registers here I went to Chichester and inspected them there. They run from Feb. 10, 1396 to 1511 and include the Register of Bp Storey, founder of the present Prebendal School. But I could find no reference to any school or to the Chancellor's scholastic duties, except as regards the latter in one passage in Bishop Rede's[1] register f.32 which is transcribed out as 95 on file by the Rev. Prebendary Stephens, an expert in ancient manuscripts, who was kind enough to refer to the passages for me which I thought likely. I had made out with great difficulty this passage myself with the exception of a word or two and this reading confirmed my reading of the passage on the Bishop's Visitation of the Cathedral AD 1402. Among other complaints "Item compertum est quod cancellarius non invenit magistrum [diligentem?] ad instruendum choristas in grammatica." In Bishop Storey's register there is, so far as I could make out, and Mr. Stephens says it also, no reference to the Prebendal School or statute, or any other school.

27. There is therefore absolutely no evidence to show that there was any school attached to the cathedral before the Prebendal School except the Choristers' School kept by the Chancellor of the Cathedral and there is nothing to show any connection between that school and the Prebendal School.

28. But in the British Museum (M.S. add 6, RR Sussex collections Sir W. Burrell) 5706 at p.136 in pencil; 338 [introduction][2] is given the extract

from Bishop Rede's register quoted above and under it is written "N.B.
To exempt the Chancellor from this expense Bp Storey founded the
Grammar School and annexed to it the Prebend of Hyleigh." This was
probably written by Sir W. Burrell and is the passage which put me on
inquiring into the Episcopal Registers. But as there is no evidence forthcoming in support of it and as it appears that the Hyleigh Statutes were
intended to furnish a substitute for the Chancellor or his "persona
idonea" and not to give an additional endowment to an existing Schoolmaster I fear that any hope of proving the existence of a grammar
school attached to the Cathedral other than the Chancellor's Choristers'
School is vain.

29. But taking the institution as it stands under the Highleigh statutes, I
would submit to the Commission whether the School does not come
within the [provisions] of V.27 of the E.S.A. 1869 and whether therefore
additional endowment to the present endowment of £ 81 a year would
not be obtained for it from the Eccl. [Commission]. The prebend was
undoubtedly a part of the endowment of Chichester Cathedral. It appears to me it is so still ... The judgment of the Cathedral [Commission]
has clearly been i) that the Prebend is a part of the Cathedral endowment
and ii) that it is permanently attached "to any school or the mastership
thereof." If so then the Prebendal School is deserving assistance out of
the endowment of such (cathedral) "Church" and has a claim upon the
Ecclesiastical [Commission] to an "increased provision." It may of course
be argued that as the Prebend had not fallen into the "Common Fund"
of the Ecclesiastical [Commission] there is no claim for increased provision such as exists in regard to Chester or Canterbury. But the provision in the ancient statutes of the Cathedral with regard to the duties
of the Chancellor "Cancellarius debet scholatizare vel dare lectiones
auscultare et terminare" show [sic] that there was a School attached to
the Cathedral at a very early date and it seems certain that teaching
was an essential part of the design of Cathedrals of the Old as much
as of the New foundation ... In any case the Prebend of Highleigh has
been diminished in value by the same process as the new Cathedral
School endowments viz the abolition of the common table, while Highleigh has been diminished in value by a flagrant application of the system
of fines ... I informally sounded some of the members of the Chapter
as to what their view would be of an application to the [Ecclesiastical
Commission] and whether they would back it up and the answer was,
perhaps upon terms but I gather that the Master of the school himself
would not be willing to accept anything from the Ecclesiastical
[Commission] and especially not through the Charity [Commission].

A.F.L.

27 July 1886

Latin Grammar

MS HARL. 1002 (fols.97v-99)

Quid est accentus? Modulacio vocis in significativa pronunciacione ... Species vero accentus prosayci sunt tres propter soni trinam divisionem, sonus enim sillabe vel deprimitur et dicitur gravis accentus, vel tendit in altum et dicitur acutus, vel est medius inter elevacionem et depressionem et dicitur moderatus. Antiqui vero utebantur accentu circumflexo qui ab ymo incipiens tendebat in altum et iterum rediebat in ymum qui adhuc a quibusdam religiosis habetur in usu ... Et nota quod nullus accentus in usu moderno potest esse predominans in primis vel in mediis sillabis nisi moderatus nec in ultimis nisi acutus sicut lectorum investigare poterit prudencia ... Nunc restat videre quot sunt instancie impedientes communem accentum que sunt novem ut ex autoritatibus Prisciano, Petro Helie et Vergilio colligi poterit, scilicet Apocopacio, Sincopacio, Interrogacio, Relacio, Equivocacio, Anostropha, Enclesia, Dirivacio et Barbaries ... Interrogacio quoque impedit accentum quia interrogativa in fine acuuntur omnia; si autem interrogativa diccio in oracione aliis societur diccionibus accentum suum ultime diccioni illius oracionis tribuit hoc modo, Quid existis videre? Quis vel qualis? ... Nota quod interrogacio amittit vim suam tribus modis: uno modo causa recitacionis unde in evangelio Johannis, conversus Petrus vidit illum discipulum quem diligebat Jesus sequentem qui et recubuit in cena supra pectus eius et dixit: Domine, quis est qui tradet te. Alio modo causa transicionis ut in Job, Indica mihi cur me ita iudices. Tercio modo causa continuacionis ut ibi, Nemo audebat interrogare eum tu quis es sciens quia Dominus est.

MS AUCT. F. 3.9 (p.9)

Quot modi sunt in verbo? Dicendum quod quinque, scilicet indicativus, imperativus, optativus, coniunctivus et infinitivus unde querendum est, quid facit indicativus: dicendum quod semper demonstrat, ut Amo I love, amas thou lovyst, amat he loveth, amamus we loven, sic discurrendo per omnia tempora indicativi modi omnium coniugacionum. Imperativus semper imperat et habet duo tempora, scilicet presens et futurum, ut ama vel amato love thou, amet vel amato love he, amemus love we, amate vel amatote love ye, ament amanto vel amantote love thei. Optativus vero desiderat ut utinam amarem Wolde God I schulde love, amares thou schuldist love, amaret he schulde love et cetera. Coniunctivus modus coniungit orationem orationi ut si amem te, tu amabis me. Infinitivus vero caret numero et persona secundum quemdam tractatum id est sine discrecione numeri et persone ut amare anglice love, amavisse anglice hadde lovyd, amatum iri anglice go to love, vel amaturum esse other to be to love et sic discurrendo per omnes coniugaciones. Item querendum est quot sunt tempora in verbo: dicendum est quod quinque, presens the tyme that is now ut doceo I teche, preteritum inperfectum the tyme that is litil agon ut docebam I taughte, preteritum perfectum the tyme that is fulli agon ut docui I have taught, preteritum plusquam perfectum the tyme that is longe agon ut docueram I hadde taught, futurum the tyme that is to come ut docebo I shal teche. Iste est modus informandi pueros per omnes coniugaciones.

MS HARL. 1002 (fol.13)
Jesus Christus filius beate Marie iuvet et expediat Laurencium de Londoniis qui coram rege Anglie vel Anglicorum et archiepiscopo Cantuariensi dimicabit infra licias cum quodam homine de Beverlaco se falso proditore accusante.

Cuius casus 'beate Marie' in latinitate premissa? Genitivi et regitur de ly filius ex vi possessoris vel possessionis. Quare? Quia omnis diccio significans possessorem vel possessionem potest regere genitivum casum ex vi possessoris vel possessionis, ut rex Anglie, equus regis. Versus:

Possessor vel possessum substans quoque nomen
Post se constructum semper poscit' genitivum
Sum dominus ville sed equus regis fuit ille.

Cuius casus "Londoniis" in latinitate premissa? Ablativi mediante ista preposicione "de." Quare? Quia per regulam, propria nomina non regunt genitivos sed ablativos mediante ista preposicione "de," licet aliquando per appellativa subintellecta regunt, ut Katerina Laurencii, id est Katerina que est uxor Laurencii, unde in evangelio Maria Iacobi et Maria Salome emerunt aromata et cetera; "Maria Iacobi," id est Maria que fuit mater Iacobi.

Cuius casus Anglie vel Anglicorum in latinitate premissa? Genitivi. Quare? Quia quando nomen dignitatis temporalis vel officii debet determinari per nomen loci tunc sumendum est genitivum proprii nominis loci vel genitivum pluralem sui possessivi, ut imperator Rome vel Romanorum, rex Anglie vel Anglicorum. Cuius casus Cantuariensi in latinitate premissa? Ablativi.

Quare? Quia per regulam, quando nomen officii vel dignitatis spiritualis debet determinari per nomen loci tunc in loco proprii nominis loci sumendum est possessivum proprii nominis loci ponendo illud in idemptitate[2] casuali cum nomine officii seu dignitatis spiritualis, ut papa Romanus, archiepiscopus Cantuariensis, archidiaconus Florentinus.

MS ADD. 37,075 (fols.191–98, 256–67, passim)

fol.191
Rosarum flores prout maturescunt iam quotidie colligimus quosdam proponentes in [festivis] affigi quibus in Sancti Antonii solemnitate ibimus perornati quosdam equidem pro aquis distilandis servabimus que multum subveniunt morbis oculorum.

fol.192v
In quanto sepius habemus licenciam eundi lusum in tanto minus adhibemus diligenciam discipline quapropter nobis sunt oportune parcitas ludi et copia correcionis donec perfecte sciamus Donatum.
Manentis multis annis Londoniis ubi aliqualiter instructus sum grammaticam interest mea manere in futuro Cantebrigie vel Oxonie ubi alie facultates capiuntur [prae] addiscere in aliis locis regni.

fol.194
In futuro beandi sunt a nobis parentes et amici qui debitas nobis provident doctrinas et correcciones quos ita omni estimaremus dignos gracia si ut instigat insolencia iuventutis ludendi haberemus libertatem si amici nostri heberent noticiam quam malivoli sumus ad vigendum ipsi numquam vellent dignari dimidium expense quam faciunt exhibendo nos ad scolas sed pocius ponere nos ad artes mechanicas vel ad vilem laborem mundi.

fol.195
Si puerorum mentes tantum prope reperirent molestiam in Anglicana loquela quantam habent dummodo opponit magistralis illos detinet in difficilibus nulla foret occasio propediendi quin omnes sermones proferendi haberentur in latinis.

fol.196
Verisimile est illos pueros non servire Deo dicendo matutinas de beata Maria quibus deest gracia reddendi partem Donati sine defectu quapropter illi vapulant diatim a magistro.

fol.197v
Super singulas regiones Christianorum hereticorum codices ignibus mandarentur nullus esset error aut heresis inter Christianos per suggestionem hereticorum quorum quidam meritus hiis nuperimis diebus ad cineres comburebantur.

In quanto magis homines honorantur in presenti vita propter abundaciam bonorum temporalium in tanto minoris honoris erunt in celo ubi miseri huius mundi erunt multo feliciores quam ditissimi auri vel auro et argenti vel argento.

fol.198
Quamvis scolas frequentantibus absque amenitate instar dolor et mesticia ubique per civitatem quam plures tamen delectat in hac urbe ac eius suburbis sibi perquirere habitacula ut diviciarum et victualium omni gaudeant fertilitate.

fol.256
Scolares colligere scienciam per quam possunt intelligere quodcumque legunt est melius multo quam colligere aurum et argentum similiter avorum vel avoros qui propter avariciam sunt pocius damnandi quam salvandi.

fol.258
Omnino coartandi sunt virga magistrali ipsi scolares qui ex malicia voluntatis sapere nolunt disciplinam quam omnibus armis magis pertimescunt etsi ex ferro vel calibe fabricentur cui ut precatur prohibet proverbium qui parcit virge odit filium.

fol.258v
Si ergo possem quamvis nunc adquirere pecuniam mihi cum qua compararem librum quem socius meus habet [venuri]³ videtur mihi quod fierem clericus instar illorum qui habent libros nam refert proverbium: haurit aquam cribris clericus absque libris.

fol.259v
Patria in qua ego eram oriundus multum distante ab urbe Londoniarum ego cogito mihi diuturnum tempus esse donec loquar cum amicis vel ad minus habeam licenciam eundi domum quia puero qui est procul ab amicis deest magna pars consolacionis sue.

Talis estimatus pena condigna corpori meo nequaquam linguam prohibentis ab Anglicana loquela qualis deputa vel scolatizantibus latino eloquio non utentibus quod in labore et exercicio a nullo perfecte perquiritur.

fol.260v
Toga quam ego vestior diebus festis multo melius decet me quam illa qua ego utor diebus profestis cum qua tamen scitis bene placet michi quando a me sedetur in scola discente grammaticam.

fol.261
Magis congruit scolaribus cum arcubus et sagittis honeste sese recreare quocienscumque licencientur quam inhoneste discurrere huiusmodi ludos exercitando qui honestati claricali minime conveniunt.

Multa est pecunia quam lucrantur causidici causantes in aula Westmo-
nasterii quibus aliquando videtur deesse consciencia quia communiter qui
discior est obtinebit intentum sive phas sive nefas.

fol.262
Omnes pro maiore parte inscribuntur latinitates que citra festi paschalis
solennitatem componebantur de quibus singulis petet racionem in fine ter-
mini examinacio magistralis ut et perfecte sciantur et ut earum respondeatur
ad partes.

fol.263
Ut per media veritatis futuris temporibus victum meum perquiram sagax
providencia amicorum me disponet erudiri arte mechanica qui multis annorum curriculis grammaticalibus imbutus minimam eiusdem facultatis particulam nondum cepi in memoria.

fol.264
Vix unus reperitur inter omnes quos modo hec scola continet qui ex libera
voluntate de beata virgine assuescit dicere matutinas aut ex devocione qua
cordibus puerorum deficiente necessario deerit et gracia scienciam adipis-
cendi.

MS ADD. 37,075 (fols. 45v, 46v, 47, 49v-50)
    Papa fidem sustinet hereses damnabit
    Cardinales consulit quando hesitabit
    Bullas dat petentibus hostes concordabit
    Vere penitentibus peccata laxabit.
    ....

    Beneficiarius clericus pulsabit
    Campanas pro mortuis et illuminabit
    Candelas epistolam frequenter cantabit
    [Et cum]⁴ aspersorio domos hic rigabit.
    ....

    Est in Alamania datus imperator
    Qui est pro republica presto propugnator
    Et tocius seculi constat gubernator
    Sed est summus pontifex eius confirmator
    Et rex regit populum quem miles defendit
    Et ab adversariis cum quis hunc offendit.
    ....

    Carpentarius sequitur fabrum, fabricando
    Domos cum securibus et ligna secando
    Et cum [penetralibus tigna perforando]⁵
    Cum coanullis ligneis tectum exaltando

Et in superficie domus collocabit
Doma in quo capita tignorum firmabit
Domum laquearibus sic fortificabit
Trabes domum laqueant postis supportabit
Fenestras et ostia debet adaptare
Per que lux et homines poterunt [intrare]⁶
Lumina et cardines debet ordinare
Et in domo perticam ibidem formare.

Dictamen

MS ADD. 17,724 (fols.59–60v)
De proverbiis et litteris quibus videntur proverbia querenda. Expedito de salutacionibus in generali attendamus ad proverbia consequenter. In primis ergo videndum quid hic appellatur proverbium et unde dicatur et in quibus epistolis interponi deceat et qualiter debeat adaptari. Hic autem advocamus proverbium illud idem quod exordium in rethoricis est vocatum quod sic diffinit Tullius: exordium est oracio quedam animum auditoris ydonee operans seu temperans ad reliquam dilectionem.[1] Est siquidem quoque quoddam persuasorium ergo moveatur animus auditoris et affectetur in eo quod sequitur ennarandum unde narracioni supponitur tamquam si fundamenti [parieti?][2] substernatur et hoc idem videtur sonare proverbium quod appellatur sic quasi prothoverbium respectu narracionis hoc est videlicet primum verbum sicut prothomartir dicitur primus martir a prothos grece quod est primum latine. Est enim proverbium maxime quedam propositio dignitate sui communiter nota vel auctoritate dicentis ratificata sit ut ei statim facile debeat audientis animus consentire. Et ad hec satis concordat illa glosa Bede super *Proverbia* Salomonis principio dicentis proverbia iure nominantur quia talia sunt que in ore colloquencium digne versari ac memoria debent retineri.[3]

Ad exhortandum aliquem ut ingrediatur[4] religionem sic: Cum iam viam suam corruperit omnis caro fere peccatorum que diluvium ceperit mundare videtur esse tucius in archa Noe salvum fieri quam iniquitatis fluctibus cum mundanis carnalibus obsorbiri.

Ad congratulandum:
Si gloriatur unum membrum sicut ait apostolus solent membra cetera congaudere quo nobis datur exemplo quod nos alter alterius bonum debemus congaudendo quasi proprium reputare.

MS TRIN. 0.5.4. (fol.76)

Quarta tabula salutacionis ad Imperatorem Reges
Principes Duces Comites Barones Marchiones
Potestates Iusticiarios Milites Capellanos
Sapientes et alios laicos minores:

Gloriosissimo Dei gratia Romanorum
      Imperatori et semper
Excellentissimo Augusto divina magni- T
      ficencia vel provid- a Rex
Victoriosissimo encia Regi Anglorum l   Salutem
      potentissimo vel   i Princeps
      felicissimo Regi Anglie s
      dignis et magnis   Dux
      laudibus commendato

Glorioso et   de inimicis
excelso viro Principi   Comes T gloriam et
Illustrissimo Potentissimo principi Marchio a triumphum
     Tarentino   l quod placet
                i pastoris pro-
                s stratis et
                 superbos
                 viriliter
                 debellare
                 suum servicium
                 et amorem

Illustri et   Duci quem orbis
preclaro viro   terrarum propria
Domino favor-   reservat vel
abili et benigno commendat merita
Magnifico et   bonitatis.   Et longi-
potenti viro Domino Comiti quem decus tudinem
Sacre regie   exornaverat honor dierum et
potestatis   fama liberalitas   vite delectabilis
Magnifico et   probitas approbata. Salutem
sublimi viro   Marchioni quem fama incrementum
Illustri et   commendat et gloria
excelso viro   militaris.
         Militi multe discrec-
         ionis conspicuo vel
         constituto vel gloria
         militari decorato vel
         dignis laudibus

commendato quem fama
militaris decorat vel
gloria recommendat

Optata felicitate [ligare][5] Amoris plenitudinem vel
felicibus felicia cumulare Prospera prosperis
congregare vel adunare Cuncta que desiderat optinere
Quod spirituales nequicias viriliter propugnare
Robore accincto fortitudinis et virtutis Per quem
reges regnant et principes dominantur Cunctis
prosperitatis opulenciam[6] Clare devocionis affectum
Pure sincere vel integre dileccionis affectum

Strenuo et potenti vel			Quicquid potest
nobilissimo viro:	Iusticiario		et cetera
Immense potencie et			voluntariam et
honoris excelso :	Imperatori		servitutem cum
Egregie viro multo			promptitudine
probitatis et sapiencie:	Domino	Talis	serviendi A
Commendabili viro et		loci	serviciis
fidelibus non medio-		quicumque	continuam vol-
criter fructuoso:	Baroni	minor	untatem cum
Generoso vel honor-			debita recom-
abili inter nobiles			mendacione se
educato :	Senescallo		totum Quicquid
Nobilibus et prudent-			potest servicii
ibus viris comitibus			et honoris
talis ville :	Castellano		Debitum fidelit-
			atis in omnibus
			obsequium
			Promptum fi-
			del-
			itatis intimum
			obsequium

Speculative Grammar

MS AUCT. F. 3.9. (pp.176–77)

Interieccio quid est: pars oracionis et cetera significans hoc est demonstrans mentis affectum hoc est intellectum voce incondita hoc est voce informata. Alii autem libri habent voce incognita hoc est voce non deliberata unde notandum est secundum Remigium quod interieccio ab interiacendo nomen sortitur quia cum de aliis partibus loquimur subito inter eas proferimus interieccionem unde nota quod dicit comentator quod alie partes que subita voce proferuntur interiecciones deputantur ut pro dolor, pro nephas, Deo gratias, verbi gratia, ite missa est: de istis bene apparebit inferius. Item nota quod quidam voluerunt hanc particulam adverbio sociari sed Donatus hoc noluit quoniam habet suam proprietatem sicut et cetere partes scilicet mentis affectum indicare. Circa partem illam primo dubitatur utrum interieccio sit pars orationis et quid constituat eam in specie partis; secundo dato quod sit pars orationis utrum sit separata ab adverbio vel non; tercio utrum per interieccionem potest assignificari affectus bruti vel non. Circa primum sic procedo et probo quod interieccio non sit pars orationis quoniam nihil aliud est esse partem orationis nisi mentis conceptum significare ut dicit Priscianus in *Maiori* set interieccio non significat mentis conceptum set affectum ut dicit Donatus; relinquitur ergo interieccionem non esse partem orationis. Preterea omnis pars orationis significat ad placitum et ab impositione sed interiecciones quedam videntur significare naturaliter et non ad placitum. Item idem apparet per hoc quod dicit Priscianus dimisit eam in *Minori* ubi de ordine parcium in linea determinat quod non fecisset si pars orationis fuisset ergo et cetera.

MS LINCOLN 88 (fol.130)

Quid est pars oracionis? Vox indicans mentis conceptum ut dicit Priscianus in tractatu participii. Contra: littere et sillabe sunt partes sermonis et tamen non indicant mentis conceptum, ergo dicta diffinitio non est competens.

Sed hec diffinitio competit diccionibus que sunt partes propinque orationis: littere vero et sillabe sunt partes remote: de quibus non datur hec diffinitio. Ad hanc contra: interieccio est pars orationis propinqua et tamen indicat mentis conceptum. Dicit non Donatus quia significat mentis affectum. Si interieccio mentis affectum [aut] animi passionem respectu sui prolatoris significat tum mentis conceptum respectu sui auditoris designat, cum enim dicitur 'heu' proferens sui animi passionem ostendit et audiens naturaliter concipit illam passionem inesse proferenti et sic interieccio secundario dicit mentis conceptum licet prius autem significet mentis affectum per quam significacionem a ceteris distinguitur partibus. Contra: hec verba letor, doleo, miror, metuo et nomina ab illis derivata, leticia, dolor, miracio, et metus significant mentis affectum id est animi passionem, ergo hec non est propria significatio interieccionis per quam a ceteris partibus distinguitur.

MS EDINBURGH 136 (fols.9–9v)
Nunc autem omnium parcium oracionis modos significandi essentiales et specificos sufficienter superius annotavi quia omnis pars oracionis ut dicit Boecius significat per modum habitus aut per modum fieri. Si primo modo aut ergo per modum distincti et sic nomen, aut per modum indistincti sed distinguibilis et sic pronomen. Si secundo modo aut per modum enunciabilis de alio et sic verbum, aut per modum uniti cum substancia et sic participium, aut per modum disponentis actum indiffinite et sic adverbium, aut per modum retorquentis casuale ad actum et sic preposicio, aut per modum coniungentis diversa et sic coniunccio, aut per modum afficientis et sic interieccio. [Unde][1] secundum Aristotilem in diffinicione essentiali alicuius rei diffinibilis non debet poni aliquod eius accidens sicut in discripcione accidentali sepe poni solet sed tantum essentialia ad sui naturam et speciem pertinencia. Iam ponam singularum parcium rectam diffinicionem constantem ex genere et differenciis ipsorum essentialibus. Nomen ergo pars oracionis significans mentis conceptum per modum habitus iam distincti. Pronomen est pars oracionis significans mentis conceptum per modum habitus distinguibilis mediante relacione vel derivacione. Verbum est pars oracionis significans mentis conceptum per modum fluxus et fieri dicibilis de alio. Adverbium est pars oracionis significans mentis conceptum per modum isponentis actionem vel passionem indiffinite. Participium est pars oracionis significans mentis conceptum per modum fluxus et fieri uniti substancie. Conniunccio est pars oracionis significans mentis conceptum per modum connectentis diversa. Preposicio est pars oracionis significans mentis conceptum per modum retorquentis casuale ad actum. Interieccio est pars oracionis significans mentis conceptum per modum afficientis. Hec sunt singularum parcium oracionis recte diffiniciones cum genus et differencias essentiales ipsarum in se concludant nec ullum accidens assumant earum nec aliquod pertinens ad naturam sive speciem earum omittant nec sunt

accidentales discripciones earum quales de eis ponunt Priscianus et Donatus aliique grammatici.

William Chartham's Speculum Parvulorum

MS LAMBETH 78 (fol. 1)

Cum essem parvulus, non tantum annorum numero, quantum moribus et
sciencia, et iuxta psalmiste admonicionem, divertere a malis et bona facere,
superna inspirante gracia animo decrevissem cepi pro viribus leccioni ope-
ram dare quae leccio docet quid cavere aut quo tendere quis debeat, lęccio
intellectum mentis erudit et a mundi vanitatibus abstractum hominem ad
amorem Dei perducit, ymmo revera omnis profectus anime ex leccione et
meditacione procedit, dum tamen quod legitur opere completur. In nobis-
metipsis namque debemus transformare quod legimus ut cum per auditum
se animus excitat ad operandum quod audierit vita concurrat. Sed quibus
putatis legendi studium adhibuit? Non ut alta sapiens summe theologie
anagogicis exposicionibus ne super verticem meterem, nec dubiis philoso-
phorum assercionibus ne in vacuum laborarem neque inanibus scurrorum
fabulis ne districtam subirem sentenciam; sed propter profundioris sciencie
insufficienciam, quia non sapiebam nisi ut parvulus, devotis narracionibus
prout in vitas patrum collacionibus et institutis eorundem in *Gestis Romanorum* et in cronicis et in aliis tractatibus salutem anime vel exemplum bone
vite propinatibus invenire potueram studiosius fueram intentus. Quia igitur
quamplurima legi in alienis codicibus et mutuatis quorum contemplacione
oportuna mora frui non potui, quamplurima vero in cedulis quasi dirutis
et vetustate consumptis que parvo temporis successu in cicius excerpta fuis-
sent et ad paucorum noticiam pervenissent, ipsa que mee parvitati placue-
runt in uno volumnie redegi ad Dei laudem et, ut speratur, ad multorum
parvulorum delectacionem et utilitatem et precipue ad fugiendum illam
sterilem immo execrabilem matrem nugarum, viciorum nutricem, novera-
cam omnium virtutum sanctarum animarum inimicam que est ociositas, hec
enim virum fortissimum precipitat in reatum, suffocat virtutem, nutrit su-
perbiam et edificat ad gehennam, necnon ad respuendum verba vana et
scurrilia mundana et inhonesta que eciam in ore sacerdotis blasphemie sunt,

quibus nec os aperire aures nec ceteros sensus permittimur accomodare, sed in omni loco et tempore coram quibuscumque personis semper sancta et religionem concernencia proferre tenemur toto que corde debemus preceptis nos salutaribus occupare ut omnium viciorum labem fugiamus.

APPENDIX SIX

Educational Documents

ACTA CAPITULARIA (2H2) 1410–1429, YORK (fol.36)

Examination of York Chapter in Grammar, 7 February 1421

Johannes Garwarby	competenter literatus
Johannes Harlesay	mediocriter literatus
Ricardus Storthwayte	competenter literatus
Thomas Ledestone	illiteratus compellatur adiscere
Stephanus Kyrkeby	illiteratus compellatur adiscere
Ricardus Prillane	mediocriter literatus compellatur exercere scolas
Ricardus Farrowr	mediocriter literatus compellatur etc.
Robertus Dyghtone	competenter literatus
Robertus Boswell	illiteratus compellatur adiscere
(Willelmus Gray	
	isti duo exercent scolas competenter
(Thomas Gednay	

Comparuerunt omnes suprascripti vii die mensis Februarii anno domini millesimo cccc° xxi° coram Venerabilibus viris dominis Thoma Haxey˛ Thesaurario Roberto Wolveden et Thoma Parkes canonicis capitulum faciendis et moniti sunt er dictos dominos canonicos quod docentes diligenter exerceant scolas grammaticales. Sub pena amercionis ab ecclesia et officio suo in casu et eventui quod si per diligentem examinacionem eorum dictorum minus habiles inveniantur. Et moniti sunt eciam. Sub pena superius annotata quod intersunt processionibus in ecclesia Eboracensis ac aliis processionibus generalibus in civitate faciendis. Et quod eciam intersunt in choro diebus dominicis et festivis videlicet matutinis missarum maiorum et vesperis sub eadem pena.

THE REGISTER OF ROBERT GILBERT (fol.191v)

Ordinance of Bishop Gilbert with regard to the teaching of grammar in London, March 1445

Robertus ... universis et singulis rectoribus vicariis capellanis curatis et non curatis notariis publicis clericis et litteratis quibuscumque per nostras civitatem et diocesim Londoniensem ... Cum tam de iure communi quam de antiqua et laudabili [?] prescripta consuetudine hactenus eciam a tempore et per tempus cuius contraria memoria hominis non existit pacifice et inconcusse usitata et observata. Ius admittendi proficiendi et deputandi quoscumque magistros ad informandum instruendum et docendum publice pueros in gramatica ubicumque infra civitatem London' infra nostram iurisdiccionem ad Episcopum Londoniensem quemcumque pro tempore existentem seu ad cencellarium ecclesie cathedralis sancti Pauli Londoniensis pertinuerit pertineat et pertinere debeat infuturum [fueritque] dicte ecclesie ... et sit ac esse deberet infra dictam civitatem London' infra nostram iurisdiccionem una [solummodo] et dumtaxat scola gramaticalis videlicet in atrio dicte ecclesie cathedralis quam una cum quatuor aliis scolis gramaticalibus infra eandem civitatem videlicet una in ecclesia collegiata regali sancti Martini magni, alia in ecclesia beate Marie de arcubus, tercia in ecclesia parochiali Sancti Dunstani in oriente et quarta in hospituli sancti [Antonii][1] eiusdem civitatis pro instruccione et informacione puerorum dicte civitatis quorumcumque et aliorum confluencium in eandem civitatem sufficere et competere estimamus pronunciamus decernimus et declaramus alias scolas gramaticales infra eandem civitatem infra iurisdictionem nostram publice exerceri prohibendo et interdicendo. Quidam tamen alii permissorum non ignari commodum eorum singularis quam utilitatem rei publice magis affectantes absque examinacione ordinacione et admissione et sine auctoritate ordinaria ad hoc non admissi in diversis aliis locis civitatis predicte ... scolas tenere et pueros in gramatica informare de facto presumpserunt et presumunt in presenti pueros nonnullos et eorum amicos eos exhibentes nequiter[2] defraudando in dicte iurisdiccionis nostre contemptu magistrorumque scolarum ... quod infra duodecim dierum spacium a tempore monicionis ... cessent penitus et desistant ... sub pena maioris excommunicacionis.

Notes

1 My interest in Leach derived from an extensive use of some of his
published source material for a doctoral thesis in history at the University of London under the supervision of the late Helena M. Chew
of Queen Mary College and the late Richard Hunt of the University
of Oxford, who put at my disposal a quite unique body of grammatical manuscripts. The aim of the thesis was two-fold: to survey the institutional organization of secondary or pre-university educational
facilities and, more importantly, to determine the Latin program of
these grammar schools in the fourteenth and fifteenth centuries. The
results of this investigation were later summarized in two periodical
publications: "The Teaching of Latin in Later Medieval England" in
Mediaeval Studies, 1961, and "Schools and Literacy in Later Medieval
England" in *British Journal of Educational Studies*, 1962.

2 Watson, "Leach, Arthur Francis (1851–1915)," *Dictionary of National
Biography* (1912–21): 327–8.

3 Ibid.

4 Leach, *Educational Charters and Documents*, Intro., ix.

5 Leach, *Schools of Medieval England*, bibliography, ix. (Cited in Part 1 as
SME with page numbers given in the text.) To this list must be added
Leach's surveys of schools in *Victoria County History of the Counties of
England, Northamptonshire* 2 and *Worcestershire* 4. Subsequent references
to the *Victoria County History* volumes will be cited as *VCH* followed by
the particular county.

6 Leach, "Memorandum," 5: 57–75. Cited in Part 1 as *M* with page
numbers given in the text.

7 Orme, *English Schools in the Middle Ages*, 4–5; Lawson and Silver, *A
Social History of Education in England*, notes on pp. 85–9.

8 Leach, *The Protectorate*, 2. Cited in Part 1 as *TP* with page numbers given in the text.

9 Both essays are considerations on the formation, management, and dissolution of clubs, with special reference to the liabilities and expulsion of members. These works can be examined in the Middle Temple Library, London.

10 Leach, *Probate Duty*, v.

11 Ibid., x-xi

12 Leach, *Club Cases*. unpaginated forward, presumably p. 3.

13 Ibid.

14 Leach, "The English Land Question." References to other countries are found on pages 14, 23–4, 29–31.

15 Ibid., 5.

16 Ibid., 6.

17 Ibid., 23.

18 Ibid., 8.

19 Fifoot, *Frederic William Maitland A Life*, 241–3.

20 Ibid.

21 Ibid.

22 Ibid., 242.

23 Ibid.

24 Leach, *Beverley Town Documents*, 14: xvii-xviii.

25 Ibid., xxxvii.

26 Fifoot, *Maitland*, 242; Fifoot, *The Letters of Frederic William Maitland*, 215–16.

27 Leach, *Beverley Town Documents*, xxxvi.

28 Ibid., xli-xlviii, passim.

29 *Proceedings of the Society of Antiquaries of London*, 2nd ser. 15 (8 March 1894): 103–18.

30 Ibid., 17 (9 December 1897): 18–21.

31 Ibid., 23 (25 November 1909): 14–17. Leach's subsequent paper, "St. Paul's School Before Colet," grew out of this presentation.

32 Leach, *Early Yorkshire Schools*, 1: vi.

33 Ibid.

34 Leach, *English Schools at the Reformation*, part i, 122. Cited in Part 1 as *ESR* with page numbers given in the text.

35 Leach, "St. Paul's School Before Colet," 191.

36 Leach, *VCH Northamptonshire* 2 (1906): 234.

37 Leach, *VCH Hertfordshire* 2 (1908): 47.

38 Leach, "Sherborne School Before, Under, and After Edward VI," 34.

39 Ibid.

40 Leach, *VCH Durham* 1 (1905): 365–413.

41 In commenting on the erroneous historical information furnished by the late charity commissioner, D.R. Fearon, relative to the school at St. Alban's, Leach's cryptic observation is that "official information depends on the information given to the particular official." *VCH Hertfordshire* 2 (1908): 47.

42 Leach, "The Reformation in England [Education]," 137.

43 Ibid., 138.

44 Ibid.

45 Ibid.

46 Ibid.

47 Ibid.

48 Ibid., 137.

49 Ibid.

50 Leach, "School Supply in the Middle Ages," 674. Cited in Part 1 as ss with page numbers given in the text.

51 Leach, *Educational Charters and Documents*, xii.

52 Leach, *VCH Hampshire and Isle of Wight* 2 (1903): 265.

53 Ibid., 264.

54 Leach, *VCH Worcestershire* 4 (1924): 476.

55 Ibid., 477.

56 Leach, *Early Yorkshire Schools* 1: xxvii.

57 Leach, *VCH Gloucestershire* 2 (1907): 317.

58 Warner, *Winchester*, 19.

59 Cox, review of *Monks of the West, from St. Benedict to St. Bernard* by Count de Montalembert, 319.

60 Leach, *Documents Illustrating Early Education in Worcester, 685 to 1700*, 1–2.

61 Leach, *Early Education in Worcester*, iv. Cited in Part 1 as *EEW* with page numbers given in the text.

62 Leach, "Sherborne School," 2–3.

63 Ibid., 3–5, passim.

64 Ibid., 15.

65 Ibid., 3.

66 Leach, *VCH Berkshire* 2 (1907): 259.

67 Leach, *VCH Gloucestershire* 2 (1907): 315; *VCH Derbyshire* 2 (1907): 210–11; *VCH Durham* 1 (1905): 371.

68 Leach, *Visitations and Memorials of Southwell Minster*, x–xi.

69 Ibid., 18 and 49, regarding the translation of obscure Latin terms.

70 Gasquet refers, for instance, to a Latin grammar belonging to Wm. Heytesbury, from *MS. Harl 79*, and speaks of *MS Arundel 249* as "a very curious book as to instruction in Latin."

71 Leach, "The Medieval Education of Women," 838.

72 Ibid., 839.

CHAPTER TWO

 1 Carlisle, *A Concise Description of the Endowed Grammar Schools in England and Wales*, 1: xviii-xix.
 2 Ibid.
 3 Ibid., xxiii-xxiv.
 4 Ibid.
 5 Ibid., xxiv.
 6 Ibid., xxv.
 7 Ibid.
 8 Ibid., xxvii.
 9 Ibid., xxx.
10 Ibid., xxxi.
11 Ibid., xxxiii.
12 Ibid., xxxv.
13 Ibid., 379–80.
14 Ibid., 402.
15 Ibid., 2: 883–5.
16 Ibid., 289.
17 Ibid., 100.
18 Leach, "St. Paul's School Before Colet," 199.
19 Hackett, *Brief Account of Cathedral and Collegiate Schools*. The correspondence bearing on the choristers of St. Paul's is all contained in a third section, pp.1–74.
20 Ibid., 3.
21 Ibid., 39–40.
22 Ibid., 41.
23 Ibid., 42.
24 Ibid., 51–2.
25 Ibid., 56–7.
26 Ibid., 63–4, passim.
27 Ibid., 66–7.
28 Bowles, *Vindiciae Wykehamicae*, title page.
29 Ibid., 7–8.
30 Ibid., 13, 16–17.
31 Ibid., 33.
32 Ibid., 35.
33 Review of *Some Account of the Foundation of Eton College, and of the Past and Present Condition of the School* by E.S. Creasy; *Public School Education* by Sir John J. Coleridge; and *Eton Reform* by William Johnson. *Edinburgh Review* 113 (April 1861): 387–8. This article, ascribed to

journalist M.J. Higgins, is not so much a review of the publications
cited as it is a general survey of the subjects treated in those works.

34 Ibid., 392.
35 Ibid., 394–5.
36 Ibid., 402–3.
37 Ibid., 407.
38 Ibid., 408.
39 Ibid., 417.
40 Ibid., 419–20.
41 Ibid., 391.
42 Ibid., 404.
43 Ibid., 425.
44 Ibid., 426.
45 Barnard, *A History of English Education From 1760*, 126–8.
46 Simon, *The Two Nations* , 305.
47 Barnard, *English Education*, 128.
48 Smith, review of *Report of Her Majesty's Commissioners, [Clarendon Commission] .4 vols. Edinburgh Review* 120 (July 1864): 148–9. Goldwin Smith, to whom this article is ascribed, was, like M.J. Higgins, at one time a student at Eton College.
49 Ibid., 157–8.
50 Ibid., 158.
51 Ibid., 159.
52 Ibid., 168.
53 Ibid., 182.
54 Leach, *Encyclopaedia Britannica*, 11th ed. (1911), s.v. "schools."
55 Ibid.
56 Ibid.
57 Ibid.
58 Ibid.
59 Ibid.
60 Ibid.
61 Simon, *The Two Nations*, 318.
62 Ibid, 319.
63 Ibid, 302, 320–1.
64 Ibid, 320.
65 Barnard, *English Education*, 129; Curtis and Boultwood, *An Introductory History of English Education Since 1800*, 87.
66 Barnard, *English Education*, 130–1; Simon, *The Two Nations*, 323–5; Young and Handcock, *English Historical Documents 1833–1874*, XII (i), 905–7.
67 Barnard, *English Education*, 131.
68 Young and Handcock, *Historical Documents*, 12(i): 908–11.

69 Barnard, *English Education*, 131; Curtis and Boultwood, *Introductory History*, 90.

70 Barnard's brief summary was that the Endowed Schools Act "gutted" the Report (*English Education*, 133–4). Curtis and Boultwood's view of the Act as "most disappointing" (*Introductory History*, 91) may be compared with Simon's more extended appraisal in *The Two Nations*, 328–36.

71 Simon, *The Two Nations*, 363–4; Brian Simon, *Education and the Labour Movement 1870–1920*, 103–6; Curtis & Boultwood, *Introductory History*, 91–3.

72 Simon, *The Two Nations*, 328–9.

73 Simon, *Education and the Labour Movement*, 99–102, and *The Two Nations*, 332–3, and n1.

74 Ibid., *The Two Nations*, 333.

75 Ibid., 325–6.

76 Leach, *A History of Winchester College*, 91–2.

77 Ibid., 92–3.

78 Ibid., 93–4.

79 Leach, *Schools Inquiry Commission*, appendix 4, p.36.

80 Ibid., 61; Leach, *Schools Inquiry Commission* 1: *Report of the Commissioners* (London: Her Majesty's Stationery Office, 1868), appendix 4: Chronological List of Endowed Schools, 36–47; Leach, *English Schools at the Reformation*, 321–7.

CHAPTER THREE

1 The commissioners' reports and related correspondence are contained in a series of boxes deposited in the Public Record Office (PRO) at Kew under the title: *Endowed Schools Acts: Reports of Assistant Commissioners*. These reports contain both written and printed material. Those of Southwell (MS ED 27/3872), Chichester (MS ED 27/4713), and Beverley (MS ED 27/5495) are in vol. 2 (1886–89); those of York (no MS reference) in vol. 3 (1890–96). An explanatory note at the beginning of the files on the history of education includes the following: "The papers comprise the administration of endowments under the Charitable Trusts Acts, 1853 to 1869, and the Endowed Schools Acts, 1869 to 1874. The records include the drafting of schemes; reports by Assistant Charity Commissioners; examination and inspection of schools; authority for the acquisition or sale of land and vesting on the Official Trustee of Charity Lands; and the sale, or transfer of stock to the Official Trustees of Charitable Funds. A few files of schemes under the Endowed Schools Acts contain the original Order in Council establishing the Scheme."

2 Report of Assistant Commissioner: Chichester Prebendal School, 786.

Cited in Part 1 as *RAC:C* with page numbers given in the text. There are at least two separate but similar printed copies of the Chichester report in the PRO. The copy used for the purposes of this study (MS ED 27/4713) is numbered – as are the other reports discussed above – from the first page; in this instance, from p.1 to 29. A second enumeration – seemingly a more recent one – from p.785 to 813 (numbered on every second page only) will be used for purposes of reference. The second copy, identical except for larger print, is catalogued as ED 27/4713. An appendix, again numbered in the two different ways, pp.30–48 and 814 to 832, consists of the Latin text of Bishop Edward Storey's statutes for his prebendal grammar school, together with the amended statutes of Bishop George Day. The second copy of the appendix, in larger print, with single enumeration, pp. 30–48, is also catalogued as ED 27/4713. These are followed by a series of extracts from both medieval and modern sources, in Latin or English as circumstances dictated, on which Leach based all or some of his arguments regarding the foundation of Bishop Storey at the end of the fifteenth century. Finally, there is extensive collection of correspondence as well as annotated reports bearing on the prebendal school, all in manuscript, again catalogued as ED 27/4713 and consisting of some 50 pages, most of which is in Leach's hand and signed by him, from 1865–66.

3 Prebendary: the holder of a "prebend," that is, a cathedral benefice or "living," usually consisting of the revenue from a manor of the cathedral estates.

4 Charles Anthony Swainson (1820–87), author of important works on the Nicene and Apostles' creeds and Greek liturgy, became principal of the theological college at Chichester in 1854 and vice-chancellor of Cambridge in 1885.

5 Both Benson's and Freeman's essays are cited from *Essays on Cathedrals*, edited by the Very Rev. J.S. Howson, D.D., Dean of Chester (London: Murray 1872).

6 Leach cites the sources as *The Foundation of Waltham Abbey*, edited, with Introduction and Notes, by William Stubbs, 1861.

7 The source is listed as *History of the University of Oxford*, by H.C. Maxwell-Lyte, M.A., F.S.A., Deputy Keeper of the Public Records, (London: Macmillan & Co., 1886).

8 The publishing data are confined to: *Dugdale's History of S. Paul's*, edited by Henry Ellis. (London: Lackington & Co., Longman & Co., 1818).

9 *Statuta et Consuetudines Eccl. Salisburiensis* by Edward A. Daymon and Wm. Rich Jones. Privately printed. (Bath: William Lewis and Sons, 1883).

10 W.H. Rich Jones, ed., *Register of St. Osmund*, Rolls Series, 1883.

11 The source is cited as *Extract from Cathedral Commission (1880) Report on Wells Cathedral*, 1883: Appendix 2.

12 Leach, ed., *Visitations and Memorials of Southwell Minster*.

13 Ibid.

14 Charity Commission, Endowed Schools Acts, vol.2. Report of the Assistant Commissioner. Cited in Part 1 as RAC:s with page numbers given in the text. MS ED 27/3872, 2: 625–6. The report on *Southwell Collegiate Grammar School, Nottinghamshire* extends through thirty pages.

15 A soke, deriving from Anglo-Saxon times, constituted a local jurisdiction.

16 A benefice with "cure" refers to property bestowed on an ecclesiastical person as his "living." Attached to the "living" is the obligation of caring for the spiritual life of the persons entrusted to him.

17 Charity Commission, Endowed Schools Acts, vol. 2. Report of Assistant Commissioner: York, E. R., Beverley, Beverley Foundation School and Other Chantries, MS ED 27/5495, which includes both printed and manuscript material. There is an identical copy of the printed and confidential report catalogued in the PRO as ED 27/5500. Leach's initial chronology of the inquiry proceedings is found on pp.1–2.

18 The letter, dated 7 January 1888, is included in the manuscript section of ED 27/5495 and is out of place.

19 A 16-page confidential printed report on "Beverley Foundation School and Other Chantries," signed by Leach on 1 February 1889; the quotation is found on p.2. The material in the report is related to many of the items in MS ED 27/5495.

20 Leach, *Memorials of Beverley Minster: Chapter Act Book of The Collegiate Church of S. John of Beverley, A.D. 1286–1347*, 1: ix-x.

21 ED 27/5495, pp.2–4, passim.

22 Poulson, *Beverlac or the Antiquities*.

23 ED 27/5495, p.7. In the interests of consistency, the usual pound sterling sign used by Leach after the respective numeral will be replaced throughout the present text by current usage (£).

24 Ibid., 7–8.

25 Ibid., 8–15, passim.

26 Ibid., 16.

27 Although included under ED 27/5495, these inserts of the related newspaper accounts are enumerated differently, that is, from p.91 to 95(b) and extending to 9 pages in all. The above references are to the body of this material, passim.

28 Ibid., 94 (b).

29 Ibid.

30 Report of Assistant Commissioner: Staffordshire, Walsall, Queen
    Mary's Schools. The manuscript section is catalogued as ED 27/4326,
    on p.155 of which is the notice of inquiry dated 1 December 1891.
31 ED 27/5495, p.835.
32 Charity Commissions, Endowed Schools Acts, vol. 3. Report of Assis-
    tant Commissioner: School of the Cathedral Church of St. Peter of
    York, York (City).(Cited in Part 1 as RAC:Y with page numbers given
    in the text.) The printed, confidential report extends through 41 pa-
    ges, with an appendix of documents included in an additional 23
    printed pages. The report has been paginated at two different times,
    the later one apparently being the stamped enumeration, from 583
    through to 623, every second page only. This will be the pagination
    used for the following references. Leach acknowledges at the outset
    the invaluable assistance afforded him by the Reverend Canon Raine,
    the cathedral chancellor, with his "unrivalled knowledge of the volu-
    minous records at York."

CHAPTER FOUR

1 Leach's definition of a chantry is perhaps too "institutional." The endowment normally called for the sung celebration of masses for the
   founder's intentions and, by extension, the term "chantry" referred to
   the chapel or altar where the masses were offered.
2 A.G. Little, review of *The Schools of Medieval England* by A.F. Leach in
   The English Historical Review 30 (1915): 527–8.
3 William Hunt, in a letter to Little dated 6 September 1915, explains his
   predicament in challenging Leach to substantiate his criticisms of several of his (Hunt's) historical statements: "I asked Leach to refer to
   what I had really written in the articles at which he jeers, and after
   pressing him was told by him that he was too unwell to answer, though
   he was then going about. Last week I wrote sharply to him, but heard
   from Mrs. Leach that he was then really very ill and had lost his son
   and was in hospital after an operation" P.F. Wallis, "Leach – Past, Present and Future," *British Journal of Educational Studies*, 12, no. 2 (May
   1964): 190.

CHAPTER FIVE

1 Leach, *Memorials of Southwell*, x–xi. Cited in Part 1 as *MS* with page
   numbers given in the text.
2 Leach, "Schools," 364.
3 Leach refers to the distinctive "educational foundation" of late fifteenth century Rotherham.
4 Leach, "Schools," 363–4.

5 Ibid., 364–5.

6 Ibid., 365.

7 Leach, "Collegiate Church Schools," *A Cyclopedia of Education,* 111–12.

8 Leach, *Memorials of Beverley Minster,* 1: ix-x.

9 Ibid., 1: xxxiv.

10 Ibid., 1: xxxv.

11 Ibid., 2: 5, 113.

12 Ibid., 1: 212.

13 Ibid., 2: 133.

14 Leach, "Schools," 364.

15 Leach, "Lincoln Grammar School, 1090–1906," 524.

16 Ibid., 524–5.

17 Ibid., 525, passim.

18 Leach, *VCH Lincolnshire* 2 (1906): 427–8.

19 Sir Walter Besant, *London City,* 385.

20 Ibid., 386–7, passim.

21 Ibid., 387–8.

22 Ibid., 391.

23 Ibid., 392.

24 Ibid., 399–400.

25 Ibid., 404–5.

26 Ibid., 405–6.

27 Ibid., 408–9.

28 Ibid., 409.

29 Ibid., 400–1, passim.

30 Ibid., 401.

31 Ibid., 403–4.

32 A.F. Leach, "St. Paul's School," 508, Leach's ellipsis points.

33 A.S. Lupton, "Colet and St. Paul's School. A Rejoinder," *The Journal of Education,* n.s., 31 (1909): 567.

34 Leach, "The Foundation and Re-foundation of Pocklington Grammar School," 5: 64. Cited in Part 1 as FRP with page numbers given in the text.

35 Leach, *VCH Hampshire* 2 (1903): 253–6, passim.

36 Ibid., 257–60, passim.

37 Ibid., 261.

38 Ibid., 263.

39 Ibid., 256.

40 Leach, "Wykeham's Models," 9.

41 Ibid., 12.

42 Ibid., 12–13.

43 Ibid., 13–14.

44 Ibid., 15.

45 Leach, *A History of Winchester College*, v. Cited in Part 1 as *HWC* with page numbers given in the text.

CHAPTER SIX

1 Leach, *English Schools at the Reformation*, 1: 15.

2 Leach, *History of Warwick School*, 71.

3 Ibid., 75.

4 Ibid., 75, n1. The reference is to Powicke and Emden, *The Universities of Europe in the Middle Ages by the late Hastings Rashdall*, 602.

5 Ibid., 77–9.

6 Ibid., 79.

7 Ibid., 80–1.

8 These, with the exception of *MS Lambeth 78*, are described in my article, "The Teaching of Latin," 1–20. To this summary must now be added that of Thomson, *Descriptive Catalogue*, part 1, in which the author discusses several of the manuscripts in question as they pertain to his emphasis on their Middle English content.

9 There is a full description of this MS in Thomson, *Descriptive Catalogue*, 158–68. For Alexander see Orme, *English Schools*, 89–90, and Thomson, *Descriptive Catalogue*, 33–4. For Lawrence of Aquileia see Murphy, *Rhetoric in the Middle Ages*, 258–63.

10 This MS is fully described in Thomson, *Descriptive Catalogue*, 219–32.

11 Thomson, *Descriptive Catalogue*, 239–53; the provenance remains undetermined. For Evrard of Béthune see Orme, *English Schools*, 90, and Thomson, *Descriptive Catalogue*, 34–5.

12 G.H. Rooke, "Dom William Ingram and his Account Book, 1504–1533," *Journal of Ecclesiastical History* 7, 1 (April 1956): 30–44, passim. The MS was discussed by Gasquet, *The Old English Bible and Other Essays*, 235–45. Gasquet, however, assumed that the school in question was that of the novices.

13 John of Cornwall is discussed by Hunt, "Oxford Grammar Masters in the Middle Ages," 174–81; Thomson, *Descriptive Catalogue*, 38–40; Orme, *English Schools*, 95–6.

14 Thomas Hanney is discussed in Thomson, *Descriptive Catalogue*, 37–8, in Orme, *English Schools*, 96, and in Hunt, "Oxford Grammar Masters," 175.

15 This MS is described in M.R. James, *A Descriptive Catalogue of the Manuscripts in the Library of Gonville and Caius College* (Cambridge University Press, 1907–08) 2: 435–37, but James despairs of any attempt at collation. See also *VCH Oxfordshire* 2 (1907): 93. Dictamen and related business letters are discussed in the writings of H.G. Richardson, as listed in Orme, *English Schools*, 335.

16 Described in Thomson, *Descriptive Catalogue*, 185–92.

17 For Priscian see Orme, *English Schools*, 91–2; Thomson, *Descriptive Catalogue*, 31–2; and Murphy, *Rhetoric*, 71–2.

18 The MS is quite fully described in Catherine Borland, *A Descriptive Catalogue of the Western Medieval Manuscripts in Edinburgh University Library* (Edinburgh University Press, 1916), 213; and was the subject of a study by Galbraith, "John Seward and his Circle," 85–104.

19 The MS is described in M.R. James, *A Descriptive Catalogue of the Manuscripts in the Library of Peterhouse* (Cambridge University Press, 1899), 99–100. For Warkeworth's career, see Emden, *A Biographical Register of the University of Oxford to 1500*, 3: 1992–93; *A Biographical Register of the University of Cambridge to 1500*, 618–19.

20 This MS is fully described by M.R. James, *Catalogue of the MSS in the Library of Lambeth Palace* (Cambridge: Cambridge University Press, 1900), 128–34.

21 Described in Thomson, *Descriptive Catalogue*, 169–78; see also Orme, *English Schools*, 104.

22 MSS *Peniarth 356*, *St. John's 163*, *Rawl. G.60*, *Add. 12195*.

23 For Thomas Hanney, see Orme, *English Schools*, 96; Hunt, "Oxford Grammar Masters;" Thomson, *Descriptive Catalogue*, 37–8.

24 MSS *St. John's 163*, *Digby 100*, and *Rawl. G.60*.

25 MSS *Add. 17,724*, *Lincoln 88*, *Add. 37,075*.

26 MSS *Trin. 0.5.4.*, *Add. 37,075*, *Auct. F.3.9.*, *Lincoln 88*, *Add. 32,425* and MSS *Caius 417*, *Hatton 58*, and *Peniarth 356*. The *Ars Minor of Donatus* was translated and printed by Wayland Johnson Chase (University of Wisconsin Studies in the Social Sciences and History, no.11, 1926).

27 MSS *Harl. 1587*, *37,075*, and *Caius 383*.

28 Orme, *English Schools*, 92–3; Thomson, *Descriptive Catalogue*, 35–7.

29 This is discussed by Thomson, *Descriptive Catalogue*, 33–7.

30 MS *Auct. F.3.9.*, pp. 414–27: referred to as *commune modum dictandi ... secundum usum Oxonie*, with its rules arranged *pro iuvenibus*, it appears to be the most elementary of the treatises on dictamen included in these manuscripts.

31 MSS *Trin. 0.5.4.*, *Harl. 1002*, *Caius 203*, *Caius 417*, *Peniarth 356*, and *Add. 37,075*.

32 MSS *Trin. 0.5.4.*, *Harl. 1002*, *Peniarth 356*, *Caius 417*.

33 MSS *Add. 37,075*, *Harl. 1002*, *Harl. 5751*, *Bodl. 837*, *Peniarth 356*.

34 MSS *Trin. 0.5.4.*, *Add. 37,075*, *Caius 203*.

35 MSS *Trin. 0.5.4.*, *Add. 37,075*, *Peniarth 356*, *Shrewsbury School 4*, *Caius 417*, *Corpus Christi 233*, *St. John's 147*, *Rawl. G.60*.

36 MSS *Lincoln 88*, *Auct. F.3.9.*, *Add. 32,425*, *Edinburgh 136*.

37 For Isidore see Murphy, *Rhetoric*, 73–6 and Orme, *English Schools*, 92. For Peter Helias see Thomson, *Descriptive Catalogue*, 32–3.

38 On Bede see Murphy, *Rhetoric*, 77–80. On Hugutio see Orme, *English Schools*, 93.

39 For Papias and Brito see Orme, *English Schools*, 92–4.

40 All the known facts of Hanbury's career and publications are included in Hunt, "Oxford Grammar Masters," 163–74.

41 Thomson, *Descriptive Catalogue*, 4–11.

42 Thomas Wright, ed., *A Volume of Vocabularies ...* (London: Private printing, 1857), 1: xiv.

43 MS *Auct. F.3.9.*, p.189. R.W. Hunt has drawn attention to other manuscripts containing Hanney's work, "Oxford Grammar Masters," 175, n3.

44 Thomson, *Descriptive Catalogue*, 177.

45 L.J. Paetow, "The Arts Course at Medieval Universities," 38.

46 *Cato* and some of the other readers are described in Orme, *English Schools*, 102–6.

47 Orme, *English Schools*, 104, n3.

48 The provenance of MS *Peniarth 356* is discussed in Thomson, *Descriptive Catalogue*. Thomson is inclined to identify it with the school attached to the Cistercian abbey of Basingwerk in Flintshire, Wales.

49 Orme, *English Schools*, 103–4.

50 *MS Harl. 5751*, fol.32: "Grammatica est ars recte loquendi, recte scribendi, recte proferendi. Quot sunt huius partes? 4. Que? Littera, sillaba, dictio et oratio."

51 *MS Add. 37,075*, fol.216v.

52 *MS Auct. F. 3.9.*, p.187: "Diasintastica, que est quarta pars et ultima gramatice, continet in se duo capitula principalia, unum de regimine, alterum de construccione et de construendi ordine."

53 *MS Add. 37,075*, fol.216v: "docet veritatem oracionis absolute per se, non ut conectuntur in oracione." This is presumably derived from the definition given in the *Catholicon*: "tractatus de veritate omnium partium orationis absolute."

54 *MS Harl. 5751*, fol.246v.

55 *MS Trin. 0.5.4.*, fol.80.

56 *MS Auct. F. 3.9.*, p.341.

57 *MS Edinburgh 136*, fol.12v. It may be observed that Richard de Bury puts prosody second in referring to the four parts of grammar in the *Philobiblon* ed. A. Altamura (Naples, 1954): cap.XII, p.114.

58 Ibid., fols.12v-19, passim. Augustine composed the *De Musica*. Marius Servius Honoratus, born c.355 A.D., composed a commentary on Virgil; Brislegh, presumably an Englishman, has not been identified. See Galbraith, "John Seward," 88–9.

59 Ibid., fol.97.

60 Galbraith, "John Seward," 90.

61 *MS Auct. F. 3.9.*, p.443. The other hymns named here, with the exception of the *Splendor paterne glorie*, are attributed by Augustine to Ambrose; see Raby, *A History of Christian-Latin Poetry* , 33–4.

62 *MS Auct. F. 3.9.*, p.444: "Nota quod quamvis metrum non observetur per totum ympnorum, tamen cadencia metri ubique observatur, et hoc sufficit, quia sancta ecclesia liberis gaudet habenis, et non subiacet regulatis libris Prisciani."

63 *MS Add. 17,724*, fol.61.

64 Ibid., fol.67v; see appendix 2.

65 *MS Harl. 1002*, fols.97v-99, passim. The definition is that given in the *Catholicon of John of Genoa* (Venice: P. Lichtenstein, publisher, 1497): "Modulacio vocis in significativa pronunciacione." See appendix 2.

66 Matthew 11: 7.

67 John 21: 20.

68 Job 10: 2.

69 John 21: 12.

70 *MS Lincoln 88*, fol.129v: "Expliciunt flores accentus iam meliores per quos lectores dicantur nobiliores."

71 Ranulph Higden, *Polychronicon*, Rolls Series, 2, 41 (1869): 161; and Emden, *Biographical Register of Oxford*, 1: 490.

72 *MS Auct. F. 3.9.*, p.9.

73 Ibid., text in appendix 2.

74 *MS Harl. 1002*, fols.1–1v, passim.

75 Ibid., fol.13; text in appendix 2.

76 Meaning "hindered."

77 By "infuirtacion" is presumably meant "inversion," that is, of the word order.

78 *MS Trin. o.5.4*, fol. 4

79 *MS Harl. 1587*, fols.69–83, passim. The original spelling has been retained except for the addition of capital letters.

80 *MS Trin. o.5.4.*, fol.4.

81 *MS Harl. 5751*, fol.146.

82 *MS Add. 37,075*, fol.70; cf. W.A. Pantin, "A Medieval Collection of Latin and English Proverbs and Riddles," reprint from *Bulletin of John Rylands Library* (1930).

83 *MS Harl. 1587*, fol.104.

84 *MS Add. 32,425*, fol.35; Psalms 50: 16.

85 Ibid., fol.76v; Psalms 42: 1.

86 Ibid., fol.82v; Matthew 25: 21.

87 *MS Harl. 1587*, fol.81: the opening verse of matins of the "Little Office" of the Blessed Virgin.

88 Ibid., fol.92v; Luke 11: 28.

89 *MS Add. 37,075*, fols.188v-198v, 256–67.
90 Ibid., fol.196.
91 The texts appear in appendix 2. Due allowance has to be made for the boy's misspelling, as well as for the idiomatic Latin; in some cases the exact sense can only be conjectured.
92 Ibid., fol.191.
93 Ibid., fol.192v.
94 Ibid.
95 Ibid., fol.194.
96 Ibid., fol.195.
97 Ibid., fol.196.
98 Ibid., fol.197v.
99 Ibid.
100 Ibid., fol.198.
101 Ibid., fol. 256.
102 Ibid., fol. 258.
103 Ibid., fol.258v.
104 Ibid., fol.259v.
105 Ibid., fol.260v.
106 Ibid., fol.261.
107 Ibid.
108 Ibid., fol.262.
109 Ibid., fol.263.
110 Ibid., fol.264.
111 *MS Caius 383*, p.103, from Psalm 65. The definition is from the *Catholicon*: "continens ponitur pro contento."
112 *MS Harl. 1002*, fol.109v. This is the example used by Alexander. Both the definition and the example are presumably from D. Reichling, ed., *Das Doctrinale des Alexander de Villa-Dei* (Berlin, 1893): lines 2566–72.
113 *MS Trin. 0.5.4.*, fol.90: "Parabola est rerum genere dissimilium comparacio." This is the definition given in the *Catholicon*.
114 Ibid: " Paradigma est narracio exempli hortantis." The example is from James 5: 17.
115 Ibid. Both the definitions and the examples are from the *Catholicon*.
116 *MS Harl. 1002*, fols.106v-107.
117 *MS Add. 37,075*, fol.276.
118 Ibid., fol.277.
119 *MS Lincoln 88*, fols.78-87v.
120 Ibid., fol.17.
121 *MS Trin. 0.5.4.*, fols.96–275.
122 *MS Harl. 1002*, fol.167.
123 Ibid., fol.171: *ru[s]ticula* for *rusticola*?

124 *MS Harl. 1587*, fol.26v.
125 *MS Trin. o.5.4.*
126 Ibid., fol.243.
127 A. Way, ed., *Promptorium Parvulorum sive Clericorum*, Camden Society Series, 3 vols., nos. 25, 54, 89 (1843–1865); L. Mayhew, ed., *Promptorium Parvulorum, The First English-Latin Dictionary*, Early English Text Society (EETS), no.102 (1908). In Way's edition the *nominale* and *verbale* were merged in the interests of simplicity, but the EETS edition retained the original arrangement. A similar dictionary, from 1483, is the *Catholicon Anglicum*, ed. S. J. H. Herrtage, EETS, (London, 1881).
128 *MS Add. 37,075*, fols.45v, 46v, 47, 49v-50; text in appendix 2.
129 This dictionary is printed in Wright, *A Volume of Vocabularies* 1: 120–38.
130 *MS Harl. 1002*, fols.111–12.
131 Ibid.
132 Text in Dr. J. Osternacher, ed., *Theoduli Ecloga* (Linz, 1902).
133 J.P. Migne, ed., *Patrologiae Cursus Completus*, 221 vols. (Paris, 1844–63), 184, col. 1307–08.
134 *MS Harl. 1587*, fol.118.
135 O. Ruffhead, ed., *The Statutes at Large* 1 (London: M. Basket, 1763), Cap.XVII, p.470. Regarding the education of girls, Gardiner, *English Girlhood at School*, 133, states: "Girls nowhere attended grammar-schools." See also her remarks on the system of "placing out," p.116. On the subject of the nuns conducting girls' schools, see Eileen Power, *Medieval English Nunneries*, 261–84 and note B, 568–81. The practice extended to boys as well.
136 *MS Trin. o.5.4.*, fol.25.
137 See, for example, *Auctores Octo Opusculorum cum Commentariis* (Lyons: P. LeMasson & B. Jean, 1494).
138 *MS Auct. F. 3.9.*, p.414.
139 Ibid. In the original manuscript the upper case is used for each part of the letter.
140 *MS Add. 17,724*, fol.39: "Diffinicio dictaminis: dictamen est sermonum dispoc[ic]io de omni re quidem cum venustate."
141 Ibid., fols.53–53v; text in appendix 3.
142 Ibid., fols.59–59v.
143 Ibid., fol.59v: Genesis 6: 12. The text of this example and the two below are in appendix 4.
144 Ibid., fol.60v: I Corinthians 12: 26.
145 Ibid., 5: 6.
146 *MS Trin. o.5.4.*, fols.70–4.
147 Ibid., fol.72v. John de Waldeby became provincial of the Augustinian Friars in 1354. He was a friend of Thomas de la Mare, Abbot

of St. Albans, for whom he wrote a series of twelve homilies on the apostolic creed. Cf. D. Knowles, *The Religious Orders in England*, 2: 41, 150.

148 *MS Trin. O.5.4.*, fols.74v-79 contains the *Practica Dictaminis*; the author taught at Paris c.1300. See Richardson, "The Oxford Law School under John," 332 & n53; text in appendix 3.

149 *MS Caius 383*, p.194.

150 Ibid. 127–8.

151 Ibid., 128.

152 Ibid., 160.

153 This whole subject is treated by Pantin, Salter, and Richardson in *Formularies which bear on the History of Oxford*, and in the following articles by Richardson: "Business Training in Medieval Oxford"; "An Oxford Teacher of the Fifteenth Century," reprint from *Bulletin of John Rylands Library* 23 (1939); and "The Oxford Law School Under John."

154 Besant, *London City*, 397.

155 Leach, "The Humanists in Education," 147.

156 Leach, "Results of Research," 477.

CHAPTER SEVEN

1 John 14: 2.

2 *MS Harl. 1587*, fol.51.

3 *MS Harl. 5751*, fol.135v.

4 Matthew 8: 9. The dative case of *alius* is *alii*.

5 John 7: 12.

6 Ibid., 2: 9.

7 *MS Caius 383*, p.52: "Queritur an melius dicitur factum vel factam. Dico indifferenter quando adiectivum ponitur inter duo substantiva diversorum generum quando unum significat materiam et aliud materiatum cum substantio significante materiatum debet concordare."

8 *MS Add. 32,425*, fol.21.

9 Cf. W.J. Chase, ed. and trans., *Aelius Donatus: The Ars Minor* (University of Wisconsin Studies in the Social Sciences & History, no. 11, 1926), 38.

10 *MS Add. 32,425*, fol.21.

11 Ibid., fol.9.

12 Ibid., fol.81v.

13 Remigius of Auxerre (d. 908) composed the *tractatus super Donatum*, Virgil being his principal Latin authority; Manitius, *Geschichte der lateinischen Literatur des Mittelalters*, 1: 504–7.

14 *MS Auct. F. 3.9.*, p.176.

15 Ibid., p.177; text in appendix 4.

16 Cf. Gilson, *History of Christian Philosophy in the Middle Ages*, 312–14.

17 *MS Lincoln 88*, fol.130; text in appendix 4.

18 Ibid., fol.139v.

19 *MS Edinburgh 136*, fols.1–10v.

20 Ibid., fol.2v.

21 Ibid., fol.9.

22 Ibid., fols.9–9v; text in appendix 4.

23 *MS Lincoln 88*, fol.148v.

24 *MS Harl. 1587*, fols.60–60v: "Non sum clericus sed sum aliqualiter litteratus ... Liber vir est litteratus [MS literarum] per manualem impressionem ... Ego sum literatus per scienciam ... Quero qui est clericus? Clericus est vir litteratus, moribus bonis, sacris ordinibus constitutus et consecratus ..."

25 The *distinctio* is defined, *MS Harl. 5751*, fol.50: "Distincte dicit qui omnia bene collocat in oracione et ex ornacionibus variat atque distinguit."

26 *MS Harl. 5751*, fol.104; the references are respectively, John 8: 2; Matthew 5: 14; Isaias 9: 2; the Introit of the Requiem Mass.

27 Ibid., fol.134; see appendix 6.

28 Ibid., fols.134–134v. It is difficult to trace precisely the source of the second example but it could refer to David near the height of his power, II Kings: 8, 15; "Et regnavit David super omnem Israel." The third example appears to be a reference to Luke 10: 24: "Dico enim vobis, quod multi prophetae et reges volverunt videre quae vos videtis, et non viderunt."

29 Ibid., fol.160.

30 Ibid., fols.139–139v. The respective references are: Luke 11: 3; Psalms 77: 25; the third example may be misquoted from Psalms 80: 17: "Et cibavit eos ex adipe frumenti"; Psalms 41: 4; John 6: 52; John 6: 41; Matthew 4: 4.

31 Ibid., fol.139v.

32 Ibid., fol.245v. See Smalley, "Stephen Langton and the Four Senses," 60–76; also, Master Rypon of Durham's explanation of the four senses in Owst, *Literature and Pulpit in Medieval England*, 59–60.

33 Ibid.

34 Ibid., fols.50v-69, passim. The quotation from Sallust is one of several in this collection that appear to have been attributed erroneously. There is no such quotation in the work of Boethius cited: there may be confusion with the educational treatise, for which see Steiner, "The Authorship of De Disciplina scholarium," 81–4. The quotation attributed to St. Paul is not found in his epistles.

35 Ibid., fol.304.

36 Ibid., fol.302.

37 Ibid.

38 Ibid., fol.302v.

39 Ibid., fols.301–301v. In a thesis of 10 entitled "La Somme Le Roi" de Frère Laurent, *Position des Thèses* 14 (Paris: École des Chartes, 10), 27–35. Edith Brayer notes in regard to this work, which was composed in French in 1279–1280: "Traité des sept vertus: l'auteur établit une concordance entre les pétitions de la Pater nôtre, les dons du Saint-Esprit, les vertus et les béatitudes."

40 Ibid., fols.290v-291.

41 Ibid., fol.290.

42 Ibid., fol.316.

43 On this subject see Ullman, "Classical Authors in Medieval Florilegia."

44 *MS Add. 37,075*, fol.308v, and entitled *nomina villarum*. The spelling has been modernized.

45 *MS Peterhouse 83*. For Warkeworth's career see Emden, *Biographical Register of Cambridge*, 3: 1992–3.

46 Ibid., fol.1.

47 Ibid.; Isaias 1: 1: "Visio Isaias, filii Amos, quam vidit super Judam et Jerusalem, in diebus Oziae, Joathan, Achaz, et Ezechiae, regum Juda."

48 Ibid., fol.41; Job 2: 4, 13: "et nemo loquebatur ei verbum, videbant enim dolorem esse vehementem."

49 Ibid., fol.8v.

50 Ibid., fol.56; Apocalypse 19: 1.

51 Ibid., fol.93; Matthew 28: 1–7.

52 Ibid.

53 Ibid., fol.55v: "[u]t lectores melius legant et intelligant."

54 Ibid., fol.56: "In omni duplici festo per annum secundum usum Sarum dicitur Kyrie eleison Christe eleison cum versibus quorum verba difficiliora et omnium sequenciarium que leguntur in ecclesia secundum usum Sarum. Hic consequenter exponuntur ut ad maiorem devocionem in Deo excitentur lectores et celebrantes."

55 *MS Trin. 0.5.4.*, fol.80.

56 *MS Lambeth 78*.

57 Ibid., fols. 1–1v; part of introduction in appendix 5.

58 Ibid., book 1, sections 2, 5, 3, 61, 56 respectively.

59 Ibid., 1, 52: "Utrum corpus Christi cum sit in loco locale faciat localem differenciam."

60 Ibid., 1, 105–12, *De oracione dominica*.

61 Ibid.

62 Ibid., 1, 115.

63 Ibid., 2, 49.

64 Ibid., 2, 126.

65 Ibid., 2, 103.

66 Ibid., 2, 6.

67 Ibid., 5, 143.

68 Ibid., 17.
69 Ibid., 4, 61.
70 Ibid., 2, 88.
71 Ibid., 4, 15.
72 Ibid., 5, 197.
73 Ibid., 4, 3.
74 Ibid., 2, 139, 149; 4, 92.
75 Ibid., 4, 70.
76 Ibid., 4, 124.
77 Ibid., 4, 71.
78 Ibid., 4, 79.

CHAPTER EIGHT

1 Knowles and Hadcock, *Medieval Religious Houses, England and Wales,* 58–208, passim; Russell, "The Clerical Population of Medieval England," 186–212, passim; Russell notes that A.G. Little thought that the Franciscans suffered "a great and steady decline throughout the fifteenth century," 206–7.
2 J. B. Sheppard, ed., *Canterbury, The Letter Books of the Monastery of Christ Church,* Rolls Series, 3 vols. (London, 1887–1889) 1: 126–7.
3 Letter to Bishop Adam Orleton, 1329: James M. Wilson, ed., *The Worcester Liber Albus* no. 1144 (London: SPCK, 1920), 229–30.
4 Walter de Gray Birch, ed., *Liber Vitae: Register and Martyrology of New Minster and Hyde Abbey, Winchester,* (London: Hampshire Record Society, 1892), lxxxi.
5 D. Wilkins, ed., *Concilia Magnae Britanniae et Hiberniae, A.D. 446–1718* 4 vols. (London, 1737) 2, no.7, p.594, *Constitutiones Benedicti XII super ordine monachorum nigrorum.* The decrees were contained in the *Summi magistri,* issued 20 June 1336. Cf. Knowles, *Religious Orders* 2: 3 and Pantin, *The English Church in the Fourteenth Century,* 106.
6 H.T. Riley, ed., *Reg. J. Whethamstede,* Rolls Series, 2 vols. (London, 1873) 2: 315. The text and translation are in Leach, *Educational Charters and Documents,* 296–7; cf. Leach, *VCH Hertfordshire* 2 (1908): 53–4.
7 Sheppard, *Canterbury Letter Books,* 1: 444–5.
8 Wilson, *Worcester Liber Albus,* no.1028, 209.
9 Leach, *Educational Charters and Documents,* 306–15, passim, for Westminster. In 1364 Hugh of Kingston forsook his charge as "petagogus" of the Christ Church almonry school in Canterbury to assume control of the public grammar school at Kingston, to the annoyance of the monastic almoner. Cf. Sheppard, *Canterbury Letter Books,* 2, no.919, and Leach, *Educational Charters and Documents,* 318–19.

10 Ethel M. Hampson, "The Grammar Schools," *VCH Cambridge and Isle of Ely* 2: 321.

11 Leach, *VCH Yorkshire* 1 (1907): 418–21; and Leach, *VCH Worcestershire* 4 (1924): 476.

12 Leach, *Educational Charters and Documents*, 298–9, the duties of the St Albans almoner c.1330.

13 For Reading and Westminster respectively, Leach, *VCH Berkshire* 2(1907): 247, and Leach, *Educational Charters and Documents*, 308.

14 Mary Dormer Harris, ed., *Coventry Leet Book, A.D. 1420–1535*, 2 vols. (London: EETS, 1907–13), 1: 90.

15 J. A. Twemlow and W. H. Bliss, eds., *Calendar of Papal Registers: Papal Letters*, vols. 5–8, 1396–1447, (London: His Majesty's Stationery Office, 1904–09), 8: 348–9.

16 Riley, *Reg. J. Whethamstede* 2, appendix C, p.305; T. Arnold, ed., *Memorials of St. Edmund's Abbey, Bury St. Edmunds*, Rolls Series, no. 96, (London, 1896) 3: 182–3. The relationship between an abbey and a town school is clearly described by Leach, *VCH Suffolk* (1907) 2: 306–12. Leach's own contribution to this volume extends from pp. 301–36; the last part, pp. 337–55, was contributed by Miss E. P. Steele Hutton.

17 *Calendar of Patent Rolls, Edward III, 1345–1348*, London: PRO Publications, 7: 362.

18 H.E. Salter, ed., *Chapters of the Augustinian Canons*, (London: Canterbury and York Society Publications, 1922), 29: 83. The constitutions were issued in the decree of May 15, *Ad decorem*, for which cf. Knowles, *Religious Orders*, 2: 3.

19 A. Hamilton Thompson, ed., *Visitations of Religious Houses in the Diocese of Lincoln*, 3 vols., (London: Canterbury and York Society Publications 1915–1927), 1: 89.

20 Ibid., 3, part 2, 372.

21 Ibid., 371.

22 Ibid., 2, part 1, 169, and n4.

23 Ibid., 171. As the editor remarks, n1, evidently the novices paid their grammar master out of their *peculium*, for which see Knowles, *Religious Orders*, 1: 287–9.

24 Thompson, *Visitations of Lincoln*, 2, part 1, 208.

25 Ibid., 86.

26 Ibid., 3, part 2, 233.

27 Ibid., 237–8.

28 Ibid., 371.

29 Ibid., 2, part 1, 214.

30 Knowles, *Religious Orders* 2: 296.

31 Leach, *VCH Derbyshire* 2 (1907): 210.

32 Leach, *VCH Gloucestershire* 2 (1907): 317–19.

33 *Rotuli Parliamentorum*, IV Henry IV, 3: 502; cf. Hinnebusch, *The Early English Friars Preachers*, 264–5.

34 Alleging undue force being employed to have him received into the Friars Preachers, Hugh Kennedy's petition to the Holy See states that his parents entrusted him to the Dominicans of Ayr in the diocese of Glasgow "that they might teach him grammar"; Twemlow and Bliss, *Calendar of Papal Registers*, 8: 553. Clerval, in reference to the higher schools of grammar in Chartres c.1460–67, says: "Les Dominicains surtout tinrent des écoles florissantes. Ils compterent jusqu'à 200 et 300 élèves." If these figures are anywhere near the truth, the friars' schools must have been open to secular clerks; Clerval, *Les Écoles de Chartres au Moyen Âge du V^E au XVIE Siècle*, 422.

35 Chettle, "The Friars of the Holy Cross," 204–20; and *Calendar of Patent Rolls, 1348–50* 8: 268.

36 A.G. Little, review of *The Schools of Medieval England* by A.F. Leach in *The English Historical Review* 30 (1915): 528.

37 Leach, *Schools of Medieval England*, 166–7.

38 Joan Simon, "A.F. Leach on the Reformation: I," *British Journal of Educational Studies* 3 (1954–55): 134–38, passim.

39 Jordan, *Philanthropy in England, 1480–1600*, 279–97, passim.

40 Knowles and Hadcock, *Medieval Religious Houses*, 325–53; and the recent article by Moran, "Clerical Recruitment in the Diocese of York, 1340–1530: Data and Commentary," 19–54.

41 See Russell, "The Clerical Population of Medieval England," 179.

42 C.J. Hefele, *Histoire des Conciles* ed. and trans. by H. Leclercq (Paris: Letouzey et Ané, 1913), vol. 5, pt.2: 1341.

43 The effect of this legislation on England is discussed in Gibbs and Lang, *Bishops and Reform, 1215–1272*, 154–7. The authors point out that three grades of schools – theology, grammar and song – were attached to the cathedrals of Lincoln, Salisbury, and York in the thirteenth century. With reference to England they say: "it would appear that the canon had little effect because the bishops considered that there were already sufficient educational centres," p.157. Similarly, Edwards, *The English Secular Cathedrals in the Later Middle Ages*, 206, states: "In the case of the grammar schools the movement to provide permanent endowments had begun before 1179; while the theological lecturers have also been found at several cathedrals about the end of the twelfth century."

44 Orme, "Education and Learning at a Medieval English Cathedral: Exeter 1380–1548," 265–83.

45 Edwards, "Cathedral of Salisbury," 176.

46 F.C. Hingeston-Randolph, ed., *Reg. J. de Grandisson*, 2 parts (London, 1894–97), 1: 123.

47 Cecil Deedes, ed., *Reg. R. Reade*, (London: Sussex Record Society Publications, 1908), 1 : 115. The instruction of the choristers in grammar at Lincoln Cathedral is discussed by Edwards, *English Secular Cathedrals*, 318–19.

48 For clerks of the second form see Edwards, *English Secular Cathedrals*, 309–13.

49 *MS Exeter 3550*, fol.61.

50 *MS York Acta Capitularia (2 H2)*, fol.36. Text in appendix 6.

51 *The Fabric Rolls of York Minster*, Surtees Society Publications, 35(1859): 250: "non curant laborare pro sciencia historiarum suarum."

52 Ibid., 252.

53 Thompson, *Visitations of Lincoln*, 1 : 139.

54 Leach, *Early Yorkshire Schools*, 1 : 151.

55 Leach, *Educational Charters and Documents*, 332–40.

56 Leach, "Results of Research," 465.

57 W. Dugdale, ed., *Monasticon Anglicanum*, new ed., 8 vols. (London: Harding, 1817–1830), vol. 6, pt.3: 1407.

58 *Reg. John Carpenter*, 1 (1443–76) fol.83v; the entry, dated 17 December 1463, is, in part, as follows: "ecclesiam parochialem de Clyfton predictam cum suis iuribus et pertinenciis universis ... ad usum exhibicionis magistri sive informatori in facultate gramatice ad informandum et instruendum ut prefertur ministros dicte ecclesie collegiatis et collegii et alios quoscumque venire volentes in gramatica ... incorporamus et appropriamus." Cf. Leach, *VCH Gloucestershire* 2 (1907): 108.

59 Thompson, *The English Clergy and Their Organisation in the Later Middle Ages*, 133.

60 In a recent study, *English Chantries: The Road to Dissolution* (Cambridge: Harvard University Press, 1979), Alan Kreider has shown that only a relatively small minority of chantry priests taught school and that Leach who, in his view, tended "to overstress" the contribution of the chantry schools to medieval education, conceded that the "great majority" of the chantry holders were not schoolmasters, 59.

61 *Calendar of Patent Rolls, Henry VI, 1429–36*, 2: 189–90.

62 Ibid., 1446–52, 5: 170.

63 Ibid, 1446–52, 5: 402.

64 W.H. Stevenson, ed., *Calendar of the Records of the Corporation of Gloucester* (Gloucester, 1893), 398.

65 Arthur Thomas Bannister, ed., *Reg. T. Spofford*, Episcopi Herefordensis, 1442–48 (London: Canterbury and York Society Publications, 1919), 281–8.

66 Ibid., 282.

67 Ibid.

68 Ibid.

69 Hingeston-Randolph, *Reg. J. de Grandisson* part 2: 666; "advowson": the right to present to an ecclesiastical benefice.

70 Ibid., 667.

71 Ibid., 66.

72 Cf. Génestal, *Le Privilegium Fori en France* 1: 11: "Le principe canonique est en effet qu'il y a incompatibilité entre clericature et servitude."

73 *MS Chancery C 47, Miscellanea*, bundle 21, no. 4.

74 Ibid.

75 Ibid and Moran, *Education and Learning in the City of York, 1300–1560*, 9.

76 Ibid., and Knowles and Hadcock, *Medieval Religious Houses*, 322.

77 *Reg. J. Thoresby*, fols.72–72v: "necnon exhibiciones puerorum pauperum scholarum proficientium in scolis gramaticalibus qui ibidem sustentari consueverunt perpetuis temporibus perdurare"

78 F. C. Hingeston-Randolph, ed., *Reg. W. de Stapledon* (London, 1892), 229.

79 Ibid., 225–6.

80 H.C. Maxwell-Lyte, and M.C.B. Dawes, eds., *Reg. T. Bekynton* (London: Somerset Record Society Publications, 1935), part 1: 20–1.

81 T.F. Kirby, ed., *Reg. W. Wykeham*, Hampshire Record Society Publications, (1896–99) 2: 195.

82 Leach, *Educational Charters and Documents*, 324.

83 The following entries are taken from the final edition of the statutes contained in a manuscript copy c.1400, referred to as *MS New College, Founder's Statutes of Winchester*. There is a description of the manuscript in Kirby, *Reg. W. Wykeham* 2: 518–19.

84 *MS New College, Founder's Statutes of Winchester*, fol.1: "Septuaginta pauperium et indigencium scolarium gramatica sciencie intendere ... in scolares eligendi sint pauperes indigentes bonis moribus ... ad studium habiles et conversacione honesti in lectura, plano cantu et antiquo donato competenter instructi."

85 Ibid.

86 Ibid., fol. lv: "Nolentes tamen quod aliquis ... patitur ... alium ... provenientem propter quem redditur omnino inhabilis ad sacros ordines suscipiendos in dictum nostrum Collegium prope Wyntoniam quomodolibet admittatur."

87 Ibid., fols. 1v-2.

88 Although theological studies are not specifically mentioned, the inference is that such candidates would have access to the usual kind of in-service training normally provided at cathedrals and collegiate

churches. Orme, in the article cited above, "Education and Learning: Exeter," 267, states, with reference to the minor clergy, that "only a small minority seem to have studied at university."

89 Leach, *History of Winchester College*, 72.

90 H.T. Riley, ed., *Thomas Walsingham, Historia Anglicana*, Rolls Series, 2 vols. (London, 1864), 2: 268.

91 Leach, *A History of Winchester College*, 73. The reception of the clerical tonsure (first tonsure) did not confer any *order*, but it did admit the recipient to clerical status and the privileges of the clerical order; cf. Génestal, *Le Privilegium Fori* 1: 3.

92 A postscript to Rubric 16 is quoted in Parry, *Education in England in the Middle Ages*, 198: "sons of noble and powerful persons ... to the number of *ten* might be instructed and informed in grammar within the college, without charge to the college."

93 Kirby, *Reg. W. Wykeham*, 2: 407–9.

94 G. Williams, ed., *Official Correspondence of Thomas Bekynton*, Rolls Series, 2 vols. (London, 1872), 2: 280–2, passim.

95 H.C. Maxwell-Lyte, *A History of Eton College, 1440–1884*, new and rev. ed. (London: Macmillan & Co. Ltd., 1889), 5. The royal charter of foundation is dated 11 October 1440.

96 Ibid., appendix A., pp.493–505, passim.

97 Ibid., 17.

98 Ibid., 497.

99 Williams, *Correspondence of Bekynton* 2: 280–2, passim.

100 Maxwell-Lyte, *History of Eton College*, 500.

101 Heywood and Wright, *The Ancient Laws of the Fifteenth Century for King's College, Cambridge, and the Public School of Eton College*, 479–80.

102 Ibid., 480.

103 Maxwell-Lyte, *History of Eton College*, 499.

104 Mullinger, *University of Cambridge* 1: 254, n1.

105 The appointment dated 15 October 1445, is one of several in Pantin, *Canterbury College, Oxford*, 101–2.

106 Powicke and Emden, *The Universities of Europe* 3: 1983, n2. F.M. Powicke and A.B. Emden, *Statutes of the Colleges of Oxford* (London: E.A. Bond, 1853), 1: cap. 2, p.24.

107 *Statutes of the Colleges of Oxford*, 1: cap. 2, pp. 14–15, 30.

108 Ibid., 2: 6, 16, 76.

109 Ibid., 77.

110 *Clare College, 1326–1926* (no author). (Cambridge: Cambridge University Press, 1928), 1: 34–5; Mullinger, *University of Cambridge* 1: 252.

111 Damian Riehl Leader, "Grammar in Late-Medieval Oxford and Cambridge," *History of Education*, 12 (1983): 10.

112 Mary Lobel has written a concise and clear account of what is known about the Oxford grammar schools in "The Grammar Schools of the Medieval University," *VCH Oxfordshire* 3 (1954): 40–3. See also Hampson, "The Grammar Schools," *VCH Cambridge and the Isle of Ely* 2 (1948): 321.

113 The relevant entries are in H.E. Salter, ed., *A Cartulary of the Hospital of St. John the Baptist*, 3 vols. (Oxford Historical Society Publications: Clarendon Press, 1914–17), 3: 137–95; cf. Emden, *Biographical Register of Oxford*, 3: 1456.

114 Lobel, "The Grammar Schools of the Medieval University," 43.

115 Leader, "Grammar in Oxford and Cambridge," 10.

116 Salter, *Mediaeval Archives of the University of Oxford*, 2: 279; Emden, *An Oxford Hall in Mediaeval Times*, 173–9, includes an account of the Oxford grammar schools.

117 Emden, *Oxford Hall*, 168–9, 174.

118 S. Gibson, ed., *Statuta Antiqua Universitatis Oxoniensis*, (Oxford:Clarendon Press, 1931), 291.

119 Leach, *Educational Charters and Documents*, 240.

120 *Records of the Borough of Nottingham, 1155–1399*, W.H. Stevenson, ed. (London and Nottingham: 1882), 262.

121 Twemlow and Bliss, *Calendar of Papal Registers*, 5: 300.

122 *Reg. T. Bourchier* fol.7v: "Te que magistrum dictarum scolarum cum potestate accipiendi salarium competens a singulis scolaribus singulis terminis iuxta consuetudinem laudabilem actenam usitatem et approbatam profecimus presencium per tenorem."

123 Orme discusses the status of the grammar masters in *Education in the West of England*, 19–20.

124 Leach, *Educational Charters and Documents*, xxxiv.

125 The text is in Leach, *Educational Charters and Documents*, 330–41.

126 *Calendar of Patent Rolls 1413–16*, pp.206–7, and T. Arnold, ed., *Memorials of St. Edmund's Abbey, Bury St. Edmunds*, Rolls Series (London, 1896), 3: 182–3.

127 *Reg. T. Arundel* 1, fol.93, and Emden, *Biographical Register*, 2: 663.

128 *Reg. Wykeham*, 2: 195.

129 *Reg. G. Welton*, fol.71, and *Calendar of Patent Rolls, Edward III, 1374–7*, 1: 80.

130 *Reg. W. Courtenay*, fol.10v, and *Reg. W. Lyhert*, fol.84.

131 *Reg. W. Lyhert*, fol.131.

132 Leach, *Educational Charters and Documents*, 280–2.

133 Leach, *VCH Lincolnshire* 2 (1906): 426.

134 *Reg. G. Welton*, fol.52: "ad tenendum et exercendum scolas gramaticales infra civitatem nostram Karliolensem et ad informandum pueros, adultos et alios quoscumque per te informari volentes in

sciencia gramaticali ac aliis super quibus tua noverit sciencia informare tibi licenciam concedimus specialem."

135 *Calendar of Inquisitions Post Mortem*, vols.5–11, Edward II – Edward
III. (Public Record Office Publications, 1908–1935), 7, no. 250,
p.192.

136 Ibid., vol. 11, no.130, p.124.

137 Ibid., vol. 7, no.172, p.140.

138 Ibid., vol. 8, no.602, p.449.

139 *Calendar of Patent Rolls, Henry VI, 1441–46*, 4: 432. The ordinance of
the bishop of London followed a similar one from the archbishop of
Canterbury, and both ordinances were given royal assent some six
weeks later. The text from Bishop Gilbert's register, fol.191v, is given in appendix 6. See Orme, *English Schools*, 219.

140 Reddan, "The Hospital of St. Anthony," 581–3, passim.

141 *Reg. R. Gilbert* fol.183: "monstrabunt unum magistrum sive ydoneum
informatorem in gramatice facultate ... qui scolas gramaticales infra
dictum precinctum vel prope ut prediciutr regere debeat et cunctos
pueros ac alios universos addiscere vel scolatizare volentes gratis do-
cere, instruere et informare."

142 *Reg. R. Gilbert*, fol.191v.

143 Leach, *Educational Charters and Documents*, 418–20.

144 Ibid.; Leach, "St. Paul's School Before Colet," 216–17.

145 Thorndike, "Elementary and Secondary Education in the Middle
Ages," 407.

146 Wilson, *Worcester Liber Albus*, no.801, p.175.

147 Orme, *English Schools*, 217–20.

148 J. H. Parry, ed., *Reg. J. de Trillek* (London: Canterbury & York Society Publications, 1912), 400.

149 *Reg. R. Clifford*, fol.67: "ad hoc duxistis eligendum quibuscumque li-
teratis primam tonsuram et aliis clericis regularibus et secularibus."

150 *Reg. R. Gilbert*, fol.191v: "universis et singulis rectoribus, vicariis, Capellanis curatis et non curatis, Notariis publicis, clericis et litteratis
quibuscumque per nostras civitatem et diocesim Londoniensem."

151 See, for example, Maxwell-Lyte & Dawes, *Reg. T. Bekynton*, 1: 65, 94,
102, 149, 187, 190, 203, 207, 291.

152 Even in regard to the "secondaries" of Exeter Cathedral, that is,
those in residence as eventual candidates for the major – or celibate
– orders of the priesthood, a sizeable minority – perhaps 35–45 percent – reverted to lay status and "augmented the fund of lay literacy," Orme, "Education and Learning: Exeter," 279–80. Pegues,
"The Clericus in the Legal Administration of Thirteenth-Century
England," 529–59. On p.557 Pegues states: "When examined more
closely, a great many of the *milites literati* may be found to have been

nuper clerici." For the conditions governing dispensation from ordination to the priesthood for purposes of study on the part of clerks not
in major orders, see the constitution *Cum ex eo* in A.F. Friedberg,
ed., *Corpus Iuris Canonici* 2 parts (Leipzig, 1879–81), 2: Sexti Decre-
tal., Lib. I. Tit. VI. cap. XXXIV. A thorough analyis of the intent
and effect of *Cum ex eo* is in Leonard E. Boyle, *Pastoral care, clerical
education and canon law, 1200–1400* (London: Variorum Reprints,
1981), 263–302, and in Roy M. Haines, "The Education of the English clergy During the Later Middle Ages: Some Obervations on the
Operation of Pope Boniface VIII's Constitution *Cum ex eo*," *Canadian
Journal of History* 4(1969): 1–22.

153 Génestal, *Le Privilegium Fori*, 7.

154 Ibid., 11. The relationship of first tonsure to serfdom is discussed by
Petot, "Servage et tonsure cléricale dans la pratique française du
Moyen Âge," 193–205.

155 The education of women is discussed in Orme, *English Schools*, 52–5.
The Statute of Labourers is in Ruffhead, *The Statutes at Large*,
Cap.17: p.470. Regarding the education of girls, Gardiner, *English
Girlhood at School*, 133, states: "Girls nowhere attended grammar-
schools;" see also her remarks on the system of "placing out," p.116.
On the subject of the nuns conducting girls' schools, see Power, *Me-
dieval English Nunneries*, 261–84 and note B, 568–81.

156 Denifle and Chatelain, *Chartularium Universitatis Parisiensis* 3: 24.

157 Ibid., no.1446, 289–91.

158 Lefèvre, *L'organisation ecclésiastique de la ville de Bruxelles au moyen-âge*,
218.

159 Ibid., 213.

160 Ibid., 218.

161 Leach, "Results of Research," 453.

162 Leach, *Educational Charters and Documents*, 424.

163 Gibson, *Statuta Antiqua* , 22. The editor's ascription of these statutes
to "before 1350" has recently been amended to "before 1313." David
Thomson, "The Oxford Grammar Masters Revisited," *Mediaeval
Studies* 45 (1983): 298 and n2.

164 Gibson, *Statuta Antiqua*, 22.

165 Ibid., 20: "nec optineat aliquis licenciam, nisi prius fuerit examinatus
de modo versificandi et dictandi et auctoribus et partibus."

166 Ibid., 23: "predicto statuto contempto, lectiones cursorias, quas vo-
cant audienciam abusive, in doctrine scolarium suorum evidens de-
trimentum legere presumpserunt."

167 Ibid.

168 Cf. the definition furnished by the 14th century German cleric and
given in Thorndike, *University Records and Life in the Middle Ages*,
217–18: "the bachelor is an arch-scholar who gives cursory lectures

in the place of the master and who goes about the classes of the doctors arguing and responding, but has not yet received the laureat of doctoral knighthood, yet is close to the degree of master."

169 Riley, *Reg. J. Whethamstede*, 2, appendix C, 312.

170 Leach, *Educational Charters and Documents*, 258–9.

171 Leach, *Memorials of Beverley Minster*, 2: 127. Additional evidence of assistant teachers at grammar schools being designated "bachelors" comes from Troyes, 1436, where, in the bishop's ordinances for the schools of his diocesan city, there are several references to them. These ordinances are printed in Gustave Carré, *L'Enseignement Secondaire à Troyes*, 305–16.

172 Riley, *Reg. J. Whethamstede*, 2, appendix C, 312.

173 Rackham, *Early Statutes of Christ's College, Cambridge*, 24.

174 Riley, *Reg. J. Whethamstede*, 2, appendix C, 312.

175 Ibid.

176 Carré, *L'Enseignement Secondaire à Troyes*, 22, states that the use of the disputation extended even to the younger students, but in view of the factual nature of their studies this claim is difficult to accept.

177 F.C. Hingeston-Randolph, ed., *Reg. T. de Brantyngham* (London, 1901), part 1, 378–9.

178 Wilkins, *Concilia*, 3: 317: "*Constitutiones domini Thomae Arundel ... contra haereticos.*"

179 Thomson states that the earliest reference to an Oxford B. Gram. that he has noticed comes from 1512, "Oxford Grammar Masters," 300. In the same article, p.301, he mentions that the computer printout in the Bodleian Library of the grammarians mentioned in A.B. Emden's *Biographical Register of the University of Oxford to 1500* has 3, 4, 6, 2 and 6 entries for each of the twenty-year periods of the fourteenth century.

180 Mullinger, *The University of Cambridge*, 1: 350, n1, distinguished between grammar schools for those "engaged upon an arts course," and a distinct faculty of grammar for those "who aimed at nothing more than a grammar degree." At Oxford, statutes ascribed to the fourteenth century speak of regent masters in grammar, *magister quiscumque regens in gramatica*, and the licentiate in grammar, *si quis licenciatus fuerit in gramatica, artibus, aut medicine*, Gibson, *Statuta antiqua*, 173–4. Paetow, *The Arts Course at Medieval Universities*, 55, 57, pointed out that grammar constituted a separate faculty at some of the universities of southern France: "at Toulouse, as early as the beginning of the fourteenth century, there was a regular succession of degrees in grammar – bachelor, licentiate, master."

181 For "God's house" see Leach, *Educational Charters and Documents*, 402–3.

182 Rackham, *Statutes of Christ's College*, i-ii, gives a brief chronology of

"God's house".

183 Leader, "Grammar in Oxford and Cambridge," 11–13.

184 See, for example, John of Trevisa's remarks in his continuation of Higden's *Polychronicon*, 159–61 regarding the decline of French.

185 Gibson, *Statuta Antiqua*, 171.

186 Ibid., 240.

187 *Reg. R. Braybrooke*, fol.404v: "Item lego Johanni consanguineo meo XL s. ad standum in scolis causa legendi, scribendi et faciendi Franciscum, Latinum, cartas et indenturas," and Rickert, "Chaucer at School," 273.

188 Pantin, Salter, Richardson, *Formularies*; Richardson, "Business Training;" "An Oxford Teacher;" and "The Oxford Law School."

189 Printed in Carré, *L'Enseignement Secondaire à Troyes*, 305–16.

190 Ibid., 316.

191 Carré, *L'Enseignement Secondaire à Troyes*, 309.

192 Ibid., 103. The text is no. 30, pp.310–11.

193 Heinr. Wilh. Heerwagen, ed., *Zur Geschichte der Nürnberger Gelehrtenschulen in dem Zeitraume von 1485 bis 1526* (Nuremberg: Fr.Campe & Sohn, 1860), 34. The *Alanus* is the *Liber Parabulorum*. For the *Summulae* of Peter of Spain see Étienne Gilson, *History of Christian Philosophy in the Middle Ages*, 319, 680–1. It is of interest to note that the Nuremberg grammar schools are called "trivial" schools, and the inclusion of Peter of Spain's work on logic, therefore, quite fitting.

CHAPTER NINE

1 Leach, "Results of Research," 436. The school in question, as recounted above, was the prebendal school at Chichester.

2 Green, *A Short History of the English People*, preface, xi.

3 Leach, "Results of Research," 35.

4 Leach, "Edward VI: Spoiler of Schools", 368–9.

5 Leach, *English Schools at the Reformation*, 1: 2.

6 Ibid., 3.

7 Leach, "Results of Research," 435.

8 Leach, "The Origin of Oxford," 93.

9 Leach, "The Monasteries and the Education of Girls," 667–79, passim.

10 Ibid., 669. The reference to "modern monks" is almost certainly a criticism of Gasquet.

11 Leach, *Schools of Medieval England*, v–vi.

12 Leach, *Memorials of Beverley Minster*, 2: v–vii, passim. The criticism of Leach had appeared in "Notes of the Month," 290–1.

13 Leach, *A Cyclopedia of Education*, s.v. "free schools."

14 Ibid.

15 Leach, "Free Grammar Schools. 1: The Case Stated," 550–2; "Free Grammar Schools. 2: Free Schools Before 1500," 577–9.

16 Leach, "Free Grammar Schools. 1," 551.

17 Leach, "Free Grammar Schools. 2," 578.

18 Ibid.

19 Leach, "The True Meaning of 'Free School'," (June 1980): 378–80; "The True Meaning of 'Free School'," (July 1980): 495–7.

20 Leach, "The True Meaning of 'Free School'," (June 1908): 378.

21 Review of *English Schools at the Reformation 1546–8* by Arthur F. Leach, *The Athenaeum* 3618 (February 1897): 272–3.

22 Ibid., 272.

23 Ibid.

24 Ibid., 272–3.

25 Ibid., 273.

26 Leach, response to review of his *English Schools at the Reformation 1546–8*, in *The Athenaeum* 3620 (March 1897): 348.

27 Arthur F. Leach, letter to reviewer of his *English Schools at the Reformation 1546–8*, in *The Athenaeum* 3622 (March 1897): 417.

28 Review of *A History of Winchester College*, by A.F. Leach, *The Athenaeum* 3738 (17 June 1899): 748.

29 Ibid.

30 Ibid.

31 Review of *Educational Charters and Documents, 598 to 1909*, by Arthur F. Leach, *The Athenaeum* 4378 (23 September 1911): 349–50.

32 Review of *Educational Charters and Documents, 598 to 1909*, by A.F. Leach, *The Times Educational Supplement* (3 October 1911): 125.

33 Ibid.

34 H. Rashdall, review of *Educational Charters and Documents, 598 to 1909*, by Arthur F. Leach, *The Oxford Magazine* (14 March 1912): 278–9.

35 Ibid., 278.

36 Ibid., 278–9, passim.

37 Ibid., 279.

38 Leach, "The Origin of Oxford," 331–2.

39 Ibid., 331.

40 Ibid., 331–2, passim.

41 Ibid., 333.

42 Foster Watson, review of *Documents Illustrating Early Education in Worcester, 685 to 1700 A.D.*, by Arthur F. Leach, *English Historical Review* 29 (1914): 341–3.

43 Ibid., 341.

44 Ibid., 342.

45 Ibid., 343.
46 Review of *Schools of Medieval England*, by A.F. Leach, *The Athenaeum* 4560 (20 March 1915): 262–3.
47 Ibid., 262.
48 Ibid.
49 Ibid., 262–3, passim.
50 Ibid., 262.
51 A.G. Little, review of *The Schools of Medieval England*, by A.F. Leach, *English Historical Review* 30 (1915): 525–9.
52 Ibid., 525.
53 Ibid.
54 Ibid., 527.
55 Ibid., 528. Little is referring to the directive in the decree enjoining not only cathedrals but other churches that "can afford" to do so to appoint grammar masters.
56 Ibid., 528–9.
57 Ibid., 529. At the end of the review A.G. Little appended a note with some errors that he thought should be corrected in the event of a second edition. For whatever reason, the errors, admittedly of a minor character, were left uncorrected in the second edition, that of 1916.
58 Foster Watson, *The English Grammar Schools to 1660*. A new edition of the publication of 1908.
59 Joan Simon, "A.F. Leach: A Reply," *British Journal of Educational Studies* 12, 1 (November 1963): 48, fn. 3.
60 Watson, *Grammar Schools*, 7–8.
61 Ibid., preface, v-vi, and 128.
62 Ibid., 139–40.
63 Ibid., 1.
64 Ibid., 3–4.
65 Ibid., 4.
66 Ibid., 143–5.
67 Parry, *Education in England in the Middle Ages*.
68 Ibid., 248–53.
69 Ibid., 69.
70 Ibid., 64.
71 Ibid., 66–7.
72 Ibid., 71–3, passim.
73 Ibid., 166–7.
74 Ibid., 71–5, passim.
75 Ibid., 160–1.
76 Ibid., 170–1.
77 Ibid., 175.

78 Margaret Deanesley, "Medieval Schools to c. 1300," *The Cambridge Medieval History* 5 (1926): 934–5.

79 G.R. Potter, "Education in the Fourteenth and Fifteenth Centuries," 985.

80 Sir Maurice Powicke, *The Thirteenth Century, 1216–1307* (Oxford: Clarendon Press, 1953), 763, n1.

81 May McKisack, *The Fourteenth Century* (Oxford: Clarendon Press, 1959), 553.

82 E.F. Jacob, *The Fifteenth Century* (Oxford: Clarendon Press, 1961), 715.

83 Joan Simon, "A.F. Leach on the Reformation: I," *British Journal of Educational Studies* 3, no. 2 (May 1955): 128–43; "A.F. Leach on the Reformation: II," *British Journal of Educational Studies* 4, no. 1 (November 1955): 32–48.

84 Joan Simon, *Education and Society in Tudor England.* G. R. Elton, in his *England under the Tudors,* 2nd ed. (London: Methuen, 1974), 505, in reference to her work says: "Solid array of facts carefully linked to social developments," and a book "that re-establishes the century as one of educational reform and advance."

85 Simon, "Leach on the Reformation, I," 128.

86 Ibid., 128–9.

87 Ibid., 129. The author notes that Sir Maurice Powicke, in *The Thirteenth Century,* had omitted *The Schools of Medieval England* from his bibliography. In commenting on the debate involving Joan Simon's estimate of pre-Reformation schooling as opposed to Leach's view, P.J. Wallis included correspondence from R.L. Poole and Rose Graham, written in the spring of 1915, encouraging Little in his criticism of Leach's monastic errors by suggesting specific points of their own: "Leach – Past, Present and Future," 184–194.

88 Ibid., 134.

89 Ibid., 143, and n3. This, at least, seems to be uppermost in Simon's mind when she thinks of the church in decline – a concept which she states to be central to Parry's treatment of the question. On p.134 of the same article she connects decline with the negligence on the part of secular colleges, even more than monastic communities, in maintaining schools as intended by "ecclesiastical legislators." She bases this opinion largely on A. Hamilton Thompson's studies on clerical organization and diocesan visitation records in the later middle ages.

90 Ibid., 138–9.

91 Simon, "Leach on the Reformation: II," 36–7, passim.

92 Ibid., 37–8.

93 Ibid., 39.

94 Ibid., 41.

95 Ibid., 42.

96 W. N. Chaplin, "A.F. Leach: A Re-Appraisal," *British Journal of Educational Studies* 11, 2 (May 1963): 99–124; Joan Simon, "A.F. Leach: A Reply," *British Journal of Educational Studies* 12, 1 (November 1963): 41–50; W. N. Chaplin, "A.F. Leach: Agreement and Difference," *British Journal of Educational Studies* 12(1964): 173–83; P. J. Wallis, "Leach – Past, Present and Future," *British Journal of Educational Studies* 12(1964): 184–94. This last contains the letters of A.L. Poole and Rose Graham to Little with respect to Leach's book *The Schools of Medieval England*.

97 Simon, "Leach: A Reply," 50. In a belated letter of condolence to Mrs.Leach (20 November 1915) on her husband's death, the secretary of the British Academy, Professor I. Gollancz, expresses the hope that the proposal outlined by Leach in the last paper read before the Academy may some day be realised "as a fitting memorial of his lifelong devotion to the problems of schools and education." He goes on to say that "those of us who were brought into close association with your revered husband feel we have lost a cherished friend; and we will never forget his generous zeal in helping other investigators, his steadfastness of purpose, & his staunch comradeship" A copy of the above letter was kindly given to me by a grandson of Leach, Mr James W. Leach.

98 W.E. Tate, *A.F. Leach as a Historian of Yorkshire Education*, St. Anthony's Hall Publications (York: St. Anthony's Press, 1963).

99 Ibid., 6–8, passim.

100 Ibid., 6–7, passim.

101 Ibid., 9.

102 Ibid., 10. The other source-book is Leach's *Early Education in Worcestershire*.

103 John Lawson, *A Town Grammar School through Six Centuries*.

104 Ibid., 100–1.

105 Ibid., 191.

106 Ibid., 210.

107 Ibid., 223–4.

108 Ibid., 16.

109 Ibid., 21–31, passim.

110 Ibid., 39.

111 John Lawson, *Medieval Education and the Reformation*

112 Ibid., 20.

113 Ibid., 26–8.

114 Ibid., 51.

115 Ibid., 3–5.

116 Ibid., 9.

117 Ibid., 93–5.

118 Ibid., 13.

119 Ibid., 75.

120 Ibid., 76. Lawson equally takes issue with Jordan's "disparagement" of later medieval education, observing that if this author's statistical evidence regarding educational bequests and donations between 1550 and 1640 were to be adjusted to the monetary values of this "notoriously inflationary" period, it might show that "the greatest expansion actually took place in the last generation of Catholic England," ibid., 81–2.

121 Ibid., 80–1.

122 Ibid., 70.

123 Margaret Spufford, *Contrasting Communities*, 188.

124 Ibid., 217.

125 Heath, *The English Parish Clergy on the Eve of the Reformation*, 71. Heath gives special attention to the sermon addressed to ordinands and their examiners by the chancellor of York, William de Melton: the text is in A. G. Dickens, *Transcriptions of the Royal Historical Society*, 5th ser. xiii, 53–4.

126 Ibid., 81.

127 Ibid., 85.

128 Ibid.

129 Ibid., 83–4.

130 Kreider, *English Chantries* .

131 Ibid., 28.

132 Ibid., 59.

133 Ibid., 28.

134 Ibid., 59.

135 Ibid., 40.

136 Ibid., 61–3.

137 Ibid., 60–1.

138 Ibid., 234, n78.

139 Ibid.

140 G.R. Elton, *Reform and Reformation England 1509–1558* (London: Edward Arnold, 1977), 400.

141 Anthony Goodman, *A History of England from Edward II to James I* (London and New York: Longman Group Ltd., 1977).

142 M.H. Keen, *England in the Later Middle Ages* (London: Methuen, 1973), 541.

143 A.R. Myers, *England in the Late Middle Ages*, 2nd rev. ed., (Penguin Books, 1963), 251.

144 L.C.B. Seaman, *A New History of England 410–1975* (Brighton: The Harvester Press, 1981), 110–13. The pre-university educational developments are confined to a single paragraph.

145 Tate, "Leach as a Historian," 6.

146 Orme, "English Schools," 6.

147 Ibid., 87–115.

148 Ibid., 106–15.

149 Ibid., 113.

150 Ibid., 48–9.

151 Ibid., 142–6.

152 Ibid., 43–5.

153 Ibid., 206.

154 Ibid., 178.

155 Orme, *Education in the West of England* . The author remarks that "a local study of this kind, more fully than a national one, throws light on the number and distribution of schools at different times and their continuity from one period to the other."

156 Ibid., 43–6, 72–4, 81–4.

157 Ibid., 43.

158 Ibid., 98.

159 Ibid., 192.

160 Ibid., 117–21, 151–2, 188–90.

161 Ibid., 152.

162 Ibid., 13–14. The author also mentions that jurisdiction in medieval England normally extended only over a single town and that it was mainly in areas like Lincolnshire and Nottinghamshire where such jurisdiction might extend to a whole county.

163 Ibid., 31.

164 Ibid., 28–9.

165 Ibid., 29.

166 Ibid., 30.

167 Ibid.

168 Ibid., 31.

169 Ibid.

170 Orme, *English Schools*, 4.

171 Ibid., 5–6.

172 Ibid., 6.

173 Ibid.

174 Ibid., 6–7.

175 Ibid., 4. Orme also would include Leach's *Educational Charters and Documents, 598–1909*, provided that "the more accurate dates and texts" added since Leach's day were taken into account.

176 Ibid., 4–5.

177 Ibid., 5.
178 Hoeppner Moran, *The Growth of English Schooling 1340–1548*. The author's studies include "Education and Learning In the City of York 1300–1560," *Borthwick Papers* (1979): 1–49; "Literacy and Education in Northern England, 1350–1550"; and "Clerical Recruitment in the Diocese of York, 1340–1530."
179 Moran, *Growth of English Schooling*, 12–13 and n28; Orme, *English Schools*, 7 and n2.
180 Moran, *Growth of English Schooling*, appendix B, 237–79. The author states that in this appendix she has assumed "that children singing in the choirs or reading in the parish church must have received some training, however informal," and further, that while such schools should not be understood to be "institutionalized," in a number of cases there was "continuity."

APPENDIX ONE

1 The usual spelling is 'Reade' but such variations are common in the MSS which Leach used.
2 The brackets indicate extensions of Leach's abbreviations.

APPENDIX TWO

1 MS *Possit*.
2 MS *edemptitate*.
3 MS reading (for some form of *vendo?*)
4 MS E aspersorio; suggested reading is that of *MS Trin. 0.5.4.*, fol.34
5 *MS Trin. 0.5.4.*, fol.34v; *MS Add. 37,075* reads: *ponatur libet ligna perforando*.
6 *MS Trin. 0.5.4.* fol. 34v; *introire* of *MS Add. 37,075* does not scan.

APPENDIX THREE

1 Cicero's word is *dictio*, not *dilectio*; *Inv*.1, 15, 20.
2 MS *piecti*.
3 Liber Proverbiorum, Cap.I: Parabolae Salomonis, filii David, regis Israel, ad sciendam sapientiam V.5 – Audiens sapiens, sapientior erit; et intelligens gubernacula possidebit.
4 MS *ingrediat*.

5 Probable reading of MS.
6 MS *epilenciam.*

APPENDIX FOUR

1 MS apparently *Uni.*

APPENDIX SIX

1 MS *Antonini.*
2 MS *nequit.*

Bibliography

PRIMARY SOURCES

The Writings of Arthur Francis Leach

BOOKS, CHAPTERS IN BOOKS, AND ARTICLES

"The Ancient Schools in the City of London," in Sir Walter Besant, *London City*. London: Adam & Charles Black, 1910, 385–429.

Beverley Town Documents. Edited for the Selden Society, vol. 14. London: Bernard Quaritch, 1900.

"A Clerical Strike at Beverley Minster in the Fourteenth Century." *Archaeologia* 55 (1896): 1–20.

Club Cases. London: Harrison, 1879.

"Colet and St. Paul's School. A Joinder of Issue." *Journal of Education*, n.s., 31 (1909): 609–12.

"Colet's Place in the History of Education." *Journal of Education*, n.s., 26 (1904):438–39.

Digest of the Law Relating to Probate Duty. London: William Maxwell & Son, 1878.

Documents Illustrating Early Education in Worcester, 685–1700. Edited for the Worcestershire Historical Society. London: Mitchell Hughes and Clarke, 1913.

"Durham School." *Journal of Education*, n.s. 28(1906):294–5.

Early Yorkshire Schools. Vol. I: *York, Beverley, Ripon*. Vol. 2: *Pontefract, Howden, Northallerton, Acaster, Rotherham, Giggleswick, Sedbergh*. The Yorkshire Archaeological Society, Record Series: vols. 27 & 33. Leeds: 1899–1903.

"Edward VI: Spoiler of Schools." *Contemporary Review* 62 (1892): 368–84.

"The English Land Question." *Political Tracts* reprinted from the *Winchester Observer and County News*. London: The National Press Agency Ltd., 1871–83. [n.d. but British Library catalogue gives 1883], 3–32.

English Schools at the Reformation 1546–8. London: Archibald Constable & Co., 1896.

"English Schools at the Reformation." *The Athenaeum*, 3622 (27 March 1897):417.

"The Foundation and Re-foundation of Pocklington Grammar School." *Transactions of the East Riding Antiquarian Society* 5 (1897):63–114.

"Free Grammar Schools. I: The Case Stated." *National Observer* 16 (Sept.1896):550–2.

"Free Grammar Schools. II: Free Schools Before 1500." *National Observer* 16 (Oct. 1896):577–9.

History of Warwick School. London: Archibald Constable & Co., Ltd., 1906.

A History of Winchester College. London: Duckworth & Co., 1899.

"The Humanists in Education." Review of *Studies in Education during the Age of the Renaissance, 1400–1600*, by William Harrison Woodward. *Classical Review* 24 (1910): 146–50.

"The Inmates of Beverley Minster." *Transactions of the East Riding Antiquarian Society*. 2 (1894):100–23.

"Lincoln Grammar School, 1090–1906." *Journal of Education*, n.s. 28(1906): 524–5.

"The Medieval Education of Women." *Journal of Education*, n.s. 32 (1910): 838–41.

"Memorandum by Mr. A.F. Leach, Assistant Charity Commissioner, on the History of Endowed Schools," in *Royal Commission on Secondary Education: Memoranda and Answers to Questions*, 57–75. London: Printed for Her Majesty's Stationery Office by Eyre and Spottiswoode, 1895.

"Milton as Schoolboy and Schoolmaster." *Proceedings of the British Academy* 3 (1909):295–318.

"The Monasteries and the Education of Girls." *Journal of Education*, n.s. 32 (1910):667–9.

"The Origin of Oxford." *National Review* 28 (1896): 93–102.

"The Origin of Westminster School." *Journal of Education*, n.s. 27(1905): 79–81.

"The Origins of Oxford." *The Oxford Magazine*. (16 May 1912): 331–3.

"Our Oldest School." *The Fortnightly Review*, n.s. 52 (1892): 638–50.

"The Pedigree of Durham School." *Journal of Education*, n.s. 27(1905): 707–9.

The Protectorate. London, Oxford & Cambridge: Rivington, 1872. (The Stanhope prize essay read in the Theatre, Oxford, 12 June 1872).

"The Records of the Borough of Beverley," in *Historical Manuscripts Commission: Report on the Manuscripts of the Corporation of Beverley*, 1–7. London: Printed for Her Majesty's Stationery Office by Mackie & Co., Ltd., 1900.

"St. Paul's School." *Journal of Education*, n.s. 31 (1909): 503–9.

"St. Paul's School Before Colet." *Archaeologia* 60 (1910):191–238.

"School Supply in the Middle Ages." *Contemporary Review* 66 (1894): 674–84.

"The Schoolboys' Feast." *The Fortnightly Review*, n.s. 59 (1896):128–41.

Schools of Medieval England. London: Methuen & Co., Ltd., 1915.

"Shakespeare's School." *Journal of Education*, n.s. 30 (Jan. 1908):23–5.

"Shakespeare's School." *Journal of Education*, n.s. 30 (March 1908):211–12.

"Sherborne School Before, Under, and After Edward VI." *Archaeological Journal*, 2nd ser., 5(1898):1–83.

"Some English Plays and Players, 1220–1548," in *An English Miscellany Presented to Dr. Furnivall*, 205–34. Oxford: Clarendon Press, 1901.

"Some Results of Research in the History of Education in England; With Suggestions for Its Continuance and Extension." *Proceedings of the British Academy* 6 (1914):433–80.

"The True Meaning of 'Free School.'" *Journal of Education*, n.s. 30 (1908):378–80.

"The True Meaning of 'Free School.'" *Journal of Education*, n.s. 30 (1908):495–7.

The Victoria History of the Counties of England. Edited by H. Arthur Doubleday [and subsequently by others]. London: Archibald Constable, 1900 – . (Leach's contributions to the *VCH* volumes are invariably titled "Schools"):

– Bedfordshire, 2 (1908): 149–85.

– Berkshire, 2 (1907): 245–84.

– Buckinghamshire, 2 (1908): 145–221.

– Derbyshire, 2 (1907): 207–81.

– Durham, 1 (1905): 365–413.

– Essex, 2 (1907): 501–64. (By C. Fell-Smith, edited by A. F. Leach.)

– Gloucestershire, 2 (1907): 313–448.

– Hampshire and Isle of Wight, 2 (1903): 251–408; 5 (1912): 14–19.

– Hertfordshire, 2 (1908): 47–102.

– Lancashire, 2 (1908): 561–624. (Edited by A. F. Leach and co-authored with Rev. H. J. Chaytor and William Farrer.)

– Lincolnshire, 2 (1906): 421–92.

– Northamptonshire, 2 (1906): 201–88.

– Nottinghamshire, 2 (1910): 179–264.

– Somersetshire, 2 (1911): 435–65, (Edited by A. F. Leach. Section on Wells written by A.F. Leach, the rest written by Rev. T. Scott Holmes.)

– Suffolk, 2 (1907): 301–36. (Edited by A. F. Leach; pp. 337–57 by Miss E. Steele Hutton.)

– Surrey, 2 (1905): 155–242.

– Sussex, 2(1907): 397–440.

– Warwickshire, 2 (1908): 297–373.

– Worcestershire, 4 (1924): 473–540.

– Yorkshire, 1 (1907): 415–500.

"Winchester College, 1393 and 1893." *Contemporary Review* 64 (1893): 74–89.

"Wykeham's Books at New College," in *Collectanea*, 3rd ser., vol. 32. Edited by Montagu Burrows. Oxford Historical Society Publications, 1896, 211–44.

"Wykeham's Models," in *Winchester College 1393–1893* by Old Wykehamists, 9–17. London: Edward Arnold, 1893.

ARTICLES IN ENCYCLOPEDIAS AND DICTIONARIES

Dictionary of English Church History. Edited by S.L. Ollard and Gordon Cross. London: Mowbray, 1912:

– "Education, the Church in relation to." 192–98.

– "Waynflete, William." 619–20.

– "Wykeham, William." 659–61.

Encyclopaedia Britannica. 11th edition, s.v. "Schools."

A Cyclopedia of Education. Edited by Paul Monroe. 5 vols. New York: Macmillan, 1911–13:

– "Abbey Schools." 1 (1911): 2–4.

– "Almonry Schools." 1 (1911): 98–100.

– "Archdeacon." 1 (1911): 175–6.

– "Bishops' Schools." 1 (1911): 386–9.

– "Boy Bishop." 1 (1911): 435–7.

– "Busby." 1 (1911): 473–4.

– "Canon Law on Education." 1 (1911): 525–7.

– "Cathedral Schools." 1 (1911): 551–3.

– "Chancellors' Schools." 1 (1911): 565–6.

– "Chantry Schools." 1 (1911): 567–9.

– "Choristers' Schools." 1 (1911): 644–5.

– "Church Schools." 2 (1911): 3–5.

– "Clerk." 2 (1911): 35–6.

– "Cloister Schools." 2 (1911): 39–40.

– "Colet, John." 2 (1911): 49–50.

– "College." 2 (1911): 51–7.

– "Collegiate Church Schools." 2 (1911): 110–12.

– "Commonwealth and Education." 2 (1911): 162–3.

– "Edward VI." 2 (1911): 419–20.

– "Endowments, Educational." 2 (1911): 452–6.

– "Eton College." 2 (1911): 509–12.

– "Exhibition." 2 (1911): 543–5.

– "Fagging." 2 (1911): 571–2.

– "Fees." 2 (1911): 583–6.

– "Free Schools." 2 (1911): 694–8.

– "Glomery." 3 (1912): 116–17.

– "Grammar School." 3 (1912): 138–44.
– "Harrow School." 3 (1912): 220–3. Co-authored with Isaac L. Kandel.
– "Henry VI." 3 (1912): 248–9.
– "High School." 3 (1912): 261–3.
– "Hospital Schools." 3 (1912): 314–18.
– "London, Education in." 4 (1913): 69–73.
– "Middle Ages, Education during the." 4 (1913): 217–24.
– "Milton as Educator." 4 (1913): 244–5.
– "Prefect and the Prefectural System." 5 (1913): 26–8.
– "Primer and Primarian." 5 (1913): 29–30.
– "The Reformation in England [Education]." 1 (1911): 135–41.
– "Rugby School." 5 (1913): 218–20.
– "School." 5 (1913): 257–60.
– "Udal Nicholas." 5 (1913): 645–6.
– "Usher." 5 (1913): 695–6.
– "Waynflete, William." 5 (1913): 755–6.
– "Winchester College." 5 (1913): 781–5.
– "Wolsey, Thomas." 5 (1913): 794–5.
– "Women, Higher Education of – Historical Sketch." 5 (1913): 795–803.
– "Wykeham, William of." 5 (1913): 828–9.
– "York School." 5 (1913): 837–9.

LETTERS IN NEWSPAPERS

"The Origin of Canterbury School." *The Times* (London), 12 September 1896,
    p.8.
Ibid., 7 September 1897, p. 5.
"Which is our oldest school? Canterbury v. York." *The Guardian*, 12 January
    1898, p.51.
Ibid., 19 January 1898, p.95.
"St. Paul's Girls' School and Its Pedigree." *The Times* (London), 2 April 1904,
    p. 6.
Ibid., 12 April 1904, p. 10.
"St. Paul's School before Colet." *The Times* (London), 7 July 1909, p. 4.
Ibid., 14 July 1909, p. 22.
Ibid., 3 August 1909, p. 4.
"Our Oldest Public School." *The Times Educational Supplement*, 3 January
    1911, p.51.
The Times (London), 6 January 1911, p. 6.
Ibid., 16 January 1911, p. 7.
"Dr. Arnold and After." *The Times Educational Supplement*, 7 March 1911,
    p. 68; *The Times Educational Supplement*, 4 April 1911, p. 73.
ed. *Educational Charters and Documents 598 to 1909.* Cambridge University
    Press, 1911.

ed. *A History of Bradfield College*. London: Henry Frowde and Oxford University Press, 1900.

ed. *Memorials of Beverley Minster: The Chapter Act Book of the Collegiate Church of S. John of Beverley, A.D. 1286–1347*, vols. 98 and 108. Printed for the Surtees Society. Durham: Andrews & Co., 1898–1903.

ed. *Visitations and Memorials of Southwell Minster*. Printed for the Camden Society. Westminster: Nichols and Sons, 1891.

REVIEWS AND CRITICISMS OF WRITINGS BY

ARTHUR FRANCIS LEACH

Review of *Chapter Act Book of Beverley Minster* by A.F. Leach. *The Antiquary* (Oct. 1898):290–1.

Review of *Educational Charters and Documents, 598 to 1909*, by Arthur F. Leach. *The Athenaeum* 4378 (23 Sept. 1911): 349–50.

"Educational Charters and Documents." Review of *Educational Charters and Documents, 598 to 1909*, by A.F. Leach. *The Times Educational Supplement* (3 Oct. 1911): 125–6.

Review of *English Schools at the Reformation, 1546–8*. *The Athenaeum* 3618 (27 Feb. 1897):272–3.

"English Schools at the Reformation." Addition to review of same in 3618, 27 Feb. 1897. *The Athenaeum* 3620 (13 March 1897): 348.

Review of *A History of Winchester College*, by A.F. Leach. *The Athenaeum* 3788 (17 June 1899): 748.

Review of *The Schools of Medieval England*, by A.F. Leach. *The Athenaeum*, 4560 (20 March, 1915): 262–3.

Chaplin, W.N. "A.F. Leach: Agreement and Difference." *British Journal of Educational Studies* 12, no. 2 (May 1964): 173–83.

– "A.F. Leach: A Re-Appraisal." *British Journal of Educational Studies* 11, no. 2 (May 1963): 99–124.

Little, A.G. Review of *The Schools of Medieval England*, by A.F. Leach. *English Historical Review* 30 (1915): 525–9.

Lupton, A.S. "Colet and St. Paul's School. A Rejoinder." *The Journal of Education*, n.s. 31 (1909): 567–8.

Rashdall, Hastings. Review of *Educational Charters and Documents: 598 to 1909*, by Arthur F. Leach. *The Oxford Magazine* (14 March 1912): 278–9.

Simon, Joan. "A.F. Leach: A Reply." *British Journal of Educational Studies* 12, no. 1 (Nov. 1963): 41–50.

– "A.F. Leach on the Reformation: I." *British Journal of Educational Studies* 3, No. 2 (May 1955): 128–43.

– "A.F. Leach on the Reformation: II." *British Journal of Educational Studies* 4, No. 1 (Nov. 1955): 32–48.

– "The Reformation and Education." *Past & Present* 11 (April 1957): 48–65.

Wallis, P.J. "Leach – Past, Present and Future." *British Journal of Educational Studies* 12, no. 2 (May 1964): 184–194.

Watson, Foster. Review of *Documents Illustrating Early Education in Worcester, 685 to 1700 A.D.*, by Arthur F. Leach. *English Historical Review* 29 (1914): 341–3.

Manuscript Sources

CAMBRIDGE

Gonville and Caius College Library, MS Caius 383 (Grammatical Miscellanea)

Peterhouse Library, MS Peterhouse 83 (Expositio Verborum Difficilium)

Trinity College Library, MS Trin. 0.5.4. (Grammatical Miscellanea)

CARLISLE

Diocesan Registry, The Register of Gilbert Welton, Bishop of Carlisle, 1353–1363

EDINBURGH

University Library, MS Edinburgh 136 (Opera Johannis Seward)

ELY

Diocesan Registry, The Register of Thomas Bourchier, Bishop of Ely, 1443–1454

EXETER

Cathedral Library, Dean and Chapter MS 3550 (Chapter Acts, 1382–1424)
– Dean and Chapter MS 3521 (Treatises of John Seward, fols. 5–85)

LINCOLN

Cathedral Library, Dean and Chapter MS Lincoln 88 (Grammatical Miscellanea)

LONDON

British Library
   MS Add. 17,724 (Grammatical Miscellanea)
   MS Add. 32,425 (Grammatical Miscellanea)
   MS Add. 37,075 (Grammatical Miscellanea)
   MS Harl. 1002 (Grammatical Miscellanea)
   MS Harl. 1587 (Grammatical Miscellanea)
   MS Harl. 5751 (Grammatical Miscellanea)
Public Record Office
   Charity Commission, Endowed Schools Acts. Reports of Assistant Commissioners
   Vol.2 (1886–89)
      Beverley Foundation School, MS ED 27/5495, MS ED 27/5500, pp.833–48.

Chichester Prebendal School, MS ED 27/4713, pp.785–832.
Southwell Collegiate Grammar School, MS ED 27/3872, pp. 623–52.
Vol.3 (1890–96)
School of the Cathedral Church of St. Peter of York, York (City),
pp. 583–657 (no MS ref.).
MS Chancery C 47, Miscellanea 21/4 (Ordinance of Archbishop Simon
Langham for St. Leonard's Hospital, York)
Guildhall Library
MS 9531/3 The Register of Robert Braybrooke, Bishop of London, 1382–
1404
MS 9531/4 The Register of Richard Clifford, Bishop of London, 1407–
1421
MS 9531/6 The Register of Robert Gilbert, Bishop of London, 1436–
1448
Lambeth Palace
MS Lambeth 78 (Speculum Parvulorum of William Chartham)
The Register of William Courtenay, Archbishop of Canterbury, 1381–
1396
The Register of Thomas Arundel, Archbishop of Canterbury, 1399–1414
Norwich Diocesan Registry
The Register of Walter Lyhert, Bishop of Norwich, 1446–1472

OXFORD
Bodleian Library MS Auct. F. 3.9. (Grammatical Miscellanea)
New College Library MS New College, Founder's Statutes of Winchester

WORCESTER
Worcestershire Record Office
The Register of John Carpenter, Bishop of Worcester, 2 vols., vol.1, 1443–
1476

YORK
Cathedral Library Dean and Chapter MS (Acta Capitularia (2 H2), 1410–
1429)
St. Anthony's Hall MS, The Register of John Thoresby, Bishop of York,
1352–1373

Printed Sources

Aelius Donatus: The Ars Minor. W. J. Chase, ed. and trans. University of
Wisconsin Studies in the Social Sciences & History, no. 11, 1926.
Auctores Octo Opusculorum cum Commentariis. Lyons: P. LeMasson & B. Jean,
publishers, 1494.
Bekynton, Official Correspondence of Thomas. Memorials of the Reign of King
Henry VI. 2 vols. G. Williams, ed. London: Rolls Series, 1872.
Brito, W. Vocabularius Biblie. Ulm: J. Zainer, publisher, c. 1473.

Calendar of Inquisitions Post Mortem. Vols. 5–11, Edward II – Edward III. London: Public Record Office Publications, 1908–35.

Calendar of Papal Registers: Papal Letters. Vols. 5–8, 1396–1447. J. A. Twemlow and W. H. Bliss, eds. London: His Majesty's Stationery Office, 1904–09.

Calendar of Patent Rolls, Edward III – Henry VI, 1327–1461. 34 vols. London: Public Record Office Publications, 1891–1911.

Canterbury, The Letter Books of the Monastery of Christ Church. J.B. Sheppard, ed. 3 vols. London: Rolls Series, 1887–89.

A Cartulary of the Hospital of St. John the Baptist. H.E. Salter, ed. 3 vols., nos. 66, 68, 69. Oxford Historical Society Publications: Clarendon Press, 1914–17.

Catholicon of John of Genoa. Venice: P. Lichtenstein, publisher, 1497.

Catholicon Anglicum. S. J. H. Herrtage, ed. London: Early English Text Society (EETS), 1881.

Catonis, Disticha. M. Boas & H.J. Botschuyer, eds. Amsterdam, 1952.

Chapters of the Augustinian Canons. H. E. Salter, ed. London: Canterbury and York Society Publications, no.29, 1922.

Clare College, 1326–1926. (no author). Vol.1. Cambridge: Cambridge University Press, 1928.

Concilia Magnae Britanniae et Hiberniae, A.D. 446–1718. D. Wilkins, ed. 4 vols. London, 1737.

Corpus Iuris Canonici. A. F. Friedberg, ed. 2 parts. Leipzig, 1879–81.

Coventry Leet Book, A.D. 1420–1555. Mary Dormer Harris, ed. 2 vols. London: EETS, 1907–13.

Das Doctrinale des Alexander de Villa-Dei. D. Reichling, ed. Berlin, 1893.

Fabric Rolls of York Minster, The. Vol.35. Surtees Society Publications, 1859.

Le Facet En Francoys. J. Morawski. Vol. 2, part I. Société Scientifique de Poznan, 1923.

Furnivall, F.J., ed. *The Babees Book.* London: E.E.T.S., 1868.

Gloucester, Calendar of the Records of the Corporation of. [W.H. Stevenson, ed.] Gloucester: J. Bellows, 1893.

Graecismus, Eberhardi Bethuniensis. Dr. J. Wrobel, ed. Vol. 1, *Corpus grammaticorum medii aeui.* Bratislava, 1887.

Hefele, C.J. *Histoire des Conciles.* H.Leclercq, ed., trans. Vol.5, part 2. Paris: Letouzey et Ané, 1913.

Isidori Hispalensis Episcopi Etymologiarum sive Originum. W. M. Lindsay, ed. 2 vols. Oxford, 1911.

Liber Vitae: Register and Martyrology of New Minster and Hyde Abbey, Winchester. Walter de Gray Birch, ed. London: Hampshire Record Society, 1892.

Memorials of St. Edmund's Abbey, Bury St. Edmunds. T. Arnold, ed. Vol.3. London: Rolls Series, 1896.

Monasticon Anglicanum. W. Dugdale, ed. 8 vols. London: Harding, 1817–30.

Papias, Grammaticus, Elementarium. Boninus Mombritius, ed. Venice, 1491.

Patrologiae Cursus Completus. J. P. Migne, ed. 221 vols. Paris, 1844–63.

Philobiblon. Richard de Bury. A. Altamura, ed. Naples, 1954.

Polychronicon. Ranulph Higden. C. Babington, ed. Vol.2. London: Rolls Series, 1869.

Promptorium Parvulorum, The First English-Latin Dictionary. L. Mayhew, ed. London: EETS, no.102, 1908.

Promptorium Parvulorum sive Clericorum. A. Way, ed. 3 vols., nos. 25, 54, 89. Camden Society Series, 1843–65.

Records of the Borough of Nottingham, 1155–1399. [W.H. Stevenson, ed.] Vol. I. Published under authority of corporation of Nottingham. London and Nottingham, 1882.

Registrum J. Whethamstede. H. T. Riley, ed. 2 vols. London: Rolls Series, 1872–73.

Rotuli Parliamentorum. Vol.3, 1377–1411. London: 1783.

Statuta Antiqua Universitatis Oxoniensis. S. Gibson, ed. Oxford: Clarendon Press, 1931.

The Statutes at Large. O. Ruffhead, ed. Vol.1. London: M. Basket, 1763.

Statutes of the Colleges of Oxford. Vol.1. London: E.A. Bond, 1853.

Theoduli Ecloga. Dr. J. Osternacher, ed. Linz, 1902.

Visitations of Religious Houses in the Diocese of Lincoln. A. Hamilton Thompson, ed. 3 vols. London: Canterbury and York Society Publications, 1915–27.

A Volume of Vocabularies. T. Wright, ed. Vol.1. London: 1857.

Walsingham, Thomas. Historia Anglicana. H.T. Riley, ed. 2 vols. London: Rolls Series, 1863–64.

The Worcester Liber Albus. James M. Wilson, ed. No. 1144. London: S.P.C.K., 1920.

Episcopal Registers

Bath and Wells: *T. Bekynton*. H. C. Maxwell-Lyte and M. C. B. Dawes, eds. London: Somerset Record Society Publications, 1934–35.

Chichester: *R. Reade*. Cecil Deedes, ed. London: Sussex Record Society Publications, 1908–10.

Exeter: *T. de Brantyngham*. F. C. Hingeston-Randolph, ed. 2 parts. London, 1901–06.

Exeter: *J. de Grandisson*. F. C. Hingeston-Randolph, ed. 2 parts. London, 1894–97.

Exeter: *W. de Stapledon*. F. C. Hingeston-Randolph, ed. London, 1892.

Hereford: *J. de Trillek*. J. H. Parry, ed. London: Canterbury and York Society Publications, 1912.

Hereford: *T. Spofford*. Arthur Thomas Bannister, ed. London: Canterbury and York Society Publications, 1919.

Winchester: *W. Wykeham*. T. F. Kirby, ed. 2 vols. Hampshire Record Society Publications, 1896–99.

SECONDARY SOURCES

Adams, The Reverend H.C. *Wykehamica. A History of Winchester College and Commoners, From the Foundation to the Present Day.* Oxford and London:James Parker and Company, 1878.

Barnard, H.C. *A History of English Education From 1760.* 2nd ed. London: University of London Press Ltd., 1961.

Besant, Sir Walter. *London City.* London: Adam and Charles Black, 1910.

Bonaventure, Brother, F.S.C. [also, J.N.T. Miner]. "Schools and Literacy in Later Medieval England." *British Journal of Educational Studies* 11, no. 1 (November 1962): 16–27.

– "The Teaching of Latin in Later Medieval England." *Mediaeval Studies* 23 (1961): 1–20.

Borland, Catherine. *A Descriptive Catalogue of the Western Medieval Manuscripts in Edinburgh University Library.* Edinburgh: Edinburgh University Press, 1916.

Bowles, Rev. W.L. *Vindiciae Wykehamicae; or, A Vindication of Winchester College, in a Letter to Henry Brougham, Esq.* Bath: Richard Cruttwell, 1818.

Bursill-Hall, G.L. "Teaching Grammars of the Middle Ages:Notes on the Manuscript Tradition." *Historiographica Linguistica* 4 (1977): 1–29.

Carlisle, Nicholas. *Bedford – Lincoln*, vol. 1, and *London – Wales*, vol. 2 of *A Concise Description of the Endowed Grammar Schools in England and Wales.* London: W. Bulmer and Co., 1818.

Carré, Gustave. *L'Enseignement Secondaire à Troyes.* Paris: Hackette, 1888.

Chettle, H.F. "The Friars of the Holy Cross." *History* 34 (1949): 204–20.

Clerval, J.A. *Les Écoles de Chartres au Moyen Age, du Ve au XVIE Siècle.* Mémoires de la Société Archaéologique d'Eure-et-Loire, vol. 11. Chartres, 1895.

Coleman, Janet. *Medieval Readers and Writers, 1350–1400.* New York: Columbia University Press, 1981.

Cox, G.W. Review of *Monks of the West, from St. Benedict to St. Bernard* by Count de Montalembert. *Edinburgh Review* 114 (October 1861): 318–47.

Curtis, S.J., and M.E.A. Boultwood. *An Introductory History of English Education Since 1800.* 4th ed. London:University Tutorial Press, 1966.

de Montmorency, J.E.G. "The Medieval Education of Women." *The Journal of Education* n.s. 32 (November 1910): 720–2.

– *State Intervention in English Education:A Short History from the Earliest Times down to 1833.* Cambridge: Cambridge University Press, 1902.

Denifle, H., and A. Chatelain, eds. *Chartularium Universitatis Parisiensis.* 3 vols. Paris, 1894.

Dobson, Barrie. "The Later Middle Ages 1215–1500." In *A History of York Minster*, G.E. Aylmer and Reginald Cant, eds. 44–109. Oxford:Clarendon Press, 1977.

Edwards, Kathleen. "Cathedral of Salisbury." *VCH Wiltshire* 3 (1956): 156–210.

– *The English Secular Cathedrals in the Later Middle Ages*. Manchester: Manchester University Press, 1949.

Emden, A. B. *A Biographical Register of the University of Cambridge to 1500*. Cambridge: Cambridge University Press, 1963.

– *A Biographical Register of the University of Oxford to A.D. 1500*. 3 vols. Oxford: Oxford University Press, 1957–9.

– *An Oxford Hall in Medieval Times*. Oxford: Clarendon Press, 1927.

Fifoot, C.H.S. *Frederic William Maitland: A Life*. Cambridge, MA: Harvard University Press, 1971.

– ed. *The Letters of Frederic William Maitland*. London: Selden Society, 1965.

Firth, J.d'E. *Winchester College*. London: Winchester Publications Limited [n.d.].

Galbraith, V. H. "John Seward and His Circle." *Mediaeval and Renaissance Studies* 1, no. 1 (1941).

Gardiner, D. *English Girlhood at School*. Oxford: Oxford University Press, 1929.

Gasquet, Francis Aidan. *Henry VIII and the English Monasteries*. 6th ed. London: J. Hodges, 1895.

Génestal, R. *Le Privilegium Fori en France du Décret de Gratien à la Fin du XIVE Siècle*. Paris: E. Leroux, 1921.

Gibbs, M., and J. Lang. *Bishops and Reform, 1215–1272*. Oxford: Oxford University Press, 1934.

Gilson, Etienne. *History of Christian Philosophy in the Middle Ages*. London: Sheed and Ward, 1955.

Green, John Richard. *A Short History of the English People*. Rev. ed. London: Dent, Everyman's Library, 1960.

Hackett, Maria. *Brief Account of Cathedral and Collegiate Schools*. London: J. Nichols and Son, 1827.

Hampson, Ethel M. "The Grammar Schools." *VCH Cambridge and the Isle of Ely* II (1948): 319–55.

Hardy, Henry John, ed. *Winchester College, 1867–1920: A Register*. Winchester: P. and G. Wells, 1923.

Heath, Peter. *The English Parish Clergy on the Eve of the Reformation*. London:Routledge and Kegan Paul, 1969.

Heywood, J., and T. Wright, eds. *The Ancient Laws of the Fifteenth Century for King's College, Cambridge, and the Public School of Eton College*. London: Longman, 1850.

Higgins, M. J. Reviews of *Some Account of the Foundation of Eton College, and of the Past and Present Condition of the School*, by E. S. Creasy, *Public School*

Education, by John J. Coleridge, and *Eton Reform*, by William Johnson. *Edinburgh Review* 113 (April 1861): 387–426.

Hinnebusch, W. A. *The Early English Friars Preachers*. Rome: Ad S. Sabinae, 1951.

Howson, J.S. *Essays on Cathedrals*. London: Murray, 1872.

Hunt, R.W. *Oxford Grammar Masters in the Middle Ages*, n.s. 16, 163–96. *Oxford Studies Presented to Daniel Callus*. Oxford: Oxford Historical Society,1964.

Jordan, W. K. *Philanthropy in England, 1480–1660*. London: Allen and Unwin, 1959.

Knowles, David. *The End of the Middle Ages*. Vol. 2 of *The Religious Orders in England*. Cambridge: Cambridge University Press, 1955.

– and R. Neville Hadcock. *Medieval Religious Houses, England and Wales*. London: Longman, 1953.

Kreider, Alan. *English Chantries:The Road to Dissolution*. Cambridge, Mass.:Harvard University Press, 1979.

Frère Laurent. "La Somme Le Roi." *Position des Thèses* 14. Paris: École des Chartes (1940): 27–35.

Lawson, John. "Beverley Minster Grammar School in the Middle Ages." *University of Hull Studies in Education* 2 (1954): 151–67.

– *Medieval Education and the Reformation*. London: Routledge and Kegan Paul, 1967.

– *A Town Grammar School through Six Centuries:A History of Hull Grammar School against its Local Background*. Oxford:Oxford University Press, 1963.

– and Harold Silver. *A Social History of Education in England*. London: Methuen and Co., Ltd., 1973.

Lefèvre, Placido Fern. *L'organisation ecclésiastique de la ville de Bruxelles au moyen-âge*. Recueil de Travaux d'histoire et de Philologie. 3rd ser., vol. 11. Louvain: Bibliothèque de l'Université, 1942.

Lobel, Mary D. "The Grammar Schools of the Medieval University." *VCH Oxfordshire* III (1954): 40–3.

McMahon, Clara P. *Education in Fifteenth-Century England*. The Johns Hopkins University Studies in Education, no. 35. New York: Greenwood Press, 1968.

Manacorda, Giuseppe. *Storia della Scuola in Italia*. 2 vols. Milan: 1913.

Manitius, Maximilianus. *Geschichte der lateinischen Literatur des Mittelalters*. 3 vols. München: Beck, 1911–31.

Maxwell-Lyte, H.C. *A History of Eton College, 1440–1884*. New and rev. ed. London: Macmillan and Co. Ltd., 1889.

– *History of the University of Oxford*. London: Macmillan and Company, 1886.

Moran, Jo Ann Hoeppner. "Clerical Recruitment in the Diocese of York, 1340–1530: Data and Commentary." *Journal of Ecclesiastical History* 34, no. 1 (1983): 19–54.

– *Education and Learning in the City of York 1300–1500*. Borthwick Papers, no. 55. York: Borthwick, 1979.

− *The Growth of English Schooling 1340–1548: Learning, Literacy, and Laicization in Pre-Reformation York Diocese*. Princeton: Princeton University Press, 1985.

− "Literacy and Education in Northern England, 1350–1550: A Methodological Inquiry." *Northern History* 17 (1981): 1–23

Mullinger, J.B. *From the Earliest Times to the Royal Injunctions of 1535*. Vol. 1 of *The University of Cambridge*. Cambridge: Cambridge University Press, 1873.

Murphy, James J. *Rhetoric in the Middle Ages*. Berkeley:University of California Press, 1974.

Nelson, W. *A Fifteenth Century School Book*. Oxford: Clarendon Press, 1956.

Orme, Nicholas. "Education and Learning at a Medieval English Cathedral: Exeter, 1380–1548." *Journal of Ecclesiastical History* 32 (1981): 265–83.

− *Education in the West of England 1066–1548*. Exeter: University of Exeter, 1976.

− *English Schools in the Middle Ages*. London:Methuen and Co., Ltd., 1973.

Owst, G.R. *Literature and Pulpit in Medieval England*. Cambridge: Cambridge University Press, 1933.

Paetow, L.J. *The Arts Course of Medieval Universities with Special Reference to Grammar and Rhetoric*. 1910. Reprint, Iowa: Reprint Library, n.d.

Pantin, W.A. *The English Church in the Fourteenth Century*. Cambridge: Cambridge University Press, 1955.

− "A Medieval Collection of Latin and English Proverbs and Riddles." *Bulletin of John Rylands Library*, reprint, 1930.

− ed. *Canterbury College, Oxford*. n.s. 3. London: Oxford Historical Society Publications, 1951.

− H.E. Salter, and H. G. Richardson. *Formularies which bear on the History of Oxford*. n.s. London: Oxford Historical Society Publications, 1942.

Parry, A.W. *Education in England in the Middle Ages*. London: W.B. Clive, 1920.

Pegues, F. "The Clericus in the Legal Administration of Thirteenth-Century England." *English Historical Review* 281 (October 1956): 529–59.

Petot, G. "Servage et tonsure cléricale dans la pratique française du Moyen Âge." *Revue d'Histoire de l'Église de France* 40, no. 135 (July-December 1954): 193–205.

Potter, G.R. "Education in the Fourteenth and Fifteenth Centuries." In vol. 8 of *The Cambridge Medieval History*, C.W. Previte-Orton and Z.N. Brooke, eds. Cambridge: Cambridge University Press, 1936, 688–717.

Poulson, George. *Beverlac or the Antiquities and History of the Town of Beverly in the County of York and of the Provostry and Collegiate and Establishment of St. John's with a Minute Description of the Present Minster and the Church of St. Mary and Other Ancient and Modern Edifices Compiled from Authentic Records, Charters, and Unpublished Manuscripts ...* London: G. Schraum, 1829.

Power, E. *Medieval English Nunneries, c.1275–1535*. Cambridge: Cambridge University Press, 1922.

Powicke, F.M., and A.B. Emden, eds. *The Universities of Europe in the Middle Ages by the late Hastings Rashdall*. New ed. Oxford: Clarendon Press, 1936.

Raby, F.J.E. *A History of Christian-Latin Poetry from the Beginnings to the Close of the Middle Ages*. 2nd ed. Oxford:Clarendon Press, 1953.

Rackham, H., ed. *Early Statutes of Christ's College, Cambridge*. Cambridge: Cambridge University Press, 1927.

Reddan, M. "The Hospital of St. Anthony." *VCH London* 1 (1909): 581–4.

Richardson, H.G. "Business Training in Medieval Oxford." *American Historical Review* 46 (1941): 259–80.

– "The Oxford Law School under John." *Law Quarterly Review* 57 (1941): 319–38.

– "An Oxford Teacher of the Fifteenth Century." Reprint from *Bulletin of John Rylands Library* 23 (1939): 436–57.

Rickert, E. "Chaucer at School." *Modern Philology Quarterly* 29, no. 3 (1932): 257–74.

Russell, J. C. "The Clerical Population of Medieval England." *Traditio* 2 (1944): 177–212.

Salter, H.E., ed. *Mediaeval Archives of the University of Oxford*. London: Oxford Historical Society Publications, 1921.

Simon, Brian. *Education and the Labour Movement 1870–1920*. London: Lawrence and Wishart, 1965.

– *The Two Nations and the Educational Structure 1780–1870*. London: Lawrence and Wishart, 1974.

Simon, Joan. *Education and Society in Tudor England*. Cambridge: Cambridge University Press, 1966.

Smalley, Beryl. "Stephen Langton and the Four Senses." *Speculum* 6 (1931): 60–76.

Smith, Goldwin. Review of *Report of Her Majesty's Commissioners appointed to inquire into the Revenues and Management of Certain Colleges and Schools, and the Studies pursued and instructions given therein; with an Appendix and Evidence*. 4 vols. *Edinburgh Review* 120 (July 1864): 147–88.

Spufford, Margaret. *Contrasting Communities:English Villagers in the Sixteenth and Seventeenth Centuries*. Cambridge: Cambridge University Press, 1974.

Steiner, Arpad. "The Authorship of *De Disciplina scholarium*." *Speculum* 12 (1937): 81–4.

Tate, W. E. *A. F. Leach as a Historian of Yorkshire Education*. St. Anthony Hall Publications. York: St. Anthony's Press, 1963.

Thompson, A. Hamilton. *The English Clergy and Their Organisation in the Later Middle Ages*. Oxford: Oxford University Press, 1947.

Thomson, David. *A Descriptive Catalogue of Middle English Grammatical Texts*. London: Garland Publishing, 1979.

– ed. *An Edition of the Middle English Grammatical Texts.* New York and London: Garland Publishing, 1984.

Thorndike, Lynn. "Elementary and Secondary Education in the Middle Ages." *Speculum* 15 (1940): 400–8.

– *University Records and Life in the Middle Ages.* Records of Civilization Series. New York: Columbia University Press, 1944.

Ullman, E.K. "Classical Authors in Medieval Florilegia." *Classical Philology* 27 (1932): 1–42.

Wainewright, John Bannerman, ed. *Winchester College 1836–1906: A Register.* Winchester: P. and G. Wells, 1907.

Wallis, P.J. "The Wase School Collection: a Neglected Source in Educational History." *Bodleian Library Record* 4 (1952): 78–104.

Warner, R. Townsend. *Winchester.* London: George Bell and Sons, 1900.

Watson, Foster. *The English Grammar Schools to 1660:their Curriculum and Practice.* Cambridge: Cambridge University Press, 1908.

– "Leach, Arthur Francis (1851–1915)." *Dictionary of National Biography* (1912–21): 327–8.

Weisheipl, James A. "The Structure of the Arts Faculty in the Medieval University." *British Journal of Educational Studies* 19 (1971): 263–71.

Wisniowski, Eugenius. "The Parochial School System in Poland towards the Close of the Middle Ages." *Acta Poloniae Historica* 27 (1973): 29–43.

Wright, Thomas, ed. *A Volume of Vocabularies.* London:by the Author, 1857.

Young, F.M., and Handcock, W.D., eds. *English Historical Documents 1833–1874*, vol. 12, no. 1 of *English Historical Documents*, edited by David C. Douglas. London:Eyre and Spottiswoode, 1953–1977; Eyre Methuen, 1979.

Index